Field Guide to

MEAT

How to Identify, Select, and Prepare Virtually Every Meat, Poultry, and Game Cut

By Aliza Green

QUIRK BOOKS
PHILADELPHIA

DISCLAIMER
The world of meat butchery is very large and varied. While we've taken care to represent the most common cuts and types of meat, the author and publisher cannot guarantee that this guide addresses every possible type of meat available worldwide.

Library of Congress Cataloging in Publication Number: 2004103016

ISBN: 1-931686-79-3

Printed in Singapore

Typeset in Adobe Garamond, Franklin Gothic, and Impact

Designed by Karen Onorato
Photographs by Steve Legato
Illustrations and Iconography by Karen Onorato
Edited by Erin Slonaker

All photographs copyright © 2005 by Quirk Productions, Inc.

Distributed in North America by Chronicle Books
85 Second Street
San Francisco, CA 94105

10 9 8 7 6 5 4 3 2 1

Quirk Books
215 Church Street
Philadelphia, PA 19106
www.quirkbooks.com

Contents

viii   *Introduction*

1   **I. BEEF**
7   Beef Rolls
9   Bones and Marrow
11   Bottom Round
14   Bottom Sirloin Butt
16   Brisket
18   Cheeks
20   Chuck Roasts and Steaks
24   Coulotte
26   Flank Steak
28   Ground Beef and Cube Steak
31   Hanging Tender
33   Knuckle
35   Oxtail
37   Rib
41   Rump
42   Shank
44   Short Ribs
47   Shoulder Center
48   Shoulder Tender
50   Skirt Steak
52   Strip Loin
55   T-Bone and Porterhouse Steaks
57   Tenderloin
60   Top Blade Steak

61	Top Round
64	Top Sirloin Butt
66	Tri-Tip
68	Variety Meats and Fat

76	**II. VEAL**
79	Breast and Ribs
81	Feet
83	Ground Veal
85	Leg
88	Loin
90	Marrow and Knuckle Bones
93	Rib
95	Shank
97	Shoulder
99	Tenderloin
101	Variety Meats

108	**III. PORK**
111	Barbecue Ribs
115	Belly
116	Chops
119	Fat
123	Feet
124	Ground Pork
126	Head, Jowl, Ear, and Tail
128	Leg
132	Loin
134	Neck Bones

135 Rack
137 Shank and Hock
140 Shoulder
143 Sirloin
144 Suckling Pig
146 Tenderloin
148 Variety Meats

153 **IV. LAMB**
156 Breast and Barbecue Ribs
158 Chops
161 Ground Lamb
163 Leg
166 Loin
168 Neck
170 Rack
172 Shank
175 Shoulder
177 Sirloin
179 Suckling Lamb
181 Tenderloin
183 Variety Meats

188 **V. POULTRY AND GAME BIRDS**
189 Chicken
195 Duck
201 Foie Gras (Duck and Goose)
204 Goose
207 Grouse

210 Guinea Fowl
212 Ortolan and Beccafico
214 Ostrich, Emu, and Rhea
217 Partridge
219 Pheasant
221 Pigeon, Dove, and Wood Pigeon
224 Quail
226 Turkey
229 Woodcock

232 **VI. GAME AND OTHER DOMESTICATED MEATS**
233 Alligator
235 Armadillo
237 Bear
239 Beaver
242 Bison and Beefalo
245 Goat and Kid
247 Hare
249 Horse and Donkey
251 Muskrat
253 Opossum
255 Rabbit
257 Raccoon
259 Rattlesnake
260 Squirrel
262 Venison
265 Wild Boar

268 **VII. SAUSAGE AND CURED MEATS**
269 Cooked Sausages
271 Cured Sausages
276 Fresh Sausages
282 Loafs, Cooked and Jellied
283 Bacon
284 Ham, Cooked
286 Ham, Country Style
287 Ham, Uncooked European Style
290 Cured Meats

294 *Roasting Chart*
297 *Index*
310 *Sources*
311 *Acknowledgments*

Introduction

Here's a compact, easy-to-carry book packed with information and photos to help you sort your way through the meat counter's offerings. It includes everything you need to know about identifying, choosing, storing, and preparing everything from common meats like beef, pork, veal, and lamb to unusual ones like goat, wild boar, and bison, along with poultry, game, cured meats and an assortment of sausages, from andouille to zungenwurst.

For professionals, the book includes the North American Meat Producers (NAMP) cut numbers and names. To make international cooking easier, I've included equivalent names in French, Spanish, Italian, British, and other languages along with many regional and colloquial names.

You will learn about London broil (marinated grilled flank steak from London), guinea fowl (a close cousin to the chicken and pheasant that tastes deliciously of both), and chorizo (Spanish and Latin American spicy pork sausage). Detailed preparation instructions and food affinities make it easy to explore new cuts and meats. Turn to the photo section to help identify your cut.

To write this book, I called on my 30 years of hands-on experience working with meats as chef, mother (and home cook), food writer, and teacher as well as conducted extensive research. While it would take a book the size of a full-grown steer to cover all the meat sold in today's ever-changing food market, I have crammed as much information about as many types of meat as possible into this little book.

I'm happy to hear from readers, with comments, questions or suggestions. Send me an e-mail at www.alizagreen.com and I'll do my best to reply quickly.

Aliza Green

I. Beef

Beef is the meat of domestic cattle (*Bos taurus*) and belongs to the Bovidae family. Modern domestic cattle evolved about 8,500 years ago from the wild aurochs, which died out as late as the early seventeenth century in Poland. Cattle is a broad term that includes beef, humped cattle, water buffalo, bison, and yak. Beef is eaten mainly in Northern Europe, North and South America, and Australia. Americans eat about 60 pounds (27 kg) a year per person compared with the Chinese at only 6 pounds (2.7 kg). Argentineans eat as much as 80 pounds (36 kg) annually.

Purebred cattle breeds have been selectively bred to possess a distinct identity and the propensity to pass these traits to their offspring. Beef usually comes from castrated males or steers slaughtered at 18 to 24 months of age. All beef cattle start out eating grass; in the United States three-fourths are "finished" (grown to maturity) in feedlots where they are fed mostly corn, while the remaining quarter are fed only grass. Beef in South America and Australia is generally grass (or pasture) fed. Corn-fed beef is richer and milder in flavor; grass-fed beef is leaner and stronger in flavor. Worldwide, antibiotics are used to treat sick animals but are prohibited as growth promoters. In the United States, hormones may be used to promote efficient growth.

Look for beef with a minimum of creamy outer fat. The bones should be soft looking with a reddish color; the meat is best when firm, fine-textured, and light cherry-red. Avoid meat with yellowish or gray fat, little to no marbling, two-toned color, or an unpleasant odor.

The U.S. government conducts stringent mandatory inspections of both live animals and carcasses. All fresh and processed meat products shipped from one state to another must be stamped "Inspected and Passed by the Department of Agriculture." However, the stamp indicates safety only, not quality or grade.

Grading is voluntary and is based on the amount and distribution of marbling (the white flecks of fat) within the muscles. The greater the marbling, the higher the grade, because marbling makes beef more tender, flavorful, and juicy. (The protein, vitamin, and mineral content are similar regardless of grade.) Much of today's supermarket meat is choice, the most popular grade. Select is the lowest retail grade and is the leanest, therefore it can be tough. Lower grades are not found at retail; they are ground or used in processed meats. Only about 2 percent of beef is graded prime (advertisements for "prime rib" are likely for choice beef rib). Prime beef is high priced and found in high-end butcher shops and fine restaurants. Because the entire animal receives the same grade, less expensive cuts and variety meats of prime-graded steers may be worth seeking out.

A special, much-prized type of beef, Kobe beef, comes from Wagyu cattle, which are genetically predisposed to intense marbling. In Japan, they are fed sake mash and beer and are sometimes massaged with sake, producing meat that is extraordinarily tender, finely marbled, and full-flavored. Kobe beef graded A5 in Japan is 20 to 25 percent fat; U.S. and Canadian prime beef is 6 to 8 percent fat. When cooking Kobe beef, sear it quickly so that it blackens on the surface but remains rare. The meat is smooth, velvety, and incomparably sweet, with a subtle tang that lingers on the palate. Kobe beef is usually sold frozen but does not suffer in texture or flavor.

About 90 percent of American beef is shipped as boxed beef (wholesale cuts that are vacuum-packed and boxed for shipping). The retailer refrigerates boxed beef until needed for sale, when the bag is opened and the meat cut. During the period the meat is in the bag, averaging about seven days, it ages. This is referred to as "aging in the bag" or "wet-aging."

Dry-aging is an old-fashioned, expensive, and slow process still done by top butcher shops and restaurant purveyors. Beef is dry-aged anywhere from ten days to six weeks to develop additional tenderness and flavor using controlled temperatures and humidity. The longer the aging, the more the benefits but also the more shrinkage and trimming. The length of time and method of aging is a personal preference. Dry-aging results in a unique flavor that may be described as "musty"; aficionados love this flavor, calling it "gamy" or "intense." The tenderizing effects of aging are more evident in older animals. Beef that is not aged at all can be metallic tasting and lacking beefy flavor.

In the early twenty-first century, Mad Cow Disease became a concern for most beef consumers. Mad Cow Disease is the common name for bovine spongiform encephalopathy (BSE), a progressive, degenerative, and fatal disease affecting the central nervous system of adult cattle. BSE is not destroyed by cooking. Research indicates that organ meat, rather than muscle meat, is the source of infectious prions (the diseased proteins). Limit risk by avoiding head and spinal meat and processed beef products that may contain nervous-system tissue, such as hot dogs, sausage, and ground beef. Organic and 100 percent grass-fed beef carry the least risk, since these cattle are not fed any animal products. Small producers are now selling grass-fed beef directly to restaurants and at farmers' markets. Kosher and Halal meat also carries less risk because it is forbidden to use animals that are ill or injured, and the hand-slaughtering method ensures that brain matter does not contaminate the meat.

There are other diseases associated with beef, though with proper handling and cooking, the food will be safe. Two of the most dangerous, *Escherichia coli* (*E. coli*) and salmonella, are both killed at 155°C (69°C). *E. coli* colonizes in the intestines of animals and can contaminate muscle meat at slaughter. *E. coli* 0157:H7 is a rare but virulent strain that can be fatal. Salmonella is a bacteria that may be found in the intestinal tracts of livestock, poultry, and other animals. Cross-contamination can occur if raw meat (or its juices) mix with cooked food that will be eaten raw, such as a salad.

Beef Primal Cuts

Beef carcasses are large—a 1,100-pound (500 kg) steer will produce a carcass of about 680 pounds (310 kg). They are divided into primal cuts at the slaughterhouse. In the United States there are eight primals.

The **chuck** weighs about 90 pounds (41 kg) and is the large shoulder section. It includes ribs 1 to 5 (numbering starts at the shoulder). Chuck cuts are plentiful and inexpensive. Many pot roasts are from the chuck, and it is generally considered the best source of ground beef. Because the many muscles in the beef forequarters are more heavily exercised and contain more connective tissue, they require slow, moist-heat cooking to tenderize. Several muscles in the chuck are often seamed out (divided), mostly for the restaurant trade. These include the shoulder tender (page 48), the shoulder center (page 47), and the flatiron (page 60).

The tender and flavorful **rib** is one of the two sought-after beef "middle cuts" (the other is the strip loin; see below). This primal weighs about 35 pounds (16 kg) and reaches from the 6th rib, adjoining the chuck, through the 12th rib, adjoining the loin, along the steer's back. The rib section includes the large rib-eye muscle and several smaller attached muscles. Because rib is always in high demand, it fetches a correspondingly high price.

The highly flavorful and moderately tender **strip loin** is the second of two sought-after "middle cuts" (the other is the rib; see above). This primal weighs about 40 pounds (18 kg) and lies along the steer's back between the rib section and the sirloin. Steaks and roasts cut from this section are prized for their superb flavor and satisfying texture. Paralleling it, beneath the ribs and next to the backbone, lies the smaller, pointed front portion of the tenderloin (page 57). Strip loin cuts are expensive.

The full-bodied **sirloin** (upper hip) is a beef lover's favorite. Weighing about 22 pounds (10 kg), it lies between the strip loin and the round (upper leg) and includes the butt end of the long muscle that runs down the back of the steer. Though not as tender as the adjoining strip loin, cuts from the sirloin are appreciated for their full-bodied flavor and firm, satisfying texture. A baron of beef is a roast of two sirloins, or two sirloins and the round, left intact at the backbone. There is a legend that King Henry VIII of England prized this cut so much that he dubbed it Sir Loin, Baron of Beef, but the term *sirloin* most likely comes from the French *surlonge*, meaning "above the loin." There are three basic parts of the sirloin: the top sirloin butt; the stub (or larger) end of the tenderloin (page 57); and the bottom sirloin. Depending on how the beef was cut up, some of the bottom sirloin can be included in the round and will be called sirloin tip (page 12).

The large **round**, which weighs about 80 pounds (36 kg), is the entire upper leg. It contains the femur and the lower portion of the aitchbone (hipbone) and ends just above the shank (shin). The round is a lean and less tender cut and makes up about 20 percent of the beef carcass. Three main subprimals, the knuckle (page 33), the top round (page 61), and the bottom or gooseneck round (page 11), are cut from the round. Most round cuts are best suited for moist-heat pot-roasting. Beef round cuts are generally moderately priced.

The **brisket** weighs about 30 pounds (14 kg) and lies between the chuck (shoulder) and the plate (belly). The boneless brisket itself weighs only about 12 pounds (5.4 kg). Brisket is moderately priced, but there is quite a bit of shrinkage because it needs long, slow cooking to tenderize. See the individual entry for beef brisket (page 16).

The **plate** weighs about 30 pounds (14 kg) and is equivalent to a slab of pork spareribs (page 111). It lies on the underside of the steer, behind the brisket, in front of the flank, and under the rib section, and it includes the inside and outside skirt (page 50) and short ribs (page 44). Plate cuts are extremely flavorful but tough; the muscle tissue is streaked with fat and layered with connective tissue. Plate cuts need moist, low heat and long, slow cooking. Though whole plate is quite inexpensive, plate short ribs can be expensive.

The **flank** primal weighs about 20 pounds (9.1 kg) and lies on the underside of the steer, between the plate, the round, and the short loin. The beef flank steak (page 26) weighs less than 2 pounds (910 g) and is moderately priced. The remainder of this primal is used for ground beef.

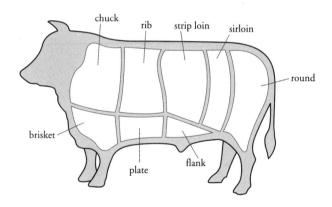

1.   **BEEF ROLLS**

Other Names:	Beef olives, *braciole* (southern Italian), *involtini* (Italian, usually veal), *paupiettes* and *roulades* (French), roll-ups, *Rouladen* (German).
General Description:	*Beef rolls are thin slices of beef that can be filled, rolled up, and then braised.* While not a specific cut of beef, beef rolls are commonly sold by butchers; the beef used for this preparation must be cut from a single muscle so that the slices cook evenly and hold together during the long cooking process. Beef rolls originated in medieval times when cooks prepared thin slices of beef, veal, or mutton with a stuffing.
Part of Animal:	These thin slices are cut from a single muscle, usually the top round or bottom round.
Characteristics:	Beef rolls are made from tough cuts of beef, which become tender when braised.
How to Choose:	Choose the largest slices of single-muscle meat sliced about 1/4 inch (.65 cm) thick.
Amount to Buy:	Allow about 4 ounces (115 g) per person.
Storage:	Because they have a large surface area, thin-cut slices spoil easily and should be used within 2 days.

Preparation: 1.   **Trim off any excess fat if necessary, then place each slice between two sheets of plastic wrap and pound lightly with a meat mallet until approximately 5 x 8 inches (13 x 20 cm).**

 2.   **Season with salt and pepper and spread cool stuffing over the meat, leaving a 1-inch (2.5 cm) border.**

3.   **Fold the sides over the stuffing, roll it up, and tie securely using butcher's string or toothpicks.**

 4.   **Brown well on all sides in a pan over medium-high heat and then remove from the pan.**

5.   **Pour off the fat, add aromatic vegetables to the pan, brown lightly, then pour in liquid to deglaze the pan.**

6.   **Return the rolls to the pan and simmer (or transfer to a Dutch oven and bake at 325°F/165°C) about 1 hour, or until fork tender.**

7.   **Allow the rolls to cool slightly in the liquid, then remove and reserve. Cook the liquid down till syrupy.**

8.   **Remove the string or toothpicks from the meat, cut the rolls into slices, and top with the cooking liquid.**

Flavor
Affinities: Basil, capers, garlic, lemons, mustard, onions, Parmesan cheese, prosciutto, red wine, tomatoes.

2.   **BONES AND MARROW**

Other Names:	**Bones:** Beef bones, bouillon bones, knuckle bones, neck bones. **Marrow:** *Médula* (Spanish), *midollo* (Italian), *moelle* (French).
General Description:	*Beef marrow is the delectable soft fatty tissue found in the center of animal leg bones.* Considered a delicacy in many countries, especially in Europe, marrow is rich, expensive, and quite perishable. Knuckle bones and other gelatin-rich beef bones (NAMP 134) are desirable for making soup, stocks, and sauces because they impart flavor and body, especially important in a reduction (sauce that is cooked until thick). Roasted marrow bones are a French bistro specialty.
Part of Animal:	Marrow bones are straight portions of leg bones that contain marrow. Knuckle bones connect the leg bones; neck bones are vertebrae from the neck.
Characteristics:	Fresh marrow has the consistency of hard butter and is whitish, with red streaks of blood and nerves.
How to Choose:	Beef leg bones, cut in 2- to 3-inch (5–7.5 cm) sections, can be used for their marrow. Marrow is also sold by weight by special order at butcher shops or from wholesale meat purveyors, and it is usually frozen. Fresh or frozen knuckle or neck bones are best used for soup, stocks, and sauces.

Amount to Buy:	Buy 1 pound (450 g) of marrow bones per person. To make it easier to extract the marrow, buy vertically cut bones. Allow about 8 ounces (225 g) per person. Allow about 2 ounces (60 g) pure marrow per person. For soups and stock, buy at least 5 pounds (2.3 kg) marrow, knuckle, or neck bones.
Storage:	Keep soup bones refrigerated and use within 2 days of purchase, or freeze. Refrigerate pure marrow soaked in cold water mixed with salt and use within 2 days.
Preparation:	***Marrow:***

1. **Soak 2- to 3-inch (5–7.5 cm) sections of marrow bone in tepid water for about 2 hours.**

2. **Push the softened marrow out of the bone and discard the bones.**

3. **Refrigerate the marrow overnight in a bowl of ice water mixed with salt to extract any blood.**

4. **Cut into slices $^{1}/_{2}$ inch (1.3 cm) thick.**

5. **Poach the marrow slices in salted, boiling water 1 to 2 minutes, then drain.**

6. **Sprinkle each slice with salt, chives, or parsley and use to top beef, veal, or fish.**

Flavor
Affinities:

Chervil, chives, fleur de sel, garlic, green onion, herb butter, lemon, paprika, parsley, salt, tarragon.

BOTTOM ROUND

Other Names:

Cara (Spanish, flat), *contra con redondo* or *cuete de res* (Spanish), gooseneck round, outside round, *semelle* or *gîte à la noix* (French), silverside (British), *sottofesa con girello* (Italian). **Roasts:** bottom round, Manhattan roast, melon roast, rump roast, silverside roast, watermelon roast, wedge-cut rump roast. **Steaks:** Breakfast steak, eye round steak, Manhattan steak.

General
Description:

The bottom round (NAMP 170) is the outer part of the round where muscles are well exercised, so it contains tough muscles and a good deal of connective tissue. When the round primal is cut, it is placed on the butcher's block with the outside on the bottom and the inside on the top, so these cuts became known as bottom and top round. Bottom round cuts are best cooked slowly with moist heat.

At wholesale, bottom round is divided into three parts: the eye of round, the flat, and the heel. The **eye of round** (NAMP 171C), which resembles a choice tenderloin but is much tougher, can make a good deli-style roast beef if thinly sliced. The **flat** (NAMP 171B) is a single, long, flattened, and rather tough muscle and is suitable for stewing and braising. The popular **rump** roast is cut from the flat (page 41). The boneless, wedge-shaped **heel** (NAMP 171F) is the toughest of all bottom round cuts because it's closest to the ground and is more heavily worked by the steer. The **silverside** is a boneless bottom round roast with a silvery membrane covering the side of the muscle adjoining the sirloin tip.

Stew meat (NAMP 135A) is lean, meaty beef, usually boneless, cut into uniform chunks of 1 to 1 1/2 inches (2.5–3.8 cm). It is cut from tougher sections like the bottom round. **Kabob meat** (NAMP 135B) is lean, boneless beef cubes cut from more tender sections of the steer.

Part of Animal: The bottom round is the outer portion of the round (upper leg) of the beef cattle.

Characteristics: Most of the bottom round consists of lean, tough, tasty muscles with a good deal of connective tissue.

How to Choose: When choosing a bottom round roast, look for one that is the best size for the number of people you will be feeding. For bottom round steaks suitable for chicken-fried steak, choose steaks about 1/2 inch (1.3 cm) thick with the least amount of connective tissue.

Amount to Buy: Allow 6 to 9 ounces (170–255 g) boneless bottom round per portion. For pot roast, 4 pounds (1.8 kg) of meat serves six.

Storage:

x2-4

Refrigerate roasts up to 4 days, steaks up to 2 days. The thinner the steak, the quicker it needs to be used.

Preparation:

Pot Roast:

1. Combine desired seasonings and rub them all over the meat, allowing the meat to absorb the seasonings for 1 to 2 hours at room temperature.

2. In a Dutch oven, brown the meat well in oil on all sides over medium-high heat. Pour off excess fat from the pan. Return the pan to the heat and add a small amount of liquid (water, wine, tomato juice, or stock), scraping up any browned bits.

3. Cover the meat with thinly sliced onions and garlic, if desired. Cover and bake for 2 hours at 300°F (150°C), adding liquid as needed to keep moist.

4. Uncover and bake 1 hour, or until the meat is tender when pierced with a fork.

5. Cool before slicing and serving; or cool, then refrigerate overnight so that the fat congeals. Remove and discard the fat, reheat, then slice and serve.

Chicken-Fried Steak:

1. Cut a thin slice off the bottom round and tenderize

by pounding with a meat mallet, then dip in seasoned flour or breadcrumbs.

 2. Skillet-fry in oil at moderate temperature till browned on both sides, about 6 minutes a side.

3. Make milk gravy from the pan drippings and serve.

Flavor
Affinities: Bacon, cinnamon, cloves, garlic, ginger, mustard, red wine, rosemary, shallots, thyme, vinegar, white wine.

BOTTOM SIRLOIN BUTT

Other Names: Bell (or ball) tip, *bola* (Spanish), bottom sirloin, butcher's heart, flap, *noce* (Italian), *pointe de surlonge* (French), thick flank (British), tri-tip.

General
Description: *One of three sirloin subprimals, the bottom sirloin butt is a boneless cut that is tougher than the top sirloin butt (page 64).* This cut is further divided into three parts: the tri-tip (page 66), the ball tip (NAMP 167A), and the flap. Though rather lean, bottom sirloin cuts have good flavor and firm texture. The **ball tip** is a small portion of the larger muscle group called the knuckle (page 33). The bottom sirloin may be found cut into various boneless steaks, including the **bottom sirloin flap steak** (NAMP 1185A), the **ball tip steak** (NAMP 1185B), and the tri-tip steak (page 66).

The **flap** (NAMP 1713) is actually a continuation of the flank (page 26) and is usually sold ground or cut up for stew. It is quite flavorful but too tough to use for steak as is; it is sometimes run through a tenderizing machine and used for cube steak (page 28).

Part of Animal: The bottom sirloin butt is the lower portion of the sirloin, or upper hip, and lies between the butt end of the tenderloin and the knuckle in the round.

Characteristics: The bottom sirloin is lean and moderately tender with good flavor and medium-fine grain.

How to Choose: Choose meat that is not overly dark. Choose a regularly shaped ball tip that is well trimmed.

Amount to Buy: Allow at least 8 ounces (225 g) of boneless meat per person because of trim waste.

Storage: Store larger cuts up to 4 days refrigerated; store steaks
x2–4 2 days refrigerated.

Preparation: 1. **Cut ball tip into 2-inch (5 cm) cubes.**

2. **Marinate overnight if desired, using bold flavorings and oil to moisten this lean cut.**

 3. **Skewer and grill over medium-high heat or broil to desired temperature.**

| Flavor Affinities: | Chile peppers, fish sauce, jerk seasoning, molasses, mushrooms, peanuts, soy sauce, wine vinegar. |

3.   **BRISKET**

| Other Names: | *Pecho* (Spanish), *petto* (Italian), *poitrine* (French). **Brisket Flat:** Deckle off, first cut, flat half, navel end brisket, thin cut. **Brisket Point:** Breast deckle, deckle point, nose, point cut, second cut, thick cut. |

| General Description: | *The brisket (NAMP 120) is the front portion of the beef breast that lies between the front legs and takes well to smoking, braising, or poaching.* This forequarter cut is associated with Jewish cooking because of prohibitions against eating hindquarter meat. Brisket is the cut of choice for Texas slow-smoked pit-cooked barbecue and is also the best cut for corned beef (page 291). While brisket is hard to beat for flavor and texture, it must be cooked slowly at low heat and will shrink significantly. Because it is a large cut that can't be cooked properly in small quantities, brisket is ideal to serve to large groups. |

Brisket consists of two distinct muscles: the larger, leaner, flat, oblong first cut (NAMP 120A) weighs 7 to 9 pounds (3.2–4.1 kg); the smaller, fattier, triangular second cut (NAMP 120B) weighs 3 to 5 pounds (1.4–2.3 kg) and lies over the first cut toward the front of the cattle. It is attached to the first cut by a large layer of fat, which keeps it juicy.

Part of Animal: The brisket is the front breast, cut from the forequarter, below the shoulder and adjoining the foreshank.

Characteristics: A whole boneless brisket is flat and roughly rectangular with long, medium-coarse grain.

How to Choose: A well-marbled whole brisket, with both the large, lean flat muscle and the smaller, fattier, triangular muscle streaked with white fat and a deep color, will cook up best. It may need to be specially ordered.

Amount to Buy: Allow about 3/4 pound (340 g) per person to allow for trimming and shrinkage.

Storage: Store brisket well wrapped and very cold in the refrigerator for up to 4 days. Both raw and cooked brisket freeze well for up to 2 months if tightly wrapped.

Preparation: 1. **Trim off excess surface fat and any thin, shiny, white connective tissue. Brisket with too little fat can become stringy and dry or mealy when cooked.**

2. **Marinate or dry-rub with spices and refrigerate for up to 3 days.**

3. **Cook slowly in a moist environment: braise (or pot-roast) for 4 to 5 hours at 300°F (150°C), cook in a**

slow cooker for 8 to 10 hours on low, poach (as for corned beef) for 4 to 5 hours, or hot-smoke up to 16 hours (as in Texas barbecue).

Flavor
Affinities:

Apricots, barbecue sauce, beer, brown sugar, chili powder, cinnamon, cumin, ketchup, mustard, onions, red wine, rosemary, sauerkraut, tomatoes.

CHEEKS

Other Names:

Guancia (Italian), *joue* (French), jowl, *mejilla* or *cachete* (Spanish).

General
Description:

Beef cheeks are rich morsels of dense, finely grained meat. Along with veal cheeks, beef cheeks are being featured on trendy restaurant menus, especially those serving French bistro cuisine. Quite inexpensive, beef cheeks can be found either by special order or in ethnic meat markets and are usually frozen. Cheeks are always braised, and they reheat beautifully.

Part of Animal:

The cheeks are the muscles on either side of the cheekbones.

Characteristics:

Cheeks are rich and dense-fleshed with a fine grain and a layer of silvery white connective tissue running through the middle.

How to Choose:	Buy well-trimmed beef cheeks.
Amount to Buy:	Allow two trimmed beef cheeks per person.
Storage:	If frozen, defrost in the refrigerator. If fresh, store up to 2 days refrigerated.

Preparation: 1. **Trim any exterior gristle off the cheeks. It is not necessary to trim the silverskin, which runs horizontally through the middle and cooks up tender.**

2. **Marinate overnight refrigerated up to 2 days in red wine, seasonings, and cut-up aromatic vegetables. Drain the meat, reserving the liquid and vegetables.**

3. **Pat dry and brown the cheeks in a Dutch oven over medium-high heat, cover with the vegetables and marinade from step 2, and then cover.**

4. **Bring to a boil and braise, partially covered with liquid, for at least 3 hours at low temperature (300°F/150°C), or until fork tender.**

5. **Allow the cheeks to cool in the liquid to firm.**

6. **When cool, remove the cheeks, strain the cooking liquid, if desired, and boil till syrupy. Reheat cheeks in sauce before serving.**

Flavor Affinities:	Bay leaves, celeriac, chives, cinnamon, cloves, garlic, horseradish, red wine, tarragon, thyme, tomatoes.

4 a–b.

CHUCK ROASTS AND STEAKS

Other Names:	**Bone-In Roasts:** Arm pot roast (round bone, or 0-bone shoulder roast), blade roast, bolar roast, cross rib roast, *épaule* (French), *paleta* (Spanish), 7-bone roast, shoulder roast, *spalla* (Italian). **Boneless Roasts:** Arm roast, boneless cross rib, center-cut chuck roast, *centro de carneza de paleta* (Spanish), chuck eye roast, chuck-wagon roast, Diamond Jim roast, English roast, *espadilla* (Spanish), *fesone di spalla* (Italian), flatiron roast, inside chuck roll, *macreuse* (French), shoulder clod roast, shoulder filet, shoulder tender. **Chuck Tender:** *Capello di prete* (Italian), *chingolo* (Spanish), Jewish filet, Jewish tenderloin, *jumeau* (French), medallion roast, mock tender. **Bone-In Steak:** Blade steak, 7-bone steak, Texas broil. **Boneless Steak:** Barbecue steak, cross rib steak, family steak, fluff steak, patio steak, shoulder clod steak.
General Description:	*The large, square-shaped chuck or shoulder (NAMP 113) is full of tough, though flavorful, muscles.* The chuck is cut into a bewildering array of moderately priced multiple-muscle pot roasts popular in retail markets. Chuck roasts, which may be sold either bone-in or boned, rolled, and tied (BRT), are used in home-style

cooking in many countries. Pot roasts from the chuck have more fat, and therefore more flavor, than those from the round.

The economical **chuck 7-bone roast** can be recognized by the shoulder blade bone (shaped like the number seven) that crosses its top third. This roast is cut 1 1/2 to 3 inches (3.8–7.5 cm) thick from the rib end. There are usually three of these roasts per chuck, with varying amounts of blade bone or part of the backbone and rib attached.

The **blade roast** is made up of different muscles with varying degrees of tenderness. It includes the prized tender top blade (or flatiron) steak (page 60) and a group of tough muscles under the blade sold separately as the **under blade roast** (NAMP 116E). On the other side of the blade bone ridge is the lean **chuck tender** (NAMP 116B), which resembles the tenderloin (page 57) in shape but is much less tender. This single muscle weighs about 2 pounds (910 g). The **chuck eye roast** includes a portion of the rib eye muscle and lies just to the front of the rib section.

The **cross rib pot roast** (or English roast) is cut out of the corner of the square chuck and includes ribs 3 to 5. It's actually the same cut as three attached chuck short ribs (page 44). If boneless, the same cut may be called **inside chuck roll** or **chuckwagon roast** (NAMP 116D). A **chuck eye steak** will include a portion of the tender rib eye muscle.

The **arm roast** (NAMP 114E) comes from the arm

side of the chuck. Because it contains only the small round arm bone, it is quite economical. It's also easy to cut up for stew. The **bolar roast** is a large boned, rolled, and tied (BRT) roast cut from the point end of the chuck blade that is popular for pot roasting.

In European-style meat cutting (also done for American restaurant sale), the whole chuck is completely boned and is called the **shoulder clod** (NAMP 114); it weighs 13 to 20 pounds (5.9–9.1 kg). The whole shoulder clod is rolled into the **boneless rolled chuck roast** (NAMP 116A). This large roast weighs 10 to 15 pounds (4.5–6.8 kg) and is often cut into three smaller roasts, the most tender of which will be the tapered end that lies closest to the rib section. The center of the shoulder clod is called the clod heart or shoulder center (page 47).

The **center-cut blade roast** is the center portion of the boned chuck. It may be cut into steaks with unrevealing names such as patio steak or family steak.

Part of Animal:	The chuck (shoulder) portion of the steer lies between the rib section and the brisket (breast).
Characteristics:	The many muscles in the chuck are heavily exercised and contain a lot of connective tissue, so they will be tough if not slow-cooked at low heat. The muscle grain is coarse; it may run in different directions within one roast and have varying degrees of tenderness and intramuscular fattiness (marbling).

How to Choose:	Pick a chuck roast with the right size and shape to suit your needs. Choose a well-trimmed roast with the least amount of connective tissue and fat.
Amount to Buy:	Allow at least ³/4 pound (340 g) of boneless chuck roast and at least 1 pound (450 g) of bone-in chuck per person.
Storage:	Refrigerate whole roasts well wrapped up to 4 days. Raw or cooked chuck freezes well for up to 2 months.
Preparation:	**All these cuts, whether roasts or steaks, must be cooked slowly for long periods of time in a moist environment, by braising (or pot-roasting), poaching, smoking, cooking in a crockpot, or stewing.**

Chuck Pot Roast:

1. **Combine herbs and spices and rub them all over the meat. Allow the meat to absorb seasonings for 1 to 2 hours at room temperature.**

2. **In a Dutch oven, brown the meat on all sides in oil over medium-high heat. Pour off excess fat. Add 1 to 2 cups (.25–.5 l) liquid to deglaze.**

3. **Cover the meat with thinly sliced onions and chopped garlic, if desired. Cover and bake for 1 hour at 300°F (150°C).**

4.   **Remove the cover and bake for 1 hour longer or until the meat is tender when pierced with a fork, adding liquid as needed to keep moist.**

 5.   **Cool before slicing and serving, or cool and then refrigerate overnight so that the fat congeals. Remove and discard fat and reheat at 300°F (150°C), covered, for about 45 minutes or until steaming hot.**

Flavor
Affinities: Anise, bay leaves, beer, coriander, cumin, onions, oyster sauce, red wine, rosemary, sage, tomatoes.

5.   **COULOTTE**

Other Names: **Whole:** Culotte, knuckle, London broil, round sirloin tip roast, *tapa del aguayón* or *picanha* (Spanish), top sirloin cap. **Steaks:** round sirloin tip steak, sirloin cap steak.

General
Description: *The coulotte (NAMP 184D) is the cap muscle on the top of the top sirloin and is well suited to grilling or pan frying.* This cut is an exceptional value and can be cut into narrow steaks or cooked whole. The coulotte has the most marbling of the whole lean top sirloin, making it flavorful, juicy, and tender. A coulotte roast or steak is best marinated or seasoned with an herb rub, then dry roasted or grilled; it can also be braised and served as a pot roast. Coulotte works well cut into large cubes

for kabobs and stews, small cubes for chili, or thin strips for stir-fry.

Part of Animal: This flat, triangular-shaped muscle lies immediately over the top butt of the sirloin.

Characteristics: The coulotte does not contain any gristle or connective tissue. Its relatively coarse grain runs lengthwise. Though tender, it is fairly lean and may need additional fat when cooking.

How to Choose: Because this muscle is long and thin, look for the largest coulotte, especially if cutting it crosswise into steaks, to increase the surface area for browning.

Amount to Buy: For a whole roast, allow 6 to 9 ounces (170–255 g) of meat per person.

Storage: Refrigerate whole coulotte for 3 to 4 days; refrigerate
x 2–4   coulotte steaks for 2 to 3 days.

Preparation: 1.   **Trim to a compact shape and then cut across the grain into steaks about 1 inch (2.5 cm) thick or leave whole to roast or cook in a covered grill. Dry-rub or marinate refrigerated for up to one day, if desired.**

 2.   **If whole, oven-roast at high temperature (450°F/230°C) for about 15 minutes, or until well browned, and then reduce heat to moderate**

(350°F/180°C) for about 25 minutes, or until it reaches desired internal temperature. (See Roasting Chart, page 294.) For steaks, grill or pan-sear at high heat and finish in a hot (400°F/200°C) oven for about 10 minutes.

Flavor Affinities:
Allspice, barbecue sauce, carrots, cumin, Dijon mustard, garlic, onions, oregano, rosemary, thyme.

6.   **FLANK STEAK**

Other Names:
Bifteck de flanc or *bavette de flanchet* (French), jiffy steak, London broil, *pancia* or *bavetta* (Italian), *redondo* or *filete de falda* (Spanish).

General Description:
The small, thin, tasty, and quick-cooking flank steak (NAMP 193) is cut from the flank primal. It is ideal for marinating and outdoor grilling over aromatic woods. Marinade can penetrate flank steak thoroughly without the meat losing its firm texture because it is relatively thin and porous. The original London broil, a name used since the 1930s and now applied to many cuts, was a tangy, marinated grilled flank steak.

Part of Animal:
The flank is a single muscle from the flank region beneath the loin and in front of the back legs.

Characteristics:
Flank steak is boneless and weighs 1 to 2 pounds (450–910 g). It is about 14 inches long (35 cm), less

than 1 inch (2.5 cm) thick at the thin, pointy end, and up to 2 inches (5 cm) thick at the thicker flat end. The muscle grain is quite coarse and runs lengthwise. There is a moderate amount of fat, though little to no connective tissue.

How to Choose: Choose a relatively large flank steak so that when cooked it is thick enough to be crusty on the outside and still rare to medium-rare. However, a smaller steak will be milder and taste less like liver.

Amount to Buy: One large flank steak will feed about four people. Allow 4 to 8 ounces (115–225 g) per person.

Storage: Store in the refrigerator for up to 3 days or up to 4 days if marinated or rubbed with oil.

Preparation: **1. Trim off any excess surface fat and silverskin; marinate or dry-rub with spices, and refrigerate for up to 2 days, if desired.**

2. Make shallow crisscross cuts on both sides of the meat to keep it from curling up.

3. Grill, broil, or pan-sear over high heat while the meat is still cold so it doesn't overcook before forming a crust, 4 to 5 minutes a side for rare to medium-rare. Like other coarse-textured meats, flank should be cooked to no more than medium-rare.

4. **Remove the meat from the heat, drape with foil, and allow to rest for about 10 minutes before slicing.**

 NOTE: **It is important to cut flank steak into thin slices against the grain or it will be tough and stringy.**

Flavor Affinities: Chile peppers, cumin, garlic, ginger, hoisin sauce, molasses, oregano, salsa, sesame oil, soy sauce.

7a. **GROUND BEEF AND CUBE STEAK**

Other Names: **Ground Beef:** *Boeuf haché* (French), *carne macinato* (Italian), *carne molida* (Spanish), ground chuck, ground round, ground sirloin, hamburger meat, hamburger patties, minced beef (British), Salisbury steak.
Cube Steak: Braising beef, minute steak.

General Description: *Ground beef (NAMP 136–137) is beef that has been cut into chunks, chilled, and put through a meat grinder.* What we call hamburger had its origin in Russia with fourteenth-century nomadic Tartar peoples who liked their beef raw, chopped fine, and seasoned. Ships based in Hamburg, Germany, brought this "Tartar steak" back home, where it eventually began to be cooked as "Hamburger Steak."

　　There are many types of ground beef, though many people believe ground chuck has the best flavor. Depending on the type, fat may have been added to the meat during grinding. Hamburger is ground beef to which seasonings and extra beef fat may be added. Salisbury steak is an oblong ground-beef patty flavored with minced onion and seasonings and then fried or broiled. It was named after nineteenth-century English physician Dr. James Salisbury, who recommended that his patients eat plenty of beef.

Cube steak (NAMP 1100–1102) is a tough cut of meat that the butcher tenderizes by pounding. Less expensive cubes may consist of pieces of meat "knitted" together. Cube steak makes for good chili and meat sauces.

Part of Animal: Ground beef may be made from the trimmings of various cuts, though ground chuck, ground round, and ground sirloin are the most popular. Cube steak may come from any tough cut but the heel or shank.

Characteristics: Fresh-cut ground meat is purplish in color, but oxygen reacts with meat pigments to form the bright red color (called beef bloom) on the surface. The interior of the meat may be grayish brown due to lack of oxygen; however, if all the ground meat in the package has turned gray or brown, it should be avoided.

Retail stores sometimes grind the meat while still frozen. Ice crystals in the frozen meat break down the cell walls so that juice is released during cooking; this also happens after ground meat is frozen at home. The amount of shrinkage will depend on fat content, the cooking temperature, and how long it is cooked. The higher the fat content and cooking temperature, the greater the shrinkage.

How to Choose: When at the store, pick up ground beef last. Choose a cold package that is not torn, with the latest sell-by date available. Use your nose: Ground beef should smell fresh and meaty, not sour or unpleasant.

Ground beef (and hamburger) is allowed up to 30 percent fat by the USDA. Ground chuck has a high fat content (20 to 25 percent), so it makes the juiciest hamburgers and meatloaf. Ground round is very lean (up to 15 percent fat). Ground sirloin is lean (15 to 20 percent fat), but it's more flavorful than ground round. An ideal percentage of fat is about 20 percent; under 15 percent will give you a dry and tasteless burger.

Amount to Buy: Allow 6 to 10 ounces (170–285 g) per person.

Storage: When meat is ground, more surfaces are exposed to

bacteria, which multiply rapidly in the "danger zone" between 40 and 140°F (4–60°C). Store at or below 40°F (4°C), and use within 2 days or freeze.

Preparation: **Ground beef is ready to cook from the package.**

Hamburgers:

1.   **If desired, combine meat with seasonings and finely**

diced onion. Mix lightly with your hands until just combined—do not overwork or the burgers will toughen.

 2. Form into the desired shape by lightly packing together the meat and patting into a round or oblong shape of even thickness. Rub lightly with oil, and season with salt and pepper.

 3. Pan-sear, grill, or broil hamburgers at high temperature for crustiness and browned flavor for 8 to 10 minutes total, or at lower temperature for 10 to 15 minutes to reduce shrinkage.

NOTE: To destroy harmful bacteria, cook ground beef to 160°F (71°C). Overcooking draws out fat and juices, making the meat dry and tasteless.

Flavor Affinities: American cheese, avocados, barbecue sauce, blue cheese, cheddar cheese, chili sauce, chutney, ketchup, mozzarella, mustard, onions, tomatoes, steak sauce.

8. **HANGING TENDER**

Other Names: Butcher's steak, butcher's tenderloin, hanger steak, *lombatello* (Italian), *onglet* (French), pillar, *solomillo de pulmon* (Spanish).

General Description:	*Hanging tender (NAMP 140) is a small, intensely flavored, odd-shaped cut that "hangs" from the diaphragm.* This popular bistro steak is better known in France than in the United States. Butchers have traditionally kept this less well-known cut for themselves. In recent years, hanger steak has become popular with chefs and steak aficionados because of its rich flavor. Like its neighbor, the skirt, this slightly chewy meat is dark in color with a beefy flavor and grainy texture. There is only one hanger steak per animal.
Part of Animal:	The hanging tender is an interior cut attached to and supporting the diaphragm. It hangs off the kidney below the tenderloin and is attached to the last rib.
Characteristics:	Hanger steak consists of two small muscles joined by a tough elastic membrane. Before trimming, this long, V-shaped strip of 1 1/2- to 2-inch (3.8–5 cm) thick muscle with a diagonal grain weighs about 1 pound (450 g), with little internal fat and abundant juices.
How to Choose:	All hanger steaks are approximately the same size and weight. The lengthwise elastic membrane should be removed by the butcher, leaving two long, thin sections about 8 ounces (225 g) each. Look for hanger steak at a specialty butcher shop.
Amount to Buy:	Because this steak is normally purchased already trimmed by the butcher and must be cooked quickly,

there is little shrinkage. Allow 6 to 9 ounces (170–255 g) per person.

Storage: Marinate if desired, and refrigerate for up to 2 days.

x2

Preparation: 1. **Drain well and pat dry. Remove the long, tough membrane from the center if necessary.**

 2. **Rub with oil, salt, and pepper, then broil, pan-sear, or grill over high heat, 10 to 15 minutes for rare to medium-rare, turning at least once.**

 3. **Remove the meat from the heat, drape loosely with foil, and allow to rest for about 10 minutes before slicing against the grain, if desired, for serving.**

Flavor Affinities: Brandy, celeriac, ginger, mushrooms, mustard, onions, parsnips, red wine, scallions, soy sauce, thyme.

KNUCKLE

Other Names: **Roasts:** Bald tip roast, ball tip roast, barbecue roast, French roll roast, *girello di noce* (Italian), *redondo de babilla* or *bola* (Spanish), *rond de tranche grasse* (French), round tip roast, sirloin butt roast, sirloin tip roast, thick flank (British), tip roast. **Steaks:** Ball tip steak, breakfast steak, minute steak, round tip steak, sandwich steak, sirloin tip steak.

General
Description:

One of the most versatile cuts of beef, the knuckle (or beef tip) is one of three main parts of the round. The trimmed tip (NAMP 167A) is found most often in retail butcher shops rather than on restaurant menus. It can be cut into countless items, from kabobs to London broil. A barbecue roast is a retail name for a solid side of sirloin tip that is cut, rolled, and tied to make a small-diameter roast suitable for spit or rotisserie roasting. Although less tender than sirloin or loin roasts, ball tip roasts can be quite tasty and are suitable for dry roasting, especially if marinated.

Stroganoff is thin strips of beef, often cut from the knuckle, used for the Russian dish beef Stroganoff, with mushrooms in a sour cream sauce. The strips may also be cut from the top round (page 61) or tenderloin tip (page 57).

Part of Animal:

The beef knuckle lies at the top of the round just beyond the sirloin and is the muscle group just above the kneecap. (A part of this muscle is included in the sirloin, depending on how the beef carcass was cut up.)

Characteristics:

Beef knuckle is a solid muscle group weighing 12 to 16 pounds (5.4–7.3 kg) that has had the small "cap" or tri-tip (page 66) muscle removed.

How to Choose:

In most retail markets at least a portion of the beef tip is sold as a roast of 4 to 8 pounds (1.8–3.6 kg). Usually it is trimmed and split down the middle and each half is tied into a rolled roast. Tip can be identified by the horseshoe- or oval-shaped line of connective tissue in the center of each cut. The center portion (NAMP 167E) is the most tender part of the round.

Amount to Buy: Allow 6 to 8 ounces (170–225 g) per portion.

Storage: Refrigerate roasts up to 4 days, steaks up to 2 days.

x2-4

Preparation: 1. **Press seasoning ingredients (salt, pepper, spices, and herbs) evenly into the surface.**

2. **Roast fat side up at 325°F (165°C), uncovered, about 1 hour for a 3-pound (1.4 kg) roast. (See Roasting Chart, page 294.)**

3. **Remove from the oven and let rest, covered with foil, for 15 to 20 minutes. The temperature will rise about 5°F (2°C). Carve roast into thin slices.**

Flavor Affinities: Allspice, cumin, garlic, hot peppers, marjoram, mushrooms, mustard, onions, oregano, paprika, thyme.

---

9. ## OXTAIL

Other Names: *Coda di bue* (Italian), *queue de boeuf* (French), *rabo de toro* (Spanish).

General
Description:
Oxtails (NAMP 1791), formerly the tails of oxen (castrated bulls used as work animals), are the tails of any beef cattle. A comfort food for many, these bits of bony meat make some of the most delicious braised beef dishes. They have an unmatched silky tenderness and give a rich, smooth consistency to their sauce because of the large amount of gelatinous collagen released during slow cooking. People from Caribbean countries have long known how delicious oxtails are; in Jamaica, they are typically seasoned with tomato, onion, habanero chiles, allspice, and thyme and then stewed.

Part of Animal:
Oxtails are the tails of any kind of beef cattle.

Characteristics:
Oxtails have small amounts of stringy, coarse-textured meat interspersed with fat and connective tissue full of collagen. There is, of course, only one oxtail per animal, which weighs 2 to 4 pounds (.9–1.8 kg). Oxtails are generally sold cut into lengths of 2 1/2 to 3 inches (6.3–7.5 cm) and resemble miniature osso buco (cut veal shanks, page 95).

How to Choose:
Oxtails are generally sold frozen and may be specially ordered or found in ethnic meat markets. If ordering oxtails wholesale, be sure to specify cut oxtails, or you may end up with a large, skinned, whole tail.

Amount to Buy:
Buy 3/4 to 1 pound (340–450 g) per person, to allow for the bone.

Storage: Keep frozen. Defrost overnight in the refrigerator.

Preparation: 1. **Season oxtails with salt, pepper, and spices, then brown well in oil over high heat, remove from pot, and reserve. Pour off fat and discard.**

2. **Add aromatic vegetables to the pot along with flavorful liquid such as stock or wine and bring to a boil.**

3. **Return the oxtails to the pan, cover, and simmer very slowly (or bake at 300°F/150°C) for about 3 hours or until fork tender.**

4. **Remove from the heat and cool, keeping the oxtails submerged by weighing them down with a plate, and refrigerate overnight or until the fat congeals.**

5. **Remove the fat and reheat gently.**

Flavor Affinities: Allspice, anise, basil, beer, ginger, mushrooms, mustard, red wine, shallots, soy sauce, white wine.

RIB

Other Names: **Roasts:** Bone-in rib-eye roast, *costillar* or *cuarto central costilla* (Spanish), fore rib (British), *insieme de costine* or *meta'schiena* (Italian), prime rib, rib-eye, rib roast, *train de côtes* (French). **Steaks:** Beauty steak,

Delmonico steak, *entrecôte* (French), market steak, rib-eye steak, shell steak, Spencer steak. **Rib Cap:** Boneless short ribs, RLM (rib lifter meat), rib lifters.

General Description:

The naturally tender, luxurious beef rib (NAMP 109–112) is one of the eight primal cuts of beef. For dramatic presentation and rich flavor, nothing beats this cut, also known mistakenly as prime rib. (Prime rib can only come from prime-graded beef.) This is the cut used to make the king of roasts for grand celebrations, the **standing rib roast**. Steaks cut from the rib section, either on the bone, including the attached smaller muscles, or completely trimmed so that only the "eye" remains, are tender and flavorful. At top butcher shops, whole prime ribs are used for dry aging.

This cut includes the large "eye" muscle and several smaller attached muscles, including the fatty but very tasty meat called variously **rib-eye lip muscle**, **cap**, **rib lifter**, or **deckle** (NAMP 112D), which lies between the eye and the thick layer of fat that covers the rib. The lean **blade meat** (NAMP 109B) lies just above and below the main rib-eye muscle at the shoulder blade end of the rib-eye. In French, **entrecôte** means "between the ribs" and refers to a steak cut from between ribs 9 and 11. In the United States, it would be called a **rib steak**, although *entrecôte* is sometimes incorrectly used in the United States to refer to a boneless strip steak. A **cowboy steak** is a bone-in rib-eye steak.

Chili meat (or diced beef) is often made from the loose-textured deckle meat or rib lifter meat from the top of the rib. It is similar to stew meat, but cut into smaller pieces. Thinly sliced rib-eye is often poached and used in Japanese and Korean dishes.

Part of Animal: The rib section spans ribs 6 through 12. (The first five ribs are in the chuck; the 13th is in the sirloin.)

Characteristics: The rib section includes several different muscles, all relatively tender; the largest is the central "eye." The rib is a relatively fatty cut, though rich in flavor. The coarse-grained muscles on top of the eye, called rib lifters, are sometimes sold separately.

How to Choose: A full 7-bone rib roast can weigh more than 15 pounds (6.8 kg). Although sold in smaller sections, the best roast includes at least three ribs. A bone-in rib-eye roast has had the external fat and smaller muscles removed so that it is smaller and easier to carve.

The front section closer to the chuck (ribs 6 to 9) is larger all around but contains a smaller eye, a large proportion of the less desirable adjoining blade muscles, and more fat. To make carving easier, be sure the chine bones (vertebrae), feather bones (sticking up from the spine), and the back strap (lengthwise tough, yellow ligament) have been removed. When choosing rib-eye steaks, look for the ones with the largest eye and least outside fat and "tail."

Amount to Buy:	For whole bone-in rib roast, allow a little more than 1 pound (450 g) per person, or one rib for every two people. For boneless rib-eye roast or steaks, allow ¹/₂ pound (225 g) per person. The back section (ribs 10 to 12) generally costs more than the front section (ribs 6 to 9).
Storage: x2~4	Store whole bone-in rib eye up to 4 days refrigerated. Store rib steaks up to 2 days refrigerated.
Preparation: 1.	**If necessary, cut away and discard excess fat.**
2.	**If desired, cut crisscross cuts though the fat but not into the meat to encourage excess fat to melt off and make crispy diamond-shaped sections of fat. Season with salt and pepper. Tie with butcher's twine for a more compact shape, if desired.**
3.	**Roast bone-side down at 450°F (230°C) for 15 minutes, reduce heat to 350°F (180°C), and roast for 1 hour, or until it reaches the desired internal temperature. (See Roasting Chart, page 294.)**
4.	**Remove from the oven, cover with foil, and let rest 15 to 30 minutes before carving. Note that the meat will rise in temperature about 5°F (2°C) as it rests.**
Flavor Affinities:	Brandy, garlic, horseradish, red wine, rosemary, soy sauce, steak sauce, thyme, truffles, wild mushrooms.

11. **RUMP**

Other Names: **Roasts:** *Cadera* (Spanish), diamond-cut roast, full rump (British), Manhattan roast, melon roast, *punta di scamone* (Italian, rump tail), round tip roast, rump roast, rump triangle, *scamone* (Italian), *tapilla* (Spanish, rump tail), watermelon roast, wedge-cut rump roast. **Steaks:** Manhattan steak, *rumsteak* (French), rump steak, Swiss steak.

General Description: *Rump roast is a triangular cut from the top end of the hindquarter, which has an unusually good flavor.* This retail cut comes from a portion of the beef that lies partially in the round and partially in the sirloin. The rump makes a delicious roast if it is graded prime or choice, or it may be pot-roasted, cut into steaks, or used for stew or ground beef.

A standing rump roast includes the hipbone. Thin slices of rump may be pounded almost paper thin and dressed with lemon and olive oil for carpaccio (see page 58). Rump steaks are sold as Swiss steaks, a name which may have come from "swissing," a British term for running cloth through rollers for smoothing. To make Swiss steak, the meat is pounded thin, floured, and then braised in a tomato-and-onion mixture.

Part of Animal: The rump is a triangular cut that includes portions of the sirloin and the flat muscle from the bottom round.

Characteristics:	The rump contains moderate amounts of fat and is fairly tender. Rump from a prime or choice steer will be moist and tender enough to dry roast.
How to Choose:	The rump is a boneless roast of 4 to 6 pounds (1.8–2.7 kg). For chicken-fried steak, choose 3/4-inch (1.9 cm) thick steaks with little connective tissue.
Amount to Buy:	Allow 6 to 9 ounces (170–255 g) rump per portion.
Storage: ☐ x2–4	Store roasts up to 4 days refrigerated. Refrigerate steaks up to 2 days. The thinner the steak, the quicker it needs to be used.
Preparation:	• **To prepare a rump pot roast, see the instructions for bottom round, page 11.**
	• **To prepare a rump roast, see the instructions for beef knuckle, page 33.**
Flavor Affinities:	Beer, brown sugar, chili sauce, garlic, mustard, onions, pancetta, red wine, rosemary, thyme, tomatoes, vinegar.

---

12. 📷   **SHANK**

Other Names:	*Garrón* or *chambarete* (Spanish), *giaretto* (Italian), *gîte de derrière* (French, rear), *gîte de devant* (French, front), shin.

General
Description:

Full of great beefy flavor though quite tough, beef shanks (NAMP 117) are cut from the bottom portion of either the front or rear leg (from the knee to the hoof). Like oxtail (page 35), crosscut shanks simmered slowly in water or broth until the tough connective tissue and tendons turn to gelatin impart full body and rich flavor to soups. Shank meat ground once through the coarse plate of a meat grinder is unbeatable for chili. Boneless shank meat is popular in Korean cuisine, where it is used to make pressed shank meat, and may be found in Asian markets.

Part of Animal:

Shanks are either the front or rear legs. More front shanks are found; rear shanks are cut up or ground.

Characteristics:

Front shanks are smaller and not as tough as rear shanks. Shanks are relatively lean, consisting of many small muscles and lots of gelatin-rich connective tissue with a round bone in the center.

How to Choose:

To make a rich beef stock, buy crosscut beef shanks, which look like gigantic osso buco rounds cut 1 to 2 inches (2.5–5 cm) thick. For Korean-style pressed beef, buy boneless shank meat, which consists of dense, cone-shaped sections of dark-colored muscle, ending in silverskin and tendon at one end and plump and open at the other. Hindshanks will be large in diameter; foreshanks are smaller, but either will work for almost every recipe. Choose center-cut shank rounds with a small round bone in the middle, if possible, because they will have more meat.

Amount to Buy:	Buy about 8 pounds (3.6 kg) of beef shank to make 1 gallon (3.8 l) of rich soup broth. Buy about 3/4 pound (340 g) boneless shank meat per person.
Storage: x2-3	Store cut beef shanks refrigerated up to 3 days. Store boneless beef shank meat refrigerated up to 2 days.
Preparation:	***Stock:***

1. **Simmer crosscut beef shanks in water to cover for 4 to 5 hours, skimming as necessary, or until the meat is tender enough to fall away from the bone.**

2. **Strain, discarding the meat or saving for another use.**

Flavor Affinities:	Black pepper, chile paste, garlic, ginger, green onions, lemons, herbs, paprika, sesame oil, soy sauce, sugar.

13a-g. **SHORT RIBS**

Other Names:	Asian-style chuck short ribs, back ribs, barbecue ribs, blade meat, braising ribs, chuck short ribs, *costata* or *costine de pancia* (Italian, back or plate ribs), *costillas del lomo* or *costillas cortas* (Spanish, back or plate ribs), *côtes de basse* or *côtes de plat* (French, back or plate

ribs), crosscut ribs, dinosaur ribs, English short ribs, flanken, Korean short ribs, plate short ribs, pony-bock ribs (British, plate ribs).

General Description:

Short ribs are cut from different sections of the 12 ribs that start at the chuck (shoulder) and continue to the loin. Relatively square, short ribs have full-bodied flavor and luscious tenderness that develop when they are slow-cooked by hot-smoking, slow-roasting, or braising. Short ribs are especially popular in Korean, Chinese, and Jewish cuisines. Although retail meat markets don't usually distinguish which section the short ribs are cut from, each kind is somewhat different. Beef **plate ribs** (NAMP 123) will be less expensive than **chuck ribs** (NAMP 130). Beef **back ribs** (NAMP 124), sometimes called dinosaur ribs, will be the most expensive. A **royal rib** is just the sixth rib with the meat cut partially from the bone, rolled, and tied.

Korean-style ribs are thin slices cut either across the ribs or accordion-cut parallel to the ribs. Eastern European Jewish flanken or crosscut ribs (NAMP 1123) are cut across the bones in strips 2 to 3 inches (5–7.5 cm) wide. English short ribs can be either bone-in or boneless. English or Asian short ribs may also be cut sections of chuck rib bones with meat attached. Boneless short ribs may be used for stew.

Part of Animal:

Short ribs are cut from the chuck (shoulder), the loin, and the plate (belly).

Characteristics:	Short ribs consist of dense layers of rather tough, medium-coarse grain meat interwoven with layers of fat and connective tissue. They usually include the rib bones.
How to Choose:	The most common short ribs come from the plate and are rather fatty but meaty and are cut from ribs 6 to 8. Chuck short ribs, cut from ribs 1 to 5 in the shoulder section, are tougher but less fatty. Back ribs, the portion left after the rib-eye is removed, are not as meaty but are more tender.
Amount to Buy:	Buy at least 1 pound (450 g) of bone-in short ribs per person to allow for bone and shrinkage. Allow 1/2 pound (225 g) of boneless short ribs per person.
Storage:	Refrigerate short ribs up to 4 days.
Preparation: 1.	**Trim excess fat. Score the fat layer in a crisscross pattern to encourage the fat to melt out.**
2.	**If desired, cure with a wet spice rub, brine, or dry-rub with spices up to 3 days before cooking to let the flavors meld. Keep refrigerated until ready to cook.**
3.	**Tie ribs with butcher's string to keep their shape and brown lightly. Slow-cook in a moist environment, braising for about 3 hours, hot-smoking for up to 10 hours, cooking in a crockpot on low for 8 to 10**

hours, or slow-roasting at 300°F (150°C) about 4
hours, or until fork tender but not falling apart.

⏳ 4.   **Chill overnight, remove fat, and reheat in liquid.**

Flavor
Affinities: Cilantro, garlic, ginger, green onions, molasses, mushrooms, onions, red wine, sesame oil, soy sauce, thyme.

---

14. 📷   **SHOULDER CENTER**

Other Names: **Whole:** Clod heart, mock brisket, *planchuela* (Spanish).
Steaks: Beef filet, ranch-cut steak, shoulder steak.

General
Description: *Shoulder center (NAMP 114E) is a new cut developed to make better use of the less utilized though flavorful and tender shoulder center muscles.* The whole trimmed shoulder center makes an excellent roast that can be sliced thinly for sandwiches. It is similar in flavor and texture to top sirloin but at lower prices. It is ideal as a breakfast or lunch steak because of its moderate size and price. It's also well suited to sandwiches and salads.

Part of Animal: This roast and steaks are from the shoulder center, an arm muscle that is part of the larger shoulder muscle group called the shoulder clod (page 22).

Characteristics: This cut is tender and juicy with moderate grain. The connective tissue should be removed by the butcher.

How to Choose:	A whole roast weighs 8 to 12 pounds (3.6–5.4 kg). Steaks are found in 4- to 10-ounce (115–285 g) portions and are 1 1/2 to 2 inches (3.8–5 cm) thick and are commonly sold frozen.
Amount to Buy:	Allow 4 ounces (115 g) for a breakfast or lunch portion and up to 10 ounces (285 g) for a dinner portion.
Storage:	Store ranch-cut steaks up to 2 days refrigerated, up to 3 days if rubbed with oil.

x2-3

Preparation: 1.	**Rub with oil and season with salt, pepper, and spices.**
2.	**Grill, pan-sear, or broil 16 to 20 minutes for medium-rare, or until it reaches the desired internal temperature. (See Roasting Chart, page 294.)**
Flavor Affinities:	Balsamic vinegar, barbecue sauce, chipotle chiles, lime, mint, oregano, red peppers, tequila, whiskey.

---

15. SHOULDER TENDER

Other Names:	Butcher's steak, chuck shoulder steak, petite filet, shoulder tender medallions, shoulder tender roast.
General Description:	*The small, juicy shoulder tender (NAMP 114F) is a versatile, lean, and quick-cooking cut from the chuck.* The method of separating out this small muscle was

recently developed to obtain one of the most tender and flavorful muscles in the beef shoulder (chuck). Introduced first in restaurants, where it works well because one muscle equals one generous portion, this cut is now reaching retail markets. There are just two of these small muscles per beef carcass.

Part of Animal:	This small oblong muscle rests atop the shoulder near the top blade and is part of the chuck shoulder clod.
Characteristics:	The shoulder tender has little connective tissue and fat. Trimmed, it weighs about 8 ounces (225 g) and is about 10 inches (25 cm) long by 3 inches (7.5 cm) wide. The medium-coarse grain curves lengthwise.
How to Choose:	Buy shoulder tender whole or precut into medallions about 3/4 inch (1.9 cm) thick. A whole shoulder tender is large enough to serve one to two people at home and will have less shrinkage than medallions. Choose the largest shoulder tender to obtain a roast with a crusty outside and juicy, tender inside.
Amount to Buy:	Allow 6 to 12 ounces (170–340 g) per person of this 100 percent usable cut. It doesn't shrink much because it is suitable for quick cooking.
Storage:	Refrigerate shoulder tender for up to 3 days. To cut into medallions, cut crosswise 3/4 inch (1.9 cm) thick while still somewhat frozen.

Preparation:	1.	**Trim off pointy tips to make a compact, even shape.**

2. **If desired, marinate overnight refrigerated, or rub with oil, garlic, and spices before cooking.**

3. **Roast whole at high temperature (425°F/220°C) for 20 to 25 minutes or pan-sear then finish in a 400°F (200°C) oven for about 10 minutes. Pan-sear medallions in oil until cooked to desired temperature.**

NOTE: **Like other coarse-grain cuts, the shoulder tender is best cooked to no more than medium-rare.**

Flavor
Affinities: Chile paste, Dijon mustard, garlic, ginger, molasses, orange, rosemary, sesame oil, shallots, soy sauce, thyme.

---

16.   **SKIRT STEAK**

Other Names: *Bavette aloyau* or *hampe* (French), *carne de falda* or *falda residual* (Spanish), *fajita* (Latin American), goose-skirt or thin skirt (British), Philadelphia steak, *spuntatura di lombata*, *bavetta oculo de aba*, or *lombatello sottile* (Italian).

General
Description: *Skirt steak is a thin, long, fan-shaped cut from the beef plate (belly) primal.* Like its neighbor the hanger steak (page 31), skirt steak is one of the most flavorful of all steaks. There are two types of skirt: inside (NAMP

121D) and outside (NAMP 121C), with inside skirt preferred because it doesn't have as much membrane to be removed. This belt-shaped flap of tender meat is the source of the word *fajita* ("belt" in Spanish). Skirt steak is the authentic meat for fajitas, preferably cooked over natural wood or charcoal. This cut is particularly delicious when marinated because its loose texture allows it to absorb flavors and its strong taste holds up to bold seasonings.

Part of Animal:	The inside skirt is cut from the plate (middle belly section) and is attached to the inside of the rib cage. The outside skirt consists of the diaphragm covered by a thick whitish membrane (the peritoneum) that is normally removed before sale.
Characteristics:	This cut is coarse textured with a pronounced grain that runs crosswise at a slight angle. The lean meat should be practically free of outside fat. There is a 3-pound (1.4 kg) inside skirt and a 1.5-pound (680 g) outside skirt steak on each side of the carcass.
How to Choose:	Skirt steak is sold rolled into pinwheel-shaped individual steaks or as is. Look for fat-free, trimmed skirt steak with the membrane removed.
Amount to Buy:	One trimmed inside skirt steak will weigh about 1 pound (450 g) and can feed two to four people.

Storage: Store up to 2 days refrigerated, up to 3 days if marinated and refrigerated.

Preparation: 1. **Marinate at least 1 hour, or up to 24 hours refrigerated. Or dry-rub the steak with spices and refrigerate,
wrapped in plastic, for 12 hours or overnight.**

2. **If marinated, drain and pat steak dry. Lightly brush
the steak with oil and grill over high heat, 3 to 5 minutes a side for medium-rare.**

 3. **Wrap the meat in a double thickness of aluminum
foil and allow it to rest for 15 minutes. Thinly slice
across the grain and serve.**

NOTE: **Skirt steak toughens if cooked to more than medium.**

Flavor Allspice, ancho chile, balsamic vinegar, cinnamon,
Affinities: cumin, garlic, lime, oregano, scallions, soy sauce.

 STRIP LOIN

Other Names: **Whole loin, Bone-In or Boneless:** Diamond cut,
faux-filet or *contre-filet* (French), *lombo* or *controfiletto*
(Italian), *lomo* (Spanish), short loin, shell loin, short-
cut beef loin, striploin (British), top loin. **Bone-In
Strip Loin Steak:** Club steak, Delmonico steak, shell
steak, sirloin strip steak. **Boneless Strip Loin Steak:**

Ambassador steak, boneless club steak, entrecôte, hotel steak, Kansas City steak, New York strip steak, *tagliata* (Italian), veiny steak.

General Description:

The high-priced strip loin is often cut into bone-in (NAMP 175, 1175) or boneless (NAMP 180, 1180) roasts or steaks that are prized by steak lovers. It is considered sacrilege to marinate this primal cut or to cook it beyond medium-rare. Whether roasted whole or cut into steaks, the strip loin is a special-occasion meat, commanding prices to match. The quality of marbling in this cut is an indicator of the quality of the entire cattle; beef grade in the United States is determined by examining the marbling at the rib end of the strip loin.

At top butcher shops, prime whole strip loins are used for dry aging. New York or Kansas City strip steaks are boneless steaks from this section. Strip steaks are ideal for dry-heat methods such as smoking and grilling. A shell steak is cut from the smaller end of the strip loin adjoining the rib. It has a bone along one side, but doesn't include any of the tenderloin.

Part of Animal:

The strip loin lies between the ribs and the upper hip (sirloin). It is the rear part of the long muscle that runs down the back on top of the ribs.

Characteristics:

The dense grain of this cut is flavorful and slightly chewy; succulence increases with the amount of marbling. Strip loin tends to be mealy if overcooked.

How to Choose: Strip steaks cut from the front end nearer the rib will be the most tender. These are rounder in shape; the muscle flattens as it nears the rear end of the beef and starts to include a section of a different muscle. Bone-in strip steaks include a portion of the "finger" bones that stick out from the side of the backbone. Veiny (or end-cut) steaks have a small piece of tough gluteus muscle above the main muscle. Steaks from farther back in the loin will have more gluteus muscle and connective tissue, and they are less desirable.

Amount to Buy: Buy meat with the most marbling, allowing 3/4 pound (340 g) of steak or roast per person. Choose steaks that are at least 1 inch (2.5 cm) thick.

Storage: Refrigerate whole strip loin up to 5 days; strip steaks will keep up to 3 days refrigerated. Vacuum-packed strip steaks may be refrigerated for up to 5 days in their packaging.

x 3–5

Preparation: 1.   **Spread a whole trimmed strip loin with a paste of oil, salt, pepper, garlic, and chopped herbs and allow it to come to room temperature.**

2.   **Roast whole strip loin for about 1 hour, fat side up, starting at 450°F (230°C) for 15 minutes, then 350°F (180°C) for 45 minutes, or until it reaches the desired temperature. (See Roasting Chart, page 294.)**

3. **Remove from the oven, cover with foil, and let rest 15 to 30 minutes before carving. The meat will increase in temperature about 5°F (2°C) as it rests.**

Flavor Affinities: Cognac, coriander seed, garlic, mushrooms, red wine, rosemary, shallots, thyme, truffles, wood smoke.

18 a–b.

T-BONE AND PORTERHOUSE STEAKS

General Description: *The T-bone and the porterhouse are steakhouse favorites adjoining each other on the loin and including portions of both the tenderloin and the strip loin.* These bone-in steaks fetch a high price. A double-thick T-bone of white Chianina beef cattle grilled rare over natural oak charcoal and served sliced for two, called La Fiorentina, is a Tuscan specialty.

The T-bone (NAMP 1174) is cut from the front section of the loin (near the rib section) and includes a smaller section of both the tenderloin and the strip loin. It may weigh 8 to 24 ounces (225–680 g) and gets its name from the T-shaped bone that includes the backbone and its attached finger bones.

The porterhouse (NAMP 1173) is cut from the middle to rear section of the loin and includes a larger section of both the tenderloin and the strip loin. It gets its name from the old coach stops called porter-houses. In 1814, Martin Morrison, a New York porterhouse keeper, began to serve this steak with ale.

Part of Animal:	Both of these bone-in steaks are cut straight through the loin section and include portions of the tenderloin and the strip loin.
Characteristics:	Both of these steaks are tender and flavorful.
How to Choose:	Choose steaks with the largest size of each of the two main muscles and with the least amount of "tail," which is actually a continuation of the skirt (page 50). Steaks should be at least 1 1/2 inches (3.8 cm) thick.
Amount to Buy:	Because the bone itself is quite dense and heavy, allow at least 1 pound (450 g) per person.
Storage:	Refrigerate T-bone and porterhouse steaks up to 3 days. Lightly oil to prevent them from drying out.

Storage icon: x3

Preparation:	1.	**If the steaks are quite thick, allow them to come to room temperature before cooking. Rub with oil and season with salt and pepper and other seasoning, if desired.**
	2.	**Grill, broil, or pan-sear at high heat and finish in a hot oven (400°F/200°C) for about 12 minutes for medium-rare or to the desired temperature. (See Roasting Chart, page 294.)**
Flavor Affinities:		Black pepper, brandy, garlic, lemon, olive oil, port wine, red wine, rosemary, shallots, thyme.

TENDERLOIN

19a–c.

Other Names: **Filet:** *Bifteck* (French, tenderloin butt), *chateaubriand* (French, large center section), filet, *filet mignon* (French, small end), filet of beef, *filete* or *solomillo* (Spanish), *filetto* (Italian), *tournedos* (French, smaller center-cut section). **Chain:** *Bavette* or *chaînette* (French), false filet, rope.

General Description: *The baseball bat–shaped tenderloin is the most tender muscle in the short loin.* This elegant cut has mellow flavor and velvety texture. The tenderloin, or filet (NAMP 189–192), is incredibly versatile and takes equally well to roasting whole, sautéing with a rich and luscious sauce, or grilling and topping with flavored butter. Though expensive, there's little waste, it's easy to prepare, cooks quickly, and is a crowd pleaser. Chateaubriand is an extra thick, 2- to 3-inch (5–7.5 cm) long steak cut from the butt end (the larger end). It may have been named after the French Vicomte de Châteaubriand.

The chain is the long thin muscle alongside the main muscle. In France, the chain is known as the *bavette*, and it is grilled. You may find *bavette* rolled and tied or cut crosswise into steaks. Tenderloin tips, small pieces cut from the smaller, pointed front end, may be a good value.

Beef carpaccio, named after Vittore Carpaccio, an Italian Renaissance painter known for his orange reds, was created at Harry's Bar in Venice. Very fresh, well-trimmed, and well-chilled beef from the tenderloin, rump (page 41), or top sirloin butt (page 64) is sliced thin enough to be almost translucent. The beef is arranged in a single layer and then sprinkled with olive oil, lemon, salt, and pepper or mustard.

Part of Animal: The filet lies underneath the ribs alongside the back-bone, paralleling the strip loin (page 52); its smaller pointed end starts just past the rib section. As the tenderloin continues down the length of the back, it becomes larger and rounder. The largest portion is the butt end, part of the top sirloin.

Characteristics: Because it is an inner muscle and gets very little exercise, the filet is quite tender, with a fine, velvety grain. It is often sold with the chain. A whole trimmed tenderloin weighs 4 to 6 pounds (1.8–2.7 kg) and is about 2 feet (60 cm) long and generally 2 to 3 inches (5–7.5 cm) across. The pointy filet tip is stringy though still tender. The center section is the most desirable. The butt end is somewhat tougher.

How to Choose: Tenderloin may be purchased in many forms. Well-marbled tenderloin will be the most succulent; a tenderloin with little marbling can be dry and flavorless.

Amount to Buy: Allow 4 to 10 ounces (115–285 g) per portion for steaks, less if roasting whole due to less shrinkage.

Storage:
x2–5

Refrigerate whole vacuum-packed tenderloin up to 5 days. Refrigerate trimmed filet up to 2 days. Rub with oil to keep it from drying out.

Preparation: 1. **Pull off all the outside fat. Remove the chain and save for another use. (Cut into thin strips against the grain for stir-frying.)**

2. **Using a sharp boning knife, cut away thin lengthwise ribbons of the silverskin, the silvery white connective tissue covering the larger end.**

3. **Fold under the thinner end for a more even shape, tying with butcher's string if desired.**

4. **Rub with oil, salt, and pepper, or herbs and chopped garlic, and bring to room temperature.**

5. **Roast at 450°F (230°C) for about 25 minutes for medium-rare, or until it reaches the desired temperature. (See Roasting Chart, page 294.)**

6. **Remove from the oven, cover with foil, and let rest 15 to 30 minutes before carving. The temperature will rise about 5°F (2°C) as it rests.**

Flavor
Affinities:

Bacon, balsamic vinegar, butter, cognac, cream, foie gras, port wine, rosemary, shallots, sherry, thyme.

20.   **TOP BLADE STEAK**

Other Names: **Steaks:** Book steak, butler steak, chicken steak, *copertina di spalla* (Italian), flatiron steak, lifter steak, *paleron* (French), *paletilla*, *planchuela*, or *parte superiore de la paleta* (Spanish), petite steak, top blade grill steak, top chuck steak. **Strips:** Fajita strips, stir-fry strips, top blade strips.

General Description: *The tender, juicy top blade steak (NAMP 114D) comes from the shoulder clod and resembles a flank steak.* Top blade steak can be grilled, skillet cooked, or stir-fried, and it is one of the most tender, richly flavored steaks. After the thick band of connective tissue is removed, the thin flat top blade is called a flatiron steak. It is popular on restaurant menus. In retail markets the meat is often cut crosswise into small sections with the tough white membrane left in. Once inexpensive, prices have risen because of high demand and the small portion of this cut in each beef carcass. Ask the butcher to trim it for quick-cooking top blade steak.

Part of Animal: The top blade comes from the uppermost portion of the shoulder clod (the large chuck muscle group) and is the muscle that lies on top of the shoulder blade.

Characteristics: Trimmed top blade ranges from ¼ to 1 inch thick (.65–2.5 cm) and is 4 to 6 inches (10–15 cm) wide and 10 to 14 inches (25–35 cm) long.

How to Choose: When looking to make steak, buy whole top blade or portion-sized steaks, which typically range from 6 to 12 ounces (170–340 g). Buy medallions of about 3 ounces (85 g) each to pan-fry with a sauce.

Amount to Buy: A whole trimmed flatiron weighs about 1 pound (450 g). This cut is 100 percent usable and doesn't shrink much because it is suitable for quick cooking. An average portion weighs 6 to 12 ounces (170–340 g).

Storage: Refrigerate flatiron steaks for up to 3 days.

Preparation: **1.**   **This cut requires no trimming; marinate overnight or rub with oil, garlic, and desired spices.**

2.   **Grill, sauté, or broil at high heat to get a crust and medium to medium-rare inside, 15 to 20 minutes. Cut into thin slices, if desired, cutting with the grain.**

Flavor Affinities: Bourbon, brown sugar, Dijon mustard, garlic, onions, teriyaki sauce, steak sauce, Worcestershire sauce.

21 a-b.   📷

TOP ROUND

Other Names: **Whole:** *Fesa interra* or *controgirello* (Italian), *filete tierno* or *cara superior* (Spanish), inside round, *tendre de tranche* (French), top round roast, topside (British), trimmed tip roast. **Steaks:** Breakfast steak, butterball steak, London broil, minute steak, round steak, round tip steak, sandwich steak.

General Description:

The large half-football-shaped top round (NAMP 169) is the most tender part of the round (upper leg). The lean top round takes well to marinades and sauces, is well suited for stews, and can be pot-roasted, braised, rotisserie-roasted, or slow-cooked in a commercial slow oven or a home crockpot. Because it contains the largest single muscle in the steer, top round is often used by delis and restaurants for roast beef. Due to its dense texture and relative leanness, top round can be dry and mealy if overcooked.

Thin strips of top round are used for sukiyaki, the Japanese one-pot meal often cooked tableside. Thick steaks cut from the top round are called top round steak; thinner steaks are called round steak. Both may include portions of the tougher bottom round and eye of round (page 11).

Part of Animal:

Top round comes from the beef round and includes large single muscle on the upper inner thigh.

Characteristics:

Whole, the top round (with the "cap" removed) weighs 10 to 18 pounds (4.5–8.2 kg). Round steaks vary in size, though they are usually large, oblong in shape, and fairly thin. The meat is dense and lean, with an even grain and relatively coarse texture.

How to Choose:	Top round can be found whole or cut into halves. It may be tied or placed into a net bag to maintain an even shape. The first steak cut off the top round, adjoining the sirloin, is the most tender and commands the highest price. It may be labeled butterball steak or London broil. Look for steaks with the largest section of the main muscle and the smallest section of the secondary muscle that appears near the top edge.
Amount to Buy:	Allow 6 to 9 ounces (170–255 g) per person of trimmed meat. Top round shrinks moderately because it's lean and because slow-cooking is more appropriate.
Storage:	Refrigerate whole or half top round up to 4 days, steaks up to 2 days.
Preparation: 1.	**Trim off excess outer fat and any visible shiny white connective tissue. Tie into a compact shape with butcher's twine and slow-roast at 200°F (100°C), allowing about 6 hours for a 5-pound (2.3 kg) roast, or until it reaches the desired temperature. (See Roasting Chart, page 294.)**
2.	**Remove from the oven, cover with foil, and let rest 15 to 30 minutes before carving. The temperature will rise about 5°F (2°C) as it rests.**
Flavor Affinities:	Barbecue sauce, bourbon, garlic, ginger, horseradish, mustard, red wine vinegar, soy sauce, steak sauce.

Storage: x2–4

22.   **TOP SIRLOIN BUTT**

Other Names: **Roasts:** Coulotte, head loin, hip sirloin, London broil, *rosbife* (Italian). **Steaks:** *Bifteck* (French), *bisteca* (Spanish), chateaubriand (American), petite top sirloin steak, sirloin butt steak.

General Description: *The top sirloin butt (NAMP 184) is a moderately priced, flavorful favorite among beef lovers.* It includes the top sirloin cap or coulotte (page 24), which is usually sold separately. This boneless cut may be found whole or cut into steaks. Its texture and intense beef flavor suit it to marinades and spice rubs. Top sirloin butt can be cut into almost any size portion for steak, made into kabobs, fajitas, or satay strips, or used in hearty soups, salads, and sandwiches. American retail butchers often call a thick top sirloin butt steak chateaubriand, although the French reserve that term for a large butt end section of the tenderloin.

Part of Animal: This cut is the largest portion of the sirloin.

Characteristics: This cut ranges from 8 to 14 pounds (3.6–6.4 kg). It is relatively tender, though less so than any short loin cuts (like strip steak or T-bone), highly flavorful, and rather lean.

How to Choose: Top sirloin steaks increase in size but decrease in tenderness as they get farther from the short loin and nearer the rump. Steaks cut from the short loin end are more juicy and flavorful than those cut from the round end. Center-cut top sirloin butt steaks have only one muscle; other steaks include multiple muscles. A whole top sirloin makes a good roast, but it can be dry if cooked to more than medium.

Amount to Buy: Allow at least 8 ounces (225 g) per person for boneless top sirloin butt, because of trim waste.

Storage: Refrigerate whole top sirloin butt up to 4 days, cut portions up to 2 days.

x 2–4

Preparation: **If you buy a whole top sirloin, you may wish to cut away the flattened top sirloin cap (or coulotte, page 24), which lies over the top of the main muscle group, and cut it up for steaks.**

1. **Season as desired, bring to room temperature, and tie into a compact shape.**

2. **Roast at 350°F (180°C) for about 16 to 20 minutes per pound to the desired temperature. (See Roasting Chart, page 294.) Or pot-roast in a moist environment with aromatic vegetables.**

Flavor Affinities: Chile peppers, fish sauce, garlic, jerk seasoning, molasses, oyster sauce, peanuts, soy sauce, wine vinegar.

23. 🎦   **TRI-TIP**

Other Names: **Whole:** Bottom sirloin butt, corner cut, knuckle cap, *punta en triángulo* (Spanish), Santa Maria barbecue, sirloin triangle muscle, triangle roast, triangle tip.
Steaks: Coulotte steak, triangle steak.

General Description: *The tri-tip (NAMP 185D) is a curved triangular muscle cut from the bottom sirloin that is just about the tastiest beef one can purchase at a reasonable price.* In the late 1950s, a butcher in Santa Maria, California, chose to rotisserie-roast this neglected cut rather than grind it. Tasters found it a perfect balance of taste and tenderness. Tri-tip's popularity quickly spread throughout the central coast of California. Because many American meat packers still ship their tri-tip to California, this cut is less easily found elsewhere. Tri-tip makes great roast beef sandwiches, takes well to dry-rubs and marinades, and adapts beautifully to bold flavors. Tri-tip is also sold cut into steaks known as triangle steaks or coulotte, although coulotte (page 24) generally refers to the top sirloin cap.

Part of Animal: The tri-tip is the butt portion of the bottom sirloin.

Characteristics: This 1 1/2- to 2 1/2-pound (680–1,140 g) roast is lean and tender, with pronounced grain that runs in a curve through its length. There is visible fat running through the muscle, which is shaped like a triangle.

When slicing, follow the grain as it changes, and always cut against the grain for tenderness.

How to Choose:
The whole tri-tip has little waste and is a perfect roast to feed four to five people. Tri-tip makes an excellent steak if it's cut at least 3/4 inch (1.9 cm) thick. Choose the largest tri-tip with moderate marbling.

Amount to Buy:
Buy 6 to 12 ounces (170–340 g) per person. This cut won't shrink much because it's cooked quickly.

Storage:
Refrigerate tri-tip for up to 3 days. Bring to room temperature before cooking.

Preparation: 1.

Trim off excess surface fat, if necessary. Marinate or dry-rub with spices and refrigerate up to 24 hours.

2.
Leave whole to roast or cook in a covered grill. (To make steaks, cut across the grain into steaks 1 inch [2.5 cm] thick.)

3.

Oven-roast at 400°F (200°C) for 20 to 30 minutes, or pan-sear over high heat and finish in a hot oven (400°F/200°C) until it reaches the desired temperature. (See Roasting Chart, page 294.)

4.
Remove from the heat, cover with foil, and let rest 5 to 10 minutes before carving. The temperature will rise about 5°F (2°C) as it rests.

Flavor
Affinities:

Allspice, chile peppers, Chinese black bean sauce, Chinese five-spice powder, cumin, Dijon mustard, garlic, horseradish, oregano, paprika, salsa.

24. 📷   **VARIETY MEATS AND FAT**

Other Names:

Innards, offal, organ meats. **Brains:** *Cervelle* (French), *cervello* (Italian), *sesos* (Spanish). **Heart:** *Coeur* (French), *corazón* (Spanish), *cuore* (Italian). **Kidneys:** *Riñones* (Spanish), *rognon* (French), *rognoni* (Italian). **Liver:** *Fegato* (Italian), *foie* (French), *hígado* (Spanish). **Testicles:** *Coglione* or *animelle* (Italian), *creadillas* (Spanish), frivolities, Rocky Mountain oysters, ranch fry, *testicules* (French). **Tongue:** *Langue* (French), *lengua* (Spanish), *lingua* (Italian), Swiss cut beef tongue. **Tripe:** *Gras-double* or *tripes* (French), *panal*, *panza*, or *cacariso* (Spanish), *trippa* (Italian).

General
Description:

Variety meats are organ meats that lie inside the body; fats lie both within and outside the muscles. Beef **brains** are located in the front of the skull and are compact and circular in shape, delicate in flavor, and soft and yielding in texture. Brains should be a bright pinkish-white color, plump, and firm. Due to fear of BSE, brains of cows and veal are not often sold; it is illegal for them to be sold in the United States. They are the key to the traditional creamy, rich meat filling used for Bolognese tortellini.

The **heart** is a large muscular organ found in the thorax region that is rather tough but quite flavorful. Hearts may be purchased with or without the cap. Cap-on hearts are surrounded by semihard white-colored fat; cap-off hearts are trimmed of visible fat and have the cap meat and bone removed. Beef heart has a strong flavor and is not for the faint of heart, but there are those who love its robust taste and chewy texture. Grilled beef heart, seasoned with rocoto chiles, cumin, oregano, red vinegar, and garlic, is popular for Peruvian anticuchos, or kabobs.

Beef kidneys are multiple-lobed organs that are more pronounced in flavor than veal kidneys and may have a lingering aroma of ammonia. The kidneys should be trimmed of all blood vessels and excess fat by the butcher. Kidneys have a firm, creamy texture when cooked. Steak-and-kidney pie is a British pub favorite.

The **liver** (NAMP 1724) consists of two lobes of substantially different sizes, which are smooth, rounded, and somewhat rectangular in shape and covered with a thin membrane. Beef liver is large, weighing up to 16 pounds (7.3 kg), and dark red to purplish in color. Beef liver is sold in slices or by the pound and is stronger tasting than veal liver, with a somewhat mealy texture when cooked, often by broiling.

Suet is fresh, hard white fat obtained from the kidney region. Melted and strained, it yields tallow, once used to create fanciful table sculptures that were not meant to be eaten, and also to make strong-smelling candles. Melted and strained suet is commonly used in Britain to make mincemeat pies, suet puddings, and suet pastry—the high melting point of suet makes this pastry light and flaky.

Testicles, typically referred to as fries, are usually pan-fried, especially on ranches in the American West. Testicles have a soft, creamy texture when cooked, which works well with a crispy coating.

The **tongue** is the long, flattened organ at the back of the mouth and weighs 2 to 5 pounds (.9–2.3 kg). It is covered with a tough outer skin that must be removed after boiling. Tongue is usually well trimmed before sale and is also available corned or smoked. Tongue, which needs long, moist cooking to make it tender, may be eaten hot or cold. Beef tongue has a chewy texture with a distinctive graininess.

Tripe is the lining of any of the animal's four stomachs. Blanket, or flat, tripe comes from the rumen (or paunch), the first and largest stomach. It is also known as double tripe because its outside and inside are quite distinct. Honeycomb tripe (NAMP 1739) comes from the reticulum, the second stomach, and is considered to be of better quality. It gets its name from the honeycomb appearance created by numerous ridges in its walls. The third stomach, or omasum, provides leaf, book, or Bible tripe; the fourth stomach, or abomasum, is rarely used by cooks. Philadelphia pepper pot is a tripe stew of Caribbean origin generously seasoned with crushed peppercorns. Menudo, a spicy Mexican tripe soup, is recommended for hangovers. Tripe has a soft, creamy yet chewy texture when slow-cooked.

Amount to Buy: All beef variety meats are inexpensive. Allow 6 to 8 ounces (170–225 g) per person for variety meats including brains, heart, kidneys, liver, and testicles. Allow 1 pound (450 g) of tripe per person. Allow 6 ounces (170 g) of suet to make pastry for one pie to feed 8 people. Allow 8 to 10 ounces (225 to 285 g) of tongue per person.

Storage: Variety meats are especially perishable and must be refrigerated and used within 1 or 2 days of purchase or frozen for later use.

x1–2

Preparation: ***Brains:***

1. **Wash well, then blanch in acidulated water (water with lemon or vinegar).**

2. **Poach, set on a plate under a weight until firm, and cut into slices for pan-frying, breading and frying, baking, or broiling.**

Heart:

1. **Wash and cut away any fat and arteries. Slice in half, then slice it into slices ¹/₂ inch (1.3 cm) thick.**

2. Season and flour, then brown in oil over medium heat on both sides. Stir in aromatic vegetables, beef broth, and wine.

3. Simmer, covered, for 1 hour or until relatively tender.

Kidneys:

1. Halve the kidney and cut out the tubes. Rinse in cold water and peel off the skin.

2. Cut a little of the kidney fat into small pieces and put it in a frying pan. Slice the kidney, sprinkle with chopped parsley and shallots, season with salt and pepper, and fry it until nicely browned.

3. Add a little flour, stir to absorb the fat, and then pour in beef stock and sherry. Simmer but do not boil (or the kidney will harden). Serve very hot.

Liver:

1. To prepare the classic dish of liver and onions, cut liver into slices less than 1/2 inch (1.3 cm) thick.

2. Brown sliced onions in butter with bay leaf, salt, pepper, and a pinch of ground cloves. Remove from the pan and reserve.

3. Add the liver and brown quickly in butter, 2 to 4 minutes. Add the reserved onions and a few drops of red wine vinegar and serve immediately.

Suet:

1. To make suet pastry, mix 3 cups (³/₄ pound/340 g) self-rising flour with a pinch of salt.

2. Cut in 1 cup (225 g) cold, shredded beef suet. When evenly blended, add ice cold water a few drops at a time until the dough comes together.

3. Knead lightly till the dough is smooth. Chill before rolling out thinly and evenly. Use as pastry for British steak-and-kidney pie or American beef, chicken, or turkey pot pie.

Testicles:

1. Use a sharp knife to split the tough skinlike muscle that surrounds the testicles. Cover with cold salt water and soak for 1 hour to remove some of the blood. Drain, then parboil in vinegared water, drain, and rinse.

2. Let cool and slice each "oyster" ¹/₄ inch (.65 cm) thick. Season with salt and pepper.

3. Dip in flour, then milk, and then flour again or breadcrumbs. Pan-fry in oil or lard till golden brown.

Tongue:

 1. Soak the tongue in cold water for 12 hours, changing the water several times.

 2. Trim, remove any fatty parts, and dip into boiling water. Remove from the water, cut slits into the skin at the base of the tongue, and peel off the skin. Sprinkle with salt and refrigerate for 24 hours.

 3. Wash again and then further cook by simmering in a broth or braising until tender, 2 to 3 hours.

Tripe:

NOTE: Tripe is always sold partially prepared by the butcher by soaking, brining, and boiling.

 1. Simmer in salted water for 2 hours in enough water to cover (flavor the water with herbs and vegetables if desired). Drain the tripe and reserve the liquid.

 2. Remove and discard fatty portions and cut into 1-inch (2.5 cm) pieces. At this point you may follow any tripe recipe.

Flavor
Affinities:

Brains: Butter, cilantro, cumin, lemons, mushrooms, red wine, shallots, tarragon, thyme, tomatoes, white wine. **Heart:** Bacon, bay leaves, cloves, cumin, garlic, lemons, nutmeg, onions, oregano, red wine. **Kidneys:** Brandy, butter, chives, Dijon mustard, garlic, mushrooms, salt pork, shallots, sherry. **Liver:** Caramelized onions, figs, lemons, onions, sage, turnips, white wine. **Tongue:** Allspice, apple cider, black pepper, cinnamon, cloves, garlic, golden raisins, tomatoes. **Tripe:** Bay leaves, Calvados, cilantro, cloves, garlic, ham, onions, oranges, oregano, red pepper flakes, tomatoes, white wine.

II. Veal

Veal, young cattle of the *Bos taurus* species, got its name from the Latin *vitellus*, meaning calf. About 2500 B.C., wealthy nobles and priests of Sumeria ate veal at elaborate banquets. In Roman times, the demand for veal and other suckling animals had to be controlled by a decree forbidding their slaughter; not enough were left to replenish stocks.

In Europe, veal is important in the cuisine of the Netherlands, France, Italy, Germany, and Switzerland. Because of longstanding humane laws, little veal is raised in Great Britain. Italian restaurants in the United States are known for their large selection of veal dishes, many of which don't exist in Italy.

Veal production in the United States is tied to the dairy industry. To remain efficient milk producers, dairy cows must give birth yearly. Female calves are raised to give milk. Until the advent of "special-fed" veal, most male Holstein calves (young dairy-breed bulls) were simply killed because they had little or no value to dairy farms and were not suitable for beef production. Now, the great majority of male Holstein calves are marketed to veal farmers for special-fed production. In the 1950s, U.S. dairy farmers sold large surpluses of skim milk to veal producers in the Netherlands. The Dutch found that calves that were special-fed skim milk, whey, and fat had increased weight and improved quality.

In recent years, veal rearing methods have been subject to objections, especially in Britain and the United States, because of cases in which calves were raised in poor conditions. However, improved animal care and feeding practices have evolved; today, calves are raised in well-lit, climate-controlled, ventilated barns. The calves are housed in individual stalls large enough for them to stand, stretch, lie down, and groom themselves. They are fed a diet formulated in stages to produce healthy animals.

In the United States, veal calves are inspected by the USDA and may also be graded for quality. (Inspection is mandatory; grading is voluntary.) There are five grades: prime, choice, good, standard, and utility. More than 93 percent of graded veal is prime or choice, with choice commonly found in supermarkets. Special-fed calves are graded choice or prime.

There are several different types of veal. Bob veal calves are milk-fed and are about 3 weeks old at slaughter. They usually weigh less than 150 pounds (68 kg) and have meat with a light pink color, a rather bland flavor, and soft texture. Meat from bob veal calves is priced low.

Special-fed calves are fed a nutritionally complete milk supplement until they reach 18 to 20 weeks of age and typically weigh 400 to 450 pounds (180–200 kg). The meat is ivory to creamy pink, with a firm, fine, and velvety texture with plenty of fat between the muscles. This type of veal is found in high-priced restaurants.

Grain-fed calves are first fed milk, then a diet of grain and hay. The meat is dark pink to red and the texture is firm, with some marbling and external fat. They have a more pronounced flavor and slightly chewy meat. These calves are marketed at 5 to 6 months of age and weigh 450 to 600 pounds (200–270 kg). Natural foods markets and restaurants tend to carry grain-fed veal.

Baby beef (petite beef, or yearling) comes from steers that are between 6 and 12 months old and weigh about 800 pounds (360 kg). The meat is generally pink to light red in color, more tender and lean than beef, but coarser and stronger-flavored than veal.

Veal Primals

Veal **chuck** (shoulder) lies forward of the rib section and above the belly and foreshank. It includes ribs 1 through 4. It is rather fatty and contains a fair number of bones, and most of its muscles are relatively tough. A whole veal chuck weighs about 25 pounds (11 kg).

Veal **rack** (rib) includes ribs 5 through 11. The rib-eye itself is extremely tender, with a very fine grain and buttery texture. It is surrounded by fattier, tougher, and coarse-grained, though flavorful, cap meat. A whole 7-rib (5 to 11) veal rack weighs about 12 pounds (5.4 kg); a 6-rib (6 to 11) rack weighs less.

Veal **loin** lies between the rib section and the sirloin at the top of the leg. It is quite tender with a buttery, somewhat dense texture and fine grain. A whole veal loin weighs about 15 pounds (6.8 kg).

Veal **leg** includes the sirloin butt (hip), the butt tenderloin, the knuckle (sirloin tip), the top or inside round, the bottom or outside round, and the shank. It is generally lean and tender, though it is made up of different muscles with different characteristics. The shank end will be tougher than the hip end. A whole special-fed veal leg weighs about 45 pounds (20 kg).

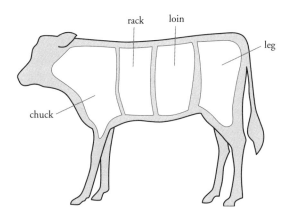

25. 📷 **BREAST AND RIBS**

Other Names: Breast roast, brisket, brisket point, flank, *pecho di ternera* (Spanish), *petto di vitello* (Italian), pocket breast, *poitrine de veau* (French).

General
Description: *Inexpensive and versatile, veal breast (NAMP 313) is especially popular in German, Italian, and French cookery and is usually stuffed and braised.* The breast, also known as brisket, consists of two distinct muscles: the larger, leaner, oblong flat and the smaller, fattier triangular point. With a matzo meal, onion, and mushroom stuffing, it is a favorite for the Jewish Passover holiday. Smaller veal short ribs, which can be braised like beef short ribs (page 44), are cut from the breast.

Part of Animal: The veal breast lies between the shoulder section above and the plate (belly) beneath.

Characteristics: Veal breast is rather fatty and tough, with a coarse grain, though quite flavorful.

How to Choose: Veal breast may be found bone-in or boneless. The smaller, fattier brisket point muscle may be found, as well as the flattened, pointed, triangular shaped flank.

Amount to Buy: A whole bone-in veal breast weighs 8 to 10 pounds (3.6–4.5 kg); a whole boneless breast weighs about 5 pounds (2.3 kg). It may also be cut into two lengthwise sections of about 2 1/2 pounds (1.1 kg) each or separated into the flat and the point.

Storage: Store veal breast refrigerated up to 3 days.

Preparation: 1.   **Trim off any excess fat and connective tissue. If stuffing the breast, cut a horizontal pocket or ask your butcher to do so.**

2.   **Rub all over with salt, pepper, and spices such as ginger, paprika, and ground coriander.**

3.   **If desired, make a stuffing. Cool the stuffing and then pack loosely into the veal pocket just before cooking. Sew or skewer the pocket closed.**

4.   **Place the breast (stuffed or not) on a bed of chopped aromatic vegetables. Add white wine and stock and cover, sealing as tightly as possible.**

5.   **Roast for 2 hours at 350°F (180°C). Uncover and roast 1 to 2 hours longer, or until it is fork tender and browned.**

6.   **Pour off the pan juices and ladle off the fat. In a small pot, reduce the juices over high heat till syrupy, then strain and season. Cut the veal into thick slices (between the bones, if applicable). Pour sauce over each portion.**

Flavor Affinities:	Apples, bacon, dill, garlic, ginger, lemons, mustard, prunes, sherry, sour cream, thyme, white wine.

FEET

Other Names:	*Pata* or *pie* (Spanish), *pied* (French), *piede* or *zampe* (Italian).
General Description:	*Known as calf's feet, rather than veal feet, these are the very bottom portion of the leg, covered partially by the hoof.* Like pig's feet (page 123), calf's feet contain large amounts of collagen, the material from which gelatin is extracted. The rich, full-bodied stock obtained from calf's feet was highly prized in early times for making jellies thought to be a restorative for invalids. They may be used to make savory or sweet calf's-foot jelly or added to the stockpot for enrichment. Though inexpensive, they often have to be specially ordered.
Part of Animal:	The feet are the lower portion of the legs.
Characteristics:	Calf's feet have small amounts of flavorful meat and much gelatinous connective tissue.
How to Choose:	Be sure the calf's feet are skinned and trimmed. They should also be split in half lengthwise and cut across into 1 1/2- to 2-inch (3.8–5 cm) chunks.

Amount to Buy:	Allow one foot per person.
Storage:	Store the calf's foot covered in cold water and refrigerated, up to 2 days.
Preparation:	***Petcha (Jewish Style Savory Calf's-Foot Jelly):***

 1. Place 6 cleaned and rinsed calf's feet in a large pot and cover with cold water. Bring quickly to a boil and cook rapidly for 2 to 3 minutes. Drain, discarding the water.

 2. Cover the calf's feet with fresh cold water, a peeled onion stuck with cloves, several carrots, a bay leaf, peppercorns, salt, parsley, and thyme in a large pot. Bring to a boil. Reduce the heat and simmer at least 3 hours, or until tender. Allow the feet to cool to room temperature in the liquid. Drain, reserving both the liquid and the feet.

3. Remove the meat from the bones, chop finely, and season with salt, pepper, and crushed garlic.

4. Slice 3 to 4 hard-cooked eggs and place them in a single layer in a serving casserole. Ladle the meat mixture on top and then pour over the reserved liquid so that it is about 1½ inches (3.8 cm) deep. Let cool and then refrigerate, covered, until the mixture jells. Cut into squares and serve with lemon wedges.

| Flavor Affinities: | Bay leaves, black pepper, cinnamon, cloves, garlic, lemons, oranges, paprika, parsley, sugar, white wine. |

7b.

GROUND VEAL

| Other Names: | Burgers, patties, *ternera molida* (Spanish), *veau haché* (French), *vitello macinato* (Italian). |

| General Description: | *The subtle flavor of ground veal (NAMP 396) makes it ideal for pairing with a wide range of seasonings.* It is often mixed with other flavorings or meats for meat loaf, meatballs, roulade or breast stuffing, cannelloni filling, or fluffy veal dumplings. Veal burgers (NAMP 1396) are light and adaptable. Ground veal patties, formed into oblong shapes and usually frozen, are used by budget restaurants for an inexpensive entrée. |

| Part of Animal: | Ground veal is made from the trimmings of veal. |

| Characteristics: | Ground veal is light colored, moist, and lean. |

| How to Choose: | Ground veal should be creamy pink in color, with milky white fat. Packages should be cold to the touch and securely wrapped with no signs of leakage. |

| Amount to Buy: | Allow 4 ounces (115 g) per serving for stuffing; 6 to 8 ounces (170–225 g) per person for meatballs, meat loaf, or patties. |

Storage: Ground veal is quite perishable; refrigerate for 1 to 2
x1–2   days.

Preparation: *Veal Meatballs:*

1.   Soak a few slices of crustless white bread in milk
     until well saturated, then squeeze it out and combine
     with 1 pound (450 g) ground veal.

2.   Add finely chopped onion, lemon juice and zest,
     chopped parsley, salt, pepper, and 1 egg.

3.   Form into rounded meatballs. Just before browning,
     roll in breadcrumbs.

4.   Brown in butter. Remove from the pan and pour off
     the excess fat.

5.   Add enough liquid, such as light beer, white wine, or
     chicken stock, to come ²/₃ of the way up the sides of
     the meatballs and simmer till the liquid is syrupy.

6.   Serve the meatballs with the sauce.

NOTE: Do not overwork the meat or it will become tough.

Flavor   Anchovies, bacon, beer, capers, cayenne, lemons,
Affinities: mushrooms, nutmeg, onions, tarragon, tomatoes.

26 a–h. 📷   **LEG**

Other Names: **Whole:** *Coscia* (Italian), *cuisseau* (French), *hind saddle*, *pierna* (Spanish). **Cutlets and Steaks:** *Escalope de veau* (French), leg cutlet, scallops, *scaloppine* (Italian), sirloin chop, sirloin steak, *Wiener Schnitzel* (German and Austrian). **Roasts:** Eye of round roast, leg center cut, leg roast, *pointe de surlonge* (French, sirloin tip or knuckle), round roast, rump roast, sirloin roast, *talon de ronde* (French, heel), top round roast.

General Description: *The choice meat of the veal leg (NAMP 334 whole, 335 boneless) is flavorful, tender, and lean and much used by Italian butchers to make thin cutlets.* A whole veal leg includes the sirloin butt, or hip section (NAMP 352), the butt tenderloin (NAMP 346), the knuckle, or sirloin tip (NAMP 351), the top or inside round (NAMP 349), the bottom or outside round (NAMP 350), and the hind shank (NAMP 337). A bone-in veal sirloin roast is rare; more common is a boned, rolled, and tied **sirloin roast**. A **sirloin chop** is a lean steak cut from the sirloin. Most often the sirloin is sold as part of the whole leg or sliced into cutlets. **Veal steak** is either sirloin steak or round steak cut from the top or bottom round muscles in the leg.

   A **center-cut leg** contains only the small round leg bone and is easy to carve or use for cutlets. The tougher but flavorful **shank half roast** is the lower leg minus the hind shank. The **knuckle** is a moderately tender, lean cut from the upper portion of the leg adjoining the sirloin. The single largest leg muscle is in the **top round**, sought after for **scaloppine** and roasting. The **bottom round** contains the regularly shaped boneless eye of round, which is lean and can be tough, the moderately tender flat, and the tougher, smaller muscles of the **heel**.

Veal is often cut into thin cutlets called scaloppine or **medallions**. Though scaloppine may come from the loin (page 88) and other parts of the calf, those cut from the leg will be largest in diameter and least expensive. They are pounded thin with a meat mallet; either flat or serrated scaloppine can be ordered.

Part of Animal:	The rear leg of the calf, including the sirloin butt, the butt tenderloin, the knuckle, the top round, the bottom round, and the hindshank.
Characteristics:	Veal leg is generally lean and tender, though it is made up of different muscles with different characteristics. The shank end, especially the heel and eye portion, will be tougher than the hip end.
How to Choose:	Look for firm, brightly colored leg meat.
Amount to Buy:	A whole special-fed veal leg weighs 20 to 40 pounds (9.1–18 kg). A whole trimmed special-fed top round weighs 3 to 8 pounds (1.4–3.6 kg). Allow 4 to 6 ounces (115–170 g) for veal scaloppine; 6 to 8 ounces

(170–225 g) for boneless veal roast; and 8 to 12
ounces (225–340 g) for bone-in veal roast per person.

Storage:
x 2–4

Refrigerate veal leg roasts up to 4 days; veal scaloppine up to 2 days.

Preparation:

Scaloppine:

1. **Purchase veal cutlets (or scaloppine). Place one cutlet
    inside a plastic zip-top bag and pound with a mallet
    to thin further. Repeat with remaining cutlets.**

2. **Season with salt and pepper and dredge lightly in
    flour. Sauté in hot oil, 1 to 2 minutes per side.
    Remove from the pan as they brown.**

3. **Pour off excess oil and add chopped shallots, white
    wine, lemon juice and zest, parsley, and capers. Scrape
    up any browned bits from the pan. Reduce the liquid
    till syrupy and pour over the veal.**

Braised Leg of Veal:

1. **Trim a 3- to 4-pound (1.4–1.8 kg) veal rump roast,
    sirloin roast, sirloin tip (or knuckle), or round roast.**

2. **Combine desired seasonings and rub all over the
    meat, allowing it to absorb the seasonings for 1 to 2
    hours at room temperature.**

3.   **In a Dutch oven, brown the meat well in oil on all sides over medium-high heat. Pour off excess fat from the pan. Return the pan to the heat and add a small amount of liquid to deglaze.**

 4.   **Add chopped aromatic vegetables to the pot. Cover and bake 2 to 3 hours at 300°F (150°C), adding liquid as needed to keep moist and partially covered, or until the meat is fork tender.**

 5.   **Remove from the oven and allow to cool somewhat in the cooking liquid before removing, slicing, and serving with some of the strained cooking juices.**

Flavor
Affinities: Bacon, capers, cream, fontina cheese, lemons, mushrooms, pancetta, parsley, prosciutto, shallots, sour cream, tomatoes, white vermouth, white wine.

27a–c.   **LOIN**

Other Names: Boneless short loin, *faux-filet*, *contre-filet*, or *longe* (French), kidney chop, loin chop and roast, *lombo* or *contrafiletto* (Italian), *lomo* (Spanish), rolled loin roast, T-bone chop.

General
Description: *An upscale restaurant favorite, veal loin is best used for quick cooking or high-temperature roasting.* One of the expensive middle cuts along with the adjoining rib

(page 93), veal loin is the source of **veal T-bone and porterhouse steaks** and **strip loin steaks**. The tender, adaptable loin is used to prepare two classic dishes: veal Oscar, sautéed loin cutlets topped with crabmeat and asparagus, and veal Orloff, sliced loin spread with puréed mushrooms and onions, topped with béchamel sauce and grated cheese, and browned. **Whole bone-in veal loin** (NAMP 332) makes an impressive, though expensive, roast. **Boneless veal loin eye** (NAMP 344) can be cut into tender scaloppine that are easy to pound into thin paillards.

Now rare, a **veal kidney chop** is a tasty old-time chop cut right through the fat-enclosed kidney inside the carcass, along the loin. These days kidney chops are assembled from two separate cuts: a loin chop and a slice of veal kidney; the tail of the chop is wrapped around the kidney to form a tight package.

Part of Animal: Veal loin lies between the rib (rack) section and the sirloin (upper hip) at the top of the leg.

Characteristics: Veal loin is tender and delicate in flavor with buttery texture and fine grain.

How to Choose: Buy whole bone-in veal loin for a roast. Buy boneless veal loin eye to roast whole or cut into cutlets, steaks, or scaloppine. Buy veal loin chops for grilling, broiling, or pan-searing and finishing in the oven.

| Amount to Buy: | Allow 4 to 6 ounces (115–170 g) per person for scaloppine; 6 to 8 ounces (170–225 g) for boneless roast; 8 to 12 ounces (225–340 g) for bone-in roast. |

Storage: Store whole veal loin 3 days refrigerated. Store cutlets
 x2–3   or steaks up to 2 days refrigerated.

Preparation: 1.   **Rub veal loin chops with a mixture of herbs, garlic,**
    shallots, salt, pepper, and olive oil. Marinate 1 hour
    at room temperature, or overnight in the refrigerator.

2.   **Grill, broil, or pan-sear for about 6 minutes on each**
    side, or until they reach the desired temperature. (See
    Roasting Chart, page 294.)

3.   **Allow the chops to rest 5 minutes covered with foil.**
    The temperature will rise about 5°F (2°C).

Flavor   Apple cider, arugula, basil, chestnuts, citrus, cranber-
Affinities: ries, garlic, hazelnuts, oregano, sage, tarragon, thyme.

28. 📷   **MARROW AND KNUCKLE BONES**

Other Names: **Marrow:** *Médula* (Spanish), *midolla* (Italian), *moelle*
    (French).

General   *Veal marrow and knuckle bones (NAMP 388–390) are*
Description: *prized by chefs wishing to prepare one of the great foun-*

dation sauces of French cuisine: demi-glace. Because it takes about 25 pounds (11 kg) of veal bones to make just one gallon (3.8 l) of sauce, and only the front and rear leg bones have enough gelatinous connective tissue and rich marrow to make the sauce, these bones fetch a high price and are seldom seen in retail markets. Demi-glace is a rich addition to sauces of all kinds. Marrow bones (NAMP 389) are the shank, femur, or humerus bones of the calf sawed into sections with the marrow exposed for easier handling. Knuckle bones have abundant connective tissue, imparting full flavor.

Veal marrow is the delectable soft fatty tissue found in the center of the front and rear leg bones. Marrow is considered a delicacy in many countries, especially in Europe. Classic Italian risotto alla milanese uses beef or veal marrow for the cooking fat.

Part of Animal:	Marrow bones are straight portions of veal leg bones. Knuckle portions connect the leg bones.
Characteristics:	Veal bones are large and somewhat unwieldy. Fresh marrow has the consistency of hard butter and is whitish, with red streaks of blood and nerves.
How to Choose:	Veal marrow bones, cut in 2- to 3-inch (5–7.5 cm) sections, can be used for their marrow, but may have to be specially ordered. To make it easier to extract the marrow, buy vertically cut marrow bones.

Amount to Buy:	Allow $1/2$ pound (225 g) of marrow bones cut in 2- to 3-inch (5–7.5 cm) sections for each person, if using for the marrow. Allow 1 pound (450 g) of the same bones for each cup (250 ml) of rich stock desired. Allow about 2 ounces (60 g) pure marrow per person.
Storage:	Store marrow bones covered in cold water and refrigerated for up to 2 days.
Preparation:	***Veal Demi-Glace:***

1. Preheat the oven to 400°F (200°C). Roast 10 pounds (4.5 kg) veal marrow and knuckle bones until brown in color, about 1 hour. Add chopped carrots, celery, and onion to the pan.

2. Continue to roast until the vegetables are brown and the veal bones are deep brown. (Take care not to burn, which will cause bitterness.)

3. Transfer the contents of the pan to a large stockpot. Deglaze the pan with white wine and transfer to the stockpot. Add tomato paste, sprigs of thyme, bay leaves, and peppercorns.

4. Fill the pot with cold water and bring to a boil. Skim as necessary and reduce the heat to a bare simmer. Cook slowly for 36 hours, skimming the surface occasionally.

5. **Strain the liquid, discarding the solids. Cool, then chill till you can remove the solidified fat, overnight if possible.**

 6. **Bring to a boil and reduce the liquid by half or until thick bubbles appear and the sauce is syrupy. Let cool completely. Keep refrigerated up to 2 weeks, or freeze till needed.**

Flavor
Affinities: Bay leaves, celeriac, garlic, Madeira, mushrooms, onions, red wine, sherry, thyme, white wine.

---

29 a–f.   **RIB**

Other Names: *Carré de veau* (French), *costilla* (Spanish), *costoletta* (Italian), crown roast of veal, French(ed) rib chop, hotel rack, rack, rib chop, rib eye.

General
Description: *A succulent, juicy veal rib chop (NAMP 1306), with its round, meaty eye and long, curving rib bone, is often the most expensive item on a restaurant menu.* This luxury cut may be grilled, broiled, or pan-seared and finished in a hot oven. A whole roasted veal rack (NAMP 306) is suitable for a splendid celebration. Veal rib is quite mild and delicate in flavor, though adaptable. In European cookery, veal is commonly paired with acidic ingredients such as lemon or with salty ingredients such as prosciutto. Boneless rib eye (NAMP 307)

makes an extra-tender roast that can be stuffed and/or wrapped in pancetta or bacon before roasting.

Rib chops from the shoulder end are larger but have a smaller eye and more of the surrounding cap meat. Chops should be cut 1 1/4 to 1 1/2 inches (3.1–3.8 cm) thick. Veal rib with the bone exposed and the side meat trimmed off is a French (or Frenched) rack and is more expensive.

Part of Animal:	The veal rib section may include seven ribs (NAMP 306), numbers 5 through 11, or six ribs (NAMP 306A), numbers 6 through 11.
Characteristics:	The rib eye is extremely tender, with a fine grain and buttery texture. It is surrounded by fattier, tougher, and coarse-grained, though flavorful, cap meat.
How to Choose:	A hotel rack is trimmed and ready for roasting. It may also be ordered cut straight across, to include both sides of the rib, for a double rack.
Amount to Buy:	Allow 14 to 16 ounces (395–450 g) for bone-in rib chops; 12 ounces (340 g) for bone-in veal roast; 8 ounces (225 g) for boneless rib eye.
Storage: ⊟ x2–3	Store rib roast up to 3 days refrigerated; store rib chops up to 2 days refrigerated.

Preparation: 1. **Trim off any excess fat and let come to room temperature. Preheat the oven to 375°F (190°C). Combine fresh breadcrumbs, parsley, minced garlic, salt, and pepper.**

2. **Brush the veal with lightly beaten egg white. Roll the meat in the breadcrumb mixture to coat.**

 3. **Brown the rack on all sides in oil in a nonstick oven-proof skillet. Place in the oven fat side up and roast about 1 1/4 hours for medium-rare. (See Roasting Chart, page 294.) Remove from the oven, drape with foil, and allow to rest for 10 minutes before slicing.**

Flavor
Affinities: Anchovies, artichokes, balsamic vinegar, cornichons, lemons, red wine, rosemary, shallots, truffle oil.

---

30 a–b. 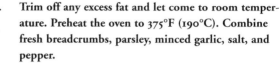 **SHANK**

Other Names: *Chambarete* or *morcillo traser* (Spanish), *jarret* (French), *stinco* (Italian).

General
Description: *Veal shank (NAMP 312 foreshank, 337 hindshank), the lower portions of both the front and rear legs, is legendary for its rich, smooth, melting texture.* When cross-cut into rounds with a section of the round bone in the middle, veal shank is called osso buco, from the classic Milanese dish. The highlight of eating osso

buco is scooping out the rich veal marrow in the center of the bone using special small spoons with a long handle. Veal shank, whether whole or cut into rounds, is best braised.

Part of Animal: Veal shanks are from the lower portion of the front or hind legs, above the hoof and below the knee.

Characteristics: Shank meat is tough and lean, with small muscles surrounded by connective tissue. Braising turns it smooth and rich.

How to Choose: Osso buco cut from the hindshank is larger, meatier, and more expensive than that from the foreshank. Be sure the rounds have a large center marrow bone that shows the inner marrow on at least one side. Shank portions cut from the bottom end will be smaller in diameter, tougher, and less meaty. For restaurant service especially, these pieces are less desirable.

Amount to Buy: Allow one crosscut round, 12 to 20 ounces (340–570 g) each, per person. A whole shank serves four.

Storage: Refrigerate osso buco up to 2 days; whole veal shank
x2–3   up to 3 days.

Preparation: 1.   **Tie with butcher's string to keep the shanks whole.**

2. Season with salt and pepper, dust with flour, and brown on all sides in hot oil. Remove and cover with foil to keep warm.

3. Drain off and discard most of the fat from the pan. Add aromatic vegetables, place the shanks back into the pot, pour in enough broth and/or wine to half cover the shanks, and bring to a boil.

4. Cover and braise in the oven for 2 to 3 hours at 300°F (150°C), turning once, until the shanks are fork tender but still whole.

5. Remove the shanks from the oven and allow to cool slightly before removing the string. Serve with the liquid, ladling off excess fat.

Flavor Affinities: Bay leaves, cilantro, cinnamon, cumin, garlic, golden raisins, lemons, marjoram, oranges, porcini mushrooms, red onion, white truffles, white wine.

SHOULDER

Other Names: Arm roast, blade roast and steak, boneless shoulder roast and steak, chuck tender, *épaule* (French), *espaldilla*, *paletilla*, or *planchuela* (Spanish), round bone steak, shoulder clod, *spalla* (Italian), square-cut shoulder, veal stew.

General
Description:
Veal shoulder (NAMP 309–311) makes excellent roasts with full, rich flavor and tender, fall-off-the-bone meat. Reasonably priced, the shoulder is often the least expensive boneless veal cut. The adaptable mild flavor of veal is complemented by a whole range of mellow flavors, and its high proportion of gelatinous collagen makes for rich, full-bodied gravy. The large veal shoulder is often cut into smaller roasts and steaks.

Veal arm roast includes the arm bone and some of the ribs and may be cut into **arm steaks**—these are a good substitute for osso buco. Arm steak resembles round steak from the hind leg because both contain round bones, but arm steak is tougher and not as lean.

The economical **veal blade roast** includes the blade bone and a fair amount of connective tissue. If boned, it can be stuffed. You may also find **veal blade steaks**. **Veal cubes** (NAMP 395) for stew are cut from any portion of the calf except the shank. **Veal cubes for kabobs** (NAMP 395A) are more regular in shape and better trimmed. The small, relatively tough **veal chuck tender** may be sold separately.

Part of Animal:
Veal shoulder lies forward of the rib section and above the belly and foreshank. It includes ribs 1 through 4, the shoulder blade section, and the upper portion of the arm (front leg).

Characteristics:
Veal shoulder is rather fatty and contains a fair number of bones, and most of its muscles are tough.

How to Choose:	A boneless veal shoulder is an entire boned, rolled, and tied shoulder. Choose a compact, well-trimmed blade roast or arm roast. Ask the butcher to cut the arm into 1 1/2- to 2-inch (3.8–5 cm) sections to use as osso buco. For veal stew, ask the butcher to cut meat from the shoulder into 2-inch (5 cm) cubes.
Amount to Buy:	Allow 12 ounces (340 g) for bone-in veal roast; 8 ounces (225 g) for boneless rib-eye.
Storage: ▯ x1–3	Store whole veal roasts up to 3 days refrigerated; store veal steaks or cutlets 1 to 2 days refrigerated. A whole chuck weighs 18 to 25 pounds (8.2–11 kg); a boneless shoulder clod weighs 1 1/2 pounds (680 g).
Preparation:	• **If using arm roast for osso buco, follow the instructions for veal shank on page 95.**
	• **If using veal shoulder for braising, follow the instructions for veal leg on page 85.**
Flavor Affinities:	Apples, cream, coriander, currants, dill, garlic, leeks, lemons, mushrooms, nutmeg, prosciutto, sage, thyme.

TENDERLOIN

Other Names:	Filet, *filete* or *solomillo corto* (Spanish), *filetto* (Italian), *grenadin* (French), short tenderloin, veal tender.

General Description:	*Like beef tenderloin, veal tenderloin is naturally tender, relatively lean, and quick cooking.* Unlike beef tenderloin, the whole veal tenderloin is generally not available; it is sold in two small sections: the **short** (NAMP 347) and the **butt** (NAMP 346). Its subtle flavor and delicate texture can quickly overcook and dry out. Cut into medallions, veal tenderloin can be sautéed with a refined pan sauce. When cut through the backbone, the smaller end of the tenderloin becomes part of veal loin chops, equivalent to beef T-bone (page 55).
Part of Animal:	The tenderloin lies underneath the ribs along the backbone, paralleling the loin.
Characteristics:	Veal tenderloin is small, extremely tender, and lean, with a fine, smooth grain.
How to Choose:	The short tenderloin is smaller and more tender than the butt tenderloin.
Amount to Buy:	The short tenderloin weighs 1/2 to 1 pound (225–450 g); butt tenderloin 1 to 1 1/2 pounds (450–680 g). Allow 6 to 8 ounces (170–225 g) per person.
Storage: ⊟ x2–3	Refrigerate uncut veal tenderloin up to 3 days; medallions, up to 2 days.
Preparation: 1.	**Season with salt and pepper, coat lightly with Dijon mustard, and roll in finely chopped mixed herbs.**

2.

Sear in olive oil on all sides. Transfer to a 375°F (190°C) oven to finish cooking, about 5 to 10 minutes or to desired temperature. (See Roasting Chart, page 294.) Short tenderloin will cook more quickly than butt tenderloin. Allow the meat to rest for 5 to 10 minutes before carving.

Flavor Affinities:
Bacon, basil, capers, cream, Dijon mustard, red onions, sage, tarragon, thyme, truffle oil, white wine.

31 a–g.

VARIETY MEATS

Other Names:
Innards, offal, organ meats. **Brains:** *Cervelle* (French), *cervello* (Italian), *sesos* (Spanish). **Cheek:** *Guancia* (Italian), *joue* (French), *mejilla* or *cachete* (Spanish). **Kidney:** *Riñones* (Spanish), *rognon* (French), *rognone* (Italian). **Liver:** *Fegato* (Italian), *foie* (French), *hígado* (Spanish). **Sweetbreads:** *Animelle* (Italian), *mollejas* (Spanish), *ris de veau* (French). **Tongue:** *Langue* (French), *lengua* (Spanish), *lingua* (Italian).

General Description:
Because veal is so young, its small-sized variety meats are sought after for their mild flavor and creamy, soft consistency. **Brains** are rich, high in cholesterol, and very perishable. Prized in European cuisines, they have a creamy texture and delicate flavor, and are similar in texture and taste to sweetbreads. Some countries are restricting sale of brains due to BSE; they are now

banned in the United States.

Cheeks are small, rich morsels of dense, finely grained meat. Along with beef cheeks (page 18), veal cheeks are showing up on restaurant menus, especially at places serving Mediterranean cuisine. Cheeks must be specially ordered and are usually frozen. Cheeks are always braised; they reheat beautifully.

The **heart** is similar to, but smaller than, beef heart (page 68).

Kidneys (NAMP 3728) in rich sauces are a French delicacy. Veal kidneys are reddish-tan in color and multilobed, concave on one side and convex on the opposite side. Kidneys are sold trimmed, with the outer membrane and the central core of hard white fat removed. Mild in flavor, they can be broiled, sautéed, or braised. Choose plump and glossy kidneys with only the slightest trace of ammonia odor.

Liver (NAMP 3724) is prized for its subtle flavor and smooth, fine-grained texture. The liver is smooth, somewhat rounded, and rectangular. It is covered with a thin membrane, which should be removed. (The butcher may do this.) Veal livers vary in color from light reddish tan to tan and have two lobes of substantially different sizes. Livers from formula-fed veal may be quite large but will be light in color. Larger, heavier, and darker livers are generally called calf liver. Sautéed veal liver topped with lots of browned onions appears in many cuisines.

Soft and creamy **sweetbreads** (NAMP 3722) are

the most desirable and highest priced of all variety meats. Sweetbreads are the culinary term for the thymus gland; they shrink as the animal grows older, becoming almost nonexistent in beef. They are multilobed and pinkish white in color. Weighing 14 to 18 ounces (395–510 g) per set of two, heart or belly sweetbreads are plump and round; throat sweetbreads are elongated and narrow.

The **tongue** (NAMP 3710) is the long, flattened organ at the back of the mouth and is covered with a tough skin. Veal tongues are smaller and more tender than beef tongue, though they share a firm, grainy texture. They may be stewed or poached, then served with a piquant sauce, or sliced for sandwiches, used for terrines, or served cold with vinaigrette or aioli.

Part of Animal:	Organ meats come from inside the carcass: the brains, sweetbreads, and tongue in the head area, the liver and kidneys from the central area.
Amount to Buy:	Organ meats are generally rich; allow 6 to 8 ounces (170–225 g) per person for brains, heart, kidneys, liver, and sweetbreads. Allow 1 pound (450 g) of cheeks per person. Allow 8 to 10 ounces (225–285 g) of tongue per person.
Storage:	Organ meats, especially those from a young animal like veal, are extremely perishable. Refrigerate and cook within 1 day of purchase.

Preparation: ***Brains and Heart:***

•   See suggested preparation for beef brains and heart, page 71.

Cheeks:

1.   Using a very sharp knife, trim the extra fat and the tough silverskin from the veal cheeks.

2.   Marinate in a mixture of red and white wine, bay leaves, pepper, rosemary, onion, celery, and garlic. Cover and refrigerate overnight, or at least 8 hours.

3.   Drain the cheeks and pat dry, reserving the marinade. Season with salt and pepper.

4.   Heat oil in a Dutch oven and brown the cheeks well. Remove from the pan and reserve.

5.   Add aromatic vegetables to the pan and cook till the vegetables are soft. Add the reserved marinade and the cheeks to the pan. Bring to a boil, skimming as necessary, and add tomato purée, red and white wine, and enough stock to partially cover the cheeks.

6.   Cover tightly and cook in a 300°F (150°C) oven for 2¹/₂ to 3 hours (adding liquid if necessary to keep the meat covered), or until the cheeks are fork tender.

Kidneys:

 1. Peel off the outer membrane. Using scissors, cut away the hard knob of fat in the center.

 2. Season with salt and pepper and cook in butter for 10 to 15 minutes, turning occasionally.

3. Add brandy to the pan, and flame. Remove the kidneys from the pan, add red wine, and bring to a boil. Cook 3 to 4 minutes, or until syrupy.

4. Remove from the heat, swirl in coarse-grain mustard and butter, and pour over the kidneys.

Liver with Onions:

 1. Peel off the outside membrane if necessary. Cut away any hard tubes. Slice into $^1/_2$ inch (1.3 cm) thick slices.

 2. Dust liver slices with flour, salt, and pepper.

 3. Pan-fry in a large, heavy skillet over medium heat in oil. Do not crowd the pan—fry in several batches if necessary. Cook to desired doneness, about $1^1/_2$ minutes per side for medium.

4. Transfer the liver to a plate and cover loosely with foil to keep warm.

5. In the same pan, melt butter and add a generous amount of sliced onions. Brown well and evenly.

6. Add beer, white wine, or sherry to the pan and cook till the liquid is syrupy. Season with salt and pepper, return the liver to the pan to heat, and then serve.

Sweetbreads:

1. Soak in cold water at least 5 hours, changing the water several times, until the water is clear.

2. Cover with cold, salted water with lemon juice or vinegar in a large pot and bring slowly to a boil. Immediately remove from the heat, drain, and rinse.

3. Remove the outer membrane and any tough sections. If desired, wrap in plastic and cover with a heavy pan to weight and firm the sweetbreads. Refrigerate 1 hour.

4. Slice into cutlets, if desired, and then dip in flour, egg, and breadcrumbs and pan-fry; flour and pan-fry in butter or olive oil; or sizzle (uncoated) in butter till evenly browned.

Tongue:

1. Wash thoroughly and then soak the tongue in cold water for 12 hours, changing the water several times.

2. **Trim any fatty parts and bony bits.**

3. **Bring a pot of water to a boil, then dip the tongue into the water to blanch it. Remove from the water. Cut slits into the skin at the base and peel off the skin.**

4. **Sprinkle with salt and refrigerate for 24 hours. Wash again, and the tongue is ready to be poached in a flavorful stock till tender, about 1½ hours.**

Flavor Affinities: **Brains:** Butter, cilantro, cumin, lemons, red wine, tarragon, tomatoes, white wine. **Cheeks:** Bay leaves, celeriac, chives, cinnamon, cloves, demi-glace, garlic, mushrooms, red wine, tarragon, thyme, tomatoes, white wine. **Heart:** Bacon, cinnamon, garlic, lemons, shallots, vinegar. **Kidneys:** Brandy, butter, chives, Dijon mustard, garlic, juniper berries, mushrooms, salt pork, shallots, sherry, parsley. **Liver:** Caramelized onions, golden raisins, lemon, Madeira, Marsala, sage, shallots, sherry, white wine. **Sweetbreads:** Bay leaves, butter, chervil, chives, hazelnuts, lemons, mushrooms, red wine, shallots, tarragon, thyme, tomatoes, white wine. **Tongue:** Allspice, apple cider, celeriac, cinnamon, cloves, garlic, Madeira, mayonnaise, port wine, sugar, tomatoes, vinaigrette, wine vinegar.

III. Pork

The domestic pig (*Sus scrofa*) is a member of the Suidae family, which also includes the wild boar and wart hog. Wild boars were an important—and dangerous—prey for prehistoric hunters, and are depicted in cave paintings at Lascaux, France. Pigs were domesticated as early as 10,000 years ago, around the same time as sheep. Apicius, the Roman epicure, provided many recipes for pork, and hams were exported from Gaul (now France) to Rome. Pork is one of the mainstays of Chinese cuisine, and the Chinese played a significant role in domesticating the pig.

Pork is eaten throughout Europe, North and South America, parts of Africa, China, and Southeast Asia. China is the world's top pork producer, followed by the European Union and the United States. Pork is forbidden to Jews and Muslims, perhaps because pork spoiled quickly in hot weather or because pigs are scavengers.

A pig weighing about 240 pounds (110 kg) will yield a carcass of about 180 pounds (81 kg), with about 100 pounds (45 kg) of meat, much of which is cured and made into ham, bacon, and sausage. Most pork is slaughtered at between 6 to 9 months. Pigs can forage for their food, but these days most American pigs are corn-fed. Today's pig has 50 percent less fat compared to the pig of the 1950s.

All pork found in retail stores is inspected. There are only two USDA grades for pork: acceptable and utility. Only acceptable pork is sold in supermarkets; utility grade is used for processing. In the United States antibiotics may be given to prevent or treat disease in pigs, but a "with-drawal" period is required before the animal may be slaughtered. Hormones may be used to promote efficient growth, but pork labeled "natural" cannot contain any artificial agent, and it cannot be more than minimally processed (ground, for example).

An important note about pork safety: Trichinosis is a parasite that lives in pork. Although people may contract trichinosis, this disease is now quite rare. To be absolutely certain of pork's safety, according to the U.S. Food Safety and Inspection Service, it should be cooked to 160°F (71°C). Because trichinosis is destroyed at 140°F (60°C), many chefs recommend cooking quick-cooking cuts (such as chops and roasts) to 150°F (65°C), so they're slightly pink and still juicy, and cooking slower-cooking cuts from the shoulder and leg to 165°F (74°C). Older recipes that recommend cooking to 180°F (82°C) will make the meat too tough.

There are several types of pig. A barrow is a castrated male hog, or boar. A gilt is a young female, while a sow is a female that has borne a litter. A pig is a young animal, 6 to 8 months old; a hog is a mature pig. In Denmark, Landrace pigs are the basis of the Danish bacon industry and are fed the skim milk created during cheese production. The famed Iberian pig, which may be a direct descendent of the original Mediterranean wild boar, is prized for the fine ham it produces. There are many different breeds of Chinese pigs because of varied geography and climate. In Britain and the United States, the majority of pigs are a cross between the Duroc, Hampshire, and Yorkshire.

Pork Primals

Pork is generally divided into four primals. Pork primals are small enough to be sold whole in some stores, especially warehouse clubs. Note that the pig has 14 ribs, while beef, veal, and lamb have just 13.

The **belly** weighs about 18 pounds (8.2 kg) and is the underside of the pig, including the side ribs, from which spareribs are cut. It is the source of pork belly, the raw form of bacon.

The **shoulder** lies between the rib section and the foreshanks. A whole pork shoulder weighs about 15 pounds (6.8 kg) and includes three to seven ribs, depending on how it was cut, along with the shoulder blade and the upper portion of the front leg bone. Pork shoulder is sometimes divided into two subprimals: the Boston butt, which is the upper shoulder, and the picnic shoulder, which is the arm.

The **loin** lies between the shoulder and the leg; it includes the blade end, rib, loin, and sirloin sections and weighs about 17 pounds (7.7 kg). Pork loin is cut extra long as compared with beef in order to maximize the number of pork chops. It is divided into three main parts: the blade end, closest to the shoulder; the blade center sirloin; and the center portion, adjoining the short loin.

Pork **leg** (or fresh ham) is the large, plump hind leg of the pig. It weighs about 22 pounds (10 kg) and contains a portion of the sirloin, the knuckle, the top round, the bottom round, and the shank, depending on how the leg is cut.

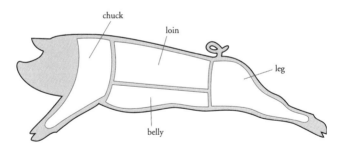

32 a–d. 📷 **BARBECUE RIBS**

Other Names:
Baby back ribs, back ribs, blade end ribs, brisket bones, button ribs, Canadian back ribs, *costa della spalla* (Italian, back ribs), *costilla ranchera* (Mexican, country-style), *costine* (Italian, spare-ribs), country-style ribs, *entero* (Mexican, spareribs), flatbone riblets, Kansas City ribs, *plat de côte* (French, back ribs), pork loin ribs, *punta de costilla* (Spanish, back ribs), riblets, spareribs, South Side ribs, St. Louis ribs.

General Description:
Pork ribs are a sought-after cut that may come from the back, side, or shoulder. There are many different traditional cutting and cookery styles for pork ribs, and each has its fanatics. In America, Carolina style uses whole hog and shoulder and is pit-cooked with a hot-and-sour vinegar-based sauce. Memphis style uses pork ribs and shoulder and features both dry and wet rubs flavored with vinegar, tomato, and mustard. Texas style uses pork ribs but also beef, especially brisket, and is pit-cooked with mesquite or hickory wood, while Kansas City style is known for gooey tomato-based sauces on pork ribs and beef brisket.

Baby back ribs or **loin ribs** (NAMP 422) are not from a baby pig; they're simply small. These are wonderful dry-rubbed with spices, then slowly baked till tender and finished under the broiler or on the grill. Baby back ribs are premium-priced and include at least eight ribs—a full slab includes 13. They are cut from either side of the ribs alongside the backbone. The tough "skin" (peritoneum) from the inside surface can be removed if requested. The meat between the ribs is called finger meat.

Country-style ribs or **blade end ribs** (NAMP 423) are cut from butterflied shoulder blade chops from the shoulder end of the loin. They have more meat than spareribs or back ribs, but they aren't as easy to eat with the fingers. They come boneless or bone-in and include three to six ribs. **Flatbone riblets** are the last four to six bones of the backbone.

St. Louis–style ribs (NAMP 416A) are cut from spareribs but are trimmed to make a more uniform, roughly rectangular rack. The brisket bones, or the belly ends of the ribs, and the top portion closer to the back are cut away and end up as **riblets**.

Spareribs (NAMP 416) are popular at barbecues because they're easy to eat with your fingers. These ribs are cut from the pork belly and may include the small, hard brisket bone at the smaller pointed end. They contain at least 11 bones and are fattier but also meatier and less expensive than baby backs. The flap of meat found on the inside of the sparerib is the skirt, which has a tendency to dry out during cooking and, if the outside edge is not trimmed off, can be very chewy. Many people remove the skirt and put it into chopped barbecue.

Pork brisket bones, **rib tips**, or **breaks** (NAMP 416B) are small, short, tasty pieces that are the trimmings from the loin, spareribs, or baby backs. **Kansas City–style**, or **barbecue cut ribs** (NAMP 416C), are spareribs with the hard front bone removed, and, in some cases, the point is squared.

Part of Animal:	Ribs may be cut from the belly (spareribs), the shoulder (country-style ribs), and the back (baby back ribs).
Characteristics:	Ribs are rather fatty and contain a significant amount of connective tissue that must be tenderized by slow cooking. Both baby back and spareribs have a skin on their interior, which is heaviest at the backbone and thinnest at the belly end. The membrane's toughness is related to the age and size of the animal and should be trimmed off of ribs from older animals.
How to Choose:	Choose ribs by your preference. Look for well-trimmed ribs with an even shape.
Amount to Buy:	Allow 1/2 pound (225 g) of country-style ribs per person. Allow 3/4 pound (340 g) of pork brisket bones per person. St. Louis–style ribs weigh 1 1/2 to 3 pounds (680–1,360 g). Spareribs weigh between 2 1/2 and 4 1/2 pounds (1.1–2 kg). Baby backs weigh 1 3/4 pounds (800 g) or less and will feed a maximum of two people; allow at least 3/4 pound (340 g) per person.
Storage:	Refrigerate pork ribs up to 3 days; vacuum-packed ribs, up to 5 days.

x3–5

Preparation: 1. **Rub spices all over, using about ¹/₄ cup (65 ml) for each slab. Refrigerate overnight, covered, so the flavors penetrate the ribs.**

2. **Prepare a covered grill, adding soaked aromatic wood chips, if desired. The temperature should stay at 200 to 250°F (100–120°C).**

3. **Cook the ribs, covered, for about 2 hours, turning occasionally. The ribs are ready when the meat comes away from the bones and the internal temperature is 165 to 175°F (74–80°C). Or slow roast, wrapped in foil in a 250°F (120°C) oven for about 2 hours.**

4. **Remove the ribs and allow them to rest at least 20 minutes, or up to 1 hour, wrapped in foil.**

5. **Cut into individual or double ribs, and toss in a large bowl with barbecue sauce. Spread onto a baking pan and heat in a 300°F (150°C) oven for 15 to 20 minutes, or until the sauce bubbles and makes a glaze.**

6. **Serve with extra barbecue sauce on the side.**

Flavor
Affinities: Allspice, brown sugar, chili powder, cumin, garlic, ginger, hoisin sauce, honey, hot sauce, ketchup, lemongrass, molasses, mustard, onions, sesame oil, soy sauce.

33. [📷]   **BELLY**

Other Names:
: *Panceta corte* (Spanish), *pancetta squadrata* (Italian), *poitrine parée* (French), pork side, *Schweinebauche* (German), trimmed belly.

General Description:
: *Pork belly (NAMP 408–409) is a rustic, flavorful cut that is popular in Italian, French, and Chinese cuisines.* A hot commodity on the futures market, pork belly is very tasty but can also be fatty. It may be braised, turned into soft, rich shreds called rillettes, turned into confit (spice-cured and slow-cooked), or made into a terrine. It is the cut from which bacon (page 283) and salt pork (page 120) are prepared.

Part of Animal:
: The belly is the underside of the pig.

Characteristics:
: Pork belly is a very fatty, tough, flavorful cut.

How to Choose:
: A whole pork belly weighs about 18 pounds (8.2 kg); a skinless pork belly weighs about 13 pounds (5.9 kg). You may also find center-cut pork belly or pork belly from which each rib has been removed.

Amount to Buy:
: Allow 4 to 8 ounces (115–225 g) per person.

Storage:
: Store pork belly and ribs refrigerated for up to 3 days.

⌁ x3

Preparation: 1.

Make a rich cooking liquid by combining stock with spices and aromatic vegetables and simmering.

2.

Add a piece of pork belly. Reduce to a gentle simmer and be careful not to boil. Simmer 2 to 3 hours, or until tender, then allow to cool in the liquid.

3.

Remove from the liquid, straining the liquid if desired. Cut the belly into slices and reheat in the liquid or pan-fry over medium heat till crisp and brown.

Flavor
Affinities:

Bay leaves, caraway, cilantro, cinnamon, cumin, fennel, garlic, leeks, paprika, sake, soy sauce, star anise.

34 a–e.

CHOPS

Other Names:

Bistecca or *bistecchine* (Italian, sirloin chop), blade chop, butterfly chop, center-cut loin chop, *chuleta* (Spanish), *côte de porc* (French), loin chop, *michigan* (Mexican, butterfly chop), rib chop, sirloin chop (or steak), *spuntatura* or *costarelle* (Italian, rib chops), top loin chop.

General
Description:

Pork chops may be cut from the shoulder, loin, sirloin, or leg and are tender pieces of meat attached to bone. Chops are cuts that are "chopped" through the bone and small enough to serve as individual portions. They are usually grilled, broiled, or pan-fried at high heat. The most tender (and most expensive) pork chops are cut from the long loin, which includes the shoulder end, rib center, short loin, and a portion of the sirloin. Both rib and loin chops are also sold boneless and can be formed into rounded shapes.

The blade or shoulder end of the loin yields **loin blade chops** (NAMP 1410B), which have more fat and connective tissue than **center-cut rib** or **loin chops**. They are made up of several muscles and can be chewy, but are improved by marinating or brining. Butterflied, or split, loin blade chops (NAMP 423) are inexpensive as well as versatile; they are equivalent to country-style ribs (page 111).

Don't confuse loin blade chops with **shoulder blade chops** or **Boston butt steak** (NAMP 1406–1407), which are somewhat tougher cuts from the adjoining upper shoulder portion known as the Boston butt (page 140). Shoulder blade chops and shoulder arm chops or steaks, which are cut from the picnic or lower arm portion of the shoulder (page 140), have full-bodied flavor, though they are relatively tough and fatty, so they are best braised.

Rib chops (NAMP 1410A) have a large eye with the rib bone attached; loin chops (NAMP 1410) include the T-bone and portions of both the loin and tenderloin. (The amount of tenderloin increases toward the back end.) Rib chops are ideal for stuffing. Loin and rib chops are great to grill, broil, or pan-fry. **Loin sirloin chops** (NAMP 1410B) come from the loin toward the rear and have more bones than rib chops, but are also tender and flavorful. They are well suited to brining or marinating and should not be overcooked because they can dry out.

Part of Animal: Pork chops may be cut from the rib, loin, shoulder, forearm, or hind leg.

Characteristics: The most tender and expensive chops come from the loin and rib sections along the back of the pig. Rib chops have more fat, so are less likely to dry out. Shoulder chops have more bones and connective tissue. Loin chops have a large single-muscle eye and less fat. Sirloin chops are relatively tender and lean. Leg chops are lean and can be dry and somewhat tough.

How to Choose: Pork chops should be 1 1/2 to 2 inches (3.8–5 cm) thick. An end-cut chop, from either the shoulder end or the sirloin end, will have more gristle.

Amount to Buy: Individual chops weigh 6 to 8 ounces (170–225 g). Allow one chop per person.

Storage: Store pork chops up to 2 days refrigerated; 3 days if
x2-3   oiled or marinated.

Preparation: 1.   **Trim off excess fat. For better flavor and juiciness,**

brine chops as follows: Combine 2 quarts (1.9 l) hot water and 1/2 cup (125 ml) kosher salt or 1/4 cup (65

ml) table salt with ¹/₂ to 2 cups (125–500 ml) sweetener. Add spices and seasonings as desired, then stir to dissolve salt. Cool liquid to room temperature. Submerge the chops in the brine for 4 to 6 hours refrigerated.

 2. **Drain and pat dry, then grill, pan-fry, or broil until slightly pink in the center, 150 to 155°F (66–69°C).**

Flavor
Affinities: Apple cider, brown sugar, coriander seed, fennel, honey, molasses, mustard seed, peaches, vanilla.

35 a–d.

FAT

Other Names: **Caul:** *Amnio* or *cuffia* (Italian), caul fat, *crépine* (French). **Fatback:** Back fat or rindless back fat (British), *bardière découennée* (French, without rind), *grasa dorsal* (Spanish), *lard gras* or *bardière* (French), *lardo* (Italian), *lardo scotennato* (Italian, without rind). **Lard:** *Flomen* or *Schweineschmalz* (German), *manteca* (Spanish), *panne* (French), *sugna* (Italian). **Salt pork:** *Petit salé* (French), *salume* (Italian), *tocino* (Spanish, also used for bacon), white bacon.

General
Description: *Fats from pork are often used in cooking and baking to add rich flavor.* **Caul,** or mesentery, is a delicate lacy net of fat about a yard (1 m) square, used to wrap lean meats while roasting, called barding. As the caul fat melts it moistens the meat and also keeps it

wrapped into a compact shape.

Fatback is a strip of fresh fat from the back of the pig, though it may also be found salted. Fresh fatback can be rendered into lard. Thin sheets of fatback are used to wrap lean roasts or to line terrines. Garlic-clove-size chunks of fatback, called *lardons*, are inserted at intervals using a larding needle into the flesh of drier cuts of meat to add succulence. Tender, flavorful, nearly transparent slices of cured *lardo*, the Italian version of fatback, are considered a delicacy. The rind (or skin) is usually cut away but is excellent added to a pot of greens, baked beans, soup, or braising meat to lend richness.

Rich and flavorful, **lard** is used in many European countries for deep- and pan-frying. It is widely used in South America and is essential for making tamales. In the American South, lard is the secret to tender, flaky biscuits. The firmest and most prized type, leaf lard, is separated into leaves from around the kidneys.

Although some **salt pork** (not to be confused with unsalted fatback) may look like slab bacon and may also be cut from the side of the pig, it is most commonly cut from the belly. Much more fatty than bacon and unsmoked, salt pork is cured with salt. It is used mostly for enrichment and flavoring and is an important ingredient in Boston baked beans.

Part of Animal: Caul is the thin fatty lining of a pig's stomach. Fatback comes from the upper portion of the back and lies between the loin eye and the skin of the back. Lard may be rendered from all pork fatty tissue; hard leaf lard surrounding the kidneys is considered best. Salt pork is cut from the sides and belly.

Characteristics: Fatback is firm and supple tissue that mostly consists of fat suspended in a network of fine connective tissue. Unprocessed lard has a strong flavor and a soft texture; processed lard is firmer with a milder, nutty flavor and longer shelf life. Salt pork is a thick block of fat usually containing some streaks of lean meat.

How to Choose: Look for caul in the meat sections of Asian or Mediterranean markets, or order it. Fatback is not as common now as it once was, because pigs are much leaner these days. You may find either rind-on or rindless fatback. Choose fresh-smelling lard. Salt pork is generally found precut into 4-inch (10 cm) square portions.

Amount to Buy: One caul will bard one bird or roast. Allow 1/4 pound (115 g) per person when using fatback or salt pork. You may need to special order fresh fatback. Purchase as much lard as is called for in your recipe. Salt pork may often be found vacuum-packed in 1-pound (450 g) packages in the meat case.

Storage: Caul is usually found frozen. It can be refrigerated for
x1 up to 1 day. Fresh fatback may be refrigerated for up

to 1 week; if cured, it may be refrigerated for up to 1 month. Lard should be tightly wrapped to prevent absorption of other flavors and may be stored at room temperature or in the refrigerator. Store salt pork refrigerated for up to a month.

Preparation: ***Caul:***

 1. **Soak the caul in warm water with a little vinegar and then stretch it out gently (it tears easily). Pat dry.**

2. **Use to wrap game birds, such as pheasant or quail, calf's liver, or pâtés to baste them as they cook.**

Fatback:

 • **To cut into sheets, freeze the fatback for about 1 hour. Using a long, thin knife, slice sheets that are as thin as possible paralleling the length of the fatback. Drape the sheets over lean meats before cooking.**

Lard:

• **Lard needs no preparation for baking. For frying, it must be melted and heated to the desired temperature.**

Salt Pork:

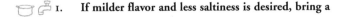 1. **If milder flavor and less saltiness is desired, bring a**

small pot of cold water to a boil. Add the salt pork
and simmer 2 to 3 minutes. Drain and rinse.

2. Cut a crisscross diamond pattern into the skin-side
surface of the salt pork, or cut into 1-inch (2.5 cm)
squares. Place in the pot when cooking beans or into
a pot of simmering soup.

Flavor
Affinities:
Caul: Bay leaves, duck, pâté, pheasant, quail, salmon,
thyme. **Fatback** and **Salt Pork:** Brown sugar, cabbage, molasses, mustard, onions, sauerkraut, turnips.
Lard: Bay leaves, caraway, corn, chile, cilantro,
cumin, garlic, onions, rosemary, thyme.

---

36. **FEET**

Other Names:
Manitas (Mexican), *pata* or *pie* (Spanish), *pied*
(French), trotter (British), white offal (Britain), *zampa*
or *piede* (Italian).

General
Description:
*Pig's feet (NAMP 420 front, 420A hind) are the front and
rear feet of the pig.* Feet are often found pickled and
are served as bar food in taverns, especially in the
American Midwest. They're also added to stocks to
lend richness and body, especially for reduction
sauces, and to make natural jellies. Pig's feet require
long, slow cooking.

Part of Animal:	The front and rear feet of the pig.
Characteristics:	The feet are bony and full of sinews, but also full of gelatinous connective tissue and small bits of meat.
How to Choose:	Pig's feet often must be specially ordered.
Amount to Buy:	Allow $1/2$ pound (225 g) per person.
Storage:	Store fresh pig's feet 2 to 3 days refrigerated.

x2–3

Preparation: **1.** **Place pig's feet, a peeled onion stuck with cloves, carrots, a bay leaf, peppercorns, salt, parsley, and thyme into a large pot of cold water. Simmer for 4 hours, or until tender. Remove from the pot and cool slightly. Strain the cooking broth and cool.**

2. **If the feet are to be grilled (or broiled), place the cooled feet between two weighted boards to press and firm them as they cool overnight. Prepare as desired.**

Flavor Affinities:	Apple cider, bay leaves, carrots, cayenne, cumin, gherkins, lemons, sage, shallots, thyme, white wine.

7c.

GROUND PORK

Other Names:	*Maiale macinato* (Italian), minced pork (British), *cerdo molido* (Spanish), *porc haché* (French).

General Description:	*Ground pork (NAMP 1495), made from trimmings of pork, is mellow and rich in flavor.* Often labeled according to percentage of fat, lean pork has less than 17 percent fat, while regular pork is about 20 percent fat. Ground pork is an easy-to-prepare, quick-cooking meat that can be used by itself or in an endless variety of casseroles, meat loaves, Chinese dumplings, patés, or other specialty dishes.
Part of Animal:	Ground pork comes from almost any part of the pig.
Characteristics:	Ground pork is finely textured and generally fatty.
How to Choose:	Choose ground pork that is pale pink-red in color; any with a brown or green tinge should be avoided.
Amount to Buy:	Allow 4 to 6 ounces ground pork (115–170 g) if mixed with other ingredients, 6 to 8 ounces (170–225 g) per person if served alone.
Storage: ⊟ x 2	Store raw ground pork in its original wrapping in the refrigerator for no more than 2 days. Do not refreeze thawed ground pork. Because bacteria live on cut surfaces of meat, ground pork should be cooked to an internal temperature of 160°F (71°C).
Preparation: 1.	**Mix ground pork with spices, chopped vegetables, and other seasonings. Form into patties or meatballs.**

2. **Fry in a skillet over medium-high heat 5 minutes per side, or until the surface of the meat is golden brown and the inside has only the faintest trace of pink.**

Flavor Affinities:

Allspice, cumin, garlic, onions, rosemary, sage, shallots, red wine, thyme, tomatoes, vermouth, white wine.

HEAD, JOWL, EAR, AND TAIL

Other Names:

Head: *Cabeza* (Spanish), *testa* (Italian), *tête* (French). **Jowl:** *Guanciale* (Italian), *joue* (French), *museau* (French, snout), *papada* (Spanish), *tempia* (Italian, jowl and throat). **Ear:** *Orecchio* (Italian), *oreille* (French), *oreja* (Spanish). **Tail:** *Coda* (Italian), *queue* (French), *rabo* (Spanish).

General Description:

The jowl, ears, head, and tail are prepared in specialty dishes and are available in ethnic markets. A fat cut of meat along the side of the head, the **jowl** is often found smoked and cured, and is used as flavoring for other foods. Jowls are sold with the skin removed.

Pig **snouts**, **ears**, and **tails** are essential for the Brazilian national dish of black beans cooked with a panoply of pork parts, called *feijoada completa*. A whole simmered pig's **head** is transformed into the German delicatessen specialty head cheese (page 282). It is also the traditional primary ingredient of Pennsylvania Dutch scrapple.

Part of Animal:	The jowls and ears are on the sides of the head, which can be found whole. The tail is at the back end.
Characteristics:	Jowl meat is rich and dense with plentiful amounts of fat. The head is made up of many different muscles and abundant amounts of gelatinous connective tissue.
How to Choose:	Look for these parts in ethnic markets, especially Caribbean, Brazilian, Spanish, and Italian.
Amount to Buy:	Allow 1/2 pound (225 g) pork parts per person.
Storage:	If fresh, refrigerate and use within 2 days. Otherwise, cure in salt and spices to keep longer.
Preparation:	*Jowl:*

- **Pork jowl is most commonly found smoked. Use like salt pork (page 122).**

Head Cheese:

1. **Place 1 pig's head, thoroughly rinsed and trimmed, along with 4 pig's feet (page 123) into a large pot. Cover with cold water and bring to a boil. Reduce heat to a simmer, skimming as necessary.**

2. **Add onion, carrots, leeks, garlic, lemon zest, a bundle of fresh herbs, and peppercorns.**

3. Simmer 2 to 3 hours, or until the meat starts to come away from the bone. Remove the head and feet from the pot and strain the liquid, discarding the solids.

 4. While still warm, pick the meat from the head (peeling and dicing the tongue) and the feet. Boil the reserved liquid down to half its original volume or until syrupy and season generously with salt. Cool till the liquid just starts to gel.

5. Line a rectangular terrine mold (or bread pan) with plastic wrap. Fill with the picked meats. Pour the liquid over top, banging the mold down several times to eliminate air pockets.

 6. Chill overnight in the refrigerator. Remove from the mold, peel off the plastic, and slice. Serve cool.

Flavor Affinities:
Bay leaves, black pepper, collard greens, garlic, kale, lemons, marjoram, mustard seed, thyme, vinegar.

---

37. **LEG**

Other Names:
Whole: *Coscia* or *cosciotto* (Italian), fillet end or knuckle end (British), fresh ham, *jambon* (French), half leg, *pierna* (Spanish). **Cuts:** Fresh ham steaks, knuckle or tip, sirloin roast, top round roast.

General
Description:

The large ham, or rear leg of the pig, is tops for robust flavor and satisfying texture. A whole roasted fresh ham (NAMP 401) is quite large and makes a perfect buffet dish for a big gathering. You may buy the leg with part of the shank (page 137) removed, as a semi-boneless pork leg (with the hip bone removed) to make it easier to carve, or completely boneless. A buffet-style fresh ham has been trimmed, leaving the shank end bone clear for use as a handle when carving.

Pork leg three-way (NAMP 402G), sold to restaurants, is divided into the three major muscles called TBS (top, bottom, and side, also known as inside round, outside round, and knuckle), which can also be sold boneless. Some butchers sell individual muscles such as top round and top sirloin boned and rolled.

Pork tip, or **knuckle**, is a lean boneless cut from the tip portion, the front part of the leg above the kneecap also known as the forecushion. It is the most economically priced boneless cut. This darker muscle is perfect for slow simmering or slow braising for pot roasts. Many chefs dice it for soups and stews.

The **inside round** (NAMP 402F) is a boneless cut from the inside of the leg. This tender cut is an attractive pale gray-pink color and is quite versatile. It makes an easy-to-carve roast and can be used for cutlets, kabobs, satay, stews, terrines, and ragouts. The **outside round** is the outer or bottom muscle of the pork leg trimmed until it is practically free of fat. It is an economical boneless cut whose toughness is good for slow roasting. **Rear leg shanks** (NAMP 417A) are the lower portion of the leg, below the knee joint.

Part of Animal: Pork leg, or fresh ham, is the hind leg, the same cut that is made into a cured and/or smoked ham (pages 284–287). It contains the knuckle, top round, bottom round, and shank, depending on how it is cut.

Characteristics: A whole ham contains many different muscles with different amounts of fat and qualities of tenderness. In general, it is a lean cut that is relatively tender and can be cooked by roasting. A half ham from the butt end is more tender and tasty than one from the shank.

How to Choose: A whole pork leg must be specially ordered; though extremely large for a family roast, it is also relatively inexpensive. Have the butcher remove the aitchbone for ease of carving. A BRT (boned, rolled, and tied) leg roast weighs 6 to 12 pounds (2.7–5.4 kg).

Amount to Buy: Allow 3/4 to 1 pound (340–450 g) per person for bone-in leg, 1/2 to 3/4 pound (225–340 g) for boneless ham. A whole leg weighs about 22 pounds (10 kg).

Storage: Refrigerate a whole fresh ham up to 3 days; up to 4
⊟ x3–4   days if marinated.

Preparation: 1.   **Rub a paste of herbs, garlic, salt, and pepper over the exposed meat of the ham, including the inside if it** has been boned. Cut small gashes into the skin and fill them with the paste.

2. Roast skin side up (if there is skin) or fat side up (if the skin has been removed) at 450°F (230°C) for 20 minutes. Reduce the heat to 325°F (165°C) and continue to roast for about 4 hours, or until the meat reaches an internal temperature of 150°F (66°C) at its thickest point.

3. Remove from the oven, cover with foil, and allow to rest for 30 to 45 minutes, for the temperature to even out and the juices to be reabsorbed. The temperature will continue to rise about 5°F (2°C).

4. Make a pan sauce, if desired, from the drippings in the pan. Pour off the drippings and ladle off the fat (there will be a lot). Add stock to deglaze the pan. Transfer the liquid to a small saucepan and add wine, stock, or water. Strain and thicken lightly with a little cornstarch mixed with water.

5. Carve the ham into slices and serve with the sauce.

Flavor Affinities: Bay leaves, cloves, cranberries, cumin, fennel seeds, oranges, oregano, shallots, thyme, white wine.

38 a–b.   **LOIN**

Other Names: Back ribs, blade end pork loin roast, center-cut loin
roast (bone-in and boneless), chump (British), crown
roast of pork, double boneless loin (tied), 5- or 7-rib
roast, *lombo* or *carré* (Italian), *lomo* (Spanish), *longe*
(French), rib end loin roast, rib roast, sirloin roast.

General
Description:
The pork loin is a meaty, relatively tender cut with a
large center eye, dense texture, and full-bodied flavor.
The pork loin does not have much fat, so this roast
can dry out if overcooked. To keep it juicy, brining is
recommended. Pork loin is quite versatile and adapts
well to many flavors. In Cuba it is marinated with
cumin, oranges, rum, and oregano; American cooks
glaze it with maple and vanilla; and the Chinese
braise it with hoisin, ginger, and scallions.

The economical **blade end loin roast**, also
known as the **5-** or **7-rib roast**, is a retail cut from the
loin end nearest the shoulder and will be fatty and
thus juicy, but the bones make it difficult to carve.
Country-style ribs (page 111) are from this section.

For many cooks, a **center-cut pork loin roast**
(NAMP 412A)—often sold boneless (NAMP 412B)—is
the best choice; it's easy to carve, doesn't take long to
roast, and is tender and lean. The **sirloin end roast**
has more bone and less fat. It has good flavor and
includes a bonus: the larger butt end of the tenderloin. A **double boneless pork loin** consists of two

loins tied one atop the other to make a large roast ideal for groups.

Part of Animal:	The pork loin is the pig's entire back, including the rib, the loin, and the sirloin.
Characteristics:	The loin muscle is shaped like an oval and is lean, tender, and quick cooking. The cap muscles covering the main eye are tougher and fattier, but add juiciness.
How to Choose:	For a bone-in roast, make sure that the butcher has cracked the backbone (chine) between the ribs or has removed the bone so it's easy to carve. Boneless loin should be well trimmed.
Amount to Buy:	Allow 6 to 8 ounces (170–225 g) of boneless pork loin, 8 to 12 ounces (225–340 g) of bone-in pork loin per person. A boneless blade end roast will weigh 3 to 4 pounds (1.4–1.8 kg).
Storage:	Store pork loin roasts refrigerated for up to 3 days.

Preparation: 1. **Trim off excess fat. Follow the directions in the section on pork chops (page 118) for brining this cut. Brine for at least 1 day and up to 3 days refrigerated, if desired, for more flavor and moistness.**

2. **Remove from the brine, rinse, and pat dry. Rub with oil, salt, and pepper, unless brined.**

3. **Roast, fat side up, at 450°F (230°C) for 15 minutes. Reduce the heat and roast at 300°F (150°C) for about 1 1/2 hours, or until it reaches an internal temperature of 150°F (66°C) at the thickest portion.**

4. **Remove from the oven and cover with foil. Allow the meat to rest 15 minutes before carving.**

5. **Prepare a pan sauce from the drippings, if desired. (See instructions for pork leg, page 128.)**

Flavor
Affinities:

Brandy, cilantro, cinnamon, ginger, limes, mustard, oregano, port wine, rosemary, sage, sake, soy sauce.

NECK BONES

Other Names: *Collo* (Italian), collar (British), *échine* or *collier* (French), *huesos del cuello* or *aguja* (Spanish).

General
Description:

Neck bones (NAMP 421) are the small bones from the head end of the backbone. Neck bones are one of the most flavorful and inexpensive parts of the pig. They consist of part of the backbone and ribs with small bits of very tender and flavorful meat. Neck bones can be used as a flavoring for cooked greens and soups or cooked in a pot of sauerkraut with lots of fried onions. They may also be found smoked (see page 293).

Part of Animal:	The bones from the neck of the pig.
Characteristics:	Neck bones have small amounts of flavorful meat.
How to Choose:	Neck bones may need to be specially ordered. They may also be found in markets with an African-American or Caribbean clientele.
Amount to Buy:	Allow 1/2 pound (225 g) per person.
Storage:	Store fresh neck bones 2 to 3 days refrigerated.

x2-3

Preparation: **1.** **Rinse and place in a large pot with water to cover. Add salt, crushed red pepper flakes, black pepper, a bay leaf, and thyme.**

2. **Bring to a boil. Simmer 2 hours, or until tender. Add peeled and chopped potatoes to the pot, if desired, about 20 minutes before the neck bones are done.**

Flavor Affinities: Bay leaves, collard greens, coriander, garlic, kale, lemons, marjoram, red wine vinegar, thyme.

39 a–b.

RACK

Other Names: *Caña regia* (Mexican, Spanish), *carré* (French), center-cut loin, *costolette* or *spuntature* (Italian), crown roast, 11-rib center-cut loin, French(ed) rack, middle loin

(British), pork rib roast, rack of pork, rack roast, 7-rib center-cut loin.

General Description:

Like rack of lamb, rack of pork (NAMP 412) is one of the fanciest and priciest cuts. The rack has a large light pink center eye covered by the darker rib lifter or cap meat. The meat from the rack will be tender and juicy, as long as it is not overcooked. The rack may include anywhere from 8 ribs (like rack of lamb) to 11 ribs. If the chine (or backbone) is removed and the ribs are Frenched, or trimmed of meat, this cut is called a rack of pork. The roast will be moister if the butcher doesn't trim the big slab of fat that comes with this cut; instead cut the fat off after the roast is cooked.

Part of Animal:

The rack contains 8 to 11 ribs cut from the center of the loin section, which runs along the backbone.

Characteristics:

This cut is quite tender and succulent, with moderate grain and a fair amount of fat in the cap muscles.

How to Choose:

For the most impressive cut, choose a rack with the chine bone removed. Buy two racks with the chine bone removed to tie into a crown roast of pork.

Amount to Buy:

Allow 1 to 2 ribs per person, or about 1 pound (450 g) of bone-in, 3/4 pound (340 g) of boneless.

Storage: x2–3

Refrigerate whole rib up to 3 days, chops up to 2 days.

Preparation: 1.

Rub a seasoning paste over the rack and between each chop. Let the meat season 2 hours at room temperature, or overnight in the refrigerator. (Or, have the butcher make a crown roast by tying two racks into a circle, leaving a hollow in the center.)

2.

Roast rib bone down at 450°F (230°C) for 20 minutes. Continue roasting at 300°F (150°C) for 1¹/₂ to 2¹/₂ hours, or until the meat reaches an internal temperature of 150°F (66°C) at its thickest point.

3.

Remove from the oven and allow the meat to rest 30 minutes. The temperature will rise about 5°F (2°C).

4.

If serving a crown roast, turn the rack rib bones up and fill the crown with a hot precooked mixture if desired. (Filling the crown roast before roasting may result in overcooked meat and undercooked filling.)

Flavor
Affinities:

Anisette, cranberries, fennel seeds, garlic, leeks, oranges, rosemary, sage, sake, sesame oil, thyme.

40.   **SHANK AND HOCK**

Other Names:

Chamorro or *codillo* (Spanish), foreshank, hindshank, hock, *jambonneau* (French, hindshank), osso buco (round bone slice), *stinco* (Italian, whole), trotter, *zampino* (Italian, lower portion).

General
Description:

Pork shanks (NAMP 401D, 417) are cut from the lower portion of the rear and front legs of the pig. This cut, with its deep flavor, can be braised whole or cut into cross sections for a less-expensive alternative to veal osso buco (page 95). Pork shank meat becomes silky and luscious when cooked slowly at low heat.

Pork hocks (NAMP 417A) are the lower portion of the shank, traditionally used in Eastern European and American Southern cooking. Hocks lend themselves to numerous comfort-foods. Pork hocks make a tasty flavoring for soups, bean dishes, and stocks.

Part of Animal:

The shank is the portion below the knee of the rear legs, above or below the knee joint for front legs.

Characteristics:

Pork shanks are composed of many small, tough muscles connected by cartilage. They are relatively lean, once the fat is trimmed, and full of natural gelatin. Front leg shanks will be smaller and milder in flavor than rear leg shanks.

How to Choose:

Fresh pork shank will probably need to be specially ordered, because much of it gets turned into smoked hocks. You may also buy crosscut sections of shank, cut at least 2 inches (5 cm) thick, which are easier and a bit quicker to cook than whole.

Amount to Buy:	A whole pork shank weighs 1 1/4 to 1 1/2 pounds (570–680 g). Allow 1/2 to 3/4 pound (225–340 g) of shank per person, because of the weight of the bone.
Storage: x4	Pork shanks are often found frozen and can be kept frozen for up to 3 months. Defrost in the refrigerator overnight. Refrigerate fresh pork shanks up to 4 days.

Preparation: 1.   **Tie shanks with butcher's string to keep whole.**

 2.   **Brown shanks on all sides in oil in a Dutch oven, turning several times. Remove and keep warm.**

3.   **Drain off and discard most of the fat from the pot. Add aromatic vegetables, then add broth or wine.**

 4.   **Place the shanks back into the pot and bring to a boil. Cover and braise in the oven for about 2 hours at low temperature (300°F/150°C), turning once, until the shanks are tender but still whole.**

5.   **Remove the shanks from the oven; allow the shanks to cool in the liquid to firm before handling them. Cut off the strings and let the shanks cool completely, then refrigerate overnight.**

 6.   **Take out of the refrigerator, remove the fat, and reheat in the braising liquid.**

| Flavor Affinities: | Caraway seed, fennel, figs, garlic, horseradish, lemons, marjoram, oranges, parsley, prosciutto, rosemary, sage, sauerkraut, thyme, tomatoes, vinegar, white wine. |

41. **SHOULDER**

| Other Names: | **Roasts:** Boston butt roast, *épaule* (French), *espadilla* (Spanish), 5- or 7-bone roast, foreshank, *hombro entero* (Spanish, picnic roast), *paleta* (Spanish, shoulder blade), picnic shoulder roast, *spalla* (Italian). **Chops:** Boston butt chop, *costilla arriera* (Spanish), picnic or arm chop, pork steak. |

| General Description: | *Meat from the pork shoulder (NAMP 403) is relatively fatty, making for juicy, tender, and flavorful roasts, and it has the perfect ratio of fat to lean meat for homemade sausage.* Chinese chefs prefer pork shoulder because it has enough fat for braising or roasting and takes well to the pungent flavors typical of Chinese cuisine. The shoulder is usually divided into the upper shoulder portion, called the Boston butt, and the lower arm portion, called the picnic shoulder. The shoulder also includes the foreleg or hock (page 137). |

The **Boston butt** (NAMP 406) produces a delicious and economical pork roast, though it has a lot of internal fat. This rectangular roast is the cut of choice for pulled pork barbecue because it's marbled with enough fat to keep the meat moist. A **pork steak** or **blade steak**, not to be confused with the more tender adjoining loin blade chop (page 116), is a cut from the upper pork shoulder. The **picnic shoulder** (NAMP 405) is sold whole, usually bone-in, or as either the meatier upper arm portion or the lower foreleg portion. Picnic shoulders usually have some skin attached. A **boneless picnic shoulder** (NAMP 405A) is meaty, relatively lean, and has outstanding flavor. It is ideal for braising because it takes on a juicy, soft texture; it is popular for barbecue.

The smaller **picnic cushion** (NAMP 405B) is cut from the picnic shoulder. It is quite lean and is often used in Mexican recipes that require slow roasting, braising, or boiling as well as in Asian entrées that call for marinating and slicing thinly.

A **5-** or **7-rib** roast is a somewhat fatty, economical retail roast sold bone-in or boneless from the shoulder blade section. If you buy it as a bone-in roast, make sure that the butcher has cracked the backbone between the ribs so it's easier to carve.

Part of Animal: The pork shoulder lies between the rib section and the foreshanks. It includes three to seven rib bones along with the shoulder blade and the upper front leg.

Characteristics: A whole pork shoulder is often divided into the Boston butt and the picnic shoulder. Both consist of different muscles with different characteristics, some more tender, some tougher.

How to Choose:	A whole pork shoulder will weigh 12 to 16 pounds (5.4–7.3 kg). A Boston butt weighs 6 to 8 pounds (2.7–3.6 kg), is also sold boneless, and will serve up to eight people. The picnic shoulder weighs 6 to 8 pounds (2.7–3.6 kg) and is also sold boneless.
Amount to Buy:	Allow 3/4 to 1 pound (340–450 g) for bone-in roast; 1/2 to 3/4 (225–340 g) pound for boneless roast.
Storage:	Store pork roasts up to 3 days refrigerated.

x3

Preparation: 1. **Trim away excess fat. Sprinkle desired seasonings on all surfaces of the roast, leaving it to marinate at room temperature for about 1 hour before roasting.**

2. **Tie, if desired, to make a compact and even shape, and sear in a very hot (450°F/230°C) oven for 15 to 20 minutes, or in oil in a large, hot skillet.**

3. **Reduce heat to low (275°F/135°C) and slow-roast for 2 to 3 hours, or until tender. Or braise, cooking covered in a small amount of flavorful liquid, for 2 to 3 hours, or until tender. Or cook in a smoker till tender and most of the fat has melted away, 6 to 10 hours; cool, then shred the meat. Reheat with barbecue sauce to make pulled pork.**

Flavor Affinities:	Barbecue sauce, chile peppers, Chinese five-spice powder, ginger, lemons, oregano, rice wine, soy sauce.

SIRLOIN

Other Names:	**Roasts:** *Chuletero* or *cadera* (Spanish), chump (British), *fondello*, *carré*, or *culatello* (Italian), hip-bone roast, loin end roast, loin pork roast, sirloin end roast, sirloin roast, *surlonge* (French). **Steaks and Cutlets:** Boneless butt steak, *costilla asadera* (Spanish, butt steak), sirloin cutlet, sirloin steak.
General Description:	*The pork sirloin (NAMP 410A) is a fairly lean and eco-nomical roast that includes parts of both the backbone and the complicated hipbone.* A whole bone-in sirloin can be difficult to carve, so it's usually best to get a rolled and tied boneless sirloin roast. A pork sirloin butt steak is made up of many different muscles, some more tender than others, but all with full-bodied pork flavor. It is a popular cut among Mexicans. Sirloin is rather lean, so be careful not to overcook.
Part of Animal:	The sirloin is the upper hip section of the loin primal, which runs along the back. A bone-in sirloin roast will also contain the larger butt end of the tenderloin.
Characteristics:	Pork sirloin is moderately tender, lean, and versatile with excellent flavor.
How to Choose:	For ease of carving, buy a boned, rolled, and tied sirloin roast. You may order a roast of two top butt sirloins tied together for a regularly shaped rolled roast.

Amount to Buy:	A boneless sirloin will weigh about 8 pounds (3.6 kg) and is large enough to feed 15 to 20 people. Allow $3/4$ pound (340 g) per person for bone-in sirloin; $1/2$ pound (225 g) per person for boneless sirloin.
Storage: x2–3	Store sirloin roasts up to 3 days refrigerated; store cutlets and cubes up to 2 days refrigerated.

Preparation:

1. Season roast with spices as desired, then place roast, fat side up, on a rack in a roasting pan, uncovered.

2. Roast at 325°F (165°C) until the internal temperature reaches 150°F (66°C) at the thickest point.

3. Remove from the oven, cover with foil, and allow to rest for 15 to 30 minutes, for the temperature to even out and the juices to be reabsorbed into the meat. The temperature will rise about 5°F (2°C).

Flavor Affinities:	Allspice, caraway, chipotle chiles, cinnamon, cloves, cumin, dark rum, garlic, limes, sage, shallots, sherry.

42. **SUCKLING PIG**

Other Names:	*Cochinillo* (Spanish), *cochon de lait* (French), *lechon* (Philippine), *leitão* (Portuguese), *maialino* (Italian), piglet, sucking pig.

General Description:	*Roast suckling pig has been a delicacy since ancient times.* In many northern European countries, roast suckling pig is a traditional Christmas entrée. It is also a special occasion dish in the Philippines, a custom brought with the Spanish. In Cuba, suckling pig is traditionally served on New Year's Day. Suckling pig is served for the Hawaiian lu'au, covered with banana leaves and cooked in a pit. Roast suckling pig is served whole at Chinese weddings as a symbol of the bride's virginity, although the same pig is said to symbolize both virility and prosperity.
Characteristics:	The meat is pale, tender, and rather gelatinous. The true delicacy is the crackling, crispy skin.
How to Choose:	Suckling pigs are slaughtered at 2 to 4 weeks of age. The entire pig is sold whole and eviscerated. The smaller the pig, the more tender and delicate it is.
Amount to Buy:	A suckling pig weighing 8 to 15 pounds (3.6–6.8 kg) serves six to twelve people, allowing 1 1/2 pounds (680 g) per person. Larger baby pigs weighing up to 30 pounds (14 kg) may be purchased whole. Suckling and baby pig usually have to be specially ordered.
Storage: x1-2	Suckling pig is quite perishable; store 1 to 2 days refrigerated.
Preparation: 1.	**Rub a paste of herbs, salt, and pepper into the cavity.**

2. Tie the cavity shut with butcher's string, positioning the front and back legs against the body. Cover the tail and ears with aluminum foil.

 3. Place the piglet in a large roasting pan and roast at 350°F (180°C) for 15 minutes per pound, about 5 hours, basting with white wine and the pan juices and turning the pig every hour, or until it reaches 165°F (74°C) at its thickest point.

4. Remove the pig from the oven, drape it with foil, and allow it to rest for about 30 minutes before slicing.

Flavor Affinities: Apples, bay leaves, garlic, ginger, honey, limes, nutmeg, onions, red wine, sauerkraut, thyme, white wine.

---

43. **TENDERLOIN**

Other Names: *Filet* (French), *filetto* (Italian), filet of pork, *solomillo* (Spanish).

General Description: *Pork tenderloin (NAMP 415) is extremely tender with a buttery texture.* This premium cut is relatively expensive compared with other cuts of pork, but it is much cheaper than tenderloin of beef and even more tender. It is quick cooking, mild in flavor, and lean (about the same amount of fat as boneless, skinless chicken breast). A single pork tenderloin will usually serve two people; they are commonly found two to a package. It is quite versatile and may be grilled, cut into medallions and sautéed, cut into slices or cubes, or skewered. Take care not to overcook this delicate, lean meat.

Part of Animal: The filet lies underneath the ribs alongside the backbone, paralleling the loin. When cut through the backbone, the tenderloin and loin become part of pork T-bone (or loin) chops (see pork chops, page 116); T-bones cut from the leg end will contain a larger portion of the filet.

Characteristics: This extremely tender meat is long and less than 1 inch (2.5 cm) in diameter. Because it is relatively lean, it will dry out very quickly if overcooked.

How to Choose: Pork tenderloins weigh 3/4 to 1 1/2 pounds (340– 680 g) each and are commonly packaged in pairs.

Amount to Buy: Allow one tenderloin for every two people, or about 1/2 pound (225 g) per person.

Storage: Tenderloin is quite perishable; refrigerate and use
x2–5 within 2 days of purchase. Vacuum-packed tenderloin may be stored for up to 5 days refrigerated.

Preparation: **1.** **Marinate up to 2 hours if the marinade is acidic (no longer, or the meat will turn mushy), or overnight in the refrigerator if the marinade is not acidic.**

2.   **Allow the meat to come to room temperature.**

 3.   **Cook quickly at high temperature, either by pan-searing, grilling, or broiling to 150°F (65°C).**

Flavor
Affinities: Balsamic vinegar, cardamom, cilantro, cinnamon, dark rum, fennel, ginger, limes, mustard, oranges, rosemary, sherry, tarragon, turmeric, yogurt.

44.   **VARIETY MEATS**

Other Names: Innards, offal, organ meats. **Chitterlings:** Chitlins. **Heart:** *Coeur* (French), *corazón* (Spanish), *cuore* (Italian), *Schweineherz* (German). **Kidneys:** *Riñones* (Spanish), *rognon* (French), *rognone* (Italian). **Liver:** *Fegato* or *fegatello de maiale* (Italian), *foie de porc* (French), *hígado* (Spanish). **Tongue:** *Langue* (French), *lengua* (Spanish), *lingua* (Italian), *Schweinezungen* (German).

General
Description: *Organ meats come from inside the carcass.* Different ethnic groups use different organ meats, so these specialty items may be found in various markets.

Pork **casings** are the salted small intestines of the pig. They are soaked in water to remove the salt and then are used to encase sausages. **Chitterlings** (large intestines) are a delicacy in parts of the American South, especially in the African-American community.

They are highly appreciated in France, particularly in the area of Lyon, for making andouille sausage.

The pork **heart** is a muscular organ with fat that is soft and white. Heart is often used as an ingredient in sausages and in Pennsylvania Dutch scrapple. It may also be simmered, sliced, and then pickled.

The **kidney** is a flat, bean-shaped, smooth, firm, and reddish-brown organ. Kidneys are rather tough and can have a strong odor. It may be used in Chinese stir-fries along with pork meat.

The **liver** is a smooth, irregularly shaped organ that consists of four lobes of varying sizes. Covered with a thin membrane, it is reddish brown and strong tasting. Pork liver is commonly used in France as part of the forcemeat (a combination of finely ground and seasoned meats) for country-style pâtés.

Pork **tongue** is soft pink in color with a whitish pink membrane covering it. It weighs about 1 pound (450 g). It must be scrubbed thoroughly before using. Cooked tongue is lean, meaty, and quite versatile. Pork tongue can be used interchangeably with other types of tongue in recipes, though cooking times vary according to size.

Amount to Buy: Organ meats are generally rich; allow 4 to 6 ounces (115–170 g) per person.

Storage: Organ meats are extremely perishable. Refrigerate and cook within 1 day, or precook by parboiling and then trimming or weighting as necessary. Finish cooking within 1 day.

Preparation: ***Chitterlings:***

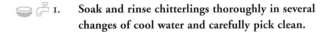 1. **Soak and rinse chitterlings thoroughly in several changes of cool water and carefully pick clean.**

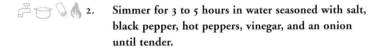 2. **Simmer for 3 to 5 hours in water seasoned with salt, black pepper, hot peppers, vinegar, and an onion until tender.**

3. **Cut cooked chitterlings into small pieces. Dip into beaten egg, and then into breadcrumbs. Fry in hot oil at about 365°F (185°C) until golden brown.**

NOTE: **Chitterlings can be bought precooked in specialty markets.**

Heart:

• **See beef variety meats (page 68) for preparation instructions.**

Kidney:

1. **To cut down on the rather strong taste and aroma of pork kidneys, skin them and then cut open without separating the halves.**

2. Remove the white central core of fat, wash under running water, and cover with milk. Soak the kidney for about 4 hours refrigerated. Drain before cooking.

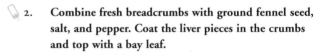 3. Season the kidney and cook in butter and oil over moderate heat, covered, for 10 to 15 minutes, or until tender but still firm. Flame, if desired, with Cognac or Armagnac. Remove the kidney and slice thinly.

4. Add butter and Dijon or coarse-grain mustard to the pan, swirling to combine into a creamy sauce. Pour sauce over kidneys.

Liver:

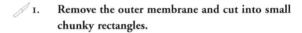 1. Remove the outer membrane and cut into small chunky rectangles.

2. Combine fresh breadcrumbs with ground fennel seed, salt, and pepper. Coat the liver pieces in the crumbs and top with a bay leaf.

 3. Wrap each piece of liver in caul (see page 119). Grill over wood embers or charcoal, if possible, or broil until the packets are crisp and brown, about 3 to 5 minutes for each side.

NOTE: Be careful not to overcook, or the liver will be dry and hard.

Tongue:

 1. Scrub well, put in a pot, and cover with cold water. Bring to a boil and simmer for 2 hours.

2. Halfway through cooking, add a carrot, a peeled onion stuck with cloves, several bay leaves, a few sprigs of thyme, and salt.

3. Remove the tongue from the broth and rinse under cool running water and remove the skin. Then put it back into the cooking broth to cool.

4. When totally cool, remove from the broth, dry, and cut thinly crosswise. Use as a sandwich filling.

Flavor Affinities: **Chitterlings:** Black pepper, hot red pepper, onions, vinegar. **Heart:** Demi-glace, garlic, hot red pepper, paprika, red wine, vinegar. **Kidneys:** Brandy, butter, chives, Dijon mustard, garlic, mushrooms, salt pork, shallots, sherry. **Liver:** Caramelized onions, fennel seed, golden raisins, lemons, onions, sherry, white wine, wine vinegar. **Tongue:** Allspice, apple cider, cloves, garlic, tomatoes, wine vinegar.

Color Plates

Icon Key

PREPARATION

caution	bowl	tap water	paper towels
scissors	knife	meat mallet	spatula
seasonings	frying pan	roasting pan	pot or Dutch oven
grill	requires waiting	STORAGE **x** number of days	

TEMPERATURE

low	medium	high

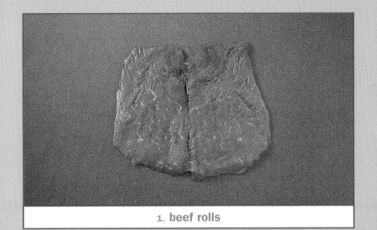

1. beef rolls

2. beef marrow

3. **brisket, whole**

4. a) **bolar roast**

4. b) **chuck eye steak**

5. **coulotte**

6. flank steak

7. **ground meat:** a) beef; b) veal; c) lamb; d) pork

8. **hanging tender, whole and trimmed**

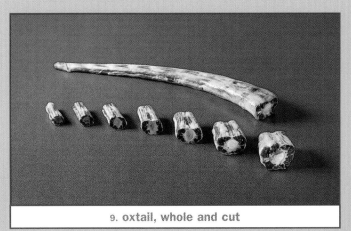

9. **oxtail, whole and cut**

10. a) **boneless rib-eye**

10. b) **boneless rib-eye steak**

10. c) **export rib of beef**

10. d) **cowboy steak**

10. e) **thin-sliced rib-eye (japanese shabu-shabu)**

11. **rump roast**

12. boneless beef shank, korean style

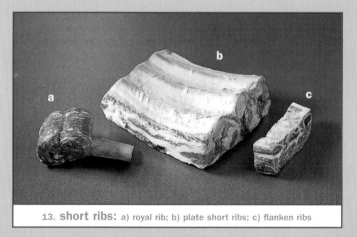

13. **short ribs:** a) royal rib; b) plate short ribs; c) flanken ribs

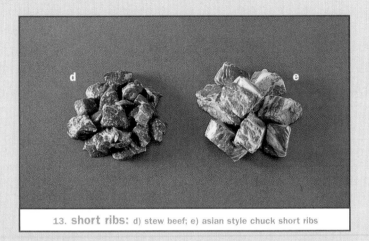

13. short ribs: d) stew beef; e) asian style chuck short ribs

13. short ribs: f) boneless short ribs; g) blade meat

14. shoulder center, ranch-cut steak

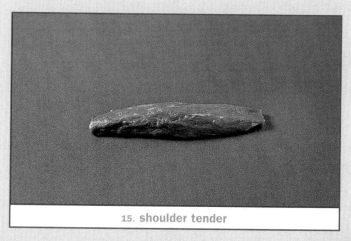

15. shoulder tender

16. **skirt steak (inside)**

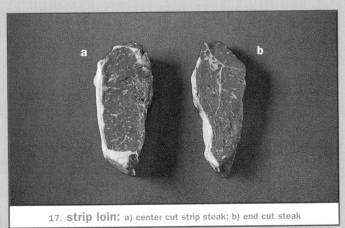

17. **strip loin:** a) center cut strip steak; b) end cut steak

17. strip loin: c) dry-aged whole sirloin strip

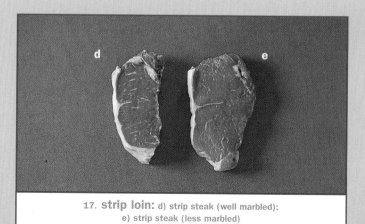

17. strip loin: d) strip steak (well marbled);
e) strip steak (less marbled)

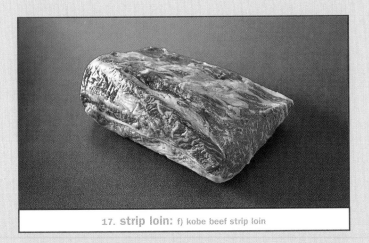

17. strip loin: f) kobe beef strip loin

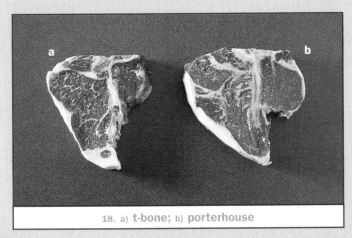

18. a) **t-bone;** b) **porterhouse**

19. **tenderloin:** a) chain, b) steaks

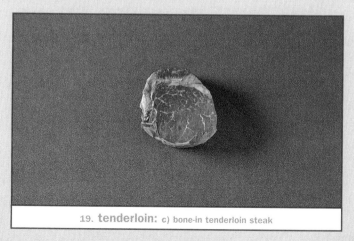

19. **tenderloin:** c) bone-in tenderloin steak

20. **top blade steak, flatiron steak**

21. **top round:** a) single muscle; b) whole

22. top sirloin butt

23. tri-tip

24. variety meat: tripe, honeycomb

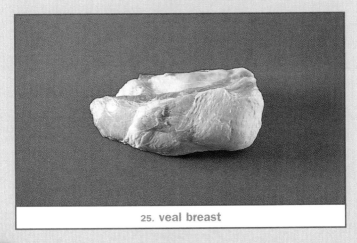

25. veal breast

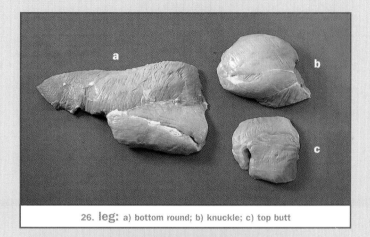

26. leg: a) bottom round; b) knuckle; c) top butt

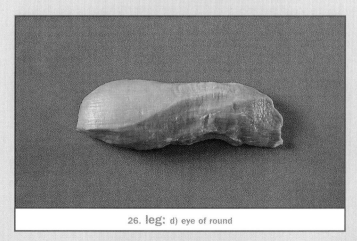

26. leg: d) eye of round

26. leg: e) top round

26. leg: f) cutlet; g) pounded cutlet; h) serrated cutlet

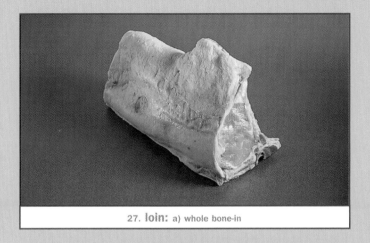

27. loin: a) whole bone-in

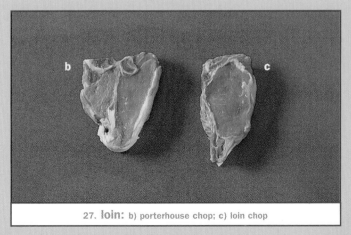

27. loin: b) porterhouse chop; c) loin chop

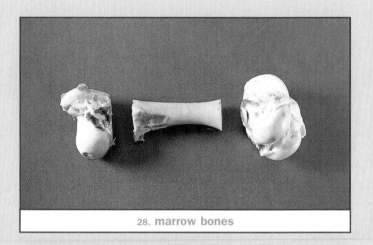

28. **marrow bones**

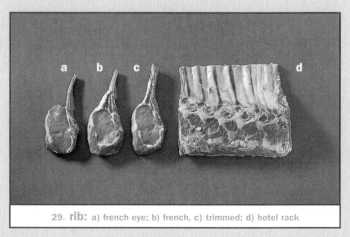

29. **rib:** a) french eye; b) french, c) trimmed; d) hotel rack

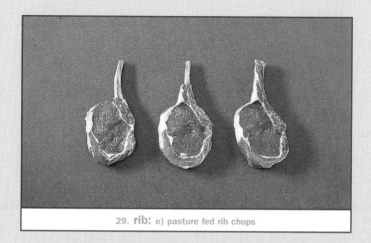

29. **rib:** e) pasture fed rib chops

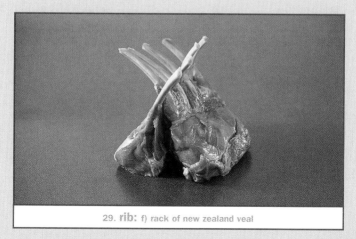

29. **rib:** f) rack of new zealand veal

30. **shank:** a) hindshank; b) veal osso buco

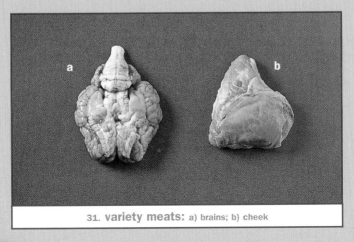

31. **variety meats:** a) brains; b) cheek

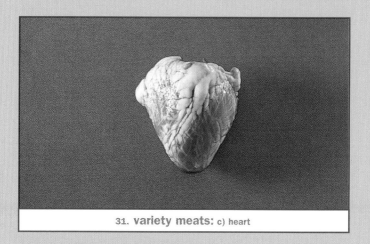

31. **variety meats:** c) heart

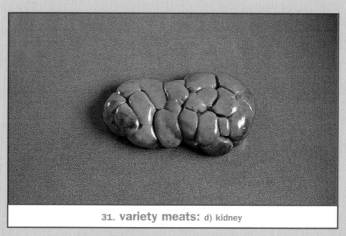

31. **variety meats:** d) kidney

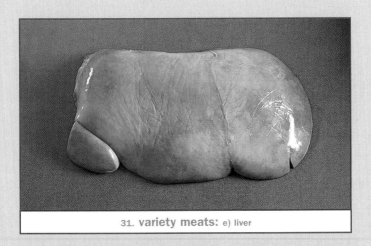

31. **variety meats:** e) liver

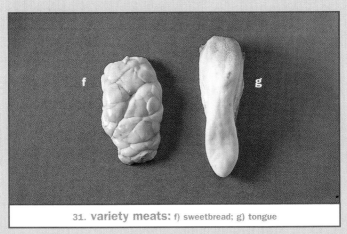

31. **variety meats:** f) sweetbread; g) tongue

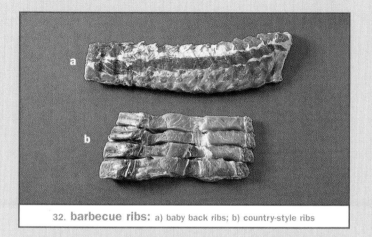

32. **barbecue ribs:** a) baby back ribs; b) country-style ribs

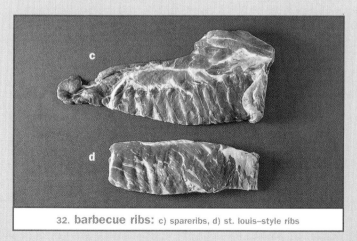

32. **barbecue ribs:** c) spareribs, d) st. louis–style ribs

33. belly

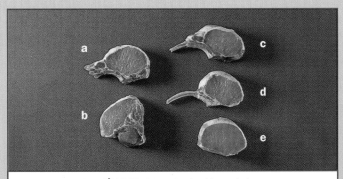

34. chops: a) bone-in shoulder end chop;
b) bone-in sirloin end chop; c) bone-in center-cut rib chop;
d) frenched center-cut rib chop; e) boneless center-cut rib chop

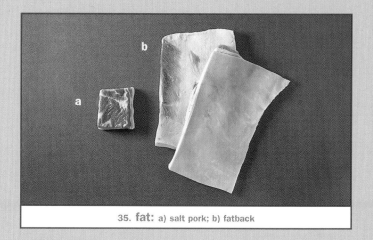

35. fat: a) salt pork; b) fatback

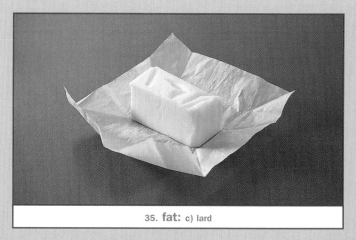

35. fat: c) lard

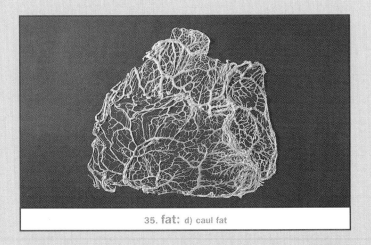

35. **fat:** d) caul fat

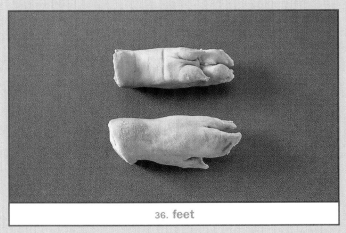

36. **feet**

37. **leg: fresh ham, buffet style**

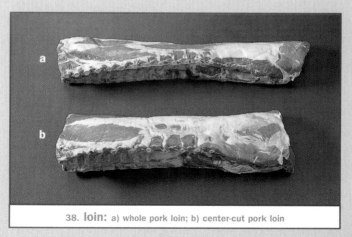

38. **loin:** a) whole pork loin; b) center-cut pork loin

39. rack: a) crown roast

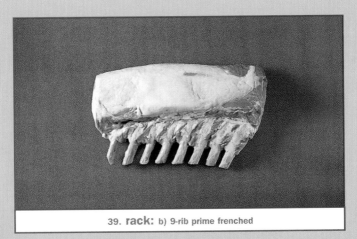

39. rack: b) 9-rib prime frenched

40. pork osso buco

41. boston butt

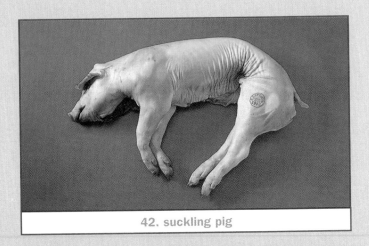

42. suckling pig

43. tenderloin

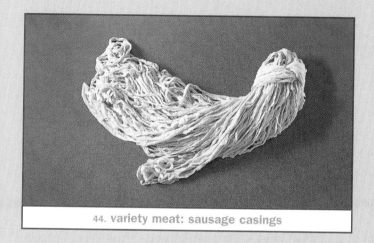

44. **variety meat: sausage casings**

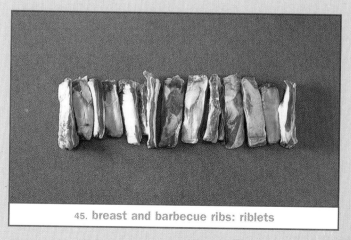

45. **breast and barbecue ribs: riblets**

46. leg: a) boneless; b) whole

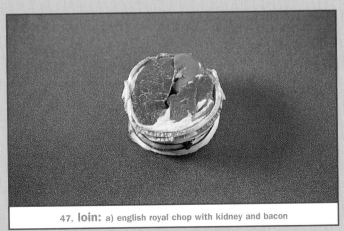

47. loin: a) english royal chop with kidney and bacon

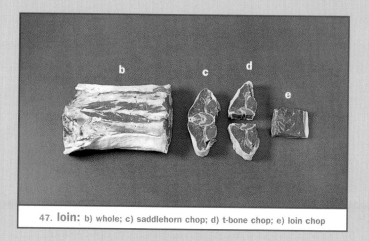

47. loin: b) whole; c) saddlehorn chop; d) t-bone chop; e) loin chop

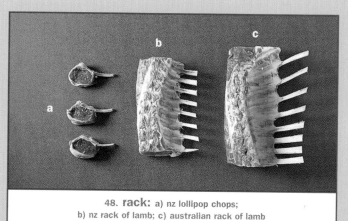

48. rack: a) nz lollipop chops;
b) nz rack of lamb; c) australian rack of lamb

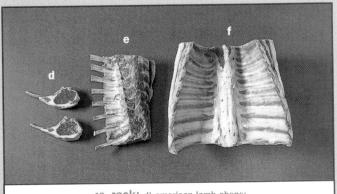

48. rack: d) american lamb chops;
e) american rack of lamb; f) american whole lamb rib

48. rack: g) baby crown rack of lamb

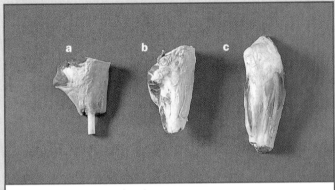

49. shank: a) australian shank;
b) american foreshank; c) american hindshank

50. shoulder: a) shoulder blade chop

50. **shoulder:** b) cushion roast

50. **shoulder:** c) lamb stew meat

51. sirloin top butt

52. tenderloin (short loin)

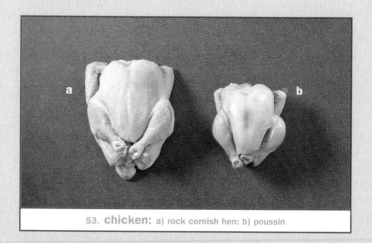

53. **chicken:** a) rock cornish hen; b) poussin

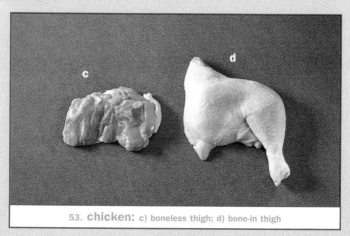

53. **chicken:** c) boneless thigh; d) bone-in thigh

53. chicken: e) wings

53. chicken: f) half

53. chicken: g) euro breast

53. chicken: h) asian-style hacked thigh; i) cutlet

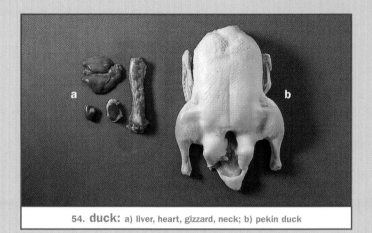

54. duck: a) liver, heart, gizzard, neck; b) pekin duck

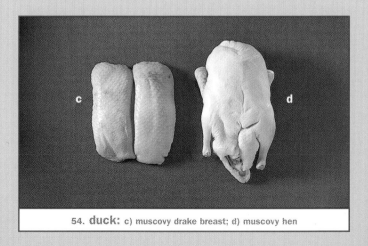

54. duck: c) muscovy drake breast; d) muscovy hen

55. foie gras: a) american (duck)

55. foie gras: b) french (duck)

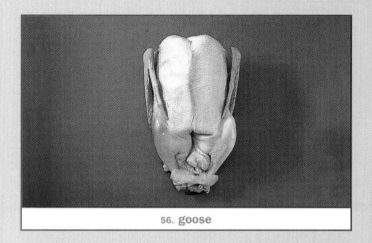

56. **goose**

57. **guinea fowl**

58. **ostrich:** a) fan; b) filet

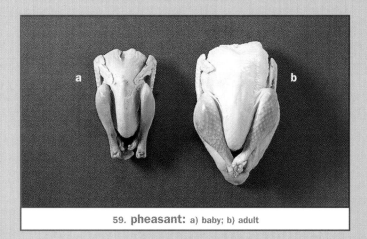

59. **pheasant:** a) baby; b) adult

60. **pigeon (squab)**

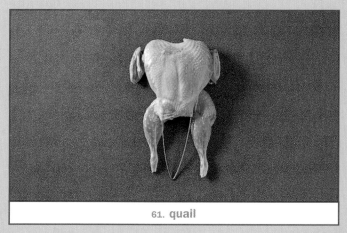

61. **quail**

62. **turkey:** a) american whole

62. **turkey:** b) american tenderloin

62. **turkey:** c) "wild" farm-raised

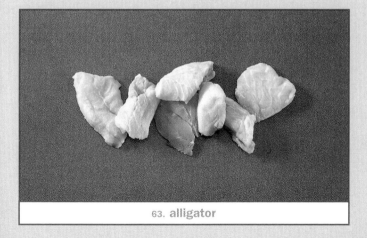

63. **alligator**

64. bison: a) strip loin

64. bison: b) short ribs

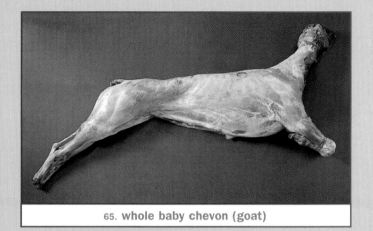

65. **whole baby chevon (goat)**

66. **rabbit:** a) whole

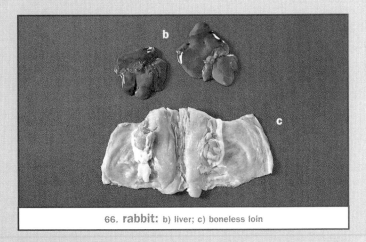

66. rabbit: b) liver; c) boneless loin

67. rattlesnake

68. venison: a) saddle (deer)

68. venison: b) elk stew meat

68. venison: c) elk pizzle

69. wild boar: boneless shoulder

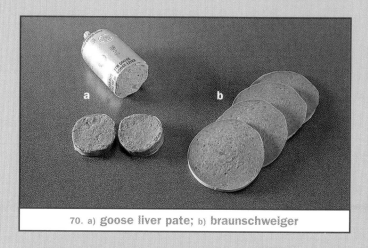

70. a) **goose liver pate**; b) **braunschweiger**

71. **polish kielbasa**

72. **italian mortadella di bologna**

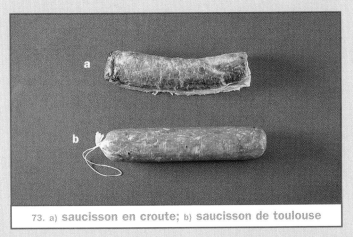

73. a) **saucisson en croute;** b) **saucisson de toulouse**

74. zungenwurst

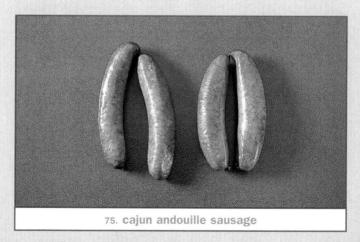

75. cajun andouille sausage

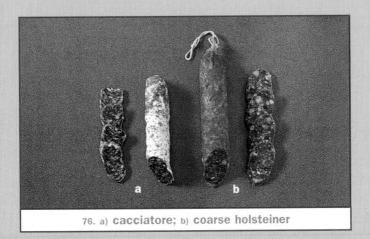

76. a) **cacciatore**; b) **coarse holsteiner**

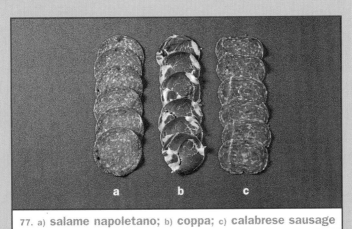

77. a) **salame napoletano**; b) **coppa**; c) **calabrese sausage**

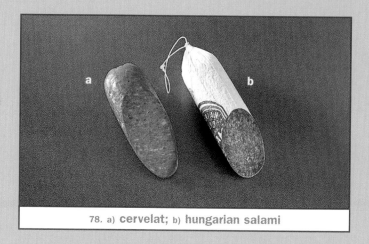

78. a) **cervelat;** b) **hungarian salami**

79. **chorizo:** a) **mexican dried;** b) **mexican fresh;** c) **spanish smoked**

80. a) **gypsy salami;** b) **russian nevskaya**

81. **landjager**

82. lap cheong

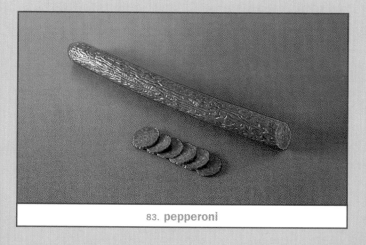

83. pepperoni

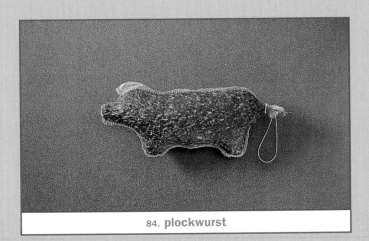

84. **plockwurst**

85. **soppressata:** a) friuli

85. soppressata: b) homemade

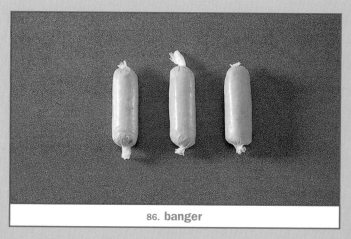

86. banger

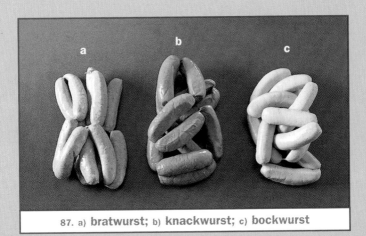

87. a) **bratwurst**; b) **knackwurst**; c) **bockwurst**

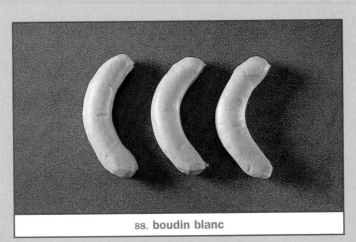

88. **boudin blanc**

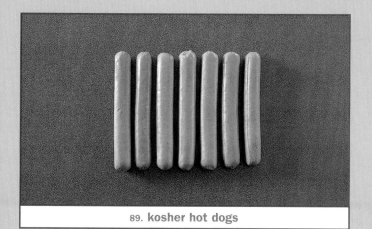

89. **kosher hot dogs**

90. **merguez sausage**

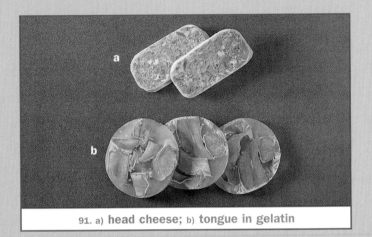

91. a) **head cheese**; b) **tongue in gelatin**

92. **scrapple**

93. **slab bacon**

94. **gypsy bacon**

95. **pancetta (italian bacon)**

96. **turkey bacon**

97. **tasso ham**

98. **smithfield ham**

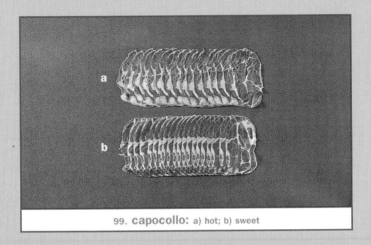

99. **capocollo:** a) hot; b) sweet

100. **lachsschinken, sliced and whole**

101. prosciutto di oca

102. prosciutto di parma

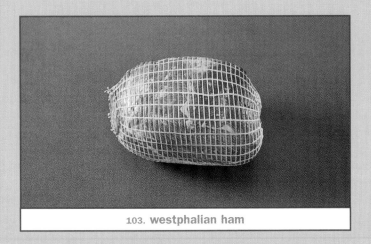

103. **westphalian ham**

104. **bresaola**

105. a) **beef jerky;** b) **tasajo;** c) **dried beef**

106. **confit of duck**

107. cracklings

108. basturma

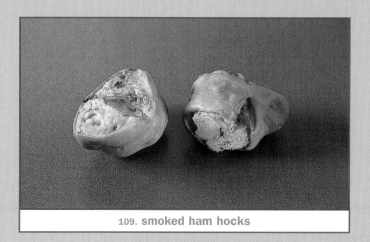

109. smoked ham hocks

110. smoked pork loin

111. smoked pork neck bones

112. smoked turkey wings

IV. Lamb

Lamb (*Ovis aries*) is a member of the Bovidae family along with cattle. It has been a popular meat ever since the beginning of domestication, as early as 10,000 years ago. Sheep herd easily, are not difficult to handle, can tolerate more severe conditions than cattle or pigs, and provide wool. Lamb is a favorite in many parts of the world, including the countries of the Mediterranean, India, Pakistan, northern China, and Indonesia.

Lamb was used for sacrifices in many different religions; it is still a favorite Easter and Passover meal (both holidays are in the spring, when young lamb is available). Older lamb, called mutton, is particularly enjoyed in Great Britain; it is rare in the United States. French pré-salé (salty pasture) lamb grazes on the salty shores of Brittany and Normandy and is considered by connoisseurs to be the finest in the world. It is rarely, if ever, available in the United States.

While American lamb is highly regarded (and is quite a bit larger than other types), it also fetches significantly higher prices because of the relatively small size of the herd and the higher cost of land, feed, and labor in the United States. The United States imported 146 million pounds (66 million kg) of lamb in 2001, almost all from Australia and New Zealand. Australia has the second largest sheep herd in the world. China has the largest sheep herd in the world, and the herd is growing rapidly. The majority of American lamb is grain-fed; lamb in Australia and New Zealand is grass-fed.

When buying lamb, the lighter the color, the younger the meat. Look for light red, finely textured meat; reddish, moist, and smooth bones; and white (not yellowed) fat. Good-quality mutton should be fine-grained and brightly colored; the fat should be white, hard, and flaky. Young lamb has red bones; as the animal ages, blood recedes from the bones.

In the United States, inspection is mandatory while grading is voluntary. USDA-graded lamb sold at the retail level is graded prime, choice, and select. As with beef, most of the lamb in supermarkets is choice or select, with prime going to fancy butcher shops, restaurants, and hotels. Lower grades are mainly ground or used in processed meat products.

There are several types of lamb. Baby lamb (hothouse or suckling lamb) is milk-fed lamb not more than 10 weeks old and weighs less than 20 pounds (9.1 kg). It is pale pink and is usually roasted whole (see suckling lamb, page 179). Spring or Easter lamb is several months old and weighs 20 to 40 pounds (9.1–18 kg). It is available fresh from spring to fall. It is a favorite for festive occasions and is often spit-roasted. Lamb is 5 months to 1 year old, the age at which most lamb is marketed. Yearling (sometimes called hogget) is lamb that is 1 to 2 years old. Its meat is darker and more flavorful than lamb. Mutton is meat from any sheep more than 2 years old. (Sometimes yearling is considered mutton.) Mutton cuts are larger, the color dark red, and the flavor more pronounced.

Lamb Primals

The **breast and foreleg** is similar in cut to, though much smaller than, brisket and foreshank of beef, and it is similar in both size and cut to pork belly and hocks. Breast of lamb is fatty and relatively tough. It includes at least seven ribs and weighs 1 to 2 pounds (450–910 g). The foreleg is usually sold separately, either whole or cut into sections.

The rear **leg** of the lamb contains the sirloin, top round, bottom round, knuckle, and shank, depending on how it is cut. Leg of lamb is generally tender, though it is made up of different muscles.

The **loin** lies just in back of the rib section. The main muscle in the loin, the "eye," is a continuation of the rib-eye. It is one of the milder tasting, lean cuts of lamb.

Lamb **rack** is cut from the rib section and includes eight ribs, numbers 5 through 12. Rack of lamb is tender and juicy and has a relatively small eye covered by a layer of rather fatty and coarse-grained, though flavorful, cap meat. An American lamb rib primal weighs about 6 pounds (2.7 kg). An Australian or New Zealand rack of lamb, sold trimmed, weighs about 1 pound (450 g).

The **shoulder** (chuck) lies between the rib section and the foreshanks. This primal includes the upper part of the front leg, the shoulder blade, and three to seven rib bones and weighs about 20 pounds (9.1 kg) for American lamb. Lamb shoulder is rather fatty, contains a fair number of bones, and is tougher than mid-section cuts like the rib or loin. It is flavorful and cooks up moist and succulent.

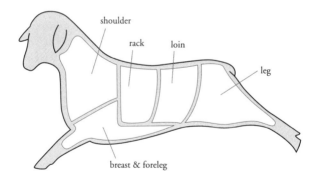

45. **BREAST AND BARBECUE RIBS**

Other Names: **Whole:** *Haut de côtelette* or *poitrine d'agneau* (French), *pechito* (Spanish), *petto d'agnello* or *costoletta superiore* (Italian), Scotch roast. **Ribs:** Denver-style ribs, riblets, spareribs.

General Description: *Breast of lamb (NAMP 209) is an often overlooked cut that is packed with flavor.* One of the cheapest cuts, breast of lamb is quite versatile. Because lamb is a young animal, the breast is more tender than that of beef. Breast of lamb is sold bone-in or boneless and may also be prepared by the butcher for stuffing, with the meat cut away from but still attached to the rib bones, leaving a pocket. If the pocket is stuffed with ground lamb, it is called a Scotch roast.

    Denver ribs or **lamb ribs** (NAMP 209A) are cut from the lamb breast and belly and include seven or eight ribs. They can be grilled or broiled and go well with spicy barbecue sauces. Lamb ribs are an excellent choice for those who don't eat pork but still want barbecue ribs. Fatty though tasty, inexpensive lamb **riblets** are individual lamb ribs on the bone.

Part of Animal: The breast is the front portion of the lamb cut from the forequarter below the shoulder and adjoining the foreshank, including the belly (plate).

Characteristics: Breast of lamb is fatty and somewhat tough, though it is more tender than beef brisket. Riblets are smaller than pork ribs but are similar: They are fatty with small amounts of flavorful meat.

How to Choose: A bone-in breast of lamb includes at least seven ribs and weighs 1 to 2 pounds (450–910 g). Make sure the breast has been skinned and trimmed.

Amount to Buy: One breast serves two. Allow 6 to 8 ounces (170–225 g) per portion of riblets.

Storage: Refrigerate for up to 3 days.

x3

Preparation: 1. **If the breast is bone-in, cut away the layer of meat that lies on top of the ribs. Discard the bones or use for stock.**

2. **Trim off excess surface fat and any thin, shiny white connective tissue.**

3. **Cook in one of the following ways:**

• **Cook slowly in a moist environment by braising in flavorful liquid (stock, wine, or tomato juice) for about 1¹/₂ hours, or until fork tender. Cool to room temperature. Chill overnight, remove and discard the fat, and reheat in liquid.**

• **Roll up the breast jelly-roll style. Cut into 1 inch (2.5 cm) thick slices and skewer to secure. Broil or grill.**

NOTE: **Lamb ribs can be marinated and grilled. Follow the instructions for pork barbecue ribs on page 111.**

Flavor
Affinities: Apricots, brown sugar, cinnamon, curry, lemons, mint, pomegranate, quinces, raisins, saffron, yogurt.

47., 48., 50a. ## CHOPS

Other Names: Best end neck chop (British, rib chop), blade chop, block chop (thick-cut shoulder chop), butterfly chop (double rib chop), *chuleta de costillar* (Spanish, rack chop), *chuleta de lomo* (Spanish, loin chop), chump chop (British, sirloin), *costola* (Italian, rack chop), *côte* (French, loin chop), *côtelette* (French, rib chop), double-cut rib chop, English chop, English royal chop, lamb steak, leg chop, loin chop, *lombo* (Italian, loin chop), *lunettes d'agneau* (French, double rib chop), middle neck chop (British, shoulder chop), rib chop, round bone chop, Saratoga chop, shoulder arm chop (or 0-bone shoulder chop), sirloin chop, sirloin steak, T-bone.

General
Description: *Lamb chops are a perfect choice for a quickly cooked dinner and are outstanding cooked on a charcoal grill.* Chops are pieces of meat that are "chopped" through

the bone and are small enough to serve as individual (or sometimes two) portions. Lamb chops are usually grilled, broiled, or pan-fried at high heat. The most elegant (and expensive) choices are rib (1204B) and loin chops (NAMP 1232A). Sirloin and leg chops (NAMP 1233E) are leaner and not quite as tender, but they're good if not overcooked.

The most economical chops come from the shoulder. **Shoulder chops** (NAMP 1207) are a bit chewy and can be fatty, but they're very flavorful and relatively inexpensive. **Round bone chops** or **arm chops** (NAMP 1207A) from the shoulder contain a cross section of the arm bone. Tender **blade chops** (NAMP 1207B) include a portion of the shoulder-blade bone and the continuation of the rib-eye muscle. A Saratoga chop is a boneless blade chop that is skewered to maintain its shape.

Rib chops, the crème de la crème of lamb chops, are quite expensive, especially if they are cut from the larger American lamb. They usually contain one rib per chop, but a double-cut rib, which includes two ribs, will be thicker and juicier. If the meat is cut away to expose the bare rib bone, it's called a French(ed) chop and is more expensive. Tiny rack chops from New Zealand lamb may be called "lollipop" chops and are popular as an hors d'oeuvre.

Loin chops usually contain sections of both the loin and the tenderloin section (like a beef T-bone), although bone-in American lamb loin chops, equivalent to bone-in beef New York strip steak, may also be found. Australian and New Zealand lamb loin is more often found boneless. An **English royal chop** is a boneless loin chop around a section of kidney and wrapped in bacon. A chop cut from the saddle (incorporating both loins) is called a double loin chop or saddlehorn chop and includes two pieces each of tenderloin and rib-eye and two T-bones.

Part of Animal:	Because lamb is relatively tender, chops may be cut from everywhere except the tough shanks and the underside or belly.
Characteristics:	Each type of chop is different, depending on which part of the lamb it was cut from.
How to Choose:	Look for a well-rounded form with light colored meat, white fat, and red-streaked bones. Choose rib and loin chops with the largest center eye muscle and the least amount of outside fat and "tail."
Amount to Buy:	Lamb chops generally run 2 to 8 ounces (60–225 g) each and should be cut at least 1 inch (2.5 cm) thick; assume one or two per person.
Storage:	Store lamb chops up to 2 days refrigerated; 3 days if oiled or marinated.

x2–3

Preparation: **1.** **Rub seasonings into the lamb and allow to rest at room temperature for 1 hour.**

2. **Grill, pan-fry, or broil to desired doneness, about 15 to 20 minutes total. Top with herb butter, if desired.**

Flavor Affinities:
Cilantro, demi-glace, fennel, garam masala, garlic, ginger, lemons, oregano, red wine, rosemary, thyme.

7d. **GROUND LAMB**

Other Names: *Agneau haché* (French), *agnello macinato* (Italian), *cordero molido* (Spanish), lamb patties.

General Description:
Ground lamb (NAMP 296) is essential to Greek moussaka, Lebanese kibbeh, Turkish kofte, and Indian keema. Mellow and mild, ground lamb takes well to aromatic seasonings. Much of the ground lamb available in supermarkets is quite fatty; it is better to buy a shoulder of lamb and have it ground by the butcher. Ground lamb is also sold preformed into patties (NAMP 1296), similar to hamburger, and can be cooked like a beef hamburger.

Part of Animal:
Ground lamb and lamb patties may come from fattier parts such as the breast or belly. Like ground beef, the best-tasting ground lamb is made from the shoulder.

Characteristics:	Ground lamb may have an overly strong taste, because the fat can be gamy. Ground lamb with a fat content of 20 percent or less is best.
How to Choose:	When buying preground lamb, look for a package that is fresh-dated, because in some markets ground lamb doesn't sell quickly. Choose a cold package that is not torn. Use your nose: Ground lamb should smell fresh and mild, not sour or unpleasant.
Amount to Buy:	When part of a casserole or other dish, allow 4 to 6 ounces (115–170 g) per person; for lamb patties allow 6 to 8 ounces (170–225 g) person.
Storage:	Refrigerate ground lamb at 40°F (4°C) or lower, and use within 2 days or freeze. Thaw frozen ground lamb in the refrigerator and cook within 1 day of thawing.
Preparation: 1.	**To prepare grilled lamb patties, combine ground lamb with seasonings and enough egg to bind. Knead until well combined and smooth. Form into patties. Chill, covered, for at least 30 minutes or up to 1 day.**
2.	**Brush the patties with olive oil and sprinkle with kosher salt. Grill, broil, or pan-fry 5 to 7 minutes on each side, or until the patties release freely when you try to turn them. The patties should be medium to medium-rare.**

Flavor
Affinities:

Allspice, caraway, chile peppers, cilantro, cumin,
curry, garlic, ginger, mint, scallions, turmeric, yogurt.

46 a–b.

LEG

Other Names:

American-style roast, *bas de gigot* (French, shank half
leg), boneless leg, bottom roast, butterflied leg, *coscia*
(Italian), *gigot* (French), *gigot raccourci* (French, short-
cut leg), half leg shank end, half leg sirloin end, haunch
(British, leg with sirloin), *haut de gigot* (French, sirloin
half leg), *jiggot* (Scottish), lamb steamship, leg center
roast, *pierna* (Spanish), short-cut leg, 3/4 French-style
leg, whole (or full) leg.

General
Description:

*Leg of lamb is the most versatile cut of lamb and makes
a beautiful roast for a large group.* A **bone-in leg of
lamb** (NAMP 233) is the most economical; one with
the aitchbone (hipbone) removed (NAMP 233E) will
be easier to carve. Boneless leg of lamb (NAMP 234)
can be stuffed or spread with a seasoning paste and
then rolled and tied. A boneless leg minus the shank
(NAMP 234A) will be more tender. A boned, rolled,
and tied (BRT) or netted leg is easy to roast.

A full American-raised leg of lamb is rather large
and unwieldy for many families, so it's often cut into
two pieces: the **shank** (lower) end is less meaty and
tougher than the **sirloin** (or upper) half, which is usually more expensive and bonier. Many people ask the

butcher to bone the sirloin half of the leg, then either roll and tie it or butterfly it. Australian and New Zealand leg of lamb is much smaller and is shipped with the aitchbone removed.

A **short leg** is partially boneless because the aitchbone has been removed along with the hindshank and the sirloin. It is smaller than a whole leg but still makes a dramatic presentation. A **lamb center roast** contains the leg bone (femur), the inside (top) round, the bottom round, and the knuckle with the shank and the sirloin removed. A **lamb bottom roast** is a boneless roast taken from the shank end of the lamb leg. A **French(ed) leg of lamb** has been cut to expose the end of the shank bone. If the bone at the end is simply chopped off, it's called an **American leg**.

An **oven-ready leg** has had the hipbone removed for ease of carving, and the leg has been netted or tied. A **butterflied leg** is completely boned and trimmed then opened up for broiling or outdoor cooking. (When spread flat, it resembles a butterfly.) Because this cut varies in thickness, it can easily satisfy many tastes with a natural range of doneness.

Lamb **cutlets** (NAMP 1234A) are thin cuts of lamb that are usually cut from the leg and should consist of a single muscle. Pound the cutlets to thin them further.

Part of Animal: Lamb leg, one of the five primal cuts, consists of the rear legs of the lamb containing the sirloin, top round, bottom round, shank, and knuckle.

Characteristics:	Leg of lamb is generally tender, though it is made up of different muscles. If you buy a boneless leg of lamb, you may wish to remove (or have the butcher remove) the shank end, which will be tougher, and use it for braising or grinding rather than roasting.
How to Choose:	Choose the size and shape of lamb leg that's right for your needs; boneless is easier to carve but takes longer to roast and won't be quite as juicy. The fell, the thin parchmentlike membrane that covers the muscles in the leg and other parts, should always be removed.
Amount to Buy:	For bone-in leg of lamb, allow about 3/4 pound (340 g) per person; for boneless leg of lamb allow about 1/2 pound (225 g) per person.
Storage:	Store whole leg of lamb up to 3 days refrigerated; up to 4 days if marinated.
Preparation: 1.	**Trim most of the outer fat from the leg. If the hip-bone has been removed, sew or skewer the opening closed. Spread a seasoning paste over the lamb, if desired, and leave at room temperature for 2 hours.**
2.	**Preheat the oven to 400°F (200°C). Brown the lamb on all sides in a large skillet over high heat.**
3.	**Roast fat side up for 40 to 60 minutes, or to the desired temperature. Test in several places, as the**

different muscles cook at different rates. (See Roasting Chart, page 294.)

⏳ 🔪 **3.** **Let stand 15 to 20 minutes before slicing. The meat will rise in temperature about 5°F (2°C) as it rests.**

NOTE: **Bone-in leg will cook faster than boneless, because the bone conducts heat to the inside.**

Flavor Affinities: Capers, cardamom, dill, ginger, lemons, mint, red wine, rosemary, shallots, tarragon, thyme, yogurt.

---

47 a–e. **LOIN**

Other Names: Double loin roast, loin roast, loin roll, *lombata* (Italian), *lomo* (Spanish), long loin (British, sirloin), *longe* (French), rolled double roast, rolled roast, saddle (double bone-in loin), short loin.

General Description: *A whole boneless loin of lamb makes an elegant, tender roast that is perfect for a small dinner party.* Loin of lamb can be specially ordered in butcher shops and is generally available from restaurant purveyors. **Saddle of lamb** (NAMP 232) is a regal bone-in cut that consists of both sides of the loin and includes both the loin eye muscle and the tenderloin. Most Australian and New Zealand lamb loin is sold boneless.

A less common but very special cut is a **double**

boneless lamb loin (NAMP 232B), in which both lamb loins are boned out and left connected. It can be stuffed and then rolled and tied for a spectacular roast that will serve at least 10 people. Most commonly, the loin is cut into small lamb T-bone steaks. The *noisette* of lamb is a French term for a boneless slice of lamb loin formed into a rounded shape that is usually sautéed and served with a pan sauce.

Part of Animal: The loin lies just in back of the rib section. The main muscle, or the eye, is a continuation of the rib-eye.

Characteristics: The long, lean loin muscle is shaped like a flattened oval and is quite tender and quick cooking. It is one of the milder tasting cuts of lamb.

How to Choose: A whole bone-in American loin of lamb weighs about 3 pounds (1.4 kg), boneless about 2 pounds (910 g). An Australian or New Zealand bone-in loin weighs about 1¹/2 pounds (680 g). An Australian or New Zealand boneless loin of lamb will weigh 10 to 14 ounces (285–395 g).

Amount to Buy: Allow ³/4 pound (340 g) of bone-in loin per person; 6 to 8 ounces (170–225 g) boneless loin per person.

Storage: Store whole loin 2 to 3 days refrigerated; store chops
x 1–3 1 to 2 days refrigerated.

Preparation: 1.

For boneless loin of lamb, wrap in caul fat (see page 119), if desired, to moisten and add flavor. For bone-in loin of lamb, trim off excess outer fat and cut criss-cross slits through the fat but not into the muscle. Season with salt, pepper, and spices.

2. **Roast at 375°F (190°C) to desired temperature, 30 to 40 minutes for medium-rare. (See Roasting Chart, page 294.)**

3. **Remove the meat from the heat, drape with foil, and allow to rest for about 10 minutes before slicing. Note that the temperature will rise 5°F (2°C) while resting.**

Flavor
Affinities:

Curry, garlic, lemons, mustard, onions, paprika, rosemary, salt, tarragon, thyme, Worcestershire sauce.

NECK

Other Names:

Collier (French), *coppa* or *collo* (Italian), *gollete* (Spanish), neck slices, *rebanada de pescuezo* (Spanish, neck slice), scrag end (British, upper neck end).

General
Description:

Lamb neck has tasty and extremely tender, fine-grained, though bony, meat. The neck is a small, tough, flavorful cut usually sold cut into crosswise slices, though it may be found whole in specialty markets. Lamb neck makes great stew and exquisite curry and is well known in countries that love lamb. The meat has plenty of collagen, which softens and dissolves to provide a rich, silky sauce and luscious meat.

Part of Animal:	Lamb neck lies between the head and the shoulder.
Characteristics:	Lamb neck is bony with bits of flavorful, soft meat.
How to Choose:	Neck may be sold as slices or bone-in stew meat, and will be found at Italian, Middle Eastern, Indian, and other ethnic meat markets. Choose the largest neck slices you can find; these will be the meatiest.
Amount to Buy:	Allow at least 1 pound (450 g) lamb neck per person.
Storage:	Store lamb neck up to 2 days refrigerated.

Preparation: 1. **Wash the necks well. Season, pat dry and toss in a little flour, shaking off any excess.**

2. **Heat a small amount of oil in a large heavy skillet. Brown the neck slices slowly over moderate heat. If desired, add chopped onions, celery, and carrots, and a little chopped garlic to the pan. Cook till soft.**

3. **Pour off and discard excess fat. Season to taste.**

4. **Add about ¹/₂ cup (120 ml) liquid, such as red wine, vegetable juice, or stock, to the pan along with**

crushed tomatoes, if desired. Cover tightly and simmer over low about 1¹/₂ hours, or until fork tender.

5. **Cool and then strain, reserving the liquid. Remove the meat from the bones and reserve, discarding the bones. Strain the liquid and chill, overnight if desired. Skim off the fat.**

 6. **Gently reheat the neck meat in the sauce.**

Flavor
Affinities: Baby carrots, bay leaves, celery, chives, curry, garlic, marjoram, onions, red wine, rosemary, sage, thyme.

---

48 a–g.   ## RACK

Other Names: *Carré* (French), *costillar* or *cuarto central costilla* (Spanish), crown roast, fore and midribs (British), French(ed) rack of lamb, *insieme di costine* or *costolette* (Italian), rack of lamb, rack roast, rib roast.

General
Description: *A standing rib of lamb (*NAMP 204A, 204B*) with eight ribs, otherwise known as rack of lamb, is the ultimate roast for lamb lovers.* This cut is possibly surpassed only by a lamb crown roast, made by curving around two (or sometimes three) rib halves and tying them to resemble a crown. When the ends of the rib bones are exposed, it is called a French(ed) rib or rack and is more expensive. For a guard of honor, stand the racks

flesh-side out and push them together so the bones cross alternately before or after cooking.

Rack of lamb is available in many forms, depending on the origin and size of the lamb, the amount of fatty belly, or "tail," left on, and how much of the outer fat and the cap muscles that cover the rib-eye have been removed. A foresaddle of lamb is cut straight across the carcass and includes both sides of the rib section. Boneless lamb rib-eye is also available. A small rack of lamb from New Zealand may be formed into an individual-sized crown roast.

Part of Animal: One of the five primal lamb cuts, the rack is cut from the rib section and includes ribs 5 through 12.

Characteristics: Rack of lamb is tender and juicy and has a relatively small eye covered by a layer of rather fatty and coarse-grained, though flavorful, cap meat that is sometimes removed. The eye itself is covered with a thin layer of silvery connective tissue called silverskin.

How to Choose: Imported racks of lamb are generally well trimmed, because shipping is expensive. Be sure the butcher cracks the chine (backbone) between the ribs or removes it so that the roast is easy to carve.

Amount to Buy: Allow one rack of lamb for two people. Imported lamb is smaller and can serve one person, albeit generously. An oven-ready American rack of lamb weighs about 2 pounds (910 g); an Australian rack of lamb may weigh 1 pound (450 g) or less.

Storage:

Store rack of lamb up to 3 days refrigerated.

Preparation: 1.

Trim off excess fat. Make crisscross cuts in the remaining fat without cutting into the muscles. Cover the exposed rib bones with foil to prevent burning

2.

Sear the lamb rack in a hot skillet, cool, and then coat with a seasoning paste, if desired.

3.

Roast bone side down at high temperature (450°F/230°C) for 15 to 20 minutes, depending on the size and the desired doneness. (See Roasting Chart, page 294.)

4.

Allow the lamb to rest 5 to 10 minutes before carving.

Flavor Affinities:

Coffee, coriander, fennel, garlic, lemons, mint, mustard, olives, oranges, rosemary, savory, thyme.

49 a–c.

SHANK

Other Names:

Foreshank, *garrón*, or *chambarete* (Spanish), *giaretto* or *stinco* (Italian), *gîte de derrière* (French, hindshank), *gîte de devant* (French, foreshank), hindshank, trotter (usually foreshank).

General
Description: *A whole braised lamb shank on the bone makes a dramatic presentation using a cut that is full of rich, flavorful meat.* Shanks are fairly lean, and if braised slowly, the meat pulls apart into delicious, juicy strands. The meat can easily be cubed for stews or ground. Lamb shanks cut into cross sections, exposing the marrow within, can be used instead of veal for the dish osso buco. Lamb shanks from imported lamb will be about half the size of American shanks. Lamb hindshanks (NAMP 233F) are large and meaty, though they take some time to cook. Lamb foreshanks (NAMP 210) are small and delicate in flavor, and they cook quickly.

Part of Animal: Lamb shanks may come from the lower portion of the arm (the front leg) or the rear leg.

Characteristics: Braised lamb shanks have dense, highly flavored meat with a creamy, rich texture.

How to Choose: Choose imported rear leg lamb shanks or American foreshanks for moderate size and mild flavor; choose American rear leg shanks for more pronounced flavor. Rear leg shanks with part of the leg above the knee joint attached may be found; called a "volcano" shank, these make a dramatic cavemanlike presentation, but they may not be as tender as smaller shanks.

Amount to Buy: A lamb shank may weigh from ¹/₂ pound (225 g) to more than 1 pound (450 g). Allow one shank per person. Your local market may have only one or two shanks available at a time; buy them as you find them and keep frozen till you accumulate enough.

Storage:
☐ x4

Lamb shanks keep well frozen for up to 3 months. Defrost in the refrigerator overnight. Refrigerate fresh lamb shanks up to 4 days.

Preparation: 1.

Tie shanks with butcher's string to insure they stay whole, then season and brown shanks well on all sides in oil in a Dutch oven. Remove and keep warm.

2.

Drain and discard most of the fat from the pan. Add aromatic vegetables, then pour in broth and/or wine.

3.

Place the shanks back into the pot and bring to a boil. Cover and braise in the oven for about 2 hours at low temperature (300°F/150°C), turning once, until the shanks are tender but still whole.

4.

Remove the shanks from the oven; allow them to cool so they don't fall apart before handling. Cut off the strings, cool completely, and chill overnight.

5.

Remove the fat and reheat in the braising liquid.

Flavor
Affinities:

Beer, chile peppers, coriander, curry, figs, garlic, ginger, honey, onions, oranges, red wine, tomatoes.

50 a–c. 📷 **SHOULDER**

Other Names: Boneless cushion roast, boneless rolled shoulder, boneless shoulder roast, *boule de macreuse* (French, arm clod), *centro de carneza de paleta* (Spanish, arm clod), *épaule* (French), *fesone di spalla* (Italian, arm clod), middle neck (British), *paleta redonda* (Spanish), presliced (precarved) shoulder roast, Saratoga roll or roast, shoulder arm roast, shoulder blade roast, shoulder roast, *spalla* (Italian), square-cut shoulder, yoke.

General Description: *Full of tasty though rather fatty meat, lamb shoulder is the most versatile lamb cut.* Because it is rich and succulent, shoulder is the preferred cut for kabobs, stew, and grinding. A **square-cut lamb shoulder** (NAMP 207) is the largest retail lamb roast with plenty of meat and usually contains four or five ribs along with the shoulder blade and arm bone. The number of ribs in a lamb shoulder varies: As few as three and as many as seven ribs may be included. The same shoulder of lamb boned out and rolled makes an easy-to-carve roast. It is called a **cushion roast** (NAMP 208) if left square and tied where the bones were.

A **Saratoga roll** (or roast) is a boneless center roast cut from the very tender blade portion of the shoulder; it's also known as **lamb chuck eye**. Though convenient, **precarved shoulder roast** can dry out in the oven and the meat may be unappetizing in color.

Lamb for kabobs (NAMP 295A) is cut into tender

1-inch (2.5 cm) cubes that are skewered for grilling, generally after being marinated. They may be cut from either the shoulder or the leg (page 163). Kabob meat from the leg is leaner, but that from the shoulder is more flavorful. **Lamb stew meat** (NAMP 295) is cut into 1-inch (2.5 cm) cubes from sections of the shoulder or leg that are too tough to grill or broil. When stewed slowly in liquid, they become tender with full-bodied flavor.

Part of Animal: The lamb shoulder lies between the rib section and the foreshanks.

Characteristics: Lamb shoulder is rather fatty and contains a fair number of bones: most of its muscles are tougher than midsection cuts like rib or loin.

How to Choose: There are many shoulder roasts sold at retail. For ease of carving, choose a boneless rolled roast; for moisture, quick cooking, and succulence, choose a bone-in roast. An arm or blade roast will be very tender. Look for a roast of the best size and shape for your needs with a well-formed, even shape (for ease of cooking), white fat, and red-streaked bones.

Amount to Buy: Allow 3/4 to 1 pound (340–450 g) for bone-in roast; 1/2 to 3/4 pound (225–340 g) for boneless roast. The largest retail lamb roast is the whole square-cut shoulder, which weighs 5 to 10 pounds (2.3–4.5 kg).

Storage: Store lamb roasts up to 3 days refrigerated.

Preparation: 1. **Cut away excess fat and sprinkle with desired seasonings.**

2. **Brown in a very hot (450°F/230°C) oven for 15 to 20 minutes.**

3. **Reduce heat to low (275°F/135°C) and slow-roast for 2 to 3 hours, or until tender.**

4. **Cool and chill overnight. Remove the fat and reheat in a little liquid.**

Flavor Affinities: Black pepper, cinnamon, cumin, curry, feta cheese, garlic, lemons, mint, oregano, red wine, rosemary, sage, thyme, turmeric, vermouth, white wine.

51. **SIRLOIN**

Other Names: **Whole:** *Aguayón* (Spanish), bone-in (or boneless) sirloin, butt, chump roast (British), *rosbif* (French), *rosbife* (Italian). **Chops and Steaks:** Chump chops (British), lamb steak, large loin lamb chops, leg chops, loin end steaks, sirloin steaks.

General Description: *The sirloin (NAMP 234G) is a meaty, flavorful, and relatively tender portion of the lamb also known as the butt.*

Like beef sirloin, this is a meat eater's delight, but because it is relatively lean, it may dry out if over-cooked. The sirloin is just above the leg, and, in many parts of the United States, it comes attached to a leg of lamb. When the sirloin is sold separately, it will usually be sliced into three or four steaks or chops, but it can be ordered whole or boneless; whole sirloin top butt may be found. Whole bone-in sirloin makes a tender, if bony, roast; whole boneless sirloin is easy to carve.

Part of Animal:	The sirloin lies between the loin (the lower back) and the upper hind leg and includes the upper portion of the aitchbone. In Europe it may be attached to the short loin; in America it may be attached to the leg.
Characteristics:	This cut is tender and lean with moderate grain and little connective tissue.
How to Choose:	A boneless lamb sirloin weighs 1 1/2 to 2 pounds (680–910 g), 2 to 3 pounds (.9–1.4 kg) bone-in. You may need to specially order a lamb sirloin roast, because it is commonly cut into chops (page 158).
Amount to Buy:	Allow 1/2 pound (225 g) of boneless meat and 3/4 to 1 pound (340–450 g) of bone-in meat per person.
Storage:	Store sirloin roasts up to 3 days refrigerated; chops up to 2 days.

2–3

| Preparation: | 1. | **Trim excess fat and marinate as desired for at least 6 or up to 24 hours, turning occasionally.** |
| | 2. | **Remove from marinade and pat dry. Roast on a rack, fat side up, at 325°F (165°C) for 40 minutes per pound, or to desired temperature, about 1 1/2 hours total. (See Roasting Chart, page 294.)** |

| Flavor Affinities: | Balsamic vinegar, black pepper, curry, feta cheese, garlic, honey, lemons, mint, olive oil, oregano, pomegranate molasses, rosemary, savory, thyme. |

SUCKLING LAMB

| Other Names: | *Abbacchio* (Italian), *agneau de lait* (French), baby lamb, Easter lamb, hot-house (or house) lamb, *lechazo* (Spanish), milk-fed lamb. |

| General Description: | *Suckling lamb is lamb that has never grazed and has been fed solely on its mother's milk, giving it pale, juicy, tender meat with an exquisite flavor.* In many countries, milk-fed lamb is an Easter specialty, and it is also served for the Muslim holiday of Eid. Roast suckling lamb is prized for its crispy skin as well as the cartilaginous texture of its small bones. It is often cooked whole, but can be cut into quarters. Suckling lamb must be specially ordered from the butcher. |

Characteristics:	Suckling lamb meat is pale pink—almost white—in color, rich in gelatin, relatively lean, tender, and mild in flavor.
How to Choose:	Suckling lamb is slaughtered at 3 to 5 weeks of age. The smaller the lamb, the more tender and mild tasting the meat.
Amount to Buy:	Allow at least 1 pound (450 g) of suckling lamb per person. A suckling lamb weighs 12 to 14 pounds (5.4–6.4 kg). Spring lambs weigh 30 to 45 pounds (14–20 kg).
Storage: 1-2	Suckling lamb is quite perishable; wrap well and refrigerate 1 to 2 days.

Preparation: 1. **Rub the meat with olive oil and season with salt and pepper. Place suckling lamb quarters in a deep roasting pan. Add aromatic vegetables, herbs, and white wine.**

2. **Sprinkle the meat with breadcrumbs and Parmigiano cheese, add stock and olive oil to the pan, and bake 45 to 50 minutes at 350°F (180°C) degrees, or until the meat is very tender and has a golden-brown crust.**

3. **Remove the lamb from the pan, and pour off excess fat. Deglaze the pan with white wine, then strain and enrich with butter. Pour the pan sauce over the lamb.**

Flavor Affinities:	Artichokes, cumin, fava beans, plums, rosemary, sage, tarragon, thyme, white vermouth, white wine.

52. **TENDERLOIN**

Other Names:	*Filet* (French), *filetto* (Italian), lamb filet, lamb tender, *solomillo* (Spanish).
General Description:	*Lamb tenderloin (NAMP 246) is extremely tender with a velvety texture.* Much smaller than beef tenderloin, lamb tenderloin is quick-cooking and delicate in flavor. Like beef tenderloin, lamb tenderloin fetches a high price. A single lamb tenderloin will usually serve one person. It may be grilled or broiled, cut into medallions and sautéed, or cut into slices or cubes and skewered. When cut through the backbone, the tenderloin and loin become part of lamb T-bone or loin chops (page 158).
Part of Animal:	The filet lies underneath the ribs alongside the backbone, paralleling the loin.
Characteristics:	This extremely tender meat is long and less than 1 inch (2.5 cm) in diameter. Because it is relatively lean, it will dry out quickly if overcooked.
How to Choose:	Lamb tenderloins may need to be specially ordered. They are commonly available from restaurant suppliers,

either whole or as the smaller short tenderloin (NAMP 232D) that lies next to the short loin.

Amount to Buy: Allow one tenderloin per person; each one weighs less than 1/2 pound (225 g).

Storage: Lamb tenderloin is quite perishable; refrigerate and use within 2 days of purchase.

Preparation: 1. **Trim tenderloins of fat and silverskin. Season with salt and pepper.**

2. **Brown tenderloins in olive oil over high heat and sauté about 8 minutes, or to the desired temperature. (See Roasting Chart, page 294.) Remove the lamb from the pan, cover with foil, and reserve.**

3. **Add chopped shallots and garlic along with julienned vegetables, if desired, to the pan, sauté 1 minute, and then pour in red or white wine. Cook the pan juices down until they are syrupy.**

4. **Season to taste and serve over the lamb.**

Flavor Affinities: Artichokes, balsamic vinegar, lemons, mint, oranges, red wine, shallots, tarragon, truffles, white wine.

VARIETY MEATS

Other Names:
Innards, offal, organ meats, pluck (liver, heart, and lungs). **Brains:** *Cervelle* (French), *cervello* (Italian), *sesos* (Spanish). **Heart:** *Coeur* (French), *corazón* (Spanish), *cuore* (Italian). **Kidneys:** *Riñones* (Spanish), *rognons* (French), *rognoni* (Italian). **Liver:** *Fegato* (Italian), *foie* (French), *hígado* (Spanish). **Sweetbreads:** *Animelle* (Italian), *mollejas* (Spanish), *ris d'agneau* (French). **Testicles:** *Coglione* (Italian), *criadillas* (Spanish), frivolities, ranch fry, Rocky Mountain oysters, *testicules* (French). **Tongue:** *Langue* (French), *lengua* (Spanish), *lingua* (Italian), Swiss-cut tongue.

General Description:
Because lamb is so young, its variety meats are quite mild in flavor and small in size. Lamb **brains** are rich, high in cholesterol, and extremely perishable. They are prized in French, Greek, and Lebanese cuisines. They have a creamy texture and delicate flavor.

Kidneys are single lobed, lima bean–shaped, and dark brown. They have a delicate flavor and can be broiled, sautéed, or braised.

Lamb's **liver** is small and pointed at the end. Its flavor is delicate, though more pronounced than veal. It is often fried with caramelized onions, and it is delicious grilled on rosemary wood skewers.

Lamb **sweetbreads** are the term for the thymus glands in the lamb's throat. They get their name because in younger animals, they are sweet and tender;

in older animals such as mutton they are tough, fibrous, and generally inedible. Throat or neck sweetbreads are elongated and irregularly shaped. Heart or belly sweetbreads and are larger and more rounded in shape.

Lamb **testicles** are typically referred to as fries. They are usually pan-fried, especially on ranches in the American West. Testicles have a soft, creamy texture when cooked. Those from smaller, younger animals are milder in flavor.

The **tongue** is the long flattened organ at the back of the mouth, which is covered with a tough outer skin. Lambs' tongues are thick and short with a smooth surface and a depression along the center. They weigh only about 1/4 pound (115 g) and are considered a delicacy. Tongue may be stewed, boiled, pickled, or made into fritters.

Part of Animal: Organ meats come from inside the carcass. The brains, sweetbreads, and tongue are from the head; the liver, testicles, and kidneys come from the central area.

Amount to Buy: Organ meats are generally rich; allow 4 to 6 ounces (115–170 g) per person.

Storage: Organ meats are extremely perishable, especially those from a young animal like lamb. Refrigerate and cook within 1 day of purchase.

Preparation: **Brains:**

• Prepare the same way as sweetbreads, below.

Kidneys:

1. Remove the outer transparent membrane and cut the kidneys in half, leaving the halves attached. Remove the white central core of fat and any tubes.

2. Skewer horizontally to keep the kidneys open, season, brush with melted butter, and roll in breadcrumbs.

3. Broil until just pink or they will toughen. Serve topped with flavored butter, if desired.

Liver:

1. Cut into slices less than ½ inch (1.3 cm) thick.

2. Season with salt and pepper and sauté in butter or olive oil. Remove from the pan and keep warm. Add chopped garlic and/or onion, and deglaze the pan with 1 tablespoon of wine vinegar per slice.

Sweetbreads:

1. Soak in cold water at least 5 hours, changing the water several times, until the water is clear.

2. Cover with cold, salted water with a little lemon juice or vinegar, and bring slowly to a boil.

 3. Immediately remove from the heat, drain, and cool under cold water. Remove the outer membrane and any tough sections. Weight for 1 hour to firm.

 4. Slice into cutlets, if desired, and then dip in flour, egg, and breadcrumbs and pan-fry.

Testicles:

 1. Use a sharp knife to split the tough skinlike muscle that surrounds the testicles. Cover with cold salted water and soak for 1 hour to remove some of the blood. Drain.

 2. Parboil in vinegared water, drain, and rinse.

 3. Let cool, then slice each "oyster" ¼ inch (.65 cm) thick. Season with salt and pepper. Dip in flour, then milk, and then flour.

 4. Pan-fry in oil or lard till golden brown.

Tongue:

 1. Wash thoroughly and then soak in cold water for 12 hours, changing the water several times.

2. **Trim off fatty parts, and dip into boiling water.**

3. **Cut slits into the skin at the base of the tongue and peel off the skin.**

 4. **Sprinkle with salt and refrigerate for 24 hours.**

5. **Wash again and the tongue is ready to be further cooked in recipes.**

Flavor Affinities: **Brains:** Butter, cilantro, cumin, garlic, lemons, shallots, tarragon, thyme, white wine. **Heart:** Bacon, garlic, onions, rosemary, sage, thyme. **Kidneys:** Brandy, chives, Dijon mustard, garlic, mushrooms, salt pork. **Liver:** Carrots, kohlrabi, lemons, onions, paprika, rosemary, sage, white wine, vinegar. **Sweetbreads:** Butter, capers, demi-glace, lemons, shallots. **Testicles:** Bacon, cornmeal, lard, lemons, onions, parsley. **Tongue:** Allspice, black pepper, celeriac, garlic, golden raisins, port wine, tomatoes, vinegar.

V. Poultry and Game Birds

Poultry is any domesticated bird used for its meat or its eggs and can refer to the flesh of all edible birds. As early as the second millennium B.C., the Chinese were raising a variety of birds, which were gradually distributed to the West via Asia, Greece, and Rome. Today there are many domesticated varieties of poultry the world over, including chicken, turkey, duck, goose, guinea fowl, and pheasant.

A game bird is any wild bird that was or is hunted for food or sport; some have been domesticated while others are farm-raised in conditions that mimic the wild. Many game birds are sold frozen, though fresh birds are available, usually by special order. Young birds will be most tender and will have a pliable breastbone that is cartilaginous, not hard and bony, at the neck end. Wild birds are much leaner than domesticated and are usually basted, barded, or larded. Older birds are best braised or used in soups or stews.

When cooking poultry and game birds, to be absolutely certain that there is no salmonella (especially important for those whose immune systems are compromised), cook whole poultry or dark meat to 180°F (82°C) measured at the thickest point of the thigh, and the breast to 170°F (77°C). Many chefs, however, cook poultry to 170°F (77°C) for dark meat and 165°F (74°C) for light meat. Unlike domesticated birds, farm-raised game birds are usually not crowded into pens and therefore are not as susceptible to salmonella bacteria; this meat can be safely cooked to below 170°F (77°C) degrees for dark meat, 165°F (74°C) for white meat. In fact, duck breast is often cooked rare like steak.

53 a–i.   **CHICKEN**

Other Names: Broiler-fryer, *coq* or *poulet* (French), *pollo* (Italian and Spanish), roaster, stewing chicken. **Black Chicken:** Black-boned chicken, *poulet soyeuse* (French), silkie bantam, silky chicken, Taihe chicken, *zook see gai* (Chinese). **Capon:** *Capón* (Spanish), *cappone* (Italian), *chapon* (French). **Poussin:** Baby chicken, spring chicken.

General Description: *The chicken* (gallus domesticus, NAMP P1000, P1100) *is a commonly eaten bird descended from the wild red jungle fowl of Southeast Asia.* Chickens may have been domesticated in India as long ago as 3200 B.C. Chicken is the most popular and widely eaten poultry in the world and may be cooked by almost any method. It can be cooked whole or cut-up, or individual parts may be cooked, seasoned, stuffed, basted, or sauced with a huge range of ingredients.

Free-range chickens, which are allowed access to the outdoors, have full-bodied flavor but are not as tender and are usually more expensive than conventionally raised commercial chickens. **Natural chickens** contain no artificial ingredients or added color and are only minimally processed. **Kosher chickens** are specially raised, fed a grain diet, and slaughtered by a ritual slaughterer using a razor-sharp knife. Then they are soaked in cold water and hand-salted with coarse salt and allowed to drain.

The small Chinese **black chicken** originated in Taihe, China, where it has been raised for more than 2,000 years. Because of their silky, furlike appearance, black chickens are cultivated as pets in some countries. These birds are usually processed Chinese style, known as Buddhist slaughter—with their head and feet left on—and are available year round in Asian markets. They are used by the Chinese to make a rich yellow chicken soup known for its curative powers and used as an energy-producing tonic for prenatal women. A black chicken is short with a small head, a short neck, and a black tongue.

Capons (namp P1200) are castrated young chickens prized for their tender white flesh. Caponization was known in ancient Greece and Rome; the procedure is done to produce a bird that is large and fat when fully grown. Capons are generally stuffed and roasted whole.

Poussin (NAMP P1400, P1401) are very small, immature chickens with delicate, moist meat. *Poussin* is French for "chick," an unfledged bird too young to have developed feathers for flying. These individually portioned birds are most popular among French and French-trained chefs. They have tender, subtly flavored lean meat due to their fast growth and young age. They may be semi-boned (removing just the rib cage) to make them suited to stuffing.

Rock Cornish game hens (NAMP P1500) are miniature chickens. They were created in 1965 by chicken mogul Donald Tyson, who cross-bred White

Rock and Cornish chickens to create a reasonably priced, single-serving whole chicken. Game hens are popular for banquet service.

Characteristics:

Chickens have both white (breast) and dark (leg, thigh, back, and neck) meat; wings contain both light and dark meat. Chicken is inexpensive and readily available, fresh or frozen, and is relatively lean and quick cooking. Kosher chickens may have some residual feathers, which must be plucked off, and their skin tends to be tough. Black chickens have small amounts of fine and tender all-dark meat that is highly flavorful and rich in nutrients. A capon is full-breasted with fine-textured, flavorful, light-colored meat covered with a layer of white fat. Poussins are very soft textured, with fragile flesh and bones, and are about 1 month old. Rock Cornish game hens are quite meaty and relatively fatty, though tender and mild in flavor. Cornish hens are easy to split in half before cooking because the bones are relatively soft.

How to Choose:

Select a chicken appropriate to your needs. All birds should be plump with unblemished skin. A **young chicken**, or **broiler-fryer**, weighs 2 1/2 to 3 1/2 pounds (1.1–1.6 kg) and is about 13 weeks old. Almost any cooking method is suitable.

A **roaster** is a young chicken, 3 to 5 months old, which weighs 3 1/2 to 5 pounds (1.6–2.3 kg). It is especially suited to roasting. A **stewing** chicken is a mature chicken, often a hen formerly used for egg production, that is more than 10 months old and weighs 2 1/2 to 8 pounds (1.1–3.6 kg).

Commonly available chicken cuts include halves; breast quarters (the breast, wing, and back); drumsticks (the part of the leg below the thigh); drummettes (the meatiest top joint of the wing); and leg quarters (including the drumstick and thigh). Cut-up chickens are broiler-fryers that have been cut into eight parts. Also available are boneless, skinless breasts; thinly sliced cutlets; boneless thighs; Buffalo wings (the top two wing joints cut apart); back and necks (good for stock and soup); chicken tenders (the tubular, rich-tasting inner muscle under the breast); and organs such as chicken livers, gizzards, and heart. For Asian-style dishes, the legs may be sold "hacked" (cut through the bone into small sections).

Ground chicken may be either dark meat, light meat, or mixed. Giblets are the bird's heart, liver, and gizzard and usually come in a package tucked inside the abdominal cavity of a packaged whole bird. The parson's (or pope's) nose is the fleshy part of a chicken or turkey's tail.

Chicken oysters, the small, rounded, dense muscle that lies between the leg joint and the back, are highly prized for their flavorful and fine-textured meat. In French, their name is *sot-l'y-laisse*, meaning "fool leaves it there."

Amount to Buy:	Allow 1 pound (450 g) bone-in chicken per person; 6 to 8 ounces (170–225 g) of boneless chicken per person. Black chicken can be found in Asian markets, usually frozen but occasionally fresh. One black chicken will make soup to serve eight. A capon weighs 6 to 9 pounds (2.7–4.1 kg). Poussin are sold as whole birds with giblets or as a boneless or semi-boneless specialty item. Allow one poussin per person. Rock Cornish game hens are sold whole only, with or without a separate packet of giblets. Allow one hen per person.

Storage: x 2–3	Refrigerate whole birds 2 to 3 days; refrigerate parts 1 to 2 days.

Preparation: **Whole Chicken:**

1. **Remove the neck and giblets from the cavity (use the neck, gizzard, and heart for stock; use the liver for stuffing). Rinse under cold water, pat dry, and season inside and out with salt, pepper, and any desired herbs.**

2. **Place lemon halves and herb sprigs inside the chicken cavity, or stuff as desired. Tie the legs together with butcher's string to keep its shape. For crispy skin, massage the chicken with softened butter or oil.**

3. **Roast at 400°F (200°C) for 15 minutes.**

4. Reduce the heat to 350°F (180°C) and cook for about 1 ½ hours for a broiler fryer, 2 hours for a capon, 2 ½ hours for a roaster, or until it reaches 170°F (77°C) on a thermometer stuck in the thickest part of the thigh and the juices run clear.

Chicken Legs and Thighs:

 1. Trim off excess fat, using a sharp knife or scissors. If desired, marinate overnight in the refrigerator.

 2. Drain and pat dry, season, and roast, broil, pan-fry, braise, or grill till well cooked, generally about 25 minutes. You may also dust with flour or roll in breadcrumbs and bake.

Chicken Breasts:

 1. Marinate briefly if desired, at room temperature, for 1 hour, or refrigerated for up to 3 hours.

 2. Drain and pat dry and then cook in any of the following ways: pan-fry; dust with flour, roll in beaten egg then breadcrumbs, and then pan-fry; rub lightly with seasoned oil and grill or broil; steam over seasoned broth; roast at 400°F (200°C); or cut into strips and stir-fry. Cook until it reaches an internal temperature of 170°F (77°C), approximately 15 to 20 minutes.

Chicken Innards:

 • Chicken livers may be sautéed with onions, shallots, wine, or other flavorful liquids and served whole or ground up for pâté. Do not add chicken livers to stock or soup, because it will make it cloudy.

 • Chicken hearts and gizzards need long, slow cooking by simmering, braising, or stewing till they are tender. They may be served as is, or chopped up and added to stuffing or rice.

 • Chicken necks may be simmered till tender, and then the mellow, fine-textured meat may be picked off and eaten as is, or added to soup.

Flavor Affinities: Balsamic vinegar, basil, black pepper, carrots, chipotle chiles, cilantro, cinnamon, cumin, garlic, ginger, honey, lemons, mushrooms, mustard, olive oil, olives, onions, red wine, rice wine, rosemary, sage, savory, soy sauce, tarragon, thyme, tomatoes, white wine.

---

 54 a–d.

DUCK

Other Names: *Anadón* (Spanish), *anatra* (Italian), broiler duckling, *canard* (French), *caneton* (French, duckling), canvasback, colvert, duckling (young duck), *Ente* (German), fryer duckling, goldeneye, mallard, *patito* (Spanish, duckling), *pato* (Spanish), pintail, teal, widgeon, wood duck. **Moulard Duck:** Magret, mulard. **Muscovy Duck:** *Canard de barbarie* (French). **Pekin Duck:** "Long Island" duck.

General Description:

Duck is a water fowl prized for its rich flavor. Duck is one of the most versatile meats and pairs well with a large range of ingredients, both sweet and savory; they may be roasted, braised, or made into confit (page 291). Ducks, along with other migratory birds, naturally gorge themselves till they double in weight, creating a thick layer of fat that helps them during their seasonal voyages.

Ducks hunted in the wild include many species of the Anas family; the most highly rated in the United States include canvasback, wood duck, mallard, and teal. The Chinese were the first to raise wild ducks, with their strong-flavored, lean meat, for food. Many hunters prefer wild duck roasted very rare.

The **Moulard** duck (*Cairina moschata X Anas pekin*) is a cross between a Muscovy male and a Pekin female artificially bred to produce foie gras. Large moulard ducks are the foundation of Gascon cuisine, in the southwest of France. Do not confuse Moulard with mallard, which is a wild duck. In the eastern United States and Canada, large and firm foie gras is produced from Moulard ducks. Moulards are especially prized for their large breasts, called magret, which are seared rare like a steak.

The **Muscovy** duck (*Cairina moschata*), which originated in Brazil, is raised for its well-flavored meat. The Muscovy duck is now Europe's most popular breed of duck, especially in France. Because they need no protection against cold weather, the Muscovy develops little fat and is by far the leanest domesticated duck, with 30 percent less fat than Pekin duck. Muscovy ducks, along with Moulard, are used to produce foie gras in California.

Pekin duck (*Anas peking*, NAMP P3001-3050) is a variety of mallard native to China and raised extensively in America for its dark, rich, flavorful meat. Peking duck is a legendary dish: To prepare it, air is pumped into the duck to separate the skin from the flesh. The bird is then hung to dry in the open air, glazed with honey and other ingredients, and air-dried again. It is then roasted in a special oven until crispy on the outside and succulent on the inside. The duck is sliced into small pieces with the skin and meat served separately spread with hoisin sauce (Chinese sweet bean barbecue sauce) and rolled with scallions in thin pancakes.

Characteristics:

Most ducks sold now are actually ducklings, or young ducks. In general, duck breast is finely textured and milder in flavor than the leg meat. Because ducks fly, their breast meat is dark—more oxygen is needed by working muscles, which is delivered by the red blood cells, giving the meat color and a stronger flavor.

Duck legs cooked long and slow will become tender and succulent without excess fat. Wild duck has lean, deep reddish-brown meat.

Moulard has the wildest game flavor of domesticated fowl and tastes of wild berries. The drake (male) is about twice as large as the hen (female). Magret breast can be dry and mealy if overcooked.

Muscovy ducks have plump breasts and a rich, distinctive flavor, making them excellent for roasting, especially the smaller females. The drakes are larger and often older, making them best suited for braising.

Young Pekin ducks are mild in flavor with tender breast meat and are excellent for roasting.

How to Choose: Restaurant buyers can find duck in almost any form: whole, half, quarters, legs, breasts, boneless breasts, giblets, livers, wings, thighs, drumsticks, and even duck feet and tongues. Home cooks will most often find whole ducks, with or without giblets, or duck breasts. Pekin duck breasts will be relatively small; breasts of other types of duck will be larger. Look for firm meat with moist-looking skin. A broiler duckling is a young bird between 6 and 8 weeks old. A roaster duckling is a somewhat older duckling less than 16 weeks old. Moulard duck breast is considered the best-tasting duck breast. Breasts from the female weigh about 1/2 pound (225 g); breasts from the male weigh as much as 1 pound (450 g). Magrets are sometimes aged up to 7 days to improve their flavor. Even though there is a lot of fat on the Moulard, the meat is quite lean.

Duck livers are valued as a delicacy, particularly for foie gras. Sometimes the livers are removed to sell separately; many are exported to France. In France, duck fat is highly regarded and is rendered for use in cooking and frying and for making confit (page 291).

Amount to Buy: Duck has a high percentage of bone and fat to meat. Allow 1 to 1 1/2 pounds (450–680 g) per person of whole duck. Allow 6 to 10 ounces (170–285 g) of breast and leg per person.

Storage: Fresh duck may be available at holiday times, but they are commonly sold frozen. Defrost in the refrigerator for 48 hours on a tray to catch drips. Refrigerate whole birds 1 to 2 days; refrigerate vacuum-packed breasts or legs up to 5 days.

Preparation: ***Duck Breast:***

 I. Score the fat deeply without piercing the skin, so it will crisp. Marinating is not recommended for magret; other varieties of duck breast can be marinated overnight in the refrigerator.

2. Sear well skin side down in a hot pan and finish in a 400°F (200°C) oven for about 10 minutes. Cook rare to medium-rare. (See Roasting Chart, page 294.)

Whole Roast Duck:

 1. Trim excess fat, rinse the bird inside and out, and pat dry. Marinate or dry-rub as desired and keep refrigerated up to 2 days, uncovered and preferably on a rack, so the skin will dry and crisp better. If possible, let the bird air-dry in front of a blowing fan as it comes to room temperature to further encourage crispy skin.

2. Trim excess fat at the base of the tail and pull out the fat packets from either side of the opening. Prick the skin all over so the fat can melt out.

3. If desired, stuff the duck with cool stuffing no more than ³/₄ full. Massage the skin with oil or butter, which will promote crispness, and then season to taste. Tie the legs together loosely with butcher's string.

 4. Place the duck, breast side up, on a rack in a roasting pan with 1 cup (.25 l) water. Roast at 375°F (190°C) for 45 minutes, then increase the temperature to 400°F (200°C) and continue roasting for 1 hour, 15 minutes, about 2 hours total, or until the thigh measures 175°F (80°C) at its thickest point and the juices run clear. Pour off the fat once or twice while the duck is roasting. (Reserve the rendered fat, refrigerated, to use for cooking; it is especially good with potatoes, chestnuts, or cabbage.)

⏳ 5.   **Transfer the duck to a platter, drape with foil, and allow it to rest 15 minutes before carving.**

Flavor
Affinities: Apples, cabbage, chestnuts, curry, figs, ginger, hoisin sauce, honey, oranges, peaches, pears, pomegranates, port wine, raspberries, sage, soy sauce, turnips.

55 a–b.   ## FOIE GRAS (DUCK AND GOOSE)

Other Names: Duck liver foie gras, *fegato grasso* (Italian), *foie gras cru* (French, raw), *foie gras entier* (French, whole), *foie gras frais* (French, fresh), foie gras parfait, foie gras purée, mousse de foie gras, pâté de foie gras.

General
Description: *Foie gras (Aiecur ficatum) is the fattened liver of either duck or goose produced by a special feeding process.* Foie gras is a luxurious product at once velvety and meaty, though actually low in saturated fat. Duck and goose foie gras have always been considered a rare delicacy and are usually reserved for special occasions.

   Egyptians enjoyed foie gras during celebrations, and the Romans perfected the art of "gavage," force-feeding figs to their geese; today corn is used.

Characteristics: Foie gras is smooth and rich with a subtle and complex flavor. Goose liver is delicate and unctuous; duck liver is rich and earthy. Goose liver is best for terrines; duck liver is best for searing. Grade A raw duck foie gras is highest in price. It weighs 1¼ to 1½ pounds (570–680 g) and is best used whole in a terrine. Grade B livers are softer, darker, and show a few bruises. They will be slightly grainy when cooked and are good for mousses and stuffings. Grade C livers are small and soft, with lower fat content and meatier texture. This least expensive grade is best used to enrich sauces.

How to Choose:

Preferably pink in color, the liver should be slightly shiny and firm yet soft to the touch. Somewhat rectangular, French foie gras is soft and easy to slice—perfect for making terrines—and holds its shape well. Fresh American foie gras is oval and is best sautéed.

To make terrine de foie gras, the whole liver is deveined, cleaned, and cooked to an internal temperature of 165°F (74°C). When imported from France it is called *foie gras entier*. This is considered to be the best, and is the most expensive, prepared foie gras.

A special 1-kilo (2.2 lb) block of foie gras that can be prepared hours in advance is produced for restaurants. Because it contains nitrates that keep the meat pink, it does not discolor when exposed to air.

Mousse is liver blended with other ingredients. It should be made with foie gras, without other less expensive types of liver. It is soft and spreadable.

French *foie gras mi-cuit* or *en semi-conserve* (part-cooked foie gras) has been cooked and pasteurized. Sold in cans, it will keep for 3 months in the refrigerator once opened. French *foie gras de conserve* (shelf-stable foie gras) improves, like wine, as it ages in the can or jar. Because higher temperature and longer cooking times tend to subdue flavor, producers often reserve the best-quality livers for this storage. Eat it cold, on a good piece of bread.

Amount to Buy: Buy as much foie gras as you can afford; a typical portion weighs 2 to 4 ounces (60–115 g).

Storage: Raw foie gras is commonly sold frozen and vacuum-packed. Keep frozen until ready to use. Defrost overnight in the refrigerator and cook within 2 days.

⊟ x1

French *foie gras mi-cuit* must be refrigerated but can keep several weeks to several months, depending on the processor. French *foie gras de conserve* (shelf-stable foie gras) is packed in glass jars or metal tins and will keep for a year without refrigeration.

Preparation: 1.   **Allow the liver to come to room temperature. Peel away the outer membrane. Gently pull apart both lobes: a large nerve connects them. This nerve/vein network runs about ¼ inch (.65 cm) below the surface of each lobe. To aid in removing the nerve, slit the liver along the nerve using the tip of a sharp knife.**

2.   **Starting with the larger lobe, grasp the nerve, and pull gently but firmly to remove it, making sure not to rip the flesh. Repeat for the small lobe. It is not**

necessary to remove all the little nerves or veins. The foie gras may now be used in other recipes.

Flavor
Affinities:

Allspice, apples, bacon, balsamic vinegar, black pepper, cloves, cognac, figs, grapes, mangoes, nutmeg, pears, port wine, raisins, shallots, truffles, white truffle oil.

56. [📷]   **GOOSE**

Other Names:

Ánsar (Spanish), gander (male goose), *Gans* (German), *ganso* (Spanish, gander), gosling (young goose), *oca* (Italian and Spanish), *oie* (French).

General
Description:

The goose (Anser anser, NAMP P4001–P4045) is a large web-footed wild or domestic bird, prized for its dark, rich, though rather fatty, meat. Geese were first bred in ancient Egypt, China, and India, became immensely popular in Europe, and then traveled across the Atlantic to the United States.

Many Europeans roast geese for their Christmas dinner. Popular methods of cooking are to roast wrapped in bacon (after removing the skin); braise with sage, rosemary, and cider; or roast goose with apples, pears, or chestnuts.

Wild geese are the big game of waterfowl. The main variety of wild geese in North America is the Canada goose; others include the snow goose, the blue goose, and the black (or brant) goose. Wild geese are extremely lean and generally smaller than the domestic type. Wild geese that feed on fish will have strong-flavored meat that may not be palatable; geese that feed mostly on grain are superb. A young goose can be roasted if barded with fatback or bacon, but an older goose is best braised.

The giblets (liver, heart, and gizzard) are usually sold with whole birds, but sometimes the liver is exported to France. In retail markets, normally only whole geese are available. Goose tongues and feet are highly esteemed in Asia and are mostly exported to Hong Kong, but some go to Asian-American markets.

Characteristics: Goose contains only small amounts of meat, which is dark, rich, and flavorful. It has very fatty skin.

How to Choose: Fresh geese are not available in the United States during February and March, because the older birds are too tough and the younger ones are newborn. In the restaurant trade, whole goose, bone-in parts such as leg and breast quarter, and boneless breast are available. Look for plump birds with light, unblemished skin.

Amount to Buy: Allow about 2 pounds (910 g) of whole goose per person to allow for the fat and the bones. Allow 1 1/2 to 2 pounds (680–910 g) whole wild goose per person. One goose breast will serve two to three people.

Storage:

□ x1-2

Goose is commonly sold frozen, though at holiday times, fresh goose may be available. Refrigerate goose immediately and use within 1 or 2 days. If frozen, defrost in the refrigerator on a tray, allowing 48 hours.

Preparation: 1. **Remove the neck and giblets from the cavity (use the neck, gizzard, and heart for stock; use the liver for stuffing).**

2. **Remove the fat from the body cavity and any excess skin. Rinse with cold running water, pat dry, and season inside and out with salt and pepper. Fold the neck skin over the back. Prick the skin in many places.**

3. **Rub seasonings inside and outside the goose. Place aromatic ingredients such as thyme sprigs, bay leaves, and orange halves in the body cavity. Tie the legs and tail together using butcher's string.**

4. **Place breast side up on a rack in a roasting pan with the wings folded under so they stay in place. Cover with foil and roast for 1½ hours at 400°F (200°C).**

5. **Reduce heat to 325°F (165°C), uncover, and roast about 1 hour longer, or until the thigh measures 170°F (77°C) at its thickest point and the juices run clear. Pour off the melted fat every 30 minutes. (A goose will yield about 1 quart (1 l) of fat, which can be refrigerated and used for cooking.)**

6. Remove the goose from the oven, cool slightly, and increase the temperature to 450°F (230°C). Brush glaze as desired over the goose and roast for 10 minutes longer, or until the skin is golden and crisp.

 7. Remove from the oven and allow the goose to rest at least 20 minutes, draped with foil, before carving.

Flavor Affinities: Allspice, apples, cabbage, Calvados, caraway seed, chestnuts, cloves, cognac, figs, mushrooms, nutmeg, onions, pears, potatoes, rum, sage, sauerkraut, truffles.

GROUSE

Other Names: Blackcock, capercaillie, *Moorhuhn* (German), partridge (New England), ptarmigan, red grouse, ruffed grouse, ruffy, *starna di montagna* (Italian), *tétras* (French), *urogallo* or *lagópodo* (Spanish), willow grouse, white-tailed grouse.

General Description: *Grouse are medium-sized wild birds that are highly sought after for their distinctly flavored meat.* The ruffed grouse, the main woodland game bird in America, is known in New England as partridge, though this is also the name for a different bird (page 217). The smallest member of the grouse family is the ptarmigan, any of three or four partridge-like birds including the willow ptarmigan (*lagopus lagopus*) and rock ptarmigan (*lagopus mutus*). The sage grouse (*centrocercus urophasianus*) is indigenous to the American Northwest. The spruce grouse (*falcipennis canadensis*), which feeds heavily on spruce trees, is found in evergreen woods and may have an overly resinous flavor in winter.

Another member of this family, the capercaillie (*Tetrao urogallus*), an ancient bird as large as a turkey, is legendary among hunters in northern Europe. The capercaillie lives in northern Europe and Asia in coniferous forests, especially in hills and mountains, and in the mountains of central eastern Europe, in the Pyrenees, and in the Scottish Highlands.

The red grouse (*Lagopus lagopus scoticus*) is a sub-species of the willow grouse that lives only in the British Isles and is widely hunted in Scotland. It is one of the most desirable of game birds, with meat that is resin-accented from their diet of young heather. A limited number of wild Scottish grouse are exported from mid-September to February by specialty purveyors. Young grouse can be roasted; older birds should be braised.

Characteristics:	Grouse is quite lean with distinctive full flavor. Their resinous flavor is something of an acquired taste.
How to Choose:	Grouse is only found wild. Ruffed grouse weigh 1 to 1 3/4 pounds (450–800 g); blue grouse weigh 2 to 2 1/2 pounds (.9–1.1 kg), and sharp-tailed grouse weigh 1 3/4 to 2 1/2 pounds (.8–1.1 kg). Male sage

grouse weigh 5 1/2 to 6 pounds (2.5–2.7 kg), almost twice as much as females. Young wild grouse from Scotland weigh 10 to 12 ounces (300–350 g) each. Look for plump birds with unblemished skin.

Amount per Portion:

Allow 1 to 1 1/2 pounds (450–680 g) whole grouse, usually 1, per person.

Storage:

Store game birds 1 to 2 days refrigerated.

Preparation: 1.

If necessary, pluck carefully to avoid tearing the skin, draw out the innards, and wipe the bird, but do not wash so as not to dilute the flavor. Cut off the head.

2.

Tie the bird with butcher's string. To increase moistness, bard (page 119) or put butter inside the cavity.

3.

Roast at 350°F (180°C), basting every 5 minutes, 30 to 35 minutes per pound (450 g), or until it reaches an internal temperature of 170°F (77°C) measured at the thickest portion of the thigh and the juices run clear.

4.

Remove the grouse from the oven, drape with foil, and allow to rest about 10 minutes.

5.

Parboil the liver and pound to a paste with butter, cayenne pepper, and salt. Toast thin slices of bread and spread with this paste. Serve the grouse with the toast and gravy made from the pan drippings.

Flavor Affinities:	Bacon, brandy, butter, cayenne, chestnuts, mushrooms, oranges, sour cream, thyme, white pepper.

57. 📷 ## GUINEA FOWL

Other Names:	African pheasant, *faraona* (Italian), *gallina de Guinea* or *pintada* (Spanish), guinea hen, *pintade* (French, mature bird), *pintadeau* (French, young bird).
General Description:	*The guinea fowl* (Numidia melagris, NAMP P5000) *is a chickenlike bird with slightly red, somewhat gamy meat.* Guinea fowl is the common name for any of several species of the Numididae family native to Africa and Madagascar. They were domesticated by the ancient Greeks and Romans and are still popular in Italy. After dying out in Egypt about 2,000 years ago, they reappeared on the Guinea (or western) coast of Africa and were brought to Europe by Portuguese navigators in the fifteenth century. Guinea fowl are extremely good runners and opt to run, rather than fly, to escape predators. Similar in size to a pheasant, they are slightly smaller than a chicken.

Cooks seek guinea fowl out because of their marvelous flavor and tender meat. For restaurant service, they are often chosen over pheasants (page 219) because they do not have hard tendons in the leg and thigh. Mostly farm-raised, they are noisy, somewhat difficult to handle, and frighten easily. A mature guinea fowl will have striking white spots on its gray feathers. Confusingly, the term guinea hen is used for males and females.

Characteristics:	Guinea fowl have light flesh with little fat. Their meat is light red and slightly dry, milder in flavor than duck, and reminiscent of pheasant without an excessive gamy flavor. They have an exceptionally high yield (50/50 ratio of meat to bone).
How to Choose:	Female guinea fowl are more tender than males. Guinea hens weigh 2 1/2 to 3 pounds (1.1–1.4 kg).
Amount to Buy:	Allow one guinea fowl for two people, or 1 to 1 1/2 pounds (450–680 g) of whole bird per person. Allow 6 to 8 ounces (170–225 g) of boneless guinea fowl per person.
Storage:	Store whole guinea fowl 1 to 2 days refrigerated.

x1–2

Preparation:

1. **Remove the neck and giblets from the cavity (use the neck, gizzard, and heart for stock; use the liver for stuffing). Rinse the bird with cool water.**

2. **Pat dry and season with salt, pepper, and herbs.**

3. **Guinea fowl is quite lean, so bard it (page 119) or butter it before roasting. Alternatively, marinate it before grilling.**

4. **In a large oven-safe pan, brown in oil on all sides. Brush all over with butter (plain or flavored).**

 5. **Transfer to the oven and roast at 450°F (230°C) for 25 minutes, basting every 5 minutes, until it reaches an internal temperature of 170°F (77°C) measured at the thickest portion of the thigh and the juices run clear when the thickest part of the thigh is pierced.**

Flavor
Affinities: Apple brandy, demi-glace, garlic, grapes, lemons, mustard, plums, sage, shallots, tarragon, thyme, truffles.

ORTOLAN AND BECCAFICO

Other Names: *Bruant ortolan* (French), *escribano cinéreo* (Spanish), ortolan bunting.

General
Description: *The ortolan (Emberiza hortulana) and beccafico (silvia hortensis) are tiny migratory songbirds that are eaten bones, innards, and all.* The ortolan has been considered since early times to be the finest and most delicate of birds to eat. A symbol of culinary luxury, ortolans are quite rare. They are considered the ultimate connoisseur's bird in France, where they are protected by laws that forbid hunting, selling, or eating them. Even so, in the Landes region of Gascony, where the birds migrate each year on their way to North Africa, ortolans are eaten with gusto.

The birds must be taken alive; once captured they are fed millet, grapes, and figs, a technique apparently taken from the decadent cooks of imperial Rome who called the same (or similar) birds, *beccafico*, or "fig-pecker." When they've reached four times their normal size, they're usually drowned in a snifter of Armagnac. Ortolans are usually roasted on spits or in a hot oven, cooked mainly in their own fat.

Traditionally, the diner's head and face are covered by a large white napkin tent over the dish to capture the full aroma of this succulent, exquisitely flavored bird. The entire bird, served so hot that you must cool it on your tongue while inhaling rapidly through your mouth, is eaten at once. It is said that part of the reason for the cloth is to hide oneself from God while eating this rare delicacy.

Characteristics: The bird's special diet and a drowning in Armagnac give it its characteristic exquisite flavor.

How to Choose: Ortolans are rarely if ever found in the United States. If you're lucky enough to find them on a restaurant menu, don't miss the opportunity to have them.

Amount per Portion: These small birds weigh no more than 1 1/4 ounces (35 g) each. One bird is served per portion.

Preparation: 1. **Season birds as desired. Tie the birds into a compact shape with butcher's string.**

2. **Roast whole in a small earthenware dish for 5 to 7 minutes at 450°F (230°C), basting with melted butter.**

Flavor
Affinities:

Armagnac, bacon, breadcrumbs, butter, ham, lemons, mushrooms, oranges.

58 a–b.

OSTRICH, EMU, AND RHEA

Other Names:

Ratites. **Ostritch:** *Autruche* (French), *avestruz* (Spanish), *Strauss* (German), *struzzo* (Italian). **Emu:** *Émeu* (French). **Rhea:** *Nandon* (French), *ñandú* (Spanish).

General
Description:

Ostrich (Struthio camelus), *emu* (Dromaius novaehollandiae), *and rhea* (Rhea Americana) *are ratites, a family of large flightless birds with small wings and flat breastbones.* The largest of the ratites, ostriches were considered a delicacy in ancient Rome, though they have only recently regained popularity. The majority of the world's ostrich comes from South Africa, where ostrich farming began originally for its feathers. The somewhat smaller emu originated in Australia, where it was used by aborigines for meat and plumage. Rhea, the smallest of the ratites, is native to South America, particularly the grasslands of Argentina. Charles Darwin wrote home from South America that he enjoyed eating ostrich dumplings (actually rhea).

All three birds are 95 percent usable as meat, feathers, oil, and leather. Although ratites are poultry, their flesh is similar to beef, lean and red with a beefy texture and flavor. Ratites may be cooked according to recipes for other lean red game meats such as venison, buffalo, and boar. The meat should be cooked quickly to rare or medium-rare; overcooking will make it tough and livery tasting.

Characteristics: Ratites have no intramuscular fat, so they are quite lean. Farm-raised ostrich, emu, and rhea have very dark cherry-red meat. Ostrich meat looks like beef with similar though slightly sweet flavor. Emu meat is fine-grained and slightly oily. Rhea meat is tender with a distinctive and pleasing flavor. With all ratites, the smaller the bird, the finer the texture.

How to Choose: Ostriches and other ratites do not have breast meat. All the ostrich meat comes from the tenderloin and major muscles in the thighs and legs, which range in size from 2 to 20 pounds (.9–9.1 kg). Ratite meat is sold as steaks, filets, medallions, roasts, and ground meat. Although the different cuts of ostrich, rhea, and emu are confusing, the most tender portions are the fan fillet (the thigh), inside strip, tenderloin, and oyster. Next in tenderness are the tip, top loin, and outside strip; tougher cuts come from the leg. Ostrich medallions, consisting of three tender muscles rolled together, are sold as steaks. Emu and rhea cuts are similar to ostrich, but somewhat smaller, more tender, and milder in flavor. Aging ratite meat for 2 to 4 days before cooking, in the refrigerator, enhances the taste and texture.

Amount to Buy: Emu, ostrich, and rhea meat are specialty items. Allow 6 to 8 ounces (170–225 g) boneless meat per person. Because the meat is so lean, there is little shrinkage.

Storage: Ratite meat is generally sold frozen and will keep well for up to 3 months. Store up to 2 days refrigerated.

Preparation: 1. **Allow the meat to come to room temperature before cooking. Season with a dry rub or marinade if desired.**

 2. **Sauté, stir-fry, or grill over hot coals to medium-rare. However, because it is so low in fat, care must be taken not to overcook the meat. As with venison, overcooking turns the meat dry and tough. Steaks and roasts can be safely cooked to medium-rare (145°F/63°C) or to medium (160°F/71°C); ground meat should be cooked to 160°F (71°C).**

3. **Remove the meat from the heat, drape with foil, and allow to rest about 10 minutes before serving.**

Flavor Affinities: Bay leaves, brandy, butter, garlic, mushrooms, onions, red wine, rosemary, shallots, thyme, white wine.

PARTRIDGE

Other Names:
Common, English, European, gray, Hungarian, or red-legged partridge, chukar (or chukkar) partridge, *Feldhuhn* (German), *perdigón* (Spanish, mature partridge), *perdiz* (Spanish, young partridge), *perdreau* (French, young partridge), *perdrix* (French, mature partridge), *pernice* (Italian), *pouillard* (French, baby partridge), *Rothuhn* (German, red-legged partridge).

General Description:
A partridge is a small, tasty, plump Old World game bird in the Phasianidae (pheasant) family. The name partridge refers to various medium-sized stout-bodied game birds, or any of the numerous American birds (such as the American ruffed grouse, or bobwhite quail) similar to Old World partridges. In Europe, the two most common species are the red-legged partridge and the gray-legged partridge. The most common partridge in America, the gray-legged, was imported from the plains of Hungary. The somewhat larger chukar partridge, native to Asia, is farm-raised. There is a significant difference in flavor and texture between high-priced wild partridge and its less interesting farm-raised cousins. In European cuisine, older partridge is classically braised with cabbage, bacon, and juniper berries.

Characteristics:
Partridge has very lean, light, highly flavorful meat comparable to pheasant but is firmer and earthier.

Young partridge are up to a year old; partridge are considered mature once they are more than 15 months old. Due to their small size, partridge are generally sold whole. Young partridge is rarely hung for aging; older birds may benefit from hanging.

How to Choose: Young birds will have flexible beaks and the pointed first feather on the wing will have a white tip. Older birds require hanging (for aging), slow cooking, and a strong sauce to counter their gamy flavor.

Amount to Buy: An average single-serving RTC (ready-to-cook) partridge will weigh about 10 to 12 ounces (285–340 g).

Storage: Store partridge up to 2 days refrigerated.

Preparation: 1. **Remove the giblets and neck and pat the partridges dry. Season inside and out with salt and pepper.**

2. **In a large Dutch oven, lightly brown cubes of bacon and reserve. Discard most of the fat and use it to wilt 1 head of shredded green cabbage. Add equal amounts apple cider and chicken stock, along with the reserved bacon cubes, and bring to a boil.**

3. **Place the partridges on top of the cabbage. Cover and cook slowly for 20 minutes. Turn off the heat and allow it to rest for 10 minutes before serving.**

Flavor Affinities:	Apple cider, cilantro, garlic, lentils, nutmeg, pancetta, pears, rosemary, shallots, tarragon, white wine.

59a–b. 📷 **PHEASANT**

Other Names:	*Fagianello* (Italian, young pheasant), *fagiano* (Italian), *faisan* (French), *faisán* (Spanish), *Fasan* (German).

General Description:	*Pheasant* (Phasianus colchicus, NAMP *P7200, P7202*) *is a long-tailed game bird related to the domestic chicken that is highly regarded for its delicious flesh.* Pheasants were first found in China but are now common worldwide. Connoisseurs prefer the smaller hen to the larger cock for its fine-grained and juicier flesh.

The ancient Romans cooked pheasants and then reassembled them in their brightly colored plumage before serving. In medieval times, pheasants were presented with gilded legs and beaks. Pheasants produced especially for restaurants and retail markets are bred for larger breasts and lighter colored flesh. The meat is versatile and complemented by a variety of sauces and seasonings. In Europe, wild pheasants are often hung for aging to gain flavor and tenderness, anywhere from 3 days to 2 weeks.

Characteristics:	Farm-raised pheasants are quite tender, with rich, wild chickenlike flavor and fine grain; they are more delicate than wild pheasant. They are lean, so bard (page 119)

before roasting. The light breast meat is the most popular portion because the legs have bony tendons. Free-range farm-raised pheasants that eat a diet closer to that of their wild cousins will be richer in flavor than purely grain-fed birds.

How to Choose:

Fresh pheasants are in season from September through March. Baby pheasants are 12 to 16 weeks of age and weigh about 1 pound (450 g). A domestic hen weighs 2 1/4 to 2 1/2 pounds (1–1.1 kg); a domestic cock weighs about 3 pounds (1.4 kg). Farm-raised free-range pheasants are available from September to April. Somewhat smaller, more flavorful wild Scottish pheasants are available from October to February.

Amount to Buy:

Allow 1 to 1 1/2 pounds (450–680 g) of whole pheasant per person; one pheasant will generally serve two people. Baby pheasants are in season in spring and summer; allow one per person.

Storage:

Store whole pheasants up to 2 days refrigerated.

x2

Preparation:

Because large cock pheasants have hard tendons in their legs, the breast is often removed and cooked quickly separately; the legs are slowly braised.

I.

Remove the neck and giblets from the cavity (use the neck, gizzard, and heart for stock; use the liver for stuffing).

2. Season inside and out with salt and pepper. Add butter to the cavity and tie the legs with butcher's string to keep its shape.

 3. Roast with a little water or stock in the bottom of the pan at 350°F (180°C) for about 1 hour, or until it reaches an internal temperature of 170°F (77°C) at the thickest part of the thigh and the juices run clear.

 4. Remove the pheasant from the oven and allow it to rest for about 15 minutes before carving.

Flavor Affinities: Bacon, basil, cinnamon, foie gras, garlic, mushrooms, nutmeg, onions, port wine, sage, tarragon, thyme.

60. ## PIGEON, DOVE, AND WOOD PIGEON

Other Names: Squab (young bird). **Pigeon:** *Piccione* (Italian), *piccione selvatico* (Italian, rock pigeon), *pichón* or *pichona* (Spanish, male/female). **Dove:** *Colomba* (Italian), *colombe* (French). **Wood Pigeon:** *Palombe* (French), *palombo* (Italian), *palomo* or *paloma* (Spanish, male/female), ring dove.

General Description: *Pigeons (Columba palumbus, NAMP P6000) are members of the large Columbidae family with stout bodies, short legs, smooth, thick plumage, and dark, strong-flavored flesh.* Pigeons originated in the Middle East and Asia and were one of the first birds to be domesticated. There are hundreds of pigeon species worldwide. New World pigeons are typically gray or brown; elsewhere they are brightly colored. A squab is a young domesticated pigeon that has never flown (unfledged) and is therefore quite tender. Pigeon is essential to the splendid Moroccan festival dish *b'stilla*, a phyllo pastry pie including almonds, sugar, cinnamon, and eggs.

Because these birds are used so much in Asian cuisine, they are sold in some special ways in Asian markets. Chinese-style (Buddhist slaughter) squab have their head and feet on; New York–dressed (Confucian slaughter) squab have their head and feet on and entrails intact.

Doves, which are found mainly in the wild, are in the same family as pigeons. Doves are smaller and have longer tails, though the names are often used interchangeably. While recipes for pigeon and dove are similar, doves are leaner so they are best braised. Wild wood pigeons are imported into America from Scotland and are native to the Old World. Not raised commercially, they are a bit larger than quail and have substantially darker, more intensely flavored meat.

Characteristics: Pigeon is dark, rich, and full-bodied with an accent of wild, almost liverlike flavor; squab is milder, very tender, and lean with a fine grain. Squab retains its moisture when cooked to medium-rare. Doves have succulent fine-grained dark meat with excellent flavor.

How to Choose: Squabs weigh 3/4 to 1 1/2 pounds (340–680 g). Fresh squab is available in the summer months (year round in some regions) in gourmet markets. Choose fresh birds by their plump, firm appearance. Frozen squab is available year round. Pigeons are over 1 month old and weigh 1 to 2 pounds (450–910 g). Doves are quite small, only about 2 3/4 ounces (78 g) dressed, and are normally found only in the wild. A limited number of wild Scottish wood pigeons, which weigh about 1/2 pound (225 g) each, are available from November to February.

Amount to Buy: Allow one squab per person, one to two wood pigeons per person. Allow two doves per person.

Storage: Refrigerate whole squab or pigeon up to 2 days.

Preparation: 1. **Remove the neck and giblets from the cavity (use the neck, gizzard, and heart for stock; use the liver for stuffing). Marinate as desired overnight, refrigerated.**

2. **To grill, split in half through the breastbone, flatten, and grill skin side down until medium and golden brown in color, then turn and grill on the other side briefly, about 30 minutes total.**

Flavor Affinities: Andouille sausage, barbecue sauce, cinnamon, hazelnuts, honey, hot sauce, peaches, rosemary, wine vinegar.

61. **QUAIL**

Other Names: *Caille* (French), *codorniz* (Spanish), *coturnix quail*, pharaoh quail, *quaglia* (Italian), *Wachtel* (German).

General Description: *The smallest of European game birds, quail* (Coturnix coturnix *and* Coturnix japonica) *belongs to the Phasianidae family, along with the partridge and pheasant, and resembles a very small partridge.* Quail are raised for both their delicious brown-and-tan spotted eggs and their meat. Even 100 years ago, Egyptian bird catchers exported more than 2 million of the birds a year to European chefs. The Israelites wandering in the wilderness after leaving Egypt may have encountered hordes of quail and called them "manna."

    Quail is the most popular game bird in the American South, where the bobwhite quail is known as partridge. The most common farm-raised quail in the United States is the Japanese or coturnix quail, which are the only farm-raised bird with females larger than males. These are small, tasty birds, usually served two per serving. Coturnix quail eggs are often pickled. Quail take well to marinades, stuffings, and bold seasonings. Because of their small size, quail are traditionally eaten with the hands.

Characteristics: Quail is plump with light tan to medium dark fine-textured meat, satisfying though subtle flavor, and an underlying sweet nuttiness.

How to Choose:	Fresh quail are in season year round, though many quail are sold frozen. Semi-boneless quail are easier to stuff and eat.
Amount to Buy:	Quail weigh 4 to 5 ounces (115–140 g) each. Allow one quail for an appetizer, two for an entrée.
Storage: x1–2	Quail are quite perishable; store 1 to 2 days refrigerated.

Preparation: 1. **Remove the neck and giblets from the cavity (use the neck, gizzard, and heart for stock; use the liver for stuffing).**

 2. **Trim off the tiny wing-bone ends, or tuck underneath. Stuff quail, as desired, before roasting. Tie with butcher's string to maintain shape. Cook in one of the following ways:**

 • **Roast at 400°F (200°C) for about 15 minutes, or till the quail is medium-rare with a crisp skin.**

 • **For grilling, cut open along the breastbone and flatten. Marinate for up to 2 hours at room temperature, or up to 6 hours refrigerated, if desired. Grill over aromatic wood for about 8 minutes, turning as needed.**

• **Sauté whole or split in two over high heat for about 15 minutes.**

| Flavor Affinities: | Almonds, apples, balsamic vinegar, chestnuts, currants, grapes, pine nuts, pistachios, rosemary, shallots. |

62 a–c.

TURKEY

| Other Names: | *Dinde* or *dindon* (French), fryer-roaster turkey, *guajolote* (Mexican), *pavo* (Spanish), *tacchino* (Italian), young (hen or tom) turkey. |

| General Description: | *Native to North America, the popular and versatile turkey* (Meleagris gallopavo, NAMP *P2000*) *is now farmed and eaten around the globe.* The word *turkey* (originally turkey-cock) came from the English, who may have had their first birds imported by Turkish merchants. In America, turkey is traditional fare for Thanksgiving, because according to legend the Pilgrims ate turkey at the first Thanksgiving dinner in 1621. Deep-frying turkeys is a Southern tradition that produces a very juicy bird with crispy skin.

Wild turkeys, among the largest game birds in North America, have lean, dark meat. In their natural state turkeys live in flocks, roosting in swampy areas and feeding on woodland berries and seeds. Wild turkeys are leaner and have denser flesh than the domesticated type. About 200,000 wild-type turkeys are farm-raised annually in the United States.

In Louisiana's Cajun country, **turducken** is a specialty. This is a deboned chicken stuffed into a |

deboned duck and lastly stuffed into a deboned turkey. A properly prepared turducken provides rich slices that present all three birds' meat in layers.

Characteristics:

A 15-pound (6.8 kg) turkey typically has about 70 percent white meat and 30 percent dark meat. Wild turkey is extremely lean, savory, and more intense in flavor than domestic turkey. Farm-raised wild turkey is somewhat more tender than the hunted type.

How to Choose:

Some people believe that smaller female (hen) turkeys are moister and plumper than males (toms); you may specify a hen or tom turkey when ordering. It's more economical to get a large bird, since a 15-pound (6.8 kg) turkey has about twice as much meat as a 10-pound (4.5 kg) turkey. Ground turkey is available as either dark meat, light meat, or a mixture of the two. Whether light or dark or mixed, it is suited to meat-balls, meat loaf, picadillo, and stuffed peppers. Cut-up turkeys are also available: The major cuts are turkey breast, tenderloin, cutlet, drumstick, and thigh. Turkey wings are an excellent and inexpensive way to enrich poultry stock. Turkey London broil is a butter-flied breast that is marinated for broiling or grilling.

Amount to Buy:

Allow 1 pound (450 g) whole turkey per person; 6 to 8 ounces (170–225 g) of boneless turkey per person. Young turkeys, which run 8 to 24 pounds (3.6–11 kg), are best.

Storage: Fresh turkeys should be used within 2 days. Frozen
□ x2   turkeys should be thawed on a tray in the refrigerator,
     allowing one day of thawing per 5 pounds (2.3 kg).

Preparation: 1. **Remove the neck and giblets from the cavity (use the
neck, gizzard, and heart for stock; use the liver for
stuffing).**

2. **Rinse the turkey under cold water. Pat dry and season inside and out with salt and pepper. Stuff as
desired—using cool or cold stuffing and never stuffing ahead of time. Tie the legs together with butcher's
string, or use trussing needles to keep its shape.**

3. **For a 12- to 18-pound (5.4–8.2 kg) turkey, roast at
425°F (220°C) for 30 minutes.**

4. **Reduce heat to 350°F (180°C) and cook for about 2
hours more, or until it reaches an internal temperature of 170°F (77°C) at the thickest part of the thigh
and the juices run clear.**

6. **Remove the turkey from the oven, drape with foil,
and allow to rest for 20 minutes before carving.**

7. **Make a pan sauce if desired and serve.**

Flavor   Allspice, apples, bacon, cranberries, garlic, grapes,
Affinities: onions, oranges, mushrooms, sage, soy sauce, walnuts.

WOODCOCK

Other Names:
Bécasse (French), *beccaccia* (Italian), bogsucker, *chocha perdiz* (European Spanish), Labrador twister, mudsnipe, timberdoodle, *Waldschnepfe* (German).

General Description:
The woodcock (Scolopax minor *and* Scolopax rusticola) *is a small juicy bird that is prized in Europe, Asia, and North America for its delectable flesh.* The European woodcock ranges from northern Spain and Britain to Siberia and Japan, and it is considered the king of game birds. Its smaller namesake, the American woodcock, is also highly esteemed and lives in woodland areas of the eastern United States. In both France and America, woodcock may be hunted and eaten, but not sold. Though rare, woodcock is a gourmet's delight because of its rich, tangy flavor, gained through a diet that includes aromatic herbs and berries. In classic French cuisine, woodcock is hung for 4 to 8 days and then used to make pâté; these days it is generally not hung, but rather roasted either dressed or complete with entrails except for the gizzard, which is not edible.

Characteristics:
Woodcocks have intensely flavored, lean dark meat. They are usually roasted, often without first being cleaned, since the entrails minus the gizzard are deemed to be essential to this bird's flavor. Their heads are normally left on for cooking.

How to Choose: A young and tender bird will have a flexible bill.

Amount per Portion: Woodcocks weigh 6 to 8 ounces (170–225 g) each, dressed. Allow one woodcock per person.

Storage: Store woodcocks at a temperature just above freezing for at least 48 hours before cooking to help tenderize them.

Preparation: **1. Pluck the bird, if necessary, and remove the entrails if desired (leaving head on).**

2. Place thyme sprigs, juniper berries, salt, and pepper inside the cavity, then cover the breasts with bacon or pork fatback (page 120). Tie with butcher's string to keep its shape, and then season on the outside.

3. Brown on all sides.

4. Roast at 400°F (200°C) for 10 to 15 minutes, or until no more than medium-rare. (The juices should run reddish-pink.)

5. Remove from the pan, cover with foil, and allow to rest 10 minutes.

6. Toast 1 slice of bread for each woodcock. Sauté the giblets and entrails (discard the gizzard) along with diced onion, pancetta, and foie gras and chop up

together. Spread the mixture on toast and serve with sliced woodcock on top.

Flavor
Affinities: Allspice, bacon, capers, cayenne, chestnuts, foie gras, lemons, nutmeg, pancetta, port, truffles, white wine.

VI. Game and Other Domesticated Meats

Game is the flesh of wild animals and birds that are hunted for food and sport. Even in early times, animals and birds worldwide were reared especially to provide a stock of game for hunting. Other "wild" animals are raised on farms for retail sale (deer, boar, and bison). These farm-raised game animals have a different diet and lifestyle, so they are generally less lean and more tender than field animals.

Game animals are divided into two groups: large game (boar, bison, and deer) and small game (squirrel, hare, and raccoon). Venison, which refers to the meat of all large antlered game animals (moose, elk, and caribou), though it is commonly associated with deer, is widely sought after by hunters. Whether the game comes from the market or the hunter, the quality is determined by the animal's age, diet, and the time of year it was killed. Younger animals are more tender, and game is best in the fall, after plentiful spring and summer feeding. If the animal is poorly handled in the field, its flesh can be damaged or even ruined. Game found in retail markets has been federally inspected, just like beef or pork. Game sold in restaurants must come from farm-raised animals.

Judge the tenderness of a particular cut of large game meat according to the corresponding cut of beef or pork. For small game, younger animals will be more tender and less "gamy" tasting overall. Wild game animals will be leaner and less tender than either farm-raised "wild" game or domesticated animals, because they get more exercise. Any fat that is present is generally rank tasting and should be removed. Most game meats should be cooked slowly, making sure to keep it moist.

63. **ALLIGATOR**

Other Names: Gator, *lagarto* (Spanish), Mississippi alligator, pike-headed alligator.

General Description: *The American alligator* (Alligator mississippiensis) *is the largest reptile in North America and is a popular meat in Cajun cooking.* This large reptile, which averages in length from 6 to 12 feet (1.8–3.6 m), is indigenous to the southeastern United States and inhabits swampy areas of the coastal plain. Most commercial alligator comes from Louisiana, where it is commonly processed in September. Alligator can be wild, though this type is less common, or farm-raised, which will be less chewy or fishy tasting. Thousands of nuisance alligators are killed annually in Florida by licensed hunters. Their meat is then processed and sold commercially. Historically, Seminole Indians would catch alligators, keep them in pens until they were large enough to eat, and then smoke them over hickory or oak.

Alligator meat can be made into cajun jambalaya or étouffée, blackened, breaded and fried, or cut into medallions and sautéed, but it should always be cooked to well-done. The body and leg meat cuts are good for burgers, casseroles, sausages, and stews. Jaw and tail meat work well for cutlets and medallions.

Characteristics: Alligator has lean, light-colored meat with a mild taste that is somewhere between chicken and rabbit with a fishy aftertaste and watery texture. The choicest alligator cuts are the jaw and the tail, which is similar to veal in texture, light pink to white in color, with bands of hard, white fat that appear circular in cross-section and run lengthwise near the tailbone. The tenderloin is a cylindrical tube inside the tail. The body meat is darker, stronger in flavor, and tougher in texture (similar to pork shoulder). The leg meat is dark with small fat deposits along the tendons.

How to Choose: Farm-raised alligators are all white meat and will be about 4 1/2 feet (1.4 m) long; wild alligators have reddish meat in the legs and the body. A young alligator that is 2 to 3 years old will be more tender than older alligators.

Amount to Buy: For boneless alligator, allow 4 to 6 ounces (115–170 g) per portion; allow 1/2 pound (225 g) or one side of ribs per person.

Storage: Almost all alligator meat is sold frozen. Defrost in the refrigerator on a tray. Use within 1 day.

Preparation: 1. **All fat and sinew must be removed, including the yellowish fat between the layers.**

2. **The tail and jaw can be cut into medallions and sautéed, fried, or grilled. The ribs can be barbecued.**

NOTE: **When using leg or body meat, the white tendons and vessels should also be removed.**

Flavor
Affinities:
Bacon, beer, Cajun andouille sausage, cayenne pepper, garlic, jalapeño chiles, lemons, onions, tomatoes.

ARMADILLO

Other Names: Gravedigger, Hoover hog, nine-banded armadillo, *tatú* (Brazil), Texas armadillo.

General
Description:
Armadillos (Dasypus novemcinctus) *are mammals, though their backs are covered by a bony shell. Armadillo,* which means "small armored thing," was given its name by Spanish conquistadors. The Aztec name was *azotochtli,* which means "turtle-rabbit." Armadillos originated in South America and belong to the same family as the sloth and anteater. They are easily captured, and they are eaten by people from Mexico to Argentina and in parts of Texas. During the Depression in Texas, armadillo was popularized under the name Hoover hog. Armadillos are sometimes called "gravediggers," especially in the South, because of their inclination to dig in soft dirt (such as a freshly dug grave) while searching for insects to eat.

The armadillo is the only animal aside from humans known to carry leprosy. For this reason it is illegal to sell a live armadillo in Texas. Armadillo is delicious pan-fried in butter, but it also takes well to spicy preparations. In Brazil, armadillo is seasoned with parsley. Armadillo sausages flavored with coriander, basil, bay leaves, garlic, and nutmeg are also common. Barbecued armadillo and armadillo chili are popular foods at various festivals in parts of Texas, Arkansas, and the southeastern United States.

Characteristics: Armadillos have tasty meat that is light in color, finely grained, and tender with generous amounts of fat. When cooked, armadillo tastes rich and porky.

How to Choose: Armadillos are not sold commercially in America. They have long been considered a legitimate game animal in Mexico, and the practice of eating armadillos was adopted by residents of south Texas when the animals migrated there. Armadillos are moderate in size, up to 2 feet (60 cm) long. Moist-heat cooking methods are recommended for the less tender, older animals. Though armadillo is notorious as roadkill, do not get your armadillo this way. Any wild animal found already dead is unsafe to eat.

Amount to Buy: Allow 1/2 to 3/4 pound (225–340 g) of bone-in armadillo per person.

Storage: Store in the refrigerator up to 2 days before cooking.

x2

Preparation: 1. **Remove the glands from the legs and back of the armadillo, then clean and cut into serving pieces.**

 2. **Brown in a little oil, covered, until light brown. Stir in enough flour to absorb the oil. Season as desired.**

3. **Add a small amount of water, barbecue sauce, or chopped tomatoes. Simmer for 5 to 10 minutes or until fork tender.**

⚠ NOTE: **Always use rubber gloves when handling raw armadillo, because it can carry leprosy.**

Flavor Affinities: Bacon, barbecue sauce, basil, chili powder, cilantro, garlic, nutmeg, onions, red wine, shallots, tomatoes.

BEAR

Other Names: *Bär* or *Brummbär* (German), glacier bear, Kermode bear, *orso* (Italian), *oso* (Spanish), *ours* (French).

General Description: *Bears are large mammals found almost exclusively in the Northern Hemisphere that are sometimes hunted for their meat.* Bears have large heads, bulky bodies, massive hindquarters, powerful limbs, short tails, and coarse, thick fur. The most numerous North American bear is the so-called black bear (*Ursus americanus*), which can range in color from light brown to black.

Bear meat from animals culled for population control in game reserves is sometimes available frozen; the paws are particularly valued. White bear fat was esteemed for cookery by French settlers in the Mississippi Valley and is said to have been preferred in New Orleans to butter or lard. Bear meat, when cooked, is very much like pork. Bear shoulder and ham also are excellent cured and hot-smoked.

Characteristics: The flavor of bear can vary greatly depending on the animal's diet and the amount of fat. Bears that have been feeding on fish will taste fishy. Bear meat is at its best in late fall when the animals have stored up fat prior to hibernation. Bear meat is best cooked slowly.

How to Choose: Bear meat can be purchased from exotic meat purveyors as ground meat, stew meat, loin, and roasts.

Amount to Buy: Allow portions similar to pork; 6 to 8 ounces (170–225 g) of boneless meat, 1/2 to 3/4 pound (225–340 g) for bone-in meat.

Storage: Bear meat is usually sold frozen; defrost overnight in the refrigerator in a pan. Use within 1 day.

x1

Preparation: **A young animal does not need to have its meat marinated, although this helps to tenderize it and remove the gamy taste. Meat from older animals should always be marinated.**

Roasts:

 1. Cut away the fat, leaving a ¹/₄ inch (.65 cm) thick layer. Cut out all sinews and other undesirable parts.

 2. To roast the shoulders, loin, and hams, marinate first overnight refrigerated.

 3. Remove from the marinade and wipe dry before roasting about 2¹/₂ hours at 300°F (150°C), or until tender. Like pork, bear should be cooked to well-done because of the danger of trichinosis.

Bear Paws:

 • Place 3 pounds (1.4 kg) skinned front paws and 1 pound (450 g) salt pork covered with cold water in a pot. Cover and simmer overnight. Drain, season, and serve.

Flavor Affinities: Apples, barbecue sauce, butter, chili powder, corn, dry mustard, garlic, onions, red wine, tarragon, thyme.

BEAVER

Other Names: *Bievre* (French, blanket beaver), blanket beaver (old beaver), *castor* (French and Spanish), *castoro* (Italian), kit (young beaver).

General
Description:

Beavers are large, aquatic, partly nocturnal rodents in the Castoridae family that are hunted for their pelts, meat, and fatty tail. Beaver was greatly relished by early trappers and explorers in North America for its fatty, rich, and tasty tail. Beaver was once considered the most valuable of furs and was also trapped for its castor glands, which produce castoreum, used in making perfume.

Beaver is versatile in the kitchen: It can be pot-roasted, barbecued, baked, fried, stewed, fricasseed, or made into meat loaf or pie, and it may be smoked to reduce the gamy flavor. Beaver may be prepared using recipes for wild goose and venison.

Characteristics:

Beaver meat is dark red, rich, fine, and soft in texture, though rather gamy in flavor. The liver is large and almost as tender and sweet as that of a goose. Fat deposits are found outside or between the muscles, much like venison. Beaver meat will dry out faster than most lean cuts of beef.

How to Choose:

Choose a young, small animal for best eating. Beavers reach maturity in 2 to 3 years; they have stout bodies about 40 inches (1 m) long including their paddle-shaped tail. A skinned and dressed beaver will be about half its live weight. Frozen farm-raised beaver that weigh 5 to 8 pounds (2.3–3.6 kg) are sold whole or as legs and saddles.

Amount to Buy:	A young beaver will serve four to six people, an older beaver will serve eight; allow 3/4 to 1 pound (340–450 g) per person.

Storage:

Before storing, the beaver needs some basic preparation. Remove the "kernels" (scent glands) in the small of the back and under the forelegs immediately after the skin has been removed, taking great care not to cut into them. Beaver fat has a strong flavor and odor and should be cut away completely before cooking. Soak the meat in enough salt water mixed with 1/4 cup (65 ml) of vinegar to cover the meat overnight, refrigerated, to draw out excess blood. Rinse the meat in cold, clear water.

Preparation: 1. **To roast, lay the legs back against the belly and secure by tying or with skewers. Place the beaver on its side in a roaster.**

2. **Cut several slits into the lean meat and stick strips of salt pork into the slits. Season with salt and pepper and dust with flour. Add a little water to the pan.**

3. **Roast at 325°F (165°C) for 1 1/2 hours with the lid on, adding more water as needed and skimming off the fat as it accumulates.**

4. **Turn the beaver. Add chopped onion, celery, and carrots to the pan. Finish roasting with the lid off, cook-**

ing until the meat falls off the bones, about 2 hours
longer. Add flour mixed with cold water to the pan
juices to thicken before serving.

NOTE: Cutting a dressed beaver into smaller roasts and
steaks requires special attention to bone structure and
will be easier if it is partially frozen.

Flavor
Affinities: Brandy, cloves, Dijon mustard, garlic, onions, parsley,
pork skin, red wine, rosemary, sage, salt pork, thyme.

---

64 a–b.   ## BISON AND BEEFALO

Other Names: **Bison:** *Bisonte* (Italian and Spanish), buffalo. **Beefalo:**
Cattalo.

General
Description: *The bison* (Bison bison), *native to North America, was
hunted extensively by Native Americans and almost to
extinction by early settlers in the West, but it is now
being farm-raised.* Although sometimes known as buffalo, the bison is not a true buffalo. The bison bull is
the largest animal indigenous to North America and
can weigh more than 1 ton (900 kg). Bison can thrive
on land considered unsuitable for domestic cattle;
they grow rapidly and have a long reproductive life.
Legal protection, the establishment of preserves, and
individuals raising bison have helped restore the bison
population to more than 350,000 animals. Buffalo

(bison) stew is a traditional dish of the Wild West that may still be found in San Francisco. While similar in many ways to beef, bison tends to have a richer, sweeter taste, and it is not gamy.

Beefalo is a cross of domestic cattle and bison developed in the 1960s. Although a hybrid species, they are not sterile like mules. Beefalo typically inherit the bison's production advantages—they can forage for feed and produce meat with little or no available grain, calving is easier, they are hardier in both cold and hot weather—but they are docile and manageable like beef cattle. Baby beefalo, similar to veal, is popular in Brazil.

Characteristics: Unlike the older, tougher animals the Native Americans ate, today's bison are custom-fed and younger at slaughter. Their meat is deep red in color, quite lean, and has a coarser grain than beef. It is high in protein, low in cholesterol, and has about half the calories and fat of beef. Bison may be cooked using almost any beef recipe, but because the meat is so lean, it is essential not to overcook it.

Beefalo meat is similar to bison, with 18 to 20 percent protein (compared with 10 percent in beef) and 5 to 7 percent fat overall (compared to 25–30 percent in beef). Its flavor and character will be closer to that of beef than bison.

How to Choose: Cuts of bison and beefalo are similar to those of beef.

Amount to Buy:	Because bison is relatively scarce, the price remains high. Bison and beefalo are denser than beef, so portions may be slightly smaller.
Storage: x2-3	Large cuts can be refrigerated for up to 3 days; small cuts and steaks can be refrigerated up to 2 days.
Preparation: 	• **For tender roasts cut from the middle section, such as tenderloin, loin, rib, top sirloin, and sirloin butt, season as desired, rub lightly with oil, and roast at 275°F (135°C) until the meat is about 5°F (2°C) below the desired temperature; rare (125°F/52°C) to medium-rare (135°F/57°C) is recommended. Remove the meat and drape with foil to keep warm, then slice.**
	• **For tougher roasts cut from the lower sections, such as sirloin tip, cross rib, inside or outside round flat, and eye of round, season as desired, rub with oil, and sear at 500°F (260°C) for 30 minutes. Reduce the heat to 275°F (135°C) and add 2 cups (500 ml) liquid to the pan, cover, and continue roasting to medium-rare (135°F/57°C) or no more than medium (145°F/63°C).**
	• **Bison hamburger should be cooked at a lower temperature than beef hamburger so that it doesn't toughen and dry out.**
	• **Bison steaks take well to marinating. Grill or pan-sear over high heat to brown, then continue cooking**

at lower heat for 6 to 15 minutes depending on thickness, turning often till rare or medium-rare; do not
cook past medium.

Flavor
Affinities:

Bay leaves, beer, chili sauce, cumin, onions, oyster
sauce, red wine, rosemary, sage, thyme, tomatoes.

65. 📷 **GOAT AND KID**

Other Names:

Goat: *Cabra* (Spanish, female goat), *capra* (Italian),
chèvre (French), *chivo* or *macho cabrío* (Spanish, male
goat), *Ziege* (German). **Kid:** *Cabrito* (Spanish and
Portuguese), *capretto* (Italian), *chevreau* (French).

General
Description:

Goat (Capra hircus) *is a mammal in the Bovidae (cattle) family closely related to the sheep with hollow horns
and coarse hair; a kid is a young goat.* The goat is
thought to have been one of the earliest animals
domesticated, along with sheep and pig. Because
goats are adaptable to hilly or mountainous environ-
ments unsuitable to other animals, they are commonly
eaten in parts of the world that don't have ready
access to other meats. Goat is usually cooked slowly
and is often marinated first or cooked in a sauce; kid
lends itself to recipes for lamb.

Characteristics:

Kid meat is light colored, mild, and lean; the meat
from older goats is darker, stronger in flavor, and less

tender but more juicy than kid. In some breeds of goat there can be color variation between males and females: the meat from males may be lighter in color and lower in fat, while the darker, more tender meat from females is desirable for steaks and chops. A well-conditioned goat has a thin coating of fat over its muscles. Goat meat is not marbled (having interspersed fat), so goat fat is easily trimmed.

How to Choose: Goat should have light pink to bright red, firm, fine-grained flesh with well-distributed white fat.

Amount to Buy: Goat meat is reasonably priced and may be found fresh or frozen, especially at halal meat markets (those selling meats slaughtered as prescribed by Islamic law). Allow about 1/2 pound (225 g) boneless goat meat and 1 pound (450 g) bone-in goat meat per person.

Storage: Refrigerate large pieces of goat 2 to 3 days. Refrigerate
x2-3 stew meat or ground meat up to 2 days.

Preparation: ***Jamaican-Style Curry Goat:***

1. **Rub cubed boneless goat meat with lime juice and then rinse off.**

2. **Marinate goat with onion, garlic, and spices refrigerated for 2 hours or overnight.**

3. **In a Dutch oven, add the goat and marinade, sliced green onions, a bay leaf, and curry powder (or Jamaican curry powder). Cover and simmer about 2 hours, or until tender.**

Flavor
Affinities:

Bacon, cinnamon, cumin, curry, ginger, habanero chiles, honey, jerk seasoning, limes, mint, onions.

HARE

Other Names:

Arctic, blue, brown, or European hare, California black-tailed jackrabbit (or hare), California white-tailed jackrabbit (or hare), *capucin* (French, more than 1 year old), *Feldhase* (German), jackrabbit, *lepre* (Italian), leveret (young hare), *liebre* (Spanish), *lièvre* (French), snowshoe hare, *trois-quarts* (French, less than 1 year old).

General
Description:

The hare, which is in the same family as the rabbit (Leporidae), has long ears, a notched (hare) lip, and powerful hind legs. Hares are larger than rabbits. The hare is native to both the Old and New Worlds, though it is much more common at the table in Europe. The Greeks and Romans enjoyed hare, and the British traditionally make jugged hare, using the blood as a thickener. The meat of hare is rich, moist, and tender when cooked by stewing or braising. Because of its assertive flavor, hare is complemented best by aggressive flavors, such as dried fruits, full-bodied red wine, and dried wild mushrooms.

Characteristics:

Hare meat is lean with a strong odor and a robust flavor redolent of berries and herbs. The meat can be tough. Hare should always be well cooked.

How to Choose:

The black-tailed hare and smaller snowshoe hare both have white meat, similar to rabbit (page 255). Wild Scottish hare has dark meat that is quite strong in flavor. A full-grown hare can weigh 12 to 14 pounds (5.4–6.4 kg). A leveret (between 2 and 4 months of age) weighs about 3 pounds (1.4 kg) and is usually roasted. A 1-year-old hare weighs about 6 pounds (2.7 kg); its saddle can be roasted or sautéed. Hares that are more than 1 year old are usually stewed.

Amount to Buy:

Hares are relatively large; one will feed four to six people. Allow 1 pound (450 g) bone-in hare per portion.

Storage:

Hares are not hung for aging because they deteriorate quickly after 48 hours. Refrigerate hare up to 2 days.

Preparation: 1.

Cut the hare into pieces. Reserve the blood if desired. Lightly dust with flour and place in a Dutch oven.

2.

Add herbs, chopped bacon and onion, ground allspice, lemon zest, port wine, salt, and pepper. Cover with water and bring slowly to a boil.

3. Remove the hare, onions, and bacon with a slotted spoon and keep warm. Discard the herbs.

4. In a small saucepan, make a roux by cooking several tablespoons of melted butter with enough flour to absorb the butter. Gradually pour in the cooking liquid and stir continuously until thickened.

5. Combine the sauce with the reserved hare, onions, and bacon. Cover and bake at 325°F (165°C) for 2 to 2 1/2 hours, or until the hare is tender.

6. Just before serving, stir in hare blood (if available) and add port to taste, mix well, and adjust the seasoning if necessary. The blood serves as a thickener. Serve with red currant jelly.

Flavor Affinities: Allspice, almonds, bacon, beer, cherries, chestnuts, cranberries, foie gras, ginger, ham, lemons, onions, port wine, raisins, red wine, truffles, vinegar.

HORSE AND DONKEY

Other Names: **Horse:** *Caballo* (Spanish), *cavallo* (Italian), *cheval* (French), *Pferd* (German), pony. **Donkey:** *Âne* (French), *asino* (Italian), *burro* (Spanish), *Esel* (German).

General
Description:

The horse (Equus caballus) is a large ungulate (or hoofed) mammal first domesticated by Central Asian nomads in the third millennium B.C. The donkey (Equus asinus) is a smaller cousin of the horse. Horses were known in ancient Mesopotamia, China, Greece, Egypt, and India. The English (and American) aversion to horse meat results from the perception that horses are noble and that they are pets or work animals. Although horse meat is rarely eaten in the United States, the American horse meat industry now rivals the beef and pork industries in the amounts of meat exported. In Sweden horse meat outsells lamb and mutton combined. Donkey meat is tough and usually stewed or made into sausages.

Characteristics:

Horse meat is lean, somewhere between beef and venison in flavor, with a dense texture and an underlying sweetness. The meat is higher in protein and lower in fat than beef, but it also spoils faster. It can be somewhat tougher than beef. Donkey meat tends to have a very strong smell, and it can be tough.

How to Choose:

Retail cuts of horse are similar to those of beef. Meat of animals more than 3 years old is a brilliant vermilion color and has better flavor. The most popular cuts of horsemeat come from the hindquarters: tenderloin, sirloin, filet steak, rump steak, and rib. Less tender cuts are ground.

Amount to Buy:	Refer to the comparable cut of beef to determine how much to purchase.
Storage:	Store horse or donkey meat up to 2 days refrigerated.

Preparation:	• **Tender cuts (rib and loin) can be roasted.**
	• **Less tender cuts should be ground, braised (roasted or simmered with a small amount of liquid in a covered pan), or stewed.**
	• **Ground meat from horse should be cooked to 160°F (71°C), or until the juices run clear with no trace of pink.**
Flavor Affinities:	Bacon, black pepper, carrots, celery, garlic, ginger, lemons, mushrooms, mustard, onions, tomatoes.

MUSKRAT

Other Names:	Marsh hare, marsh rabbit, mud beaver, mud cat, *musquash* or *ondatra* (Native American).
General Description:	*Muskrat* (Ondatra zibethica) *is trapped for both its dark brown fur and its flavorful meat.* The muskrat is the largest of the voles, a North American family of mouselike rodents. Muskrats live in swamps, marshes, and wetlands from northern North America as far

south as the Gulf of Mexico and the Mexican border. Although not widely perceived as a source of meat (it is trapped for its dark brown fur), if properly cleaned, muskrat is one of the most tender and flavorful of all wild meats. Toledo, Ohio, is the center of a large muskrat trapping and eating area, and "muskrat suppers" are held in the winter, sponsored by churches and volunteer fire departments to raise money. Muskrats may be cooked using rabbit or chicken recipes and are good fried, barbecued, spit-roasted, and braised.

Characteristics:	Muskrat meat is tasty, fine-grained, and tender.
How to Choose:	One muskrat will serve two people; allow 1 pound (450 g) per portion.
Amount to Buy:	An adult muskrat is about 15 inches long (38 cm) and weighs 2 pounds (910 g). Muskrats are sold from January through March in some parts of America.
Storage:	Store muskrat 1 to 2 days refrigerated.

x1–2

Preparation: 1. **Skin and clean the muskrat, removing all fat, the two musk glands near the base of the tail, and the white tissue inside each leg.**

2. **Soak the muskrat overnight in a brine solution of 1 tablespoon (15 ml) salt to 1 quart (1 l) water.**

3. **Drain, cut up the muskrat into serving pieces, and pat dry. Dust the pieces in flour seasoned with salt, pepper, and paprika.**

 4. **Heat oil in a Dutch oven, add the muskrat pieces, and brown slowly over medium heat.**

 5. **Cover with sliced onions and sour cream, season with salt, pepper, and cayenne, cover, and simmer 1 to 2 hours, or until tender.**

Flavor Affinities: Apples, bacon, brown sugar, cabbage, cayenne, lemons, mustard, potatoes, red wine, salt pork, vinegar.

OPOSSUM

Other Names: Possum.

General Description: *The opossum* (Didelphis virginiana) *is a large rodentlike animal that is found from South America to Canada and is frequently hunted.* Opossums are favorite game animals of the Southern states in the United States and are the subject of many folktales. The phrase "playing possum" comes from this animal's ability to appear dead when an enemy approaches. A favorite Southern dish is "possum and taters"; the opossum is parboiled, then seasoned and roasted with sweet potatoes.

Characteristics:	Opossum meat is light in color, fine-grained, and tender with generous fat deposits between the bands of muscle. Its liver may also be eaten.

How to Choose:	An opossum is about 20 inches (50 cm) long and may weigh 13 pounds (5.9 kg).

Amount to Buy:	One opossum will feed three to four people; allow 3/4 to 1 pound (340–450 g) per portion.

Storage:	Some people freeze a fresh-killed possum overnight before brining and cooking to further cut down on gaminess. Before storing, remove the reddish gland kernels under the forelegs and at the small of the back. Remove as much of the fat as possible and soak overnight, refrigerated, in a brine of 1 tablespoon (15 ml) salt in 1 quart (1 l) of water. Drain and pat dry.

Preparation:

1. **Dust the opossum all over with flour seasoned with salt, pepper, and ground thyme.**

2. **Place in a roasting pan, add red wine or other liquid, cover, and roast at 350°F (180°C) for 1 hour.**

3. **Pour off all but 1 cup (250 ml) of liquid. Add peeled sweet potatoes, split lengthwise, and peeled, cored halved apples to the pan. Sprinkle with brown sugar, allspice, cinnamon, and nutmeg. Continue to roast, uncovered, for 30 minutes longer, or until tender.**

| Flavor Affinities: | Allspice, apples, beer, chili powder, garlic, onions, red wine, rosemary, sauerkraut, thyme, white wine, yams. |

66 a–c.

RABBIT

| Other Names: | Bunny, *conejo* (Spanish), *coniglio* (Italian), coney, cony, cottontail, *Kaninchen* (German), *lapin* (French). |

| General Description: | *The rabbit* (Oryclolagus cuniculus) *is a small burrowing animal native to Morocco and the Iberian peninsula that is closely related to its darker-meat cousin, the hare.* Now widespread due partly to their legendary mating habits, rabbits have long been domesticated and are popular for the table in Europe. Rabbit in mustard sauce is a French Sunday tradition, and rabbit recipes abound in Spanish and Italian cookbooks. Rabbits are popularly hunted in the wild. Rabbit may substitute for chicken, pheasant, or squirrel in most recipes and takes well to subtle marinades. Smaller rabbits are often fried; larger rabbits are best cooked in stews or pies. Rabbit liver is sometimes used for stuffing or pâté. |

| Characteristics: | Rabbit is mild flavored, finely grained, and practically all white meat; it is like a cross between veal and chicken with a nutty aftertaste. Because it is quite lean, it may be dry if overcooked. The saddle of rabbit is the most tender and juicy part; the legs are meatier with delicate bones and a more pronounced |

muscle structure. Older rabbits should be soaked overnight in strong salt water to tenderize.

How to Choose:
Rabbit is sold fresh or frozen, whole or cut up, and may be either farm-raised or wild; farm-raised has a higher ratio of meat to bone. Rabbit should be well covered in meat, with a rounded back, springy pale pink flesh, a light-colored unblemished liver, and pure white fat surrounding the kidneys. Like chickens, rabbits are sold as fryers and roasters: Young rabbits, or fryers, are more tender than mature rabbits, or roasters. Rabbit parts may also be available; boneless loin will be the most expensive, legs the least.

Amount to Buy:
One young rabbit will serve two people; allow 1 pound (450 g) of bone-in rabbit per person.

Storage:
Store rabbit in the coldest part of the refrigerator for up to 2 days.

Preparation: 1.
Wash rabbit thoroughly in cold water and pat dry with paper towels.

• **Marinate boneless loin briefly and grill to medium-rare, about 5 minutes.**

• **Cook legs by poaching in stock until the meat falls off the bone, or prepare confit by slow-cooking in pork or duck fat.**

⚠ NOTE: **Rabbits occasionally carry tularemia, a bacterial dis-
            ease that can be transmitted to humans (it is destroyed
            through cooking). For safety, wear gloves when
            preparing rabbit.**

Flavor   Bacon, basil, beer, black pepper, cream, garlic, mus-
Affinities: tard, onions, prunes, red wine, tarragon, white wine.

RACCOON

Other Names: *Aroughcun* (one of many Native American names),
                coon, *mapache* (Spanish), *orsetto lavatore* or *procione*
                (Italian), *raton laveur* (French).

General   *The raccoon* (Procyon lotor) *is a nocturnal black-
Description: masked, ring-tailed animal that belongs to the same
                family as Chinese pandas and is hunted mostly for its
                fur.* The raccoon prefers wooded areas near water but
                is commonly found close to large cities. They are
                indigenous throughout most of North and South
                America. With proper preparation, raccoons provide
                good eating and are popular as food in the Midwest
                and the South. Raccoon is good barbecued, stuffed,
                or roasted. They are mostly nocturnal and are omniv-
                orous, feeding on crayfish, crabs, frogs, fish, and plants.

Characteristics: Raccoons have lean, dark, strong-flavored meat that
                  has long fibers and a coarse texture. Its fat is strong in

flavor and smell and should be carefully removed. Young raccoons, 6 to 8 pounds (2.7–3.6 kg), can be brined overnight. Older raccoons, up to 13 or 14 pounds (5.9–6.4 kg), should be soaked in brine for 24 hours and then parboiled in one or two changes of water to mellow the flavor.

How to Choose: A raccoon that weighs 6 to 8 pounds (2.7–3.6 kg) dressed will be less than 1 year of age and more tender than older racoons.

Amount to Buy: Allow 1 pound (450 g) of raccoon per portion.

Storage: Remove the waxy brown bean-shaped kernels (scent glands) from under the forelegs and each thigh, making sure to keep them whole. Trim off the inside and outside layers of fat. Cut the carcass into pieces and soak in brine of 1 tablespoon (15 ml) salt to 1 quart (1 l) water overnight, or up to 2 days, refrigerated.

Preparation: 1. **Dust the pieces with flour seasoned with salt and pepper.**

2. **In a Dutch oven, brown the pieces in fat. Add sliced onions, bay leaves, and thyme. Cover and bake at 350°F (180°C) for 2 hours or until the meat is tender. Make gravy by adding flour mixed with water to the pan drippings.**

Flavor Affinities:	Apples, barbecue sauce, brown sugar, butter, celery, cinnamon, cream, garlic, ginger, onions, oranges, raisins, red wine, sage, yams.

67. 📷 **RATTLESNAKE**

Other Names:	*Crotalo* or *serpente a sonagli* (Italian), *Klapperschlange* (German), musical jack, rattler, *serpent à sonnettes* (French), *crótalo* or *serpiente de cascabel* (Spanish), western rattlesnake, *yarará* (Latin American Spanish).
General Description:	*Rattlesnakes* (Crotalus viridis *and others) are indigenous to the Americas and have been a delicious source of meat for centuries.* Rattlesnakes are the only animal in the United States that can be hunted and sold without restriction. Rattlesnake hunts are popular in Western states, such as Texas, Oklahoma, and Nevada. The meat goes to purveyors who sell it to restaurants as a high-priced delicacy. Rattlesnake may be cooked in ways similar to rabbit or chicken, but it should be brined overnight before cooking. By far the most popular rattlesnake dish in America is rattlesnake chili.
Characteristics:	Rattlesnake is bony and has delicate white meat that is somewhat stringy and rather like chicken mixed with shrimp. After being cooked, the meat comes away from the bones in flakes, almost like crabmeat. The meat is low in fat and cholesterol.

How to Choose:	Large rattlesnakes of 3 to 5 pounds (1.4–2.3 kg) live weight are preferred.
Amount to Buy:	Quite expensive, rattlesnake meat can be purchased skinned, gutted, and frozen in 2- to 3-pound (.9–1.4 kg) packages.
Storage:	Rattlesnake meat is generally sold frozen. Defrost overnight in the refrigerator on a tray.
Preparation: 1.	**Cut the rattlesnake into 2-inch (5 cm) sections and soak in vinegar for 10 minutes. Remove and pat dry. Sprinkle with hot sauce, salt, and pepper.**
2.	**Dust with flour, cornmeal, or breadcrumbs, then deep-fry till well browned, about 10 minutes. Serve with salsa or other dipping sauce, as desired.**
Flavor Affinities:	Ancho chiles, bacon, corn, cumin, garlic, honey, onions, poblano chiles, tarragon, thyme, tomatoes.

SQUIRREL

Other Names:	*Ardilla* (Spanish), *écureuil* (French), *Eichhörnchen* (German), *scoiattolo* (Italian).
General Description:	*The squirrel is a tree-dwelling rodent that is widely hunted and eaten.* The squirrel's name comes from the

Greek meaning "he who sits in the shadow of his tail." Squirrels have a global distribution and are one of the few wild animals to have adapted to humans. The gray squirrel (*Sciurus carolinensis*), the most common of the tree squirrels, has been traced back 50 million years. Squirrel meat, properly prepared, is delicious and succulent. It lends itself to savory braises and stews, can be pan-fried, fricasseed (simmered in gravy), or broiled. Stewing or braising is best for older animals.

Characteristics:	Young squirrel has rosy pink to light red flesh that is tender with a pleasing flavor and little gaminess. The flesh of older squirrels is darker red and may require marinating or long cooking for tenderness.
How to Choose:	The average gray squirrel is 15 inches (38 cm) long and weighs about 1 pound (450 g).
Amount to Buy:	One small squirrel will serve one person.
Storage: x1–2	Store refrigerated 1 to 2 days.
Preparation:	***Brunswick Stew:***

1. **Cut up and trim the squirrel and place the pieces in a large kettle. Cover with water. Bring slowly to a boil, then reduce heat and simmer 1½ to 2 hours, or until the meat is tender, skimming the surface occasionally.**

2. **Remove the meat from the bones and return to the liquid. Add chopped bacon, onions, tomatoes, potatoes, and whole small lima beans to the pot. Season with salt, pepper, and cayenne. Simmer 1 hour.**

3. **Add corn (frozen or fresh cut from the cob) and cook 10 minutes longer, or till tender.**

Flavor Affinities: Bacon, barbecue sauce, cayenne, dry mustard, red wine, rosemary, sherry, sour cream, white wine.

68 a–c. **VENISON**

Other Names: Antelope, caribou, deer, elk, moose, pronghorn, reindeer, wapiti, white-tailed deer. **Deer:** *Cervo* (Italian), *chevreuil* (French), *ciervo* (Spanish), *Hirsch* (German), *venado* (Latin American Spanish). **Elk:** *Alce* (Italian and Spanish), *élan* (French), *Elch* (German). **Caribou:** *Caribú* (Spanish), *Karibu* (German), *renna* (Italian), *renne* (French).

General Description: *The word venison, derived from the Latin* venari, *meaning "to hunt," refers to all large, antlered game animals.* Farm-raised venison are generally more tender and less gamy than their wild counterparts; ranched venison are leaner and their flavor more complex. Venison makes an excellent chili. Less tender cuts can be made into juniper berry–seasoned sausages or burgers.

Deer is the most popular type of venison and is farmed and ranched in many countries worldwide, especially in New Zealand. New Zealand venison is the number-one worldwide source for farm-raised venison and accounts for about 85 percent of the venison served in U.S. restaurants.

Caribou (*Rangifer tarandus*), also known as reindeer, is a member of the deer family that lives from Newfoundland to Alaska in North America. Caribou may be farm-raised or harvested from the wild.

North American **elk** (*Cervus canadensis*) are also called "wapiti," a Shawnee word meaning "white rump," because of their distinguishing white patch. Confusingly, in Europe, moose are referred to as elk. While elk are not raised commercially in America, farm-raised elk are imported from New Zealand. Elk pizzle (penis) is sought after in some Asian markets because it is believed eating it increases male virility.

Moose (*Alces alces*), the largest member of the venison family, weighing up to 1,800 pounds (810 kg), are native to North America.

Antelope are farmed in Texas, where blackbuck (*Antilope cervicapra*) and nilgai antelope (*Boselaphus tragocamelus*), native to India, roam on huge preserves. Blackbucks are among the smallest members of the venison family. The nilgai, sometimes called South Texas antelope, are more commonly sold commercially.

The **pronghorn's** Latin name, *Antilocapra americana*, means "American antelope goat," though it is related to neither antelope or goat, nor to any other living animal. It is the only surviving species of the Antilocapra family. The pronghorn, which is the second most popular game animal in North America after white-tailed deer, has horns. It is reddish-brown above and tan or white below, with a short black mane and two white stripes across the front.

Characteristics: Deer meat has an aftertaste of berries and juniper. Firm to the touch, the meat is lean though moist. It is finely grained and much leaner but more watery than beef. The gamy flavor can be mellowed if the meat is soaked overnight in water, brine, or a vinegar solution.

Antelope, elk, and moose are similar in taste, texture, and cooking methods to deer. Nilgai meat is somewhat more delicate in flavor than blackbuck and is light enough in color to resemble veal. Elk is considered by some to be the best venison of all and is sometimes compared to prime beef. Moose meat is sweeter than deer. Caribou meat is quite lean, juicy, flavorful, and somewhat sweeter than deer, with a fine texture. Pronghorn meat is dark and rich in flavor with fine texture; it is a bit lighter but similar in taste to deer. Extremely lean (1 percent fat), pronghorn meat can be quite strong in flavor; some hunters prefer to use it for sausage or jerky.

How to Choose: Cervena is a trademark name for farm-raised deer from New Zealand that is between 18 and 30 months old. Vacuum-packed, either fresh or frozen, it is commonly sold to the restaurant trade in parts similar to lamb: saddle, rack, leg, and chops. Venison is available in specialty retail markets or by special order.

Amount to Buy: Venison is comparable to similar cuts of lamb or beef.

Storage: Refrigerate vacuum-packed venison 3 to 4 days.

 x 3–4

Preparation: • **For all venison, the meat on the upper hind legs and along the backbone is the most tender and is suitable for quick-cooking steaks cut about 1 inch (2.5 cm) thick. Tender cuts of venison should be cooked rare to medium-rare.**

• **Cuts from the lower leg, shoulder, and belly will be tougher and require long, slow moist-heat cooking; they may be ground for burgers or sausage.**

Flavor Affinities: Blueberries, brandy, chestnuts, cinnamon, cranberries, ginger, juniper berries, mustard, onions, oranges, port wine, raisins, red wine, rosemary, shallots.

 69.

WILD BOAR

Other Names: *Cerdo or verraco* (Spanish), *cinghiale* (Italian), *Keiler* (German), *marcassin* (French, young wild boar), *sanglier* (French, older wild boar).

General
Description:
The wild boar (Sus scrofa) *is the ancestor of the domestic pig and was brought to North America by Spanish explorers.* Wild boars have been found from Europe to Central Asia and from the Baltic to North Africa since ancient times and were domesticated in northern Europe by about 1500 B.C. Often reaching 300 pounds (135 kg) with tusks up to 12 inches (30 cm) long, boars have a fierce disposition, a long mobile snout, a heavy, relatively short-legged body, a thick bristly hide, and a small tail.

In medieval times wild boar was often the main attraction of the Christmas feast; special songs about boar accompanied the meal. Wild boar meat is lean and exceptionally flavorful. Wild boar prosciutto and salami (pages 289 and 276) are much appreciated in Italy. Free-range wild boars forage on wild greens, acorns, and roots, and are lean with a mild, sweet, slightly nutty taste.

Characteristics:
The lean meat of boar can range in flavor from mild and delicate to gamy, depending on variety, season, diet, and age. The most tender cuts come from the loin. Boar may be prepared using pork or venison recipes, but it must always be cooked well-done.

How to Choose:
Younger animals, less than 1 year of age, are preferred for their tenderness. Boar may be purchased from specialty purveyors in many of the same cuts as domestic pig, including smoked bacon and sausage.

Amount to Buy:	A 2 1/4-pound (1 kg) cut of boneless wild boar will serve four.
Storage: x3–4	Store vacuum-packed fresh wild boar for 3 to 4 days refrigerated.
Preparation: 1.	**Trim the meat of nerves, gristle, and fat, and cut into medium-sized chunks.**
2.	**Marinate overnight in a mixture of red wine, thyme, bay leaves, or other desired flavors.**
3.	**Drain the meat and pat dry. Season with salt and pepper. Brown in oil, remove from the pan, and brown aromatic vegetables (such as onions and carrots) in the same pan.**
4.	**Pour in red wine to partially cover the meat along with chopped resinous herbs (such as rosemary, sage, or thyme) and salt and pepper, and bring to a boil, then reduce to a simmer. Half-cover and cook for 2 to 3 hours, or until the meat is tender.**
Flavor Affinities:	Apples, bitter chocolate, brandy, chestnuts, cloves, grappa, juniper berries, prunes, red wine vinegar, rosemary, sage, savory, sugar, thyme.

VII. Sausage and Cured Meats

At its simplest, sausage is a chopped meat mixture stuffed into a tubular casing usually made from intestines, although stomach is used for haggis and beef bladder is used for mortadella. These days artificial casings are also used. Sausage making originated in antiquity as a way of preserving the innards, blood, and bits and pieces of meat, especially from pigs.

There are thousands of different types of sausages worldwide (1,000 in Germany alone), but they fit into three main categories: fresh sausages that must be cooked; cured sausages that are meant for long storage and are eaten without cooking; and cooked sausages that are either meant to be eaten cold or further cooked and eaten hot. (Some types of sausage can be found in a variety of forms.) Preparing fresh sausage is relatively simple: the meat is cut up, seasoned, and ground. Preparing cured sausage is more complex because it must first be salted, then dried (and sometimes smoked), and the process depends on controlled lactic-acid fermentation to achieve particular results. Potassium nitrate (saltpeter) is added to keep the meat an attractive pink color (rather than turning brown or gray) and also inhibit the growth of dangerous bacteria. Once the cured sausage has been properly fermented and dried, it may develop a harmless white coating called "bloom" made of yeast cells.

There are many other types of cured meats, including bacon, loafs, and even duck prosciutto. Others are prepared from whole muscles, rather than made from ground meats like sausage. The most important type worldwide is ham, classically made from the upper rear leg of a pig, though wild boar, deer, sheep, goat, or even bear are also made into hams. A ham is always cured, but it may also be dry-cured (like Italian prosciutto), or smoked (like Westphalian ham from Germany). Poultry is often preserved by making it into confit, or by smoking.

COOKED (CAN BE EATEN AS IS OR FURTHER COOKED) SAUSAGES

Bierwurst (Beerwurst, Beer Salami)

This dark red, chunky, tubular German sausage is made with pork and beef and lots of garlic, though no beer. It is cooked, then smoked and served cold sliced for sandwiches.

Bologna (Baloney, Balogna)

This soft, mild sausage is derived from the Bolognese specialty mortadella. Light pinkish brown in color, bologna is made from finely ground cured beef and pork and is usually smoked. A sandwich staple, it is usually sold sliced and ready-to-eat; it can also be fried. Beef bologna has a garlic flavor. Chub bologna is a smooth mixture of beef, pork, and bacon. Ham bologna contains large cubes of lean cured pork.

70b. Braunschweiger

This medium-large German sausage is a type of liverwurst, or smooth liver sausage enriched with eggs and milk, which is cooked and then smoked. Named after the German town of Braunschweig, it is soft enough to be spreadable and is usually served at room temperature.

Gelbwurst

This German pork and veal sausage, seasoned with nutmeg, white pepper, and ginger, is very mild and fine-grained. Its name means "yellow sausage" in German, referring to the color of the casing. Gelbwurst is called "diet bologna" in Germany since it's relatively low in fat. It can be sliced for sandwiches or pan-fried.

70a. Goose Liver Pate (Gaenseleberwurst)

This smooth, creamy pate is made from goose liver and goose meat. It is soft enough to spread on bread and is highly regarded by conoisseurs.

71. Kielbasa (Kolbasa, Polish Sausage, Knublewurst, Polnische Wurst)

This smoked Polish sausage is made with pork (and sometimes beef) flavored with garlic, pimento, and cloves. Made in long, chunky links about 2 inches (5 cm) across, it is sold precooked but is usually reheated before serving. A Hungarian version called kolbasz has paprika added to it.

Krakauer

This German-style sausage originated in the city of Krakow, Poland. It is similar to bologna studded with ham. It can be sliced and served cold or fried.

Leberkäse

Despite its name ("liver cheese" in German), this Bavarian specialty contains neither liver nor cheese. It's a cooked pork, beef, and veal loaf similar to bologna. Germans like to fry thick slices and serve them with potatoes.

Liverwurst (Liver Sausage, Leberwurst)

This is a family of German liver sausages that are creamy enough to spread. It is made in many variations, including pork, goose, and calf's liver.

72. 📷 Mortadella di Bologna

The origin of mortadella goes back to the Middle Ages, when the seasonings included myrtle berries—thought to be the origin of its name. Mortadella is made in different sizes with the choicest being the larger ones. To make it, finely ground pork is mixed with diced backfat, preserving agents, salt, finely ground white pepper, black pepper, coriander seed, mixed spices, shelled pistachios, and wine. It is packed into a beef or hog bladder, then hung in an oven and cooked slowly. Mortadella is quite perishable and must be kept cool; after being cut it should be refrigerated up to 4 days.

Ringwurst (Ring Bologna, Fleischwurst)

This German pork and beef ring-shaped sausage looks and tastes like bologna. Germans like to heat it up and serve it with potato salad or bread.

73a–b. 📷 Saucisson de Toulouse

This exquisite, rich, delicate French sausage is usually made with pork, smoked bacon, wine, garlic, and other seasonings. Saucisson à l'ail is heavily flavored with garlic. Saucisson en croute has been wrapped in puff pastry and baked. Toulouse sausage is usually braised or fried.

Schinkenwurst (Bier Schinken, Ham Bologna)

This Westphalian sausage is made from flaked ham in a bologna-like emulsion smoked over beech wood and juniper berries. It is usually sliced cold for sandwiches.

Sobrasada

This famous soft spreadable sausage from the island of Majorca, Spain, is made from finely chopped loin, filet, and leg of pork seasoned with nutmeg and lemon. It is irregularly shaped, spicy, and a reddish orange color.

74. 📷 **Zungenwurst**

(Blutwurst, Blut Zungenwurst, Blood Tongue Sausage)

This German blood sausage includes pieces of pickled tongue. This dried sausage comes ready to eat, but it's often sliced and browned in butter or bacon fat before serving.

CURED (READY-TO-EAT) SAUSAGES

75. 📷 **Andouille Sausage, Cajun**

This spicy, smoked Cajun sausage is coarse-textured and seasoned with cayenne pepper, mustard, paprika, and garlic. It is made from lean chopped pork smoked with hickory wood. It is added to gumbo and jambalaya and also served cold as an hors d'oeuvre.

Andouille Sausage, French

Andouille is a mild French sausage originally from Normandy made from chitterlings. Much loved by the French, andouille has a penetrating odor and chewy texture. Pig intestines and stomach are cleaned, cut into strips, bundled, rolled, and tied with string. Next they are marinated in salt and pepper and rolled into an intestine to form. It is then smoked, preferably over apple or beech wood, soaked in water, simmered slowly in well-seasoned stock, and finally hung for the flavor to develop. Andouille, which can be recognized by its lumpy whitish skin, is eaten cold cut into thin slices, or warm with sautéed apples and cider. Andouillette is a smaller version.

Bologna, Lebanon

This highly seasoned, slightly sweet, tangy chopped beef sausage is semi-dry, heavily smoked, and tart and tangy in flavor. A large, dark reddish brown sausage, it is a Pennsylvania Dutch specialty that originated in the nineteenth century in Lebanon County, Pennsylvania.

76a. 📷 Cacciatore (Cacciatorino, Hunter Salame)

Cacciatore is a small salami 5 to 7 inches (12.5–17.5 cm) long made from pork and beef with pancetta (page 284). Seasoned with black pepper, spices, garlic, and dry white wine, it is dried over charcoal, then aged.

77c. 📷 Calabrese Sausage

This small spicy dry Italian salame is made from pork seasoned with hot chile peppers and fennel seeds. There are about five links to the pound (450 g).

76b., 78a-b. 📷 Cervelat (Summer Sausage)

Cervelat is a general classification for mildly seasoned, smoked, semi-dry German sausages that are also called summer sausage. They get their name from *cervelle*, the French word for brains, one of their original ingredients. These sausages are good for summer because they're light in flavor and don't need to be cooked. Holsteiner is a cervelat from northern Germany that is heavily smoked.

79c. 📷 Chorizo Sausage, Spanish

Spanish chorizo is a highly seasoned, coarsely ground pork sausage flavored with garlic, sweet and hot paprika, and other spices. It is usually dry-cured and ready-to-eat and may be smoked. A picante chorizo will be hot and spicy. Large chorizos may be sliced and eaten like salami; smaller ones are usually further cooked. Don't confuse it with Mexican chorizo (page 278), which is a fresh sausage and must be cooked. Bilbao is soft chorizo, suitable for paella, from the Basque country; fuet is Catalonian-style chorizo.

Chouriço (Chourico)

This heavily seasoned Portuguese wood-smoked pork sausage is closely related to Spanish chorizo. Linguiça is a type of chouriço that includes chopped or ground pork and is often used in cozidos (meat and vegetable stews), although it may be eaten uncooked. These sausages are seasoned with sweet paprika, garlic, salt, white or red wine, and the hot pepper sauce from Angola called *piri-piri*.

Csabai

This Hungarian smoked pork sausage is heavily seasoned with sweet and hot paprika, garlic, and cumin. It is dried and then cold-smoked over beech wood. Ripening takes 3 months. Look for it sold in rings in German delis.

Cserkesz (Boy Scout Sausage)

This thin Hungarian sausage is slightly dry and makes a good snack. It is called "boy scout sausage" because it was carried by Hungarian Boy Scouts in their backpacks.

Finocchiona (Salame with Fennel Seeds)

This Italian salame is made from finely ground pork (and sometimes beef) seasoned with salt, pepper, garlic, and fennel seeds, and dry-aged for about 3 months. It is thick and 8 to 10 inches (20–25 cm) long. It should be sliced fairly thick.

80a. Gypsy Salami (Tziganskaya)

This large, dry-cured sausage is made entirely of pork. It is hand-rolled in a peppery spice mixture.

Gyulai and Debrecini

This Hungarian smoked pork sausage is made with coarsely chopped meat blended with sweet and hot Hungarian paprika, garlic, and cumin, smoked over beech wood, and dried for 3 months. Debrecini is a small version of Gyulai.

Jagdwurst

This coarse, mild German hunter's sausage is made of pork, beef, and sometimes garlic and pistachios. It's often sliced for sandwiches and served with mustard.

Kosher Salami

This is a large cooked salami and is made with ground chuck—only forequarter cuts are used in kosher cooking—and seasoned with salt, sugar, black pepper, paprika, ginger, nutmeg, garlic, and white wine.

81. Landjager (Landjaeger, Landjaeger Cervelat)

The name for this German sausage means "hunter," perhaps because it needs no refrigeration and is handy to take on hunts. A semi-dry sausage of Swiss origin, it is made from beef and pork, heavily smoked, and has a black, wrinkled appearance.

82. Lap Cheong (Chinese Dried Sausage)

These Chinese pork sausages look and feel like pepperoni, but they're much sweeter. They include soy sauce, sugar, monosodium glutamate, and Chinese rice wine. Cassia is commonly added as a preservative.

80b. 📷 Nevskaya

Nevskaya is a deep reddish brown, dry-cured pork sausage studded with dry-cured beef. It is traditional to areas around St. Petersburg, Russia, and is named for the Neva river.

83. 📷 Pepperoni

This spicy Italian sausage is made with beef and pork dried till it is hard and chewy. Cut into thin slices, it makes a popular pizza topping.

84. 📷 Plockwurst (Bear Salami)

This small, bear-shaped salami is made of beef and bear meat and often includes whole peppercorns. It is popular in Eastern Europe, where bear is hunted. Serve with pumpernickel bread.

Rosette de Lyon

This is a dry-cured sausage with coarse texture made of pork. It is probably the most prestigious salami-type sausage in France. It has a rich wine flavor and a long finish.

Salame Brianza

Salame Brianza, made from pork, is easy to find throughout Italy. It is cylindrical in shape and varied in size. The slices are homogenous and uniformly ruby-red, with a delicate, distinctive, sweet flavor.

Salame di Genoa (Genoa Salami)

This popular dry sausage of Genoese origin is usually made entirely from pork but may contain beef. It is moistened with wine and seasoned with garlic. A cord is wrapped lengthwise around the sausage at regular intervals to form its shape.

Salame di Milano (Milano Salami)

This salame typical of Milan is made with finely ground pork, beef, and fat in equal quantities, spiced only with salt and pepper. Weighing up to 3 pounds (1.4 kg) and aged for at least 3 months, it should be sliced fairly thin.

Salame d'la Duja (Preserved Salame)

This small salame, from the northern Italian province of Piedmont, is made with lean pork meat seasoned with salt and pepper. It is kept soft and fresh in a terra-cotta jar (called a *duja*) filled with melted pork fat, then sealed for 3 months. This method of preserving is used in this region because it is too humid for dry aging.

77a. 📷 **Salame Napoletano (Neapolitan Salame)**

This salame from Naples is prepared with finely ground lean pork mixed with a small quantity of fat and heavily spiced with ground peperoncino. It is stuffed into a 1 inch (2.5 cm) wide, 20 inch (50 cm) long casing and dry-aged for a minimum of 6 months.

Salami (Plural for Salame)

This family of Italian ready-to-eat sausages is made with beef and/or pork heavily seasoned with garlic and spices. Some producers use wine for moisture and to develop a special character during the cure, while others use nothing but pork, fatback, and white peppercorns. They're often thinly sliced and used in sandwiches or antipasto plates. Many types of salami, like the popular Genoa salami, are air-dried and somewhat hard. Others, like salami cotto and kosher salami, are cooked, which makes them softer and more perishable. In Italian, salame is the singular form and salami the plural, but Americans often talk of one salami and many salamis.

79b. 📷 **Salami, Hungarian**

The Hungarian sausage manufacturer Pick is famed for its mildly spiced salami. Weighing about 2 pounds (910 g), this salami includes paprika and is heavily smoked.

Salcisson

This Spanish dry-cured sausage is hard and differs from chorizo in that it has more garlic and less paprika. Different towns in Spain are famed for their particular types of salcisson, which may also include black pepper and wine.

Saucisson

This is a general French term for large sausages. Saucisson sec is French-style dry-cured salami that does not need cooking. The traditional preparation involves boning and trimming the meat, pounding the fat and lean meat with spices, predrying the sausage, and then drying and maturing for at least 4 weeks. A good saucisson is firm or hard to the touch and has a pronounced aroma. Bloom, or dark color on the outside, indicates that it has been properly matured. Some types have hazelnuts or walnuts mixed in.

Saucisson de Lyon

This dry salame from the hills near Lyon, France, is made from pork leg and shoulder cut into relatively large cubes mixed with diced fresh bacon, sea salt, and pepper. The mixture is stuffed into natural skins and dried in a low oven, and then air-dried.

85a-b. 📷 **Soppressata (Capocchia, Copa di Testa, Head Sausage)**

Soppressata, a pressed Italian sausage, is made with lean meat taken from the pig's head that is coarsely chopped, mixed with lard, and then stuffed into a natural casing. The most famous version comes from Siena and is flavored with coriander, black pepper, nutmeg, cloves, and cinnamon. It is compressed, knotted, pulled very tightly, and aged for at least 40 days. It is stored under melted back fat and is sliced by hand. Friuli-style soppressata is quite large and tart. Often, homemade soppressata is hand-tied and uneven in shape.

Teewurst (Teawurst)

Germans like to spread this smoky "tea sausage" on crackers or bread at teatime. Always a smooth, very fine-textured paste, it is made from pork or pork and beef and is highly seasoned with paprika and other spices.

Wild Boar Salame

Wild boar salame is popular in Tuscany and Umbria, where game animals are plentiful. It is flavored with local wines and ingredients such as wild myrtle berries, black truffles, or walnuts. It is made from the belly and shoulder of boars raised in the semi-wild and fed on barley and wheat germ in winter and plums, prunes, and tomatoes in summer. The meat is trimmed of all the strong-flavored fat and ground to a medium consistency with pancetta fat then seasoned, stuffed into pork intestines, and aged for 1 to 2 months.

FRESH (MUST BE COOKED) SAUSAGES

86. 📷 **Banger**

This medium-sized, mild British pork and veal sausage is seasoned with thyme, marjoram, sage, lemon peel, onion, salt, and pepper and may contain up to 35 percent rusks (dried cracker meal). Bangers originated during World War II when meat shortages led to sausages with high water content. They explode when steamed unless pricked.

Bauerwurst (Bauernwurst)

This coarse-textured German farmer's sausage is seasoned with mustard seed and marjoram and then smoked. It is steamed, sautéed, or grilled and served on a bun or cooked with sauerkraut.

Blood Sausage (Black Pudding, Black Sausage, Blood Pudding, Boudin Noir, Louisiana Boudin Rouge, Spanish Morcilla)

These large eggplant-colored link sausages are made of pig's blood mixed with fat such as suet, fillers like breadcrumbs or oatmeal, and other regional flavorings. Blood sausages are generally sold precooked, but they are traditionally sautéed and served with mashed potatoes, sauerkraut, or beans. Spanish morcilla uses rice as a filler and is heavily salted and seasoned with cinnamon, cloves, and nutmeg.

87c. 🍲 **Bockwurst**

This mild German sausage made with ground veal and pork, milk, and eggs, seasoned with chives and chopped parsley, is traditional in Munich. Similar to French boudin blanc, it is quite perishable and must be cooked within 2 or 3 days, or frozen. Traditionally served with sweet mustard, it is frequently accompanied with sliced radishes, rye bread, and Munich Beer.

Boerewors (Boeries, Wors, Boerewurst)

This spicy South African farmer's sausage is made with beef, pork, and pork fat seasoned with coriander.

Boterhamworst

This Dutch sausage is made of finely chopped veal and pork blended with coarsely chopped pork fat and seasonings.

88. 📷 **Boudin Blanc (White Boudin)**

This medium-sized delicate white sausage is made of pork, chicken, or veal. French versions are bread- and milk-based, and Cajun versions include rice. It is quite perishable and must be kept refrigerated and cooked within 2 to 3 days, or frozen.

87a. 🍲 **Bratwurst**

This medium-sized German pork and veal sausage is seasoned with spices such as ginger, nutmeg, coriander, or caraway. It usually needs to be cooked by grilling or sautéing, though some markets carry precooked bratwurst. In Germany the many varieties of bratwurst are distinguished by their seasonings and size and may also be smoked.

Breakfast Sausage

These American-style fresh pork breakfast sausages may be formed into patties or small links. They are seasoned with black pepper, nutmeg, sage, and/or marjoram. They're usually fried before serving with eggs and hash-brown potatoes.

Butifarra (Butifarró, Butifarron)

This family of names covers a large range of Spanish sausages made from pork, lard, garlic, and spices. Butifarra negra is a blood sausage seasoned with mint; butifarra blanca is a white sausage that is a specialty of the region of Catalonia. Butifarra and mongetes (a type of white bean) is a typical Catalonian dish.

Carnatzlach

This Romanian Jewish specialty is a homemade sausage made from ground beef mixed with garlic, black pepper, paprika, salt, other spices (allspice, cloves, cumin, or coriander), and herbs (oregano and thyme), formed into a sausage shape, and broiled.

Cervelas de Lyon

The elegant French cervelas is thought to have originated in Florence and originally included brains (*cervelle*), the source of its name. Made from lean pork shoulder mixed with belly and bacon, it is seasoned with salt, pepper, nutmeg, and sugar. It may also include port, Madeira, or Cognac and truffles, pistachios, or morels. It is uncooked and must be kept refrigerated 1 to 2 days and simmered for 30 to 40 minutes per pound, or until it bubbles when pricked. It is closely related to German cervelat (page 272).

Chaurice

This spicy pork sausage from Louisiana is used in jambalaya and other Creole and Cajun dishes. It's available either in links or patties, but it's hard to find outside of Louisiana. It is related, at least in name, to Spanish and Mexican chorizo.

Chipolata Sausage

Sometimes called "little fingers," these 2- to 3-inch (5–7.5 cm) long, coarse-textured pork sausages are highly spiced with thyme, chives, coriander, cloves, and sometimes hot red-pepper flakes and enclosed in natural sheep's casing. Their name comes from the Italian *cipolla* (onion) and was originally applied to a stew made with onions and small sausages. Chipolatas are eaten fried or grilled.

79a-b. 🍳 Chorizo Sausage, Mexican

Mexican chorizo is made from coarsely ground fresh pork mixed with garlic, chiles, and other spices. Don't confuse it with Spanish chorizo (page 272), which is usually dry-cured and ready-to-eat. When fresh, this sausage must be cooked. The casing is usually removed and the sausage crumbled before cooking. It may also be found dry-cured.

Cocktail Wieners

These are a type of hot dog that is smaller than a standard hot dog, but larger than a Vienna sausage. They must be cooked prior to serving, despite having been precured.

Cotechino

Cotechino is a mild and fatty Italian pork sausage. It dates back to the early sixteenth century, when the people of Modena made it in preparation for an oncoming siege. Pigskin, pork meat, and lung are ground, blended with red wine and various spices, and packed into beef intestines then dried. Cotechino and the closely related zampone are mottled pinkish-red in color, with fine-textured meat in uniform pieces. Cotechino must be poached before eating, and it should be pricked to allow some of the fat to drain out.

Cumberland Sausage

This British pork sausage is usually displayed in markets as a long coil, and it's sold by the length. It is made of coarse-cut pork, is somewhat spicy, and contains special baked rusks (dried cracker meal). It's often baked with cabbage and potatoes.

Haggis

This large Scottish sausage of ancient heritage is made by stuffing a sheep's stomach with chopped heart, lungs, and liver mixed with oatmeal, onion, fat, and seasonings. It's usually steamed before serving.

Hot Dogs

The hot dog, an American staple, is a mild, smoked, and usually skinless sausage traditionally served on a bun with relish and mustard. It is an emulsified sausage, meaning that finely ground meat is whipped together with fat and seasonings to form a creamy, smooth consistency. Studies have shown a high level of the harmful bacteria Listeria on hot dogs, so although they are fully cooked, reheat them till hot before serving.

Italian Sausage (Salsicce, Sweet Italian Sausage, Hot Italian Sausage)

This fresh pork sausage often added to pasta sauces is 70 percent lean meat and 30 percent fat. Sweet Italian sausage is flavored with garlic and fennel seed. Hot Italian sausage also contains crushed chile peppers. It's sold either as links or in bulk and must be cooked thoroughly before serving. Store refrigerated for 1 to 2 days, or freeze.

87b. 📷 Knackwurst (Knockwurst, Knoblauch, Garlic Sausage)

These short, thick links of precooked beef and/or pork sausage are flavored with garlic and cumin and usually boiled or grilled before serving, often with sauerkraut. Knackwurst gets its name from the German knack (crack) and wurst (sausage), because of the crackling sound it makes when eaten. Kosher knockwurst is made, of course, from beef—no pork—with plenty of garlic.

89. 📷 Kosher Hot Dogs

These hot dogs are made from beef (or poultry) slaughtered according to Jewish dietary laws only. They are heavily seasoned with garlic and must be cooked prior to serving.

Linguiça

This small, thin Portuguese sausage is made from coarsely ground pork butt seasoned with garlic, cumin seed, and cinnamon, then cured in a vinegar pickling solution before stuffing into thin lamb casings. It must be cooked before serving. It is related to Greek Loukanika and Italian Luganega.

Longaniza, Llangonissa, or Llonganissa

This long, thin dry-cured Spanish sausage is called *fuet* in Catalonia and is about 1 inch (2.5 cm) thick. It is typically seasoned with paprika, cinnamon, aniseed, garlic, and vinegar. Mexican, Cuban, and Puerto Rican versions are also made. It is a wonderful ingredient for sandwiches and excellent either grilled or in soups. A Filipino type called Longaniza Adobo Recado is also known as hot, or red Filipino, sausage.

Loukanika

This small, thin, spicy Greek sausage is made with lamb and pork, flavored with orange zest, and stuffed into small lamb casings. Loukanika is a fresh sausage that is quite perishable and must be cooked before eating; it is usually cut into chunks and sautéed. It is traditionally made after the pig slaughter, between mid-November and New Year's Day, and is closely related to Italian luganega and Portuguese linguiça.

Luganega

This famous raw pork sausage of Lombardy and the Veneto is flavored with cloves and cinnamon and may also contain nutmeg and Parmigiano Reggiano cheese. Made in long, thin rings and stuffed into lamb casings, it is usually sold by the length.

90. ◉ **Merguez Sausage (Mirkâs)**

This North African sausage is made of coarsely ground lamb seasoned with garlic, hot red chile pepper, and other spices. It's often used in couscous dishes and is now popular in the south of France as a pizza topping.

Mettwurst (Metts)

In Cincinnati, mettwurst is a kielbasa-like sausage that's made with beef and pork, seasoned with pepper and coriander, and smoked. It is often grilled and served on a bun. Elsewhere, mettwurst is made from ground cured beef and pork lightly spiced with allspice, ginger, mustard, and coriander seed.

Pinkelwurst

This German sausage is made with beef and/or pork, onions, oats, and bacon and is often served with potatoes and kale.

Potato Korv

This is a Swedish pork (or pork and beef) sausage that includes potatoes, onions, milk, allspice, salt, and white pepper. Potato korv is often cooked for holidays.

Salame da Sugo (Liver, Beef, and Tongue Sausage)

This Italian sausage is made with liver, beef, tongue, and lard seasoned with salt, pepper, nutmeg, and Sangiovese wine. It is dried, then aged for at least 1 year and periodically coated with a mixture of oil and vinegar. Before cooking, it is soaked in cold water, then simmered for at least 4 hours. When ready, cut it open along the seam and remove the meat from the casing. Serve with mashed potatoes in winter and melon in summer.

Salamelle (Sausage Rolled in Pancetta)

Salamelle is made with the same ingredients as cotechino (page 279), substituting pancetta (page 284) for pigskin and white for red wine. The meat is ground coarsely and sometimes flavored with garlic. Salamelle are generally split and grilled.

Salchicha

Salchicha is fresh Spanish pork sausage in links. It is a smoked sausage made from chopped lean pork and pork fat seasoned with salt and black pepper. In Catalonia and the Balearic Islands this sausage is known as llonganissa.

Vienna Sausages and Vienna-Style Frankfurters

These small, squat, cooked sausages are made in the style of and with similar ingredients to hot dogs (page 279). They are often used to make hors d'oeuvres. They must be cooked through before serving.

Weisswurst (Weißwürste, White Sausage)

German for "white sausage," weisswurst is a delicate, mildly seasoned sausage related to boudin blanc made with veal, cream, and eggs. A specialty of Munich, the links are about 4 inches (10 cm) long, plump, and light in color. Germans like to eat them with special sweet mustard, rye bread, beer, and potato salad during Oktoberfest.

Zampone (Stuffed Hog Foreleg)

Zampone is a mild and fatty pork sausage that is a seasonal specialty from Emilia Romagna in central Italy. Zampone must be wrapped in cheesecloth and then poached very slowly. Closely related to cotechino (page 279), it is classically accompanied by stewed lentils, a dish that is eaten for good luck at midnight on New Year's Eve.

LOAFS, COOKED AND JELLIED

Goetta

This mixture of ground pork and/or beef, oats, herbs, and spices of German origin is Cincinnati's version of scrapple. It's generally cut into slices and pan-fried.

91a-b. Head Cheese (Sulz, Sülze, Souse, Brawn)

Head cheese is a jellied loaf originally made entirely from the head of a pig or calf, but now can include edible parts of the feet, tongue, and heart. The head is cleaned and simmered until the meat falls from the bones, and the liquid is cooked down into a concentrated gelatinous broth. The meat is removed, chopped, seasoned, and mixed with broth then placed in a mold and chilled until set. When cool, it is unmolded and thinly sliced. It's usually eaten at room temperature as an appetizer. Souse or sulz is similar to head cheese except that sweet-sour flavor is added by a vinegar pickling liquid. Russians favor a type of head cheese with large chunks of tongue suspended in gelatin.

Loaf, Olive

This cooked loaf resembles bologna (page 269) embedded with stuffed green olives.

Loaf, Pepper

This cooked pork and beef loaf is heavily seasoned with cracked peppercorns.

Loaf, Tongue (Tongue Sausage)

Well-stocked delis often carry loaves of pork, lamb, veal, or beef tongues that have been cooked, pressed, jellied, and/or smoked.

92. Scrapple

A Pennsylvania Dutch specialty, this mixture of sausage (traditionally head meat) and cornmeal is molded into a rectangular or cylindrical shape and then sliced. It's often fried and served with eggs and grits.

BACON

93. Bacon is a cut from the fatty pork belly that is usually cured and smoked over aromatic woods such as apple, hickory, and mesquite. It is available pre-sliced (thin or thick) or whole, called slab bacon. Bacon is often fried and served with eggs or in sandwiches, and it may be wrapped around lean meats to keep them moist while cooking, called barding. Bacon may be flavored with ingredients like maple, peppercorns, or paprika. Like many cured meats, bacon contains nitrates, which contribute to the characteristic cured flavor and reddish-pink color of cured meats and act as a preservative to prevent rancidity. Nitrates and salt inhibit the growth of botulism. Nitrate-free bacon is available in natural foods stores.

94. Gypsy Bacon (Ciganyszalonna)

This Hungarian specialty consists of a double thick firm slab of bacon that's roasted and seasoned with paprika and cured so that it may be eaten without cooking. It may be cooked Gypsy style: cut into squares, skewered, and cooked over an open fire, topped with chopped sweet onion, and served with rye bread.

Lardo

Lardo is creamy white pork fatback cured for several months with rock salt, rosemary, and cloves. A specialty of Tuscany, Italian lardo is cut into thin, almost transparent slices and served on warm toast rubbed with garlic and dressed with a little olive oil.

95. 🔲 Pancetta (Italian Bacon)

Pancetta, which is sold rolled up into a fat cylinder, is the Italian equivalent of bacon, though it is cured but usually not smoked. At its simplest, pancetta is cured with salt and pepper; some types are prepared with cinnamon, cloves, and other local spices. It is leaner and saltier than bacon, with a chewy texture because it is uncooked. Smoked pancetta, best when smoked over oak or beech wood, is similar to American bacon.

35a. 🔲 Salt Pork (White Bacon)

Salt pork is a hunk of salt-cured pork belly fat that is traditionally added to Boston baked beans and used to flavor soups and stews. It may be blanched (briefly boiled) to remove excess salt before using.

Tocino

Tocino is Spanish for bacon, but in the Philippines, it refers to cured pork that's been marinated in a sweet red sauce. Look for it in Asian markets.

96. 🔲 Turkey Bacon, Duck Bacon, Veal Bacon, etc.

Many different meats are now used to make bacon-like products, usually with less fat and therefore less rich flavor than pork bacon, and it isn't as crispy when cooked. Veal and turkey bacon are common pork bacon substitutes.

Ventrèche (French Pancetta)

Like bacon, ventrèche—which means belly—is made with pork belly. Like pancetta, it is cured rather than smoked and is meatier than bacon. It can be sliced thin, seared, and used in salads or canapés, or used to wrap lean meats for flavor and moistness.

HAM, COOKED

Ham is a meaty, plump hog's upper hind leg that is commonly cured and smoked; it may be cooked or raw. Fully cooked brine-cured hams are the most common, and, if smoked, they are only lightly smoked. The smoking process not only adds flavor but also aids in aging. The longer the aging, the more flavorful the ham. Some hams are aged up to 2 years. Partially cooked hams must be cooked to be safe for eating. Fully cooked and canned hams can be eaten straight from the package.

Black Forest Ham

This moist, boneless German-style ham made from the top and bottom round only is smoked over pine and fir and coated with beef blood to give it a black exterior. Very lean and tender, it is fully cooked, weighs 4 to 6 pounds (1.8–2.7 kg), and is often sliced thin and used for upscale sandwiches.

Boneless Ham

This ham is easy to carve but is not as flavorful as bone-in ham; it takes longer to cook.

Canadian and Irish Bacon

Canadian bacon is made from the eye of the loin, formed into a rounded shape about 3 inches (7.5 cm) in diameter. More akin to ham, this cut is much leaner than American bacon made from the belly. Irish bacon is similar to Canadian bacon. It is simply called bacon in Britain. American bacon is called streaky bacon in Ireland and Britain.

Canned Ham

This boneless ham is sealed in a can and then cooked. It may consist of a whole piece of meat or pieces pressed together into a form and fused with a gelatin mixture. Less expensive than other types of ham, canned hams are less flavorful and have a higher moisture content, which makes them more perishable. It needs no futher cooking.

City-Cured Ham

Deep rose or pink, moist, and sweet, this type is America's most popular ham. Made by soaking the ham in brine and then boiling or lightly smoking, these hams may be injected—an industrial process used to speed up curing time—and then tumbled, or massaged, to produce a more tender product. City hams are less expensive and milder in flavor than country hams (page 286) because the processing is shorter and simpler.

Half Ham

Whole hams are quite large, so manufacturers often cut them in half. The larger butt half (or butt end), the upper leg, is meatier, fattier, easier to carve, and more expensive. The smaller shank half (shank end, or hock half) is said to be sweeter.

Partially Boned Ham

Partially boned hams have the difficult-to-carve hipbone and/or shank bones removed. Bone-in hams will be juicier, more flavorful, and quicker cooking then boneless.

Picnic Ham (Picnic Shoulder)

This cut from the hog's shoulder is cured and smoked like a ham. Similar to traditional hams, it is less tender and fattier than a true ham and cooks much quicker. Picnic ham is a good, inexpensive choice for soups, spreads, and casseroles.

Prosciutto Cotto (Italian Cooked Ham)

This Italian version of cooked ham is cured in brine with sugar, bay leaves, cloves, cinnamon, and nitrates. It is then rinsed, dried, pressed into a mold, and simmered until fully cooked.

Spiral-Sliced Ham

This popular partially boned ham is precarved in a spiral around the central leg bone and combines good flavor and convenience.

Sweet-Pickle Cured Ham

These hams are cured in seasoned sweet brine (usually a secret recipe of the producer). They may be called "sugar-cured" if brown sugar or molasses is added to the cure.

97. Tasso Ham

Made from lean strips of boneless pork shoulder, tasso ham is marinated in spiced brine, coated with Cajun spices to make a spicy, peppery rind, and heavily smoked. Tasso is often diced and added to beans, vegetables, gumbos, or red beans and rice.

HAM, COUNTRY STYLE

Country-style ham is a specially cured and smoked ham that is traditionally prepared in rural sections of Virginia, Georgia, Tennessee, Kentucky, Vermont, and other states. Country ham refers to a style, rather than a location, and needs long soaking and cooking before eating. Hogs for these hams are generally fed beechnuts, hickory nuts, acorns, and fruit to produce more flavorful and tender meat. They are dry-cured in salt, smoked over fragrant hardwoods, and aged at least six months. These hams are meant to be cooked before eating.

Irish Ham
Belfast is famous for its pickled hams, which get their unique flavor from smoking over peat fires. This ham must be prepared like American country ham before eating.

98. Smithfield Ham
According to the 1926 Statute passed by the General Assembly of Virginia, "Genuine Smithfield hams [are those] cut from the carcasses of peanut-fed hogs, raised in the peanut-belt of the State of Virginia or the State of North Carolina, and which are cured, treated, smoked, and processed in the town of Smithfield, in the State of Virginia." Considered a gourmet's choice, these hams are rather expensive with deep red meat that is dry, with a pungent flavor.

York Ham (Wet-Cured Ham)
This mild-flavored ham originally from York, England, has delicate pink meat. In England, it is traditionally served with Madeira sauce.

HAM, UNCOOKED EUROPEAN STYLE

Uncooked European-style hams are world-famed dry-cured hams. They are similar to American country hams in that they are heavily cured and then air-dried. However, these hams are cured in a way that makes them safe to eat without any further preparation.

Ardennes Ham (Jambon d'Ardennes)
This is an air-dried ham similar to prosciutto that comes from the Ardennes woods in Belgium. These hams are manually dry-salted with sea salt, juniper berries, thyme, and coriander, smoked over beech and oak till dark brown, and then long-aged to acquire full-bodied flavor and soft texture. Every ham has a yellow-numbered leaden seal as a guarantee of quality and origin.

Bauerschinken

This German-style dry-cured ham is made from the top round that is dipped in caramel and double cold smoked. Quite lean, it is dark red in color with a rich smoky taste.

Bayonne Ham (Jambon de Bayonne)

This mildly smoked, boneless ham comes from Bayonne, the capital of the French Basque country. It is salted using local sea salt and then dried in that region for at least 7 months so that it develops its characteristic aroma and becomes tender. When sliced thinly, it melts in the mouth and has a delicate, slightly salty taste.

99a–b. 📷 **Capocollo**

Originating in the southern Italian province of Calabria, this spicy dry-cured pork shoulder can take up to 3 months to cure. The Italian-government-controlled product is called "Capocollo di Calabria." When prepared without hot pepper it is called "sweet."

Chinese Ham (Yunnan Ham, Xuanwei Ham)

Chinese dry-cured hams produced in China's western provinces of Yunnan and Hunan are world famous. They are extremely popular in China, although they are not permitted to be imported into the United States. Smithfield ham is the closest substitute.

77b. 📷 **Coppa**

This cylindrical Italian dry-cured salami is made of pork neck flavored with dry white wine and features red meat flecked with pinkish white. It is a labor-intensive, time-consuming sausage to make, which gives it a high price.

Culatello

Culatello is one of the most prized and expensive cured meats in Italy. It is produced in a small area around Parma. An entire hind leg of pork is boned and rubbed with salt, herbs, and spices, then wrapped in a layer of fresh pork fat and stuffed into a natural casing. It is aged for at least 1 year, then soaked in white wine for a few days. It has an unmistakable, intense scent, sweet, delicate taste, and distinctive soft texture. The meat is uniformly red and speckled with pieces of white fat.

Jamón Iberico

This artisanal ham is dry-cured and accounts for only 5 percent of Spain's hams.

100. 📷 Lachsschinken

The luxurious lachsschinken is a cured and cold-smoked center-cut boneless loin of pork, rolled in a thin layer of fat for tenderness and moisture. It is named for its similarity to smoked salmon (lachs, or lox).

Prosciutto

Prosciutto is an Italian delicacy, both bone-in and boneless, cured by salting a pork leg and then air-drying it for 1 year or more. Italian prosciutto marked for export to the United States must be aged an extra 100 days to meet American specifications. Italian-style prosciutto is also produced in North America.

Prosciutto di Capriolo (Roe Buck Prosciutto)

This artisanal specialty, also called violino (violin) because of its shape, is a deer's leg seasoned with salt, pepper, garlic, and peperoncino and then aged for about 50 days. It is usually thinly sliced and served with olive oil, lemon, salt, and pepper.

Prosciutto di Cinghiale

Prosciutto di cinghiale, Italian wild boar prosciutto, is processed like prosciutto, but the skin is kept on so that the ham absorbs salt and spices only through the inner side of the leg. It will be displayed with its dark gray fur still attached. This lean ham has a rich and intense flavor of the forest and is not overly salty. It is not available in America.

101. 📷 Prosciutto di Oca, Prosciutto di Anatra

There is a tradition among Italian Jews to produce prosciutto from goose (*oca*) or duck (*anatra*) breast, because of the prohibition against eating pork. These "hams" are dry-cured and air-dried in a similar manner to prosciutto but are ready much quicker.

102. 📷 Prosciutto di Parma

The world-famous prosciutto di Parma is made from the legs of pigs that have fed on the whey left over from making Parmigiano Reggiano cheese. The Consortio del Prosciutto di Parma carefully controls the entire production process in the designated region. Fairly round in shape, Parma prosciutto is cut with a short shank and may be identified by the trademark used by the consortium: a ducal crown.

Prosciutto di San Daniele

The origins of prosciutto di San Daniele, from the area north of Venice, go back to

Celtic-Roman times. It is characterized by its flat guitar shape and dark red color. It has a pronounced aroma, a sweet and delicate flavor, and an unmistakable aftertaste.

Schinkenspeck

This German specialty from the Black Forest is lean pork cut from the bottom round with a thin layer of fat on one side. It is dry-cured, dipped in caramel, and heavily smoked. It's normally sliced paper-thin and served cold.

Serrano Ham

This violin-shaped, dry-cured ham is omnipresent in Spain. Like prosciutto, it's cured with salt and then air-dried for a long period of time. It's not meant to be cooked and is usually cut into paper-thin slices. This term refers only to hams of white pig breeds made in the mountainous southwest of Spain.

103. ⬚ Westphalian Ham (Westfalischer Schinken)

Made in the Westphalia forest of Germany from pigs fed with acorns, this high-priced choice ham is cured and then slowly smoked over beech and juniper wood. A deep brown, dense ham, it's usually sliced thin and eaten without further cooking.

CURED MEATS

These other cured meats are not sausages or ham; they can come from different animals, can be specially cured, or are otherwise prepared.

104. ⬚ Bresaola and Bünderfleisch

Bresaola, a specialty of the Valtellina in Italy's Alps, is beef round cured with salt and spices and air-cured. Bresaola comes in a thick block of deep red, dense meat that is moist and delicate with a faintly musty bouquet. Though similar, the Swiss version, bünderfleisch, is saltier and denser. Both bresaola and bünderfleisch are completely lean. Bresaola is sliced paper-thin and dressed with olive oil and lemon.

105c. ⬚ Chipped Dried Beef

Made from cured, smoked, dehydrated, and thinly sliced beef round, it is available in cans, jars, and vacuum packages. Mix with cream sauce to make creamed chipped beef.

106. Confit

Confit, a specialty of Gascony, France, is an ancient method of preserving meat (usually goose, duck, rabbit, or pork), especially tougher cuts such as gizzards and legs. The meat is salted—sometimes spices are added—drained, and cooked slowly in its own fat. It is then cooled, packed into a container, and covered with its cooking fat (for sealing and preserving) and ripened for several weeks. If kept covered by fat, confit can be refrigerated up to 6 months. To eat confit, wipe off the excess fat and brown slowly in a skillet till crispy. (Restaurants often deep-fry confit to get it to crisp up quickly.)

Corned Beef

Corned beef gets its name from Anglo-Saxon times when meat was dry-cured in coarse "corns" of salt, although today they are usually brined (with the addition of spices like mustard seed, peppercorns, and bay leaf). Corned beef is associated with Irish and British cookery, and also with Jewish deli fare. Because it is made from less-tender cuts of beef, especially brisket, it requires long, moist cooking. Because nitrate is used in the curing, corned beef may still be pink after cooking. Uncooked corned beef sold in a pouch complete with pickling spices will keep 5 to 7 days refrigerated, unopened. After cooking, corned beef may be refrigerated for 3 to 4 days.

107. Cracklings

Cracklings are small bits of pork fat cooked until the fat melts away and the remaining tissue crisps. They are eaten like potato chips in North and South America.

Creole Pickled Pork (Pickled Pork, Pickle Meat)

This Louisiana specialty is made of fresh ham hocks or boneless pork butt pickled with spices and vinegar. The quintessential seasoning meat for red beans and rice, pickle meat is hard to find outside of Louisiana, but it is fairly easy to make.

Guanciale

Guanciale is a Roman specialty of pork jowl and cheek cured with salt, pepper, spices, sugar, and saltpeter and then air-dried. High in fat and full of gelatinous connective tissue, guanciale is used to enrich and flavor pasta sauces.

105a. Jerky

Jerky comes from the Spanish word *charque* and is thin strips of meat that are salted and air-dried. Though beef jerky is most common, it may be made from beef, venison, ostrich, buffalo, salmon, and other game. Native Americans used this drying process to preserve meats and fish for winter or traveling. One pound (450 g) of meat or poultry will produce 4 ounces (115 g) of jerky. Because most of the moisture has been removed, jerky can be stored without refrigeration, making it a lightweight, flavorful, and protein-rich favorite of campers. Commercially packaged jerky will keep one year at room temperature; homemade is more perishable.

Kishke (Derma, Stuffed Derma)

This Jewish specialty consists of beef intestines stuffed with matzo meal, onion, and suet or chicken fat. It may be baked with onions or added to long-cooked dishes.

108. Pastrami (Bastirma, Basturma, Pastirma, and Others)

Pastrami is a Romanian specialty adapted from Turkish basturma—spiced, pressed, and dried meat—brought to the United States by Jewish immigrants in the late nineteenth century. Originally made with goose, pastrami is now commonly made with a fatty cut of beef brisket or plate. The meat is dry-cured with kosher salt, garlic, peppercorns, cinnamon, red pepper, cloves, allspice, and coriander, smoked, and steamed.

Qadid (Kedid)

A type of preserved lamb from Algeria and Tunisia, qadid is rubbed with salt and garlic and left to dry for 1 day. It is then seasoned with salt, harissa (Tunisian hot pepper, garlic, and caraway paste), coriander seed, and mint. It is sun-dried for several days, cut up and simmered in olive oil, and then stored in glass or earthenware jars with the oil.

109. Smoked Ham Hocks

Hocks are usually cured and smoked and cut into 2- to 3-inch (5–7.5 cm) lengths. They are added to Southern stews to lend smoky flavor and rich, gelatinous consistency.

Smoked Hog Jowl

The jowl (pronounced "jole" in the American South) is the hog's cheek, which is cut into squares then cured and smoked. It is commonly available in the South. Tightly wrapped, jowl can be kept refrigerated 2 weeks. It's used to flavor stews and beans, and it can be cut into thin strips and fried like bacon.

110. Smoked Pork Loin

A whole hot-smoked pork loin may be gently heated whole, cut into bone-in or boneless chops, or simmered with sauerkraut or beans.

111. **Smoked Pork Neck Bones**

Smoked, meaty neck bones of pork are a specialty in the American South that are often added to beans, slow-cooked greens, and soup.

112. **Smoked Poultry**

Duck, goose, pheasant, turkey, and other game birds are often hot-smoked for preserving and for flavor. In this method, the smoking also cooks the meat, so that it is ready to eat. Chinese smoked duck is flavored with tea leaves and camphor. Smoked turkey legs or wings are an excellent substitute for ham hocks.

Soujouk (Yershig, Sujuk, and Others)

This long thin, spicy beef sausage with a complex, earthy flavor is of Armenian origin. It is made from salted beef meat mixed with fat, ground with garlic, black and red pepper, cumin, and Lebanese seven-spice mixture and then dried.

105b. **Tasajo**

Tasajo is very dry, heavily salted beef sold in small blocks. Found throughout Central and South America, it is a specialty of Brazil. Add it to dishes such as beans and stew.

Meat Roasting Charts

General Roasting Tips:

- Allow small cuts to rest at room temperature for 1 hour (30 minutes in hot weather) before cooking; allow large cuts to rest at room temperature 2 hours (1 hour in hot weather).

- Season meat on all sides before roasting, including inside birds.

- Use a roasting pan that is just large enough to hold the meat, so bare areas don't smoke and burn.

- Roast fat side up.

- Use an instant-read thermometer to check doneness. Insert the thermometer into the thickest part of the roast to check temperature.

- For roasts, remove from the oven and allow the meat to rest, covered loosely with foil, from 15 minutes (for smaller roasts) to as long as 30 minutes (for large roasts).

Beef or Lamb Steaks

Doneness	Description	Chef's Ideal Temp
Extra-rare (blue, Pittsburgh)	Center soft and raw; outside bright red and juicy	115–120°F/46–49°C
Rare	Red with cold, soft center	125–130°F/52–55°C
Medium-rare	Red with warm, somewhat firm center	130–140°F/55–60°C
Medium	Pink and firm throughout	140–150°F/60–65°C
Medium-well	Pink line in center, quite firm	150–155°F/65–69°C
Well-done	Gray-brown throughout and completely firm	160–165°F/71–74°C

Beef or Lamb Roasts

Doneness	Description	Cook	Chef's Ideal Temp
Rare	Red with cold, soft center	125°F/52°C	125–130°F/52–55°C
Medium-rare	Red with warm, somewhat firm center	130°F/55°C	135–140°F/57–60°C
Medium	Pink and firm throughout	135°F/57°C	140–150°F/60–65°C
Medium-well	Pink line in center, quite firm	145°F/63°C	150–155°F/65–69°C
Well-done	Gray-brown throughout and completely firm	155°F/69°C	160–165°F/71–74°C

Veal Chops

Doneness	Description	Chef's Ideal Temp
Medium-rare	Pink with warm center	130–140°F/58–61°C
Medium	Pink throughout	140–150°F/61–65°C
Medium-well	Slight pink in center	150–155°F/65°C
Well-done	Beige-pink throughout	160–165°F/71–74°C

Veal Roasts

Doneness	Description	Cook	Chef's Ideal Temp
Medium-rare	Pink with warm center	130°F/55°C	135–140°F/57–60°C
Medium	Pink throughout	140°F/60°C	150°F/65°C
Medium-well	Slight pink in center	150°F/65°C	160°F/71°C
Well-done	Beige-pink throughout	160°F/71°C	170°F/77°C

Pork Chops

Doneness	Description	Chef's Ideal Temp
Medium	Pink throughout	155°F/69°C
Medium-well	Slightly pink in center	160°F/71°C
Well-done	Beige-pink throughout	165°F/74°C

Pork Roasts

Doneness	Description	Cook	Chef's Ideal Temp
Medium	Pink throughout	150°F/66°C	155°F/69°C
Medium-well	Slightly pink in center	155°F/69°C	160°F/71°C
Well-done	Beige-pink throughout	160°F/71°C	165°F/74°C

Poultry and Rabbit

Doneness	Description	Cook	Chef's Ideal Temp
Rabbit	Opaque throughout	155–160°F/69–71°C	160°F/71°C
Poultry (white meat)	Opaque throughout	160°F/71°C	165°F/74°C
Poultry (dark meat)	Clear juices in leg; leg jiggles easily in joint	165°F/74°C	170°F/77°C
Whole bird	Clear juices in leg; leg jiggles easily in joint	165°F/74°C	170°F/77°C

Index

Numbers in **bold** (for example, **18**) are meat numbers, and can be used to locate meat in the photograph section. All other numbers are page numbers.

A

alligator, **63**, 233–35
American lamb chops, **48d**
American rack of lamb, **48e**
American whole lamb rib, **48f**
andouille sausage, **75**, 149, 271
antelope, 263
Ardennes ham, 287
arm chops (lamb), 159
arm roast
    beef, 21–22
    veal, 98
armadillo, 235–37
Australian rack of lamb, **48c**

B

baby back ribs (pork), **32a**, 111–12
back ribs (beef), 45
bacon, **93**, 283–84
    Canadian, 285
    Gypsy, **94**, 283
    Irish, 285
    Italian, **95**, 284
    turkey, duck, veal, etc., **96**, 284
    white, 284
ball tip (beef), 14
ball tip steak (beef), 14
baloney. *See* bologna
banger, **86**, 276
barbecue ribs
    lamb, **45**, 156–58
    pork, **32a–d**, 111–14
    See also ribs; short ribs
barding, 119, 283

basturma, **108**
bauerschinken, 288
bauerwurst, 276
Bayonne ham, 288
bear, 237–39
bear salami, **84**, 274
beaver, 239–42
beccafico, 212–14
beef, 1–75
    arm roast, 21–22
    beef rolls, **1**, 7–8
    bones and marrow, **2**, 9–11
    bottom round, 11–14
    bottom sirloin butt, 14–16
    brains, 68, 71
    brisket, **3**, 5, 17–18
    butt, 14–16, **22**, 64–65
    cheeks, 19–20
    chipped dried, **105c**, 291
    chuck, 4
    chuck roasts and steaks, **4a–b**, 21–24
    corned, 291
    coulotte, **5**, 25–26
    diced, 39
    export rib, **10c**
    flank, 5–6
    flank steak, **6**, 27–28
    ground beef and cube steak, **7a**, 29–31
    hanging tender, **8**, 31–33
    heart, 69, 71–72
    kidneys, 69, 72
    knuckle, 33–35
    liver, 69, 72–73
    oxtail, **9**, 35–37

primal cuts, 4–6
rib, **10a–e**, 37–40
rump, **11**, 12, 41–42
shank, **12**, 42–44
short ribs, **13a–g**, 45–47
shoulder center, **14**, 47–48
shoulder tender, **15**, 49–50
skirt steak, **16**, 51–52
stew meat, 12, **13d**
strip loin, **17a–f**, 53–55
T-bone and porterhouse steaks, **18a–b**, 55–56
tenderloin, **19a–c**, 57–59
testicles, 70, 73–74
tongue, 70, 74
top blade steak, **20**, 60–61
top round, **21a–b**, 61–63
top sirloin butt, **22**, 64–65
tri-tip, **23**, 66–68
variety meats and fat, **24**, 68–75
beef jerky, **105a**, 291–92
beef rolls, **1**, 7–8
beefalo, 242–45
beer salami, 269
belly (pork), 33, 109, 115–16
bierwurst, 269
birds. *See* poultry and game birds
bison, **64a–b**, 242–45
Black Forest ham, 285
blade chops (lamb), 159
blade end loin roast (pork), 132
blade end ribs (pork), 112
blade meat (beef), 38
blade roast
    beef, 21
    veal, 98
blade steak
    pork, 141
    veal, 98
blood sausage, 277

blood tongue sausage, **74**, 271
blutwurst, **74**, 271
boar. *See* wild boar
bockwurst, **87c**, 277
boerewors, 277
bolar roast (beef), **4a**, 22
bologna, 269
    ham, 270
    Lebanon, 271
    mortadella di, **72**, 270
    ring, 270
bone-in
    leg of lamb, 163
    shoulder end chop, **34b**
boneless cuts
    beef shank, Korean style, **12**
    center-cut rib chop, **34e**
    chicken thigh, **53c**
    ham, 285
    lamb loin, double, 166–67
    leg, **46a**
    picnic shoulder, 141
    pork loin, double, 132–33
    rabbit loin, **66c**
    rib-eye, **10a–b**
    rolled chuck roast, 22
    short ribs, **13f**
    veal loin eye, 89
    wild boar shoulder, **69**
bones and marrow (beef), **2**, 9–11
Boston butt (pork), **41**, 117, 140
boterhamworst, 277
bottom round
    beef, 11–14
    veal, **26a**, 86
bottom sirloin butt, 14–16
boudin blanc, **88**, 277
boy scout sausage, 272
brains
    beef, 68, 71

lamb, 183, 185
veal, **31a**, 101–102, 104
See also variety meats
bratwurst, **87a**, 277
braunschweiger, **70b**, 269
breakfast sausage, 277–78
breaks (pork), 112–13
breast
    chicken, **53g**
    duck, **54c**
    lamb, **45**, 154, 156–58
    veal, 79–81
bresaola, **104**
brisket (beef), **3**, 5, 17–18
brisket bones, pork, 112–13
broiler-fryer (chicken), 191
Brunswick stew, 261–62
butifarra, 278
butt
    beef, 14–16, **22**, 64–65
    lamb, **51**, 177–79
    pork, **41**, 117, 140
    veal, 100
butterflied leg (lamb), 164

C

cacciatore, **76a**, 272
Cajun andouille sausage, **75**, 271
calabrese sausage, **77c**, 272
Canadian bacon, 285
cap (beef), 38
capocollo, **99a–b**, 288
capon, 190
caribou, 263
carnatzlach, 278
casings (pork), 148
caul, **35d**, 119–20, 122
center cuts
    blade roast (beef), 22
    leg (veal), 85

pork loin roast, 132
    rib (pork), 117
cervelas de Lyon, 278
cervelat, **78a**, 272
chaurice, 278
cheeks
    beef, 19–20
    veal, **31b**, 102
chevon (goat), whole baby, **65**
chicken, **53a–i**, 189–95
    Asian-style hacked thigh, **53h**
    black, 190
    bone-in thigh, **53d**
    boneless thigh, **53c**
    breasts, **53g**, 194
    broiler-fryer, 191
    cutlet, **53i**
    free-range, 189
    half, **53f**
    innards, 195
    kosher, 189
    legs and thighs, 194
    natural, 189
    poussin, **53b**
    Rock Cornish hen, **53a**, 190–91
    whole, 193–94
    wings, **53e**
chicken-fried steak, 13–14
chili meat, 39
Chinese dried sausage, **82**, 273
Chinese ham, 288
chipolata sausage, 278
chipped dried beef, **105c**, 291
chitterlings, 148–49, 150
chops
    lamb, **47a**, **47c–e**, **48a**, **48d**,
      50a,158–61
    pork, **34a–e**, 116–19
    round bone (lamb), 159
    veal, **27b**, 85, 89

chorizo sausage
    Mexican, **79a–b**, 278–79
    Spanish, **79c**, 272
chouriço, 272
chuck
    beef, 4
    veal, 77–78
chuck ribs (beef), 45
chuck roasts and steaks (beef), **4a–b**,
21–24
chuck tender
    beef, 21
    veal, 98
chuckwagon roast (beef), 21
coarse holsteiner, **76b**
cocktail wieners, 279
confit, **106**, 291
coppa, **77b**, 288
corned beef, 291
Cornish game hens, **53a**, 190–91
cotechino, 279
coulotte, **5**, 25–26
country-style ribs (pork), **32b**, 112
cowboy steak, **10d**, 38
cracklings, **107**, 291
Creole pickled pork, 291
csabai, 272
cserkesz, 272
cube steak, 29–31
cubes for stew (veal), 98
culatello, 288
Cumberland sausage, 279
cured meats, 290–93
    See also sausage and cured meats
cured sausages, 271–76
    See also sausage and cured meats
cushion roast (lamb), 175
cutlets
    chicken, **53i**
    lamb, 164

D
Debrecini, 273
deckle (beef), 38
deer, **68a**, 263
demi-glace, veal, 92–93
Denver ribs (lamb), 156
derma, 292
domesticated meats. *See* game and
    other domesticated meats
donkey, 249–51
dove. *See* pigeon, dove, and wood pigeon
duck, **54a–d**, 195–201
    breast, **54c**, 199
    confit, **106**
    foie gras, **55a–b**, 201–204
    liver, heart, gizzard, neck, **54a**
    Moulard, 196
    Muscovy, **54c–d**, 197
    Pekin, **54b**
    whole roast, 200

E
E. Coli, 3
ears (pork), 126–28
elk, North American, 263
elk pizzle, **68c**
elk stew meat, **68b**
emu, 214–16
English royal chop (lamb), 160
entrecôte, 38
Euro chicken breast, **53g**
European style ham, 287–90
eye of round
    beef, 11
    veal, **26a**, **26d**

F
fat (pork), **35a–d**, 119–23
fatback (pork), **35b**, 120, 122
feet
    pork, **36**, 123–24

veal, 81–83
finocchiona, 273
flank (beef), 5–6
flank steak (beef), **6**, 27–28
flap (beef), 15
flap steak (beef), 14
flat (beef), 11
flatbone riblets (pork), 112
flatiron steak, **20**
foie gras (duck and goose), **55a–b**, 201–4
foreleg (lamb), 154
frankfurters, Vienna-style, 282
French andouille sausage, 271
French pancetta, 284
Frenched 9-rib prime rack, **39b**
Frenched center-cut rib chop, **34d**

G

game and other domesticated meats,
    232–67
    alligator, **63**, 233–35
    armadillo, 235–37
    bear, 237–39
    beaver, 239–42
    bison and beefalo, **64a–b**, 242–45
    goat and kid, **65**, 245–47
    hare, 247–49
    horse and donkey, 249–51
    muskrat, 251–53
    opossum, 253–55
    rabbit, **66a–c**, 255–57
    raccoon, 257–59
    rattlesnake, **67**, 259–60
    squirrel, 260–62
    venison, **68a–c**, 262–65
    wild boar, **69**, 265–67
game birds. *See* poultry and game birds
garlic sausage, **87b**, 280
gelbwurst, 269
Genoa salami, 274

gizzard (duck), **54a**
goat and kid, **65**, 245–47
goetta, 282
goose, **56**, 204–207
    foie gras, 201–204
    liver pate, **70a**, 269
ground meat
    beef, **7a**, 29–31
    lamb, **7c**, 161–63
    pork, **7d**, 124–26
    veal, **7b**, 83–84
grouse, 207–10
guanciale, 291
guinea fowl, **57**, 210–12
Gypsy bacon, **94**, 283
Gypsy salami, **80a**, 273
Gyulai, 273

H

haggis, 279
ham, 130–31
    Ardennes, 287
    Bayonne, 288
    Black Forest, 285
    canned, 285
    Chinese, 288
    city-cured, 285
    cooked, 284–86
    country style, 286–87
    half, 285
    Irish, 287
    Italian cooked, 286
    partially boned, 286
    serrano, 290
    Smithfield, **98**, 287
    spiral-sliced, 286
    sweet-pickle cured, 286
    tasso, **97**, 286
    uncooked European style, 287–90
    Westphalian, **103**, 290

York, 287
ham bologna, 270
ham hocks, smoked, **109**, 292
hamburgers (beef), 30
hanging tender, **8**, 31–33
hare, 247–49
head cheese, **91a**, 127–28, 282
head (pork), 126–28
head sausage, **85a–b**, 276
heart
    beef, 69, 71–72
    duck, **54a**
    pork, 149, 150
    veal, **31c**, 102, 104
    See also variety meats
heel
    beef, 12
    veal, 86
hock (pork), 137–40
holsteiner, coarse, **76b**, 272
honeycomb tripe, **24**
horse, 249–51
hot dogs, **89**, 279, 280
Hungarian salami, **78b**
hunter salame, **76a**, 272

I
inside round (pork), 129
Irish bacon, 285
Irish ham, 287
Italian bacon, **95**, 284
Italian cooked ham, 286
Italian mortadella di bologna, **72**
Italian sausage, 279

J
jagdwurst, 273
Jamaican-style curry goat, 246–47
jamón iberico, 288
Japanese shabu-shabu, **10e**

jerky, **105a**, 291–92
Jewish style savory calf's-foot jelly, 82
jowl
    pork, 126–28
    smoked hog, 292

K
kabobs
    beef, 12
    lamb, 175–76
    veal cubes, 98
Kansas City–style ribs (pork), 113
kedid, 292
kid (goat), 245–47
kidney chop, veal, 89
kidneys
    beef, 69, 72
    lamb, **47a**, 183, 185
    pork, 149, 150–51
    veal, **31d**, 102, 105
kielbasa, **71**, 269
kishke, 292
knackwurst, **87b**, 280
knuckle
    beef, 33–35
    pork, 129
    veal, **26b**, 85–86
knuckle bones (veal), 91–93
kolbasa, **71**, 269
kosher meat
    chickens, 189
    hot dogs, **89**, 280
    salami, 273
krakauer, 270

L
lachsschinken, **100**, 289
lamb, 153–87
    American leg, 164
    arm chops, 159

bottom roast, 164
brains, 183, 185
breast and barbecue ribs, **45**, 154, 156–58
butt, **51**, 177–79
center roast, 164
chops, **47a**, **47c–e**, **48a**, **48d**, **50a**, 158–61
Denver ribs, 156
English royal chop, 160
ground, **7c**, 161–63
for kabobs, 175–76
kidneys, **47a**, 183, 185
leg, **46a–b**, 163–66
liver, 183, 185
loin, **47a–e**, 154–55, 166–68
neck, 168–70
primals, 154–55
rack, **48a–g**, 155, 170–72
ribs, 158
saddle of, 166
shank, **49a–c**, 163, 172–74
shoulder, **50a–c**, 175–77
sirloin, **51**, 177–79
stew meat, **50c**, 176
suckling, 179–81
T-bone chop, **47d**
tenderloin, **52**, 181–82
testicles, 184, 186
tongue, 184, 186–87
variety meats, 183–87
landjager, **81**, 273
lap cheong, **82**, 273
lard (pork), **35c**, 120, 122
lardo, 283–84
leberkäse, 270
leg
  lamb, **46a–b**, 154, 163–66
  pork, **37**, 110, 128–31
  veal, **26a–h**, 78, 85–88

linguiça, 280
liver
  beef, 69, 72–73
  duck, **54a**
  lamb, 183, 185
  pork, 149, 151
  rabbit, **66b**
  sausage, 270
  veal, **31e**, 102, 105–106
  See also variety meats
liver, beef, and tongue sausage, 281
liver pate, goose, **70b**, 269
liverwurst, 270
loafs, cooked and jellied, 282–83
loin
  lamb, **47a–e**, 154–55, 166–68
  pork, **38a–b**, 110, 110, 117–18, 132–34, 292
  rabbit, boneless, **66c**
  veal, **27a–c**, 78, 88–90
loin chops
  lamb, 159–60
  pork, 117
  veal, 90
  See also chops
longaniza, 280
luganega, 280

M
Mad Cow Disease, 3
marrow
  beef, **2**, 9–11
  veal, **28**, 91–93
meatballs, veal, 84
medallions (veal), 86
merguez sausage, **90**, 281
mettwurst, 281
Mexican chorizo sausage, **79a–b**, 278–79
Milano salami, 274
mirkâs, **90**, 281

moose, 263
mortadella di bologna, **72**, 270
Moulard duck, 196
Muscovy duck, **54c–d**, 197
muskrat, 251–53

N

Neapolitan salame, **77a**, 275
neck
    duck, **54a**
    lamb, 168–70
neck bones (pork), **111**, 134–35, 293
nevskaya, **80b**, 274
New Zealand lollipop chops, **48a**
New Zealand rack
    lamb, **48b**
    veal, **29f**
noisette (lamb), 167

O

olive loaf, 282
opossum, 253–55
ortolan, 212–14
osso buco
    pork, **40**
    veal, **30b**
ostrich, **58a–b**, 214–16
outside round (pork), 129–30
oxtail, **9**, 35–37

P

pancetta, **95**, 281, 284
partridge, 217–19
pate, goose liver, **70b**, 269
Pekin duck, 197
pepper loaf, 283
pepperoni, **83**, 274
petcha, 82
pheasant, **59a–b**, 219–21
pickled pork, Creole, 291

picnic cushion, 141
picnic ham/shoulder, 141, 286
pigeon, dove, and wood pigeon, **60**, 221–23
pinkelwurst, 281
plate (beef), 5
plate ribs (beef), 45
plockwurst, **84**, 274
Polish sausage, **71**, 269
pork, 108–52
    5- or 7-rib roast, 141
    barbecue ribs, **32a–d**, 111–14
    belly, **33**, 109, 115–16
    brisket bones, 112–13
    butt, **41**, 117, 140
    chops, **34a–e**, 116–19
    country-style ribs, **32b**, 112
    fat, **35a–d**, 119–23
    feet, **36**, 123–24
    flatbone riblets, 112
    ground, **7d**, 124–26
    head, jowl, ear, and tail, 126–28
    heart, 149, 150
    jowl, 126–28
    kidneys, 149, 150–51
    knuckle, 129
    leg, **37**, 128–31
    liver, 149, 151
    loin, **38a–b**, 110, **110**, 117–18, 132–34, 292
    neck bones, **111**, 134–35, 293
    osso buco, **40**
    outside round, 129–30
    pickled, 291
    primals, 109–10
    rack, **39a–b**, 135–37
    shank and hock, **40**, 137–40
    shoulder, **41**, 140–42
    sirloin, 143–44
    steak, 141–42

suckling pig, **42**, 144–46
    tenderloin, **43**, 146–48
    tongue, 149, 152
    variety meats, **44**, 148–52
pork tip, 129
porterhouse chops (veal), **27b**
porterhouse steaks
    beef, **18b**, 55–56
    veal, 89
pot roast, 13, 21, 23–24
potato korv, 281
poultry and game birds, 188–231
    chicken, **53a–i**, 189–95
    duck, **54a–d**, 195–201
    foie gras (duck and goose), **55a–b**, 201–204
    goose, **56**, 204–207
    grouse, 207–10
    guinea fowl, **57**, 210–12
    ortolan and beccafico, 212–14
    ostrich, emu, and rhea, **58a–b**, 214–16
    partridge, 217–19
    pheasant, **59a–b**, 219–21
    pigeon, dove, and wood pigeon, **60**, 221–23
    quail, **61**, 224–26
    smoked, 293
    turkey, **62a–c**, 226–28
    woodcock, 229–31
poussin, 190
primals
    beef, 4–6
    lamb, 154–55
    pork, 109–10
    veal, 77–78
pronghorn, 263–64
prosciutto, 289
prosciutto cotto, 286
prosciutto di anatra, 289

prosciutto di capriolo, 289
prosciutto di cinghiale, 289
prosciutto di oca, **101**, 289
prosciutto di Parma, **102**, 289
prosciutto di San Daniele, 289–90

Q
qadid, 292
quail, **61**, 224–26

R
rabbit, **66a–c**, 255–57
raccoon, 257–59
rack
    crown roast, **39a**
    hotel, **29d**
    lamb, **48a–g**, 155, 170–72
    pork, **39a–b**, 135–37
    veal, **29f**, 78
rattlesnake, **67**, 259–60
rear leg shanks (pork), 130
rhea, 214–16
rib chops
    lamb, 159
    pork, **34d–e**, 117
    veal, **29e**
    See also chops
rib-eye, **10e**
rib-eye lip muscle (beef), 38
rib lifter (beef), 38
rib roast
    beef, 38
    pork, 141
rib steak (beef), 38
rib tips (pork), 112–13
riblets
    flatbone (pork), 112
    lamb, **45**, 156
ribs
    baby back (pork), **32a**, 111–12

back (beef), 45
barbecue cut (pork), 113
beef, 4, **10a–e**, 37–40, 45
country-style (pork), **32b**, 112
Denver (lamb), 156
Kansas City–style (pork), 113
lamb, 158
plate (beef), 45
St. Louis–style, **32d**, 112
veal, **29a–f**, 79–81, 93–95
See also barbecue ribs; short ribs
ringwurst, 270
roaster (chicken), 191
roasts
arm, 21–22, 98
blade, 21, 98, 132
bolar (beef), **4a**, 22
chuck roasts and steaks, **4a–b**, 21–24
crown roast, **39a**
cushion (lamb), 175
duck, 200
lamb, 164, 175
pork loin roast, 132
rib, 38, 141
rump, **11**
shank half roast (veal), 85
shoulder roast (lamb), 175
sirloin end roast (pork), 133
sirloin roast (veal), 85
veal, 98
Rock Cornish game hens, **53a**, 190–91
roe buck prosciutto, 289
rosette de Lyon, 274
round
beef, 5
pork, 129–30
veal, **26a**
round bone chops (lamb), 159
royal rib (beef), 45
rump (beef), **11**, 12, 41–42
Russian nevskaya, **80b**, 274

S
saddle of lamb, 166
salame brianza, 274
salame da sugo, 281
salame di Genoa, 274
salame di Milano, 274
salame d'la duja, 274
salame Napoletano, **77a**, 275
salamelle, 281
salami, 275
bear, **84**, 274
beer, 269
with fennel seeds, 273
Genoa, 274
Gypsy, **80a**, 273
Hungarian, **78b**
hunter, **76a**, 272
kosher, 273
Milano, 274
Neapolitan, **77a**, 275
preserved, 274
wild boar, 276
salchicha, 281
salcisson, 275
salt pork, **35a**, 120, 122–23, 284
Saratoga roll (lamb), 175
saucisson, 275
saucisson de Lyon, 275
saucisson de toulouse, **73b**, 270
saucisson en croute, **73a**, 270
sausage
andouille, Cajun, **75**, 271
andouille, French, 271
blood, 277
boy scout, 272
breakfast, 277–78
calabrese, **77c**, 272
casings, **44**
Chinese dried, **82**, 273
chipolata, 278
cooked, 269–71

Cumberland, 279
cured, 271–76
fresh, 276–82
garlic, **87b**, 280
head, **85a–b**, 276
Italian, 279
liver, 270
liver, beef, and tongue, 281
merguez, **90**, 281
Polish, **71**, 269
rolled in pancetta, 281
summer, **78a**, 272
tongue, 283
Vienna, 282
white, 282
sausage and cured meats, 268–93
bacon, 283–84
cooked sausages, 269–71
cured meats, 290–93
cured sausages, 271–76
fresh sausages, 276–82
ham, cooked, 284–86
ham, country style, 286–87
ham, uncooked European style,
287–90
loafs, cooked and jellied, 282–83
scaloppine (veal), 86, 87–88
schinkenspeck, 290
schinkenwurst, 270
scrapple, **92**, 283
serrano ham, 290
shank
beef, **12**, 42–44
lamb, **49a–c**, 163, 172–74
pork, **40**, 137–40
veal, **30a–b**, 85, 95–97
short leg (lamb), 164
short ribs
Asian style chuck, **13e**
beef, **13a–g**, 45–47

bison, **64b**
blade meat, **13g**
boneless, **13f**
flanken rib, **13c**
plate, **13b**
royal rib, **13a**
stew beef, **13d**
See also barbecue ribs; ribs
short (veal), 100
shoulder
lamb, **50a–c**, 155, 175–77
pork, **41**, 109–10, 140–42
veal, 97–99
wild boar, **69**
shoulder blade chops (pork), **50a**, 117
shoulder center (beef), **14**, 47–48
shoulder chops (lamb), 159
shoulder clod (beef), 22
shoulder roast (lamb), 175
shoulder tender, **15**, 49–50
silverside (beef), 12
sirloin
beef, 4–5, **22**, 64–65
lamb, **51**, 177–79
pork, 133, 143–44
veal, 85
sirloin end roast (pork), 132
skirt steak, **16**, 51–52
Smithfield ham, **98**, 287
smoked meat
chorizo, Spanish, **79c**
ham hocks, **109**, 292
hog jowl, 292
pork loin, **110**, 292
pork neck bones, **111**, 293
poultry, 293
turkey wings, **112**
snouts (pork), 126
sobrasada, 271
soppressata, **85a–b**, 276

soujouk, 293
Spanish smoked chorizo sausage, **79c**
spareribs, **32c**, 112
squab. *See* pigeon, dove, and wood
    pigeon
squirrel, 260–62
St. Louis–style ribs, **32d**, 112
standing rib roast (beef), 38
steak
    ball tip (beef), 14
    blade (pork), 141
    blade (veal), 98
    bone-in tenderloin, **19c**
    chicken-fried, 13–14
    flank (beef), **6**, 27–28
    flap (beef), 14
    flatiron, **20**
    pork, 141–42
    rib (beef), 38
    strip loin (veal), 89
    tenderloin, **19b**
    top blade, **20**, 60–61
    veal, 85
stew, Brunswick, 261–62
stew meat
    beef, 12, **13d**
    elk, **68b**
    lamb, **50c**, 176
    veal, 98
stock (beef), 44
strip loin
    beef, 4, **17a–f**, 53–55
    bison, **64a**
    veal, 89
stuffed hog foreleg, 282
suckling lamb, 179–81
suckling pig, **42**, 144–46
suet (beef), 69–70, 73
summer sausage, **78a**, 272

sweetbreads
    lamb, 183–84, 185–86
    veal, **31f**, 102–103, 106

T
T-bone
    beef, **18a**, 55–56
    lamb chop, **47d**
    veal, 89
tail (pork), 126–28
tasajo, **105b**, 293
tasso ham, **97**, 286
teewurst, 276
tenderloin
    beef, **19a–c**, 57–59
    lamb, **52**, 181–82
    pork, **43**, 146–48
    turkey, **62b**
    veal, 99–101
testicles
    beef, 70, 73–74
    lamb, 184, 186
    See also variety meats
tocino, 284
tongue
    beef, 70, 74
    in gelatin, **91b**
    lamb, 184, 186–87
    pork, 149, 152
    veal, **31g**, 103, 106–107
    See also variety meats
tongue loaf, 283
tongue sausage, 283
top blade steak, **20**, 60–61
top round
    beef, **21a–b**, 61–63
    veal, **26e**, 86
top sirloin butt, **22**, 64–65
tri-tip, **23**, 66–68
tripe (beef), **24**, 70–71, 74

turkey, **62a–c**, 112, 226–28
turkey bacon, **96**, 284

U
under blade roast (beef), 21

V
variety meats
    beef, **24**, 68–75
    lamb, 183–87
    pork, **44**, 148–52
    veal, **31a–g**, 101–107
    See also specific organs
veal, 76–107
    arm roast, 98
    blade roast, 98
    blade steaks, 98
    brains, **31a**, 101–102, 104
    breast, 79–81
    breast and ribs, **25**, 79–81
    butt, 100
    cheeks, **31b**, 102
    chops, **27b**, 85, 89
    chuck tender, 98
    cubes for kabobs/stew, 98
    demi-glace, 92–93
    feet, 81–83
    ground, **7b**, 83–84
    heart, **31c**, 102, 104
    kidney, **31d**, 102, 105
    knuckle, **26b**, 85–86
    leg, **26a–h**, 85–88
    liver, **31e**, 102, 105–106
    loin, **27a–c**, 78, 88–90
    marrow and knuckle bones, **28**, 91–93
    meatballs, 84
    primals, 77–78
    rack, **29f**, 78
    rib, **29a–f**, 93–95
    scaloppine, 86, 87–88
    shank, 30a–b, 85, 95–97
    shoulder, 97–99
    steak, 85
    sweetbreads, **31f**, 102–103, 106
    T-bone, 89
    tenderloin, 99–101
    tongue, **31g**, 103, 106–107
    top round, **26e**, 86
    variety meats, **31a–g**, 101–107
veal osso buco, **30b**
venison, **68a–c**, 262–65
ventrèche, 284
Vienna sausages, 282
Vienna-style frankfurters, 282

W
weisswurst, 282
Westphalian ham, **103**, 290
wet-cured ham, 287
white boudin, **88**, 277
white sausage, 282
wild boar, **69**, 265–67
wild boar salame, 276
wood pigeon. *See* pigeon, dove, and
    wood pigeon
woodcock, 229–31

Y
York ham, 287

Z
zampone, 282
zungenwurst, **74**, 271

Sources

Aidells, Bruce, and Denis Kelly. *The Complete Meat Cookbook*. New York: Houghton Mifflin, 1998.

Cameron, Angus, and Judith Jones. *L. L. Bean Game and Fish Cookbook*. New York: Random House, 1983.

Daguin, Ariane, George Faison, and Johanna Pruess. *D'Artagnan's Glorious Game Cookbook*. Bosto: Little Brown and Company, 1999.

Davidson, Alan. *The Oxford Companion to Food*. Oxford: Oxford University Press, 1999.

Ellis, Merle. *Cutting-Up in the Kitchen*. San Francisco: Chronicle Books, 1975.

Ellis, Merle. *The Great American Meat Book*. New York: Alfred A. Knopf, 1996.

Gerrard, Frank, and F. J. Mallion, eds. *The Complete Book of Meat*. London: Virtue & Company, 1980.

Grigson, Jane. *The Art of Charcuterie*. New York: Alfred A Knopf, 1968.

Henderson, Fergus. *The Whole Beast: Nose to Tail Eating*. New York: Ecco, 2004.

Hibler, Janie. *Wild About Game*. New York: Broadway Books, 1998.

Kinsella, John, and David T. Harvey. *Professional Charcuterie*. New York: John Wiley & Sons, 1996.

Lang, Jennifer, ed. *Larousse Gastronomique*. New York: Crown Publishers, 1988

Nathan, Joan. *Jewish Cooking in America*. New York: Alfred A. Knopf, 1996.

Romans, John, William Costello, Wendell Carlson, Marion Greaser, and Kevin Jones. *The Meat We Eat*. Danville, Illinois: Interstate Publishers, Inc., 2000.

Rombauer, Irma S., Marion Rombauer Becker, and Ethan Becker. *The (All New All Purpose) Joy of Cooking*. New York: Scriber, 1997.

Schlesinger, Chris, and John Willoughby. *How to Cook Meat*. New York: William Morrow, 2000.

Time-Life Books, ed. *Time Life Good Cook Series: Beef and Veal; Variety Meats; Poultry; Lamb; Pork*. Alexandria, Virginia: Time-Life Books, 1978.

Wright, Clarissa Dickson, and Johnny Scott. *Sunday Roast: The Complete Guide to Cooking and Carving*. London: Headline Book Publishing, 2002.

www.aidells.com
www.alligatorfur.com
www.ansi.okstate.edu
www.australian-lamb.com
www.beefitswhatsfordinner.com
www.broadleafgame.com
www.catellibrothers.com
www.citterio-usa.com
www.colemanmeats.com
www.dangelobros.com
www.dartagnan.com
www.exoticmeats.com
www.fsis.usda.gov/OA/pubs/
    consumerpubs.htm#80
www.hormel.com

www.hudsonvalleyfoiegras.com
www.kobe-beef.com
www.lambchef.com
www.lobels.com
www.nimanranch.com
www.nzlamb.com
www.polarica.com
www.porkboard.org
www.porktimes.org
www.rossfarm.com
www.schallerweber.com
http://meat.tamu.edu/jeff.html
www.vealusa.com
www.wellsmeats.com

Acknowledgments

Like all good books, this one is a collaboration between some very talented and dedicated people. Erin Slonaker, my intrepid editor, helped make sense of this huge subject with her incisive comments. Steve Legato, photographer extraordinaire, took on the challenge of photographing everything from rattlesnake to rump roast. Karen Onorato and Andrea Stephany, photography directors, were with me all the way with their superb design sense. Their sense of humor helped us through the long days of taking all 160 meat photos.

   I could never have written this book without the help of some extraordinarily knowledgeable people in the meat business. My special thanks go to the people at George Wells Meats (the top-rated meat purveyor in the Philadelphia area), especially owner James Conboy, sales director Shawn Padgett, and head of production Jerry Booth, who provided the magnificent cuts we used for the photos along with answers to my endless questions. My participation in Beef 101, a course, given at Texas A&M University, was invaluable to my understanding. Tony Catelli, owner of Catelli Brothers Veal and Lamb, showed me his entire state-of-the-art cutting and packing facility so I could understand how it all gets put together for the customer.

More Quirk Field Guides

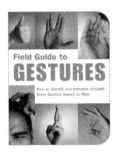

Field Guide to GESTURES

How to Identify and Interpret Virtually
Every Gesture Known to Man

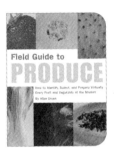

Field Guide to PRODUCE

How to Identify, Select, and Prepare Virtually
Every Fruit and Vegetable at the Market
By Aliza Green

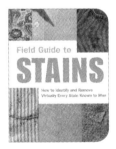

Field Guide to STAINS

How to Identify and Remove
Virtually Every Stain Known to Man

Field Guide to TOOLS

How to Identify and Use Virtually Every
Tool at the Hardware Store
By John Kelsey

Available Wherever Books Are Sold

PRINCIPLES OF ACCOUNTING 1
Financial Statements 1
    Income statement................................ 2
    Statement of owner's equity 3
    Balance sheet.................................... 4
    Statement of cash flows 5
The Accounting Equation 6
    Assets.. 6
    Liabilities 7
    Owner's equity 8
    Stockholders' equity 9
Financial Reporting Objectives 9
Generally Accepted Accounting Principles 10
    Economic entity assumption 10
    Monetary unit assumption........................ 11
    Full disclosure principle 11
    Time period assumption 11
    Accrual basis accounting......................... 12
    Revenue recognition principle 12
    Matching principle 12
    Cost principle 12
    Going concern principle 13
    Relevance, reliability, and consistency 13
    Principle of conservatism 13
    Materiality principle 14
Internal Control 14
    Control environment 14
    Control activities................................ 15

ANALYZING AND RECORDING
TRANSACTIONS 17
Analyzing Transactions 17
T Accounts 18
Double-Entry Bookkeeping 20
Journal Entries.................................... 22
The General Ledger 23

The Recording Process Illustrated 25
The Trial Balance 38

ADJUSTMENTS AND FINANCIAL STATEMENTS. 41

Accrued Revenues 41
Accrued Expenses 44
Unearned Revenues 46
Prepaid Expenses 47
Depreciation. 48
The Adjustment Process Illustrated 50
Financial Statements 60
    Income statement. 60
    Statement of owner's equity 62
    Balance sheet. 63
    Statement of cash flows 65

COMPLETION OF THE ACCOUNTING CYCLE. 67

The Work Sheet. 67
Closing Entries. 70
The Post-Closing Trial Balance. 76
A Summary of the Accounting Cycle 77
Reversing Entries. 78
Correcting Entries 82

ACCOUNTING FOR A MERCHANDISING COMPANY 85

Recording Sales 85
Sales Returns and Allowances 86
Sales Discounts 88
Net Sales 89
Inventory Systems 90
Recording Purchases 90

Purchases Returns and Allowances 91
Purchases Discounts 92
Net Purchases and the Cost of Goods Purchased.......... 93
The Cost of Goods Available for Sale
    and the Cost of Goods Sold........................ 93
Gross Profit 94
Financial Statements for a Merchandising Company 94
Adjusting the Inventory Account 96
Inventory Adjustments on the Work Sheet............... 98
Closing Entries for a Merchandising Company........... 98
The Work Sheet When Closing Entries
    Update Inventory 102

SUBSIDIARY LEDGERS
AND SPECIAL JOURNALS 103

Subsidiary Ledgers 103
Special Journals 105
    Sales journal 106
    Purchases journal............................. 108
    Cash receipts journal 110
    Cash disbursements journal 112
    General journal entries 114

CASH 115

Cash Controls..................................... 115
The Petty Cash Fund 117
Bank Reconciliation............................... 120
    Deposits in transit 121
    Outstanding checks 121
    Automatic withdrawals and deposits.............. 122
    Interest earned 125
    Bank service charges 126
    NSF (not sufficient funds) checks 127
    Errors 128
Credit Card Sales 129

RECEIVABLES **133**
  Evaluating Accounts Receivable 133
    Direct write-off method 134
    Allowance method............................ 134
  Estimating Bad Debts Under the Allowance Method 140
    Percentage of total accounts receivable method 140
    Aging method 141
    Percentage of credit sales method 142
  Factoring Receivables 142
  Notes Receivable 143
    Calculating interest 144
  Recording Notes Receivable Transactions 146
  Discounting Notes Receivable 149

INVENTORY **153**
  Determining Quantities of Merchandise Inventory 153
    Consigned merchandise......................... 154
    Goods in transit.............................. 154
  The Cost of Inventory 155
  The Valuation of Merchandise 155
  Comparing Perpetual and Periodic Inventory Systems 158
  Inventory Subsidiary Ledger Accounts 160
  Cost Flow Methods 162
    Specific cost 162
    Average cost 164
    First-in, first-out 165
    Last-in, first-out 166
    Comparing the assumed cost flow methods 168
  The Effect of Inventory Errors on Financial Statements ... 169
    Income statement effects........................ 169
    Balance sheet effects 169
  Estimating Inventories 170
    Gross profit method 170
    Retail inventory method 172

OPERATING ASSETS **175**

The Cost of Property, Plant, and Equipment............ 176

Land 176

Land improvements............................. 177

Buildings 177

Equipment, vehicles, and furniture................. 177

Depreciation....................................... 178

Straight-line depreciation 178

Units-of-activity depreciation 182

Sum-of-the-years'-digits depreciation 183

Declining-balance depreciation 184

Comparing depreciation methods 185

Partial-year depreciation calculations 186

Revising depreciation estimates 188

Depreciation for income tax purposes............. 189

Repairs and Improvements......................... 190

The Disposition of Depreciable Assets 191

Retirement of depreciable assets 192

Sale of depreciable assets 193

Exchange of depreciable assets 193

Natural Resources 196

Cost of natural resources........................ 197

Depletion..................................... 197

Intangible Assets 199

Patents 199

Copyrights.................................... 200

Trademarks and trade names..................... 201

Franchise licenses 201

Government licenses 201

Goodwill 201

Accounting is the language of business. It is the system of recording, summarizing, and analyzing an economic entity's financial transactions. Effectively communicating this information is key to the success of every business. Those who rely on financial information include internal users, such as a company's managers and employees, and external users, such as banks, investors, governmental agencies, financial analysts, and labor unions. These users depend upon data supplied by accountants to answer the following types of questions:

- Is the company profitable?
- Is there enough cash to meet payroll needs?
- How much debt does the company have?
- How does the company's net income compare to its budget?
- What is the balance owed by customers?
- Has the company consistently paid cash dividends?
- How much income does each division generate?
- Should the company invest money to expand?

Accountants must present an organization's financial information in clear, concise reports that help make questions like these easy to answer. The most common accounting reports are called financial statements.

Financial Statements

The financial statements shown on the next several pages are for a **sole proprietorship,** which is a business owned by an individual. Corporate financial statements are slightly different. The four basic financial statements are the income statement, statement of owner's equity, balance sheet, and statement of cash flows. The income statement, statement of owner's equity, and statement of cash flows report activity for a specific period of time, usually a month, quarter, or year. The balance sheet reports balances of certain elements at a specific time. All four statements have a three-line heading in the following format:

Name of Company
Name of Statement
Time Period or Date

Income statement. The **income statement,** which is sometimes called the statement of earnings or statement of operations, is prepared first. It lists revenues and expenses and calculates the company's net income or net loss for a period of time. **Net income means total** revenues are greater than total expenses. **Net loss** means total expenses are greater than total revenues. The specific items that appear in financial statements are explained later.

The Greener Landscape Group
Income Statement
For the Month Ended April 30, 20X2

Revenues		
Lawn Cutting Revenue		$845
Expenses		
Wages Expense	$280	
Depreciation Expense	235	
Insurance Expense	100	
Interest Expense	79	
Advertising Expense	35	
Gas Expense	30	
Supplies Expense	25	
Total Expenses		784
Net Income		$ 61

Statement of owner's equity. The statement of owner's equity is prepared after the income statement. It shows the beginning and ending owner's equity balances and the items affecting owner's equity during the period. These items include investments, the net income or loss from the income statement, and withdrawals. Because the specific revenue and expense categories that determine net income or loss appear on the income statement, the statement of owner's equity shows only the total net income or loss. Balances enclosed by parentheses are subtracted from unenclosed balances.

The Greener Landscape Group
Statement of Owner's Equity
For the Month Ended April 30, 20X2

J. Green, Capital, April 1		$ 0
Additions		
Investments	$15,000	
Net Income	61	15,061
Withdrawals		(50)
J. Green, Capital, April 30		$15,011

Balance sheet. The balance sheet shows the balance, at a particular time, of each asset, each liability, and owner's equity. It proves that the **accounting equation** (Assets = Liabilities + Owner's Equity) is in balance. The ending balance on the statement of owner's equity is used to report owner's equity on the balance sheet.

The Greener Landscape Group
Balance Sheet
April 30, 20X2

ASSETS		
Current Assets		
Cash		$ 6,355
Accounts Receivable		200
Supplies		25
Prepaid Insurance		1,100
Total Current Assets		7,680
Property, Plant, and Equipment		
Equipment	$18,000	
Less: Accumulated Depreciation	(235)	17,765
Total Assets		$25,445
LIABILITIES AND OWNER'S EQUITY		
Current Liabilities		
Accounts Payable		$ 50
Wages Payable		80
Interest Payable		79
Unearned Revenue		225
Total Current Liabilities		434
Long-Term Liabilities		
Notes Payable		10,000
Total Liabilities		10,434
Owner's Equity		
J. Green, Capital		15,011
Total Liabilities and Owner's Equity		$25,445

Statement of cash flows. The statement of cash flows tracks the movement of cash during a specific accounting period. It assigns all cash exchanges to one of three categories—operating, investing, or financing—to calculate the net change in cash and then reconciles the accounting period's beginning and ending cash balances. As its name implies, the statement of cash flows includes items that affect cash. Although not part of the statement's main body, significant noncash items must also be disclosed.

According to current accounting standards, operating cash flows may be disclosed using either the direct or the indirect method. The direct method simply lists the net cash flow by type of cash receipt and payment category. The indirect method is explained in *Cliffs Quick Review Accounting Principles II*. For purposes of illustration, the direct method appears below.

The Greener Landscape Group
Statement of Cash Flows
For the Month Ended April 30, 20X2

Cash Flows from Operating Activities	
Cash from Customers	$ 870
Cash to Employees	(200)
Cash to Suppliers	(1,265)
Cash Flow Used by Operating Activities	(595)
Cash Flows from Investing Activities	
Purchases of Equipment	(8,000)
Cash Flows from Financing Activities	
Investment by Owner	15,000
Withdrawal by Owner	(50)
Cash Flow Provided by Financing Activities	14,950
Net Increase in Cash	6,355
Beginning Cash, April 1	0
Ending Cash, April 30	$ 6,355

Noncash Financing and Investing Activity
The company purchased a used truck for $15,000, paying $5,000 in cash and signing a note for the remaining balance. The note payable portion of the transaction is not included on this statement.

The Accounting Equation

The ability to read financial statements requires an understanding of the items they include and the standard categories used to classify these items. The accounting equation identifies the relationship between the elements of accounting.

$$\boxed{\text{Assets}} = \boxed{\text{Liabilities}} + \boxed{\begin{array}{c}\text{Owner's}\\\text{Equity}\end{array}}$$

Assets. An **asset** is something of value the company owns. Assets can be tangible or intangible. **Tangible assets** are generally divided into three major categories: current assets (including cash, marketable securities, accounts receivable, inventory, and prepaid expenses); property, plant, and equipment; and long-term investments. **Intangible assets** lack physical substance, but they may, nevertheless, provide substantial value to the company that owns them. Examples of intangible assets include patents, copyrights, trademarks, and franchise licenses. A brief description of some tangible assets follows.

- **Current assets** typically include cash and assets the company reasonably expects to use, sell, or collect within one year. Current assets appear on the balance sheet (and in the numbered list below) in order, from most liquid to least liquid. **Liquid assets** are readily convertible into cash or other assets, and they are generally accepted as payment for liabilities.

1. **Cash** includes cash on hand (petty cash), bank balances (checking, savings, or money-market accounts), and cash equivalents. **Cash equivalents** are highly liquid investments, such as certificates of deposit and U.S. treasury bills, with maturities of ninety days or less at the time of purchase.

2. **Marketable securities** include short-term investments in stocks, bonds (debt), certificates of deposit, or other securities. These items are classified as marketable securities—rather than long-term investments—only if the company has both the ability and the desire to sell them within one year.

3. **Accounts receivable** are amounts owed to the company by customers who have received products or services but have not yet paid for them.

4. **Inventory** is the cost to acquire or manufacture merchandise for sale to customers. Although service enterprises that never provide customers with merchandise do not use this category for current assets, inventory usually represents a significant portion of assets in merchandising and manufacturing companies.

5. **Prepaid expenses** are amounts paid by the company to purchase items or services that represent future costs of doing business. Examples include office supplies, insurance premiums, and advance payments for rent. These assets become expenses as they expire or get used up.

- **Property, plant, and equipment** is the title given to long-lived assets the business uses to help generate revenue. This category is sometimes called fixed assets. Examples include land, natural resources such as timber or mineral reserves, buildings, production equipment, vehicles, and office furniture. With the exception of land, the cost of an asset in this category is allocated to expense over the asset's estimated useful life.

- **Long-term investments** include purchases of debt or stock issued by other companies and investments with other companies in joint ventures. Long-term investments differ from marketable securities because the company intends to hold long-term investments for more than one year or the securities are not marketable.

Liabilities. **Liabilities** are the company's existing debts and obligations owed to third parties. Examples include amounts owed to suppliers for goods or services received (accounts payable), to employees for work performed (wages payable), and to banks for principal and interest on loans (notes payable and interest payable). Liabilities are generally classified as short-term (current) if they are due in one year or less. Long-term liabilities are not due for at least one year.

Owner's equity. **Owner's equity** represents the amount owed to the owner or owners by the company. Algebraically, this amount is calculated by subtracting liabilities from each side of the accounting equation. Owner's equity also represents the **net assets** of the company.

$$\boxed{\text{Assets}} - \boxed{\text{Liabilities}} = \boxed{\begin{array}{c}\text{Owner's}\\\text{Equity}\end{array}} = \boxed{\begin{array}{c}\text{Net}\\\text{Assets}\end{array}}$$

In a sole proprietorship or partnership, owner's equity equals the total net investment in the business plus the net income or loss generated during the business's life. **Net investment** equals the sum of all investment in the business by the owner or owners minus withdrawals made by the owner or owners. The owner's investment is recorded in the owner's capital account, and any withdrawals are recorded in a separate owner's drawing account. For example, if a business owner contributes $10,000 to start a company but later withdraws $1,000 for personal expenses, the owner's net investment equals $9,000. **Net income** or **net loss** equals the company's revenues less its expenses. **Revenues** are inflows of money or other assets received from customers in exchange for goods or services. **Expenses** are the costs incurred to generate those revenues.

Components of Owner's Equity in a Sole Proprietorship

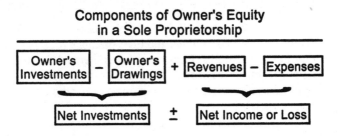

Capital investments and revenues increase owner's equity, while expenses and owner withdrawals (drawings) decrease owner's equity. In a partnership, there are separate capital and drawing accounts for each partner.

Stockholders' equity. In a corporation, ownership is represented by shares of stock, so the owners' equity is called **stockholders' equity** or **shareholders' equity.** Corporations use several types of accounts to record stockholders' equity activities: preferred stock, common stock, paid-in capital (these are often referred to as contributed capital), and retained earnings. **Contributed capital** accounts record the total amount invested by stockholders in the corporation. If a corporation issues more than one class of stock, separate accounts are maintained for each class. **Retained earnings** equal net income or loss over the life of the business less any amounts given back to stockholders in the form of dividends. Dividends affect stockholders' equity in the same way that owner withdrawals affect owner's equity in sole proprietorships and partnerships.

Components of Stockholders' Equity
in a Corporation with Two Classes of Stock

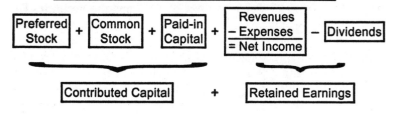

Financial Reporting Objectives

Financial statements are prepared according to agreed upon guidelines. In order to understand these guidelines, it helps to understand the objectives of financial reporting. The objectives of financial reporting, as discussed in the Financial Accounting Standards Board (FASB) *Statement of Financial Accounting Concepts No. 1,* are to provide information that

1. is useful to existing and potential investors and creditors and other users in making rational investment, credit, and similar decisions;

2. helps existing and potential investors and creditors and other users to assess the amounts, timing, and uncertainty of prospective net cash inflows to the enterprise;

3. identifies the economic resources of an enterprise, the claims to those resources, and the effects that transactions, events, and circumstances have on those resources.

Generally Accepted Accounting Principles

Accountants use **generally accepted accounting principles (GAAP)** to guide them in recording and reporting financial information. GAAP comprises a broad set of principles that have been developed by the accounting profession and the Securities and Exchange Commission (SEC). Two laws, the Securities Act of 1933 and the Securities Exchange Act of 1934, give the SEC authority to establish reporting and disclosure requirements. However, the SEC usually operates in an oversight capacity, allowing the FASB and the Governmental Accounting Standards Board (GASB) to establish these requirements. The GASB develops accounting standards for state and local governments.

The current set of principles that accountants use rests upon some underlying assumptions. The basic assumptions and principles presented on the next several pages are considered GAAP and apply to most financial statements. In addition to these concepts, there are other, more technical standards accountants must follow when preparing financial statements. Some of these are discussed later in this book, but others are left for more advanced study.

Economic entity assumption. Financial records must be separately maintained for each economic entity. Economic entities include businesses, governments, school districts, churches, and other social organizations. Although accounting information from many different entities may be combined for financial reporting purposes, every economic event must be associated with and recorded by a specific entity.

In addition, business records must not include the personal assets or liabilities of the owners.

Monetary unit assumption. An economic entity's accounting records include only quantifiable transactions. Certain economic events that affect a company, such as hiring a new chief executive officer or introducing a new product, cannot be easily quantified in monetary units and, therefore, do not appear in the company's accounting records. Furthermore, accounting records must be recorded using a stable currency. Businesses in the United States usually use U.S. dollars for this purpose.

Full disclosure principle. Financial statements normally provide information about a company's past performance. However, pending lawsuits, incomplete transactions, or other conditions may have imminent and significant effects on the company's financial status. The full disclosure principle requires that financial statements include disclosure of such information. Footnotes supplement financial statements to convey this information and to describe the policies the company uses to record and report business transactions.

Time period assumption. Most businesses exist for long periods of time, so artificial time periods must be used to report the results of business activity. Depending on the type of report, the time period may be a day, a month, a year, or another arbitrary period. Using artificial time periods leads to questions about when certain transactions should be recorded. For example, how should an accountant report the cost of equipment expected to last five years? Reporting the entire expense during the year of purchase might make the company seem unprofitable that year and unreasonably profitable in subsequent years. Once the time period has been established, accountants use GAAP to record and report that accounting period's transactions.

Accrual basis accounting. In most cases, GAAP requires the use of accrual basis accounting rather than cash basis accounting. **Accrual basis accounting,** which adheres to the revenue recognition, matching, and cost principles discussed below, captures the financial aspects of each economic event in the accounting period in which it occurs, regardless of when the cash changes hands. Under **cash basis accounting,** revenues are recognized only when the company receives cash or its equivalent, and expenses are recognized only when the company pays with cash or its equivalent.

Revenue recognition principle. Revenue is earned and recognized upon product delivery or service completion, without regard to the timing of cash flow. Suppose a store orders five hundred compact discs from a wholesaler in March, receives them in April, and pays for them in May. The wholesaler recognizes the sales revenue in April when delivery occurs, not in March when the deal is struck or in May when the cash is received. Similarly, if an attorney receives a $100 retainer from a client, the attorney doesn't recognize the money as revenue until he or she actually performs $100 in services for the client.

Matching principle. The costs of doing business are recorded in the same period as the revenue they help to generate. Examples of such costs include the cost of goods sold, salaries and commissions earned, insurance premiums, supplies used, and estimates for potential warranty work on the merchandise sold. Consider the wholesaler who delivered five hundred CDs to a store in April. These CDs change from an asset (inventory) to an expense (cost of goods sold) when the revenue is recognized so that the profit from the sale can be determined.

Cost principle. Assets are recorded at cost, which equals the value exchanged at the time of their acquisition. In the United States, even if assets such as land or buildings appreciate in value over time, they are not revalued for financial reporting purposes.

Going concern principle. Unless otherwise noted, financial statements are prepared under the assumption that the company will remain in business indefinitely. Therefore, assets do not need to be sold at fire-sale values, and debt does not need to be paid off before maturity. This principle results in the classification of assets and liabilities as short-term (current) and long-term. **Long-term assets** are expected to be held for more than one year. **Long-term liabilities** are not due for more than one year.

Relevance, reliability, and consistency. To be useful, financial information must be relevant, reliable, and prepared in a consistent manner. **Relevant information** helps a decision maker understand a company's past performance, present condition, and future outlook so that informed decisions can be made in a timely manner. Of course, the information needs of individual users may differ, requiring that the information be presented in different formats. Internal users often need more detailed information than external users, who may need to know only the company's value or its ability to repay loans. **Reliable information** is verifiable and objective. **Consistent information** is prepared using the same methods each accounting period, which allows meaningful comparisons to be made between different accounting periods and between the financial statements of different companies that use the same methods.

Principle of conservatism. Accountants must use their judgment to record transactions that require estimation. The number of years that equipment will remain productive and the portion of accounts receivable that will never be paid are examples of items that require estimation. In reporting financial data, accountants follow the **principle of conservatism,** which requires that the less optimistic estimate be chosen when two estimates are judged to be equally likely. For example, suppose a manufacturing company's Warranty Repair Department has documented a three-percent return rate for product X during the past two years, but the company's Engineering Department insists this return rate is just a statistical anomaly and less than one percent of product X will require service during the coming year. Unless the Engineering

Department provides compelling evidence to support its estimate, the company's accountant must follow the principle of conservatism and plan for a three-percent return rate. Losses and costs—such as warranty repairs—are recorded when they are probable and reasonably estimated. Gains are recorded when realized.

Materiality principle. Accountants follow the **materiality principle,** which states that the requirements of any accounting principle may be ignored when there is no effect on the users of financial information. Certainly, tracking individual paper clips or pieces of paper is immaterial and excessively burdensome to any company's accounting department. Although there is no definitive measure of materiality, the accountant's judgment on such matters must be sound. Several thousand dollars may not be material to an entity such as General Motors, but that same figure is quite material to a small, family-owned business.

Internal Control

Internal control is the process designed to ensure reliable financial reporting, effective and efficient operations, and compliance with applicable laws and regulations. Safeguarding assets against theft and unauthorized use, acquisition, or disposal is also part of internal control.

Control environment. The management style and the expectations of upper-level managers, particularly their control policies, determine the control environment. An effective **control environment** helps ensure that established policies and procedures are followed. The control environment includes independent oversight provided by a board of directors and, in publicly held companies, by an audit committee; management's integrity, ethical values, and philosophy; a defined organizational structure with competent and trustworthy employees; and the assignment of authority and responsibility.

Control activities. Control activities are the specific policies and procedures management uses to achieve its objectives. The most important control activities involve segregation of duties, proper authorization of transactions and activities, adequate documents and records, physical control over assets and records, and independent checks on performance. A short description of each of these control activities appears below.

- **Segregation of duties** requires that different individuals be assigned responsibility for different elements of related activities, particularly those involving authorization, custody, or recordkeeping. For example, the same person who is responsible for an asset's recordkeeping should not be responsible for physical control of that asset. Having different individuals perform these functions creates a system of checks and balances.

- **Proper authorization** of transactions and activities helps ensure that all company activities adhere to established guidelines unless responsible managers authorize another course of action. For example, a fixed price list may serve as an official authorization of price for a large sales staff. In addition, there may be a control to allow a sales manager to authorize reasonable deviations from the price list.

- **Adequate documents and records** provide evidence that financial statements are accurate. Controls designed to ensure adequate recordkeeping include the creation of invoices and other documents that are easy to use and sufficiently informative; the use of prenumbered, consecutive documents; and the timely preparation of documents.

- **Physical control** over assets and records helps protect the company's assets. These control activities may include electronic or mechanical controls (such as a safe, employee ID cards, fences, cash registers, fireproof files, and locks) or computer-related controls dealing with access privileges or established backup and recovery procedures.

- **Independent checks** on performance, which are carried out by employees who did not do the work being checked, help ensure the reliability of accounting information and the efficiency of operations. For example, a supervisor verifies the accuracy of a retail clerk's cash drawer at the end of the day. Internal auditors may also verify that the supervisor performed the check of the cash drawer.

In order to identify and establish effective controls, management must continually assess the risk, monitor control implementation, and modify controls as needed. Top managers of publicly held companies must sign a statement of responsibility for internal controls and include this statement in their annual report to stockholders.

Analyzing Transactions

The first step in the accounting process is to analyze every transaction (economic event) that affects the business. The accounting equation (Assets = Liabilities + Owner's Equity) must remain in balance after every transaction is recorded, so accountants must analyze each transaction to determine how it affects owner's equity and the different types of assets and liabilities before recording the transaction.

Assume Mr. J. Green invests $15,000 to start a landscape business. This transaction increases the company's assets, specifically cash, by $15,000 and increases owner's equity by $15,000. Notice that the accounting equation remains in balance.

Assets	=	Liabilities	+	Owner's Equity
+ 15,000 (Cash)				+ 15,000 (Owner's Capital)

Mr. Green uses $5,000 of the company's cash to place a downpayment on a used truck that costs $15,000, and he signs a note payable that requires him to pay the remaining $10,000 in eighteen months. This transaction decreases one type of asset (cash) by $5,000, increases another type of asset (vehicles) by $15,000, and increases a liability (notes payable) by $10,000. The accounting equation remains in balance, and Mr. Green now has two types of assets ($10,000 in cash and a vehicle worth $15,000), a liability (a $10,000 note payable), and owner's equity of $15,000.

Assets	=	Liabilities	+	Owner's Equity
+ 15,000 (Cash)				+ 15,000 (Owner's Capital)
− 5,000 (Cash)		+ 10,000 (Notes Payable)		
+ 15,000 (Vehicles)				
25,000	=	10,000	+	15,000

Given the large number of transactions that companies usually have, accountants need a more sophisticated system for recording transactions than the one shown on the previous page. Accountants use the double-entry bookkeeping system to keep the accounting equation in balance and to double-check the numerical accuracy of transaction entries. Under this system, each transaction is recorded using at least two accounts. An **account** is a record of all transactions involving a particular item.

Companies maintain separate accounts for each type of asset (cash, accounts receivable, inventory, etc.), each type of liability (accounts payable, wages payable, notes payable, etc.), owner investments (usually referred to as the owner's capital account in a sole proprietorship), owner drawings (withdrawals made by the owner), each type of revenue (sales revenue, service revenue, etc.), and each type of expense (rent expense, wages expense, etc.). All accounts taken together make up the **general ledger.** For organizational purposes, each account in the general ledger is assigned a number, and companies maintain a **chart of accounts,** which lists the accounts and account numbers.

Account numbers vary significantly from one company to the next, depending on the company's size and complexity. A sole proprietorship may have few accounts, but a multinational corporation may have thousands of accounts and use ten- or even twenty-digit numbers to track accounts by location, department, project code, and other categories. Most companies numerically separate asset, liability, owner's equity, revenue, and expense accounts. A typical small business might use the numbers 100–199 for asset accounts, 200–299 for liability accounts, 300–399 for owner's equity accounts, 400–499 for revenue accounts, and 500–599 for expense accounts.

T Accounts

The simplest account structure is shaped like the letter *T.* The account title and account number appear above the T. Debits (abbreviated Dr.) always go on the left side of the T, and credits (abbreviated Cr.) always go on the right.

Account Title	Acct. #
Debit side	Credit side

Accountants record increases in asset, expense, and owner's drawing accounts on the debit side, and they record increases in liability, revenue, and owner's capital accounts on the credit side. An account's assigned **normal balance** is on the side where increases go because the increases in any account are usually greater than the decreases. Therefore, asset, expense, and owner's drawing accounts normally have debit balances. Liability, revenue, and owner's capital accounts normally have credit balances. To determine the correct entry, identify the accounts affected by a transaction, which category each account falls into, and whether the transaction increases or decreases the account's balance. You may find the chart below helpful as a reference.

Assets		Expenses		Owner's Drawing	
Debits	Credits	Debits	Credits	Debits	Credits
Increase	Decrease	Increase	Decrease	Increase	Decrease
Normal Balance		Normal Balance		Normal Balance	

Liabilities		Revenues		Owner's Capital	
Debits	Credits	Debits	Credits	Debits	Credits
Decrease	Increase	Decrease	Increase	Decrease	Increase
	Normal Balance		Normal Balance		Normal Balance

Occasionally, an account does not have a normal balance. For example, a company's checking account (an asset) has a credit balance if the account is overdrawn.

The way people often use the words *debit* and *credit* in everyday speech is not how accountants use these words. For example, the word *credit* generally has positive associations when used conversationally: in school you receive credit for completing a course, a great hockey player may be a credit to his or her team, and a hopeless romantic may at least deserve credit for trying. Someone who is familiar with these uses for *credit* but who is new to accounting may not immediately associate credits with decreases to asset, expense, and owner's drawing accounts. If a business owner loses $5,000 of the company's cash while gambling, the cash account, which is an asset, must be credited for $5,000. (The accountant who records this entry may also deserve credit for realizing that other job offers merit consideration.) For accounting purposes, think of *debit* and *credit* simply in terms of the left-hand and right-hand side of a T account.

Double-Entry Bookkeeping

Under the double-entry bookkeeping system, the full value of each transaction is recorded on the debit side of one or more accounts and also on the credit side of one or more accounts. Therefore, the combined debit balance of all accounts always equals the combined credit balance of all accounts.

Suppose a new company obtains a long-term loan for $50,000 on August 1. The company's cash account (an asset) increases by $50,000, so it is debited for this amount. Simultaneously, the company's notes payable account (a liability) increases by $50,000, so it is credited for this amount. Both sides of the accounting equation increase by $50,000, and total debits and credits remain equal.

Cash	100	Notes Payable	280
Debits	Credits	Debits	Credits
Aug. 1 50,000			Aug. 1 50,000

Some transactions affect only one side of the accounting equation, but the double-entry bookkeeping system nevertheless ensures that the accounting equation remains in balance. For example, if the company pays $30,000 on August 3 to purchase equipment, the cash account's decrease is recorded with a $30,000 credit and the equipment account's increase is recorded with a $30,000 debit. These two asset-account entries offset each other, so the accounting equation remains in balance. Since the cash balance was $50,000 before this transaction occurred, the company has $20,000 in cash after the equipment purchase.

Cash		100
Debits	Credits	
Aug. 1 50,000	Aug. 3 30,000	
Balance 20,000		

Equipment		110
Debits	Credits	
Aug. 3 30,000		

A **compound entry** is necessary when a single transaction affects three or more accounts. Suppose the company's owner purchases a used delivery truck for $20,000 on August 6 by making a $2,000 cash down payment and obtaining a three-year note payable for the remaining $18,000. This transaction is recorded by debiting (increasing) the vehicles account for $20,000, crediting (increasing) the notes payable account for $18,000, and crediting (decreasing) the cash account for $2,000.

Vehicles		120
Debits	Credits	
Aug. 6 20,000		

Notes Payable		280
Debits	Credits	
	Aug. 1 50,000	
	Aug. 6 18,000	
	Balance 68,000	

Cash		100
Debits	Credits	
Aug. 1 50,000	Aug. 3 30,000	
	Aug. 6 2,000	
Balance 18,000		

The debits and credits total $20,000, and the accounting equation remains in balance because the $18,000 net increase in assets is matched by an $18,000 increase in liabilities. After these three transactions, the company has $68,000 in assets (cash $18,000; equipment $30,000; vehicles $20,000) and $68,000 in liabilities (notes payable).

Journal Entries

Tracking business activity with T accounts would be cumbersome because most businesses have a large number of transactions each day. These transactions are initially recorded on **source documents**, such as invoices or checks. The first step in the accounting process is to analyze each transaction and identify what effect it has on the accounts. After making this determination, an accountant enters the transactions in chronological order into a journal, a process called **journalizing** the transactions. Although many companies use specialized journals for certain transactions, all businesses use a **general journal**. In this book, the terms *general journal* and *journal* are used interchangeably.

The journal's page number appears near the upper right corner. In the example below, GJ1 stands for page 1 of the general journal. Many general journals have five columns: Date, Account Title and Description, Posting Reference, Debit, and Credit.

	General Journal			GJ1
Date	Account Title and Description	Ref.	Debit	Credit
20X1				
Aug. 1	Cash		50,000	
	Notes Payable			50,000
	Borrowed $50,000			
3	Equipment		30,000	
	Cash			30,000
	Purchased equipment			
6	Vehicles		20,000	
	Notes Payable			18,000
	Cash			2,000
	Purchased delivery truck			

To record a **journal entry,** begin by entering the date of the transaction in the journal's date column. For convenience, include the year and month only at the top of each page and next to each month's first entry. In the next column, list each account affected by the transaction on a separate line, and enter a short description of the transaction immediately below the list of accounts. The accounts being debited always appear above the accounts being credited, which are indented slightly. The posting reference column remains blank until the journal entry is transferred to the accounts, a process called **posting**, at which time the account's number is placed in this column. Finally, enter the debit or credit amount for each account in the appropriate columns on the right side of the journal. Generally, one blank line separates each transaction.

The General Ledger

After journalizing transactions, the next step in the accounting process is to post transactions to the accounts in the general ledger. Although T accounts provide a conceptual framework for understanding accounts, most businesses use a more informative and structured spreadsheet layout. A typical account includes date, explanation, and reference columns to the left of the debit column and a balance column to the right of the credit column. The reference column identifies the journal page containing the transaction. The balance column shows the account's balance after every transaction.

| | Account Name | | | | Acct. # |
Date	Explanation	Ref.	Debit	Credit	Balance

When an account does not have a normal balance, brackets enclose the balance. Assets normally have debit balances, for example, so brackets enclose a checking account's balance only when the account is overdrawn.

As the numbered arrows below indicate, you should post a transaction's first line item to the correct ledger account, completing each column and calculating the account's new balance. Then you should enter the account's reference number in the journal. Repeat this sequence of steps for every account listed in the journal entry.

General Journal   GJ1

Date	Account Title and Description	Ref.	Debit	Credit
20X1				
Aug. 1	Cash	100	50,000	
	Notes Payable	280		50,000
	Borrowed $50,000			

Cash   100

Date	Explanation	Ref.	Debit	Credit	Balance
20X1					
Aug. 1	Borrowed $50,000	GJ1	50,000		50,000

Notes Payable   280

Date	Explanation	Ref.	Debit	Credit	Balance
20X1					
Aug. 1	Borrowed $50,000	GJ1		50,000	50,000

Referencing the account's number on the journal *after* posting the entry ensures that every line item that has a reference number in the journal has already been posted. This practice can be helpful if phone calls or other distractions interrupt the posting process.

The Recording Process Illustrated

To understand how to record a variety of transactions, consider the description and analysis of the Greener Landscape Group's first thirteen transactions. Then see how each transaction appears in the company's general journal and general ledger accounts.

Transaction 1: On April 1, 20X2, the owner of the Greener Landscape Group, J. Green, invests $15,000 to open the business. Therefore, an asset account (cash) increases and is debited for $15,000, and the owner's capital account (J. Green, capital) increases and is credited for $15,000.

General Journal GJ1

Date	Account Title and Description	Ref.	Debit	Credit
20X2				
Apr. 1	Cash	100	15,000	
	J. Green, Capital	300		15,000
	Owner investment			

Cash 100

Date	Explanation	Ref.	Debit	Credit	Balance
20X2					
Apr. 1	Owner investment	GJ1	15,000		15,000

J. Green, Capital 300

Date	Explanation	Ref.	Debit	Credit	Balance
20X2					
Apr. 1	Owner investment	GJ1		15,000	15,000

Notice that the cash account has a debit balance and the J. Green, capital account has a credit balance. Since both balances are normal, brackets are not used.

Transaction 2: On April 2, Mr. Green purchases a $15,000 used truck by paying $5,000 in cash and signing a $10,000 note payable, which is due in eighteen months. One asset account (vehicles) increases and is debited for $15,000. Another asset account (cash) decreases and is credited for $5,000. A liability account (notes payable) increases and is credited for $10,000.

The shaded areas below (and in other illustrations in this book) provide a reference for the transaction's position in the journal and ledger accounts. They are not part of the current entry.

General Journal — GJ1

Date	Account Title and Description	Ref.	Debit	Credit
20X2				
Apr. 1	Cash	100	15,000	
	J. Green, Capital	300		15,000
	Owner investment			
2	Vehicles	155	15,000	
	Cash	100		5,000
	Notes Payable	280		10,000
	Purchased truck			

Vehicles — 155

Date	Explanation	Ref.	Debit	Credit	Balance
20X2					
Apr. 2	Acquired truck	GJ1	15,000		15,000

Cash — 100

Date	Explanation	Ref.	Debit	Credit	Balance
20X2					
Apr. 1	Owner investment	GJ1	15,000		15,000
2	Truck downpayment	GJ1		5,000	10,000

Notes Payable — 280

Date	Explanation	Ref.	Debit	Credit	Balance
20X2					
Apr. 2	Loan for truck	GJ1		10,000	10,000

Transaction 3: On April 3, Mr. Green purchases lawn mowers for $3,000 in cash. One asset account (equipment) increases and is debited for $3,000, and another asset account (cash) decreases and is credited for $3,000.

General Journal — GJ1

Date	Account Title and Description	Ref.	Debit	Credit
2	Vehicles	155	15,000	
	Cash	100		5,000
	Notes Payable	280		10,000
	Purchased truck			
3	Equipment	150	3,000	
	Cash	100		3,000
	Lawnmower purchase			

Equipment — 150

Date	Explanation	Ref.	Debit	Credit	Balance
20X2					
Apr. 3	Lawnmower purchase	GJ1	3,000		3,000

Cash — 100

Date	Explanation	Ref.	Debit	Credit	Balance
20X2					
Apr. 1	Owner investment	GJ1	15,000		15,000
2	Truck downpayment	GJ1		5,000	10,000
3	Lawnmower purchase	GJ1		3,000	7,000

Transaction 4: On April 5, Mr. Green purchases $30 worth of gasoline to power the mowers during April. Since the gas is a cost of doing business during the present accounting period, an expense account (gas expense) increases and is debited for $30. (Remember: increases in asset, expense, and drawing accounts are made with debit entries.) In addition, an asset account (cash) decreases and is credited for $30.

General Journal — GJ1

Date	Account Title and Description	Ref.	Debit	Credit
3	Equipment	150	3,000	
	Cash	100		3,000
	Lawnmower purchase			
5	Gas Expense	510	30	
	Cash	100		30
	Gas for lawnmowers			

Gas Expense — 510

Date	Explanation	Ref.	Debit	Credit	Balance
20X2					
Apr. 5	Gas for lawnmowers	GJ1	30		30

Cash — 100

Date	Explanation	Ref.	Debit	Credit	Balance
20X2					
Apr. 1	Owner investment	GJ1	15,000		15,000
2	Truck downpayment	GJ1		5,000	10,000
3	Lawnmower purchase	GJ1		3,000	7,000
5	Gas for lawnmowers	GJ1		30	6,970

Transaction 5: On April 5, Mr. Green pays $1,200 for a one-year insurance contract that protects his business from April 1 until March 31 of the following year. Given the length of time this contract is in effect, the matching principle requires that the contract's cost initially be recorded as an asset since it provides a future benefit. Therefore, an asset (prepaid insurance) increases and is debited for $1,200. Another asset account (cash) decreases and is credited for $1,200.

General Journal — GJ1

Date	Account Title and Description	Ref.	Debit	Credit
5	Gas Expense	510	30	
	Cash	100		30
	Gas for lawnmowers			
5	Prepaid Insurance	145	1,200	
	Cash	100		1,200
	Annual insurance premium			

Prepaid Insurance — 145

Date	Explanation	Ref.	Debit	Credit	Balance
20X2					
Apr. 5	Insurance premium	GJ1	1,200		1,200

Cash — 100

Date	Explanation	Ref.	Debit	Credit	Balance
20X2					
Apr. 1	Owner investment	GJ1	15,000		15,000
2	Truck downpayment	GJ1		5,000	10,000
3	Lawnmower purchase	GJ1		3,000	7,000
5	Gas for lawnmowers	GJ1		30	6,970
5	Insurance premium	GJ1		1,200	5,770

Transaction 6: On April 5, Mr. Green purchases $50 worth of office supplies, placing the purchase on his account with the store rather than paying cash. Supplies are a prepaid expense (an asset) until they are used and thereby become a cost of doing business (an expense). Therefore, an asset account (supplies) increases and is debited for $50. Since Mr. Green places the purchase on his account with the store, a liability account (accounts payable) increases and is credited for $50. Accounts payable differ from notes payable. Accounts payable are amounts the company owes based on the good credit of the company or the owner, whereas notes payable are amounts the company owes under formal obligations.

General Journal   GJ1

Date	Account Title and Description	Ref.	Debit	Credit
5	Prepaid Insurance	145	1,200	
	Cash	100		1,200
	Annual insurance premium			
5	Supplies	140	50	
	Accounts Payable	200		50
	Bought office supplies			

Supplies   140

Date	Explanation	Ref.	Debit	Credit	Balance
20X2					
Apr. 5	Bought office supplies	GJ1	50		50

Accounts Payable   200

Date	Explanation	Ref.	Debit	Credit	Balance
20X2					
Apr. 5	Bought office supplies	GJ1		50	50

Transaction 7: On April 14, the Greener Landscape Group cuts grass for seven customers, receiving $50 from each. An asset account (cash) increases and is debited for $350, and a revenue account (lawn cutting revenue) increases and is credited for $350.

General Journal   GJ1

Date	Account Title and Description	Ref.	Debit	Credit
5	Supplies	140	50	
	Accounts Payable	200		50
	Bought office supplies			
14	Cash	100	350	
	Lawn Cutting Revenue	400		350
	Cut seven lawns			

Cash   100

Date	Explanation	Ref.	Debit	Credit	Balance
20X2					
Apr. 1	Owner investment	GJ1	15,000		15,000
2	Truck downpayment	GJ1		5,000	10,000
3	Lawnmower purchase	GJ1		3,000	7,000
5	Gas for lawnmowers	GJ1		30	6,970
5	Insurance premium	GJ1		1,200	5,770
14	Cut seven lawns	GJ1	350		6,120

Lawn Cutting Revenue   400

Date	Explanation	Ref.	Debit	Credit	Balance
20X2					
Apr. 14	Cut seven lawns	GJ1		350	350

Transaction 8: On April 20, Mr. Green receives $270 from a customer for six future maintenance visits. An advance deposit from a customer is an obligation to perform work in the future. It is a liability until the work is performed, at which time it becomes revenue. Therefore, the advance deposit is called unearned revenue. An asset account (cash) increases and is debited for $270, and a liability account (unearned revenue) increases and is credited for $270.

General Journal — GJ1

Date	Account Title and Description	Ref.	Debit	Credit
14	Cash	100	350	
	Lawn Cutting Revenue	400		350
	Cut seven lawns			
20	Cash	100	270	
	Unearned Revenue	250		270
	Prepayment			

Cash — 100

Date	Explanation	Ref.	Debit	Credit	Balance
20X2					
Apr. 1	Owner investment	GJ1	15,000		15,000
2	Truck downpayment	GJ1		5,000	10,000
3	Lawnmower purchase	GJ1		3,000	7,000
5	Gas for lawnmowers	GJ1		30	6,970
5	Insurance premium	GJ1		1,200	5,770
14	Cut seven lawns	GJ1	350		6,120
20	Prepayment	GJ1	270		6,390

Unearned Revenue — 250

Date	Explanation	Ref.	Debit	Credit	Balance
20X2					
Apr. 20	Prepayment	GJ1		270	270

Transaction 9: On April 22, the Greener Landscape Group cuts grass for eight customers, billing each one $50 but receiving no cash. In accordance with the revenue recognition principle, revenue is recognized upon the completion of a service or the delivery of a product, even if no cash changes hands at that time. Therefore, an asset account (accounts receivable) increases and is debited for $400, and a revenue account (lawn cutting revenue) increases and is credited for $400.

General Journal   GJ2

Date	Account Title and Description	Ref.	Debit	Credit
20X2				
Apr. 22	Accounts Receivable	110	400	
	Lawn Cutting Revenue	400		400
	Cut eight lawns			

Accounts Receivable   110

Date	Explanation	Ref.	Debit	Credit	Balance
20X2					
Apr. 22	Cut eight lawns	GJ2	400		400

Lawn Cutting Revenue   400

Date	Explanation	Ref.	Debit	Credit	Balance
20X2					
Apr. 14	Cut seven lawns	GJ1		350	350
22	Cut eight lawns	GJ2		400	750

Notice the new journal page and the corresponding change in posting references on the accounts.

Transaction 10: On April 26, Mr. Green pays $200 in wages to a part-time employee. An expense account (wages expense) increases and is debited for $200, and an asset account (cash) decreases and is credited for $200.

General Journal   GJ2

Date	Account Title and Description	Ref.	Debit	Credit
20X2				
Apr. 22	Accounts Receivable	110	400	
	Lawn Cutting Revenue	400		400
	Cut eight lawns			
26	Wages Expense	500	200	
	Cash	100		200
	Wages through 4-26			

Wages Expense   500

Date	Explanation	Ref.	Debit	Credit	Balance
20X2					
Apr. 26	Wages through 4-26	GJ2	200		200

Cash   100

Date	Explanation	Ref.	Debit	Credit	Balance
20X2					
Apr. 1	Owner investment	GJ1	15,000		15,000
2	Truck downpayment	GJ1		5,000	10,000
3	Lawnmower purchase	GJ1		3,000	7,000
5	Gas for lawnmowers	GJ1		30	6,970
5	Insurance premium	GJ1		1,200	5,770
14	Cut seven lawns	GJ1	350		6,120
20	Prepayment	GJ1	270		6,390
26	Wages through 4-26	GJ2		200	6,190

Transaction 11: On April 28, Mr. Green pays $35 to print advertising fliers. An expense account (advertising expense) increases and is debited for $35, and an asset account (cash) decreases and is credited for $35.

General Journal GJ2

Date	Account Title and Description	Ref.	Debit	Credit
26	Wages Expense	500	200	
	Cash	100		200
	Wages through 4-26			
28	Advertising Expense	520	35	
	Cash	100		35
	Printed advertisements			

Advertising Expense 520

Date	Explanation	Ref.	Debit	Credit	Balance
20X2					
Apr. 28	Printed advertisements	GJ2	35		35

Cash 100

Date	Explanation	Ref.	Debit	Credit	Balance
20X2					
Apr. 1	Owner investment	GJ1	15,000		15,000
2	Truck downpayment	GJ1		5,000	10,000
3	Lawnmower purchase	GJ1		3,000	7,000
5	Gas for lawnmowers	GJ1		30	6,970
5	Insurance premium	GJ1		1,200	5,770
14	Cut seven lawns	GJ1	350		6,120
20	Prepayment	GJ1	270		6,390
26	Wages through 4-26	GJ2		200	6,190
28	Printed advertisements	GJ2		35	6,155

Transaction 12: On April 29, Mr. Green withdraws $50 for personal use. The owner's drawing account (J. Green, drawing) increases and is debited for $50, and an asset account (cash) decreases and is credited for $50.

General Journal

GJ2

Date	Account Title and Description	Ref.	Debit	Credit
28	Advertising Expense	520	35	
	Cash	100		35
	Printed advertisements			
29	J. Green, Drawing	350	50	
	Cash	100		50
	Owner withdrawal			

J. Green, Drawing

350

Date	Explanation	Ref.	Debit	Credit	Balance
20X2					
Apr. 29	Owner withdrawal	GJ2	50		50

Cash

100

Date	Explanation	Ref.	Debit	Credit	Balance
20X2					
Apr. 1	Owner investment	GJ1	15,000		15,000
2	Truck downpayment	GJ1		5,000	10,000
3	Lawnmower purchase	GJ1		3,000	7,000
5	Gas for lawnmowers	GJ1		30	6,970
5	Annual ins. premium	GJ1		1,200	5,770
14	Cut seven lawns	GJ1	350		6,120
20	Prepayment	GJ1	270		6,390
26	Wages through 4-26	GJ2		200	6,190
28	Printed advertisements	GJ2		35	6,155
29	Owner withdrawal	GJ2		50	6,105

Transaction 13: On April 30, five of the eight previously billed customers each pay $50. Therefore, one asset account (cash) increases and is debited for $250, and another asset account (accounts receivable) decreases and is credited for $250.

General Journal   GJ2

Date	Account Title and Description	Ref.	Debit	Credit
29	J. Green, Drawing	350	50	
	Cash	100		50
	Owner withdrawal			
30	Cash	100	250	
	Accounts Receivable	110		250
	Received customer payments			

Cash   100

Date	Explanation	Ref.	Debit	Credit	Balance
20X2					
Apr. 1	Owner investment	GJ1	15,000		15,000
2	Truck downpayment	GJ1		5,000	10,000
3	Lawnmower purchase	GJ1		3,000	7,000
5	Gas for lawnmowers	GJ1		30	6,970
5	Insurance premium	GJ1		1,200	5,770
14	Cut seven lawns	GJ1	350		6,120
20	Prepayment	GJ1	270		6,390
26	Wages through 4-26	GJ2		200	6,190
28	Printed advertisements	GJ2		35	6,155
29	Owner withdrawal	GJ2		50	6,105
30	Customer payments	GJ2	250		6,355

Accounts Receivable   110

Date	Explanation	Ref.	Debit	Credit	Balance
20X2					
Apr. 22	Cut eight lawns	GJ2	400		400
30	Customer payments	GJ2		250	150

The Trial Balance

After posting all transactions from an accounting period, accountants prepare a **trial balance** to verify that the total of all accounts with debit balances equals the total of all accounts with credit balances. The trial balance lists every open general ledger account by account number and provides separate debit and credit columns for entering account balances. The Greener Landscape Group's trial balance for April 30, 20X2 appears below.

The Greener Landscape Group
Trial Balance
April 30, 20X2

	Account	Debit	Credit
100	Cash	$ 6,355	
110	Accounts Receivable	150	
140	Supplies	50	
145	Prepaid Insurance	1,200	
150	Equipment	3,000	
155	Vehicles	15,000	
200	Accounts Payable		$ 50
250	Unearned Revenue		270
280	Notes Payable		10,000
300	J. Green, Capital		15,000
350	J. Green, Drawing	50	
400	Lawn Cutting Revenue		750
500	Wages Expense	200	
510	Gas Expense	30	
520	Advertising Expense	35	
		$26,070	$26,070

Although dollar signs are not used in journals or ledger accounts, trial balances generally include dollar signs next to the first figure in each column and next to each column's total. Trial balances usually include accounts that had activity during the accounting period but have a zero balance at the end of the period.

An error has occurred when total debits on a trial balance do not equal total credits. There are standard techniques for uncovering some of the errors that cause unequal trial balances. After double-checking each column's total to make sure the problem is not simply an addition error on the trial balance, find the difference between the debit and credit balance totals. If the number *2* divides evenly into this difference, look for an account balance that equals half the difference and that incorrectly appears in the column with the larger total. If the Greener Landscape Group's $50 accounts payable balance were mistakenly put in the debit column, for example, total debits would be $100 greater than total credits on the trial balance.

If the number *9* divides evenly into the difference between the debit and credit balance totals, look for a transposition error in one of the account balances. For example, suppose the cash account's balance of $6,355 were incorrectly entered on the trial balance as $6,535. This would cause total debits to be $180 greater than total credits on the trial balance, an amount evenly divisible by *9* ($180 ÷ 9 = $20). Incidentally, the number of digits in the resulting quotient—the quotient *20* has two digits—always indicates that the transposition error begins this number of digits from the right side of an account balance. Also, the value of the leftmost digit in the quotient—*2* in this case—always equals the difference between the two transposed numbers. Test this by transposing any two adjacent numbers in the trial balance and performing the calculations yourself.

If the difference between the debit and credit balance totals is not divisible by *2* or *9*, look for a ledger account with a balance that equals the difference and is missing from the trial balance. Of course, two or more errors can combine to render these techniques ineffective, and other types of mistakes frequently occur. If the error is not apparent, return to the ledger and recalculate each account's balance. If the error remains, return to the journal and verify that each transaction is posted correctly.

Some errors do not cause the trial balance's column totals to disagree. For example, the columns in a trial balance agree when transactions are not journalized or when journal entries are not posted to the general ledger. Similarly, recording transactions in the wrong accounts does not lead to unequal trial balances. Another common error a trial balance does not catch happens when a single transaction is posted twice. The trial balance is a useful tool, but every transaction must be carefully analyzed, journalized, and posted to ensure the reliability and usefulness of accounting records.

Before financial statements are prepared, additional journal entries, called **adjusting entries,** are made to ensure that the company's financial records adhere to the revenue recognition and matching principles. Adjusting entries are necessary because a single transaction may affect revenues or expenses in more than one accounting period and also because all transactions have not necessarily been documented during the period.

Each adjusting entry usually affects one income statement account (a revenue or expense account) and one balance sheet account (an asset or liability account). For example, suppose a company has a $1,000 debit balance in its supplies account at the end of a month, but a count of supplies on hand finds only $300 of them remaining. Since supplies worth $700 have been used up, the supplies account requires a $700 adjustment so assets are not overstated, and the supplies expense account requires a $700 adjustment so expenses are not understated.

Adjustments fall into one of five categories: accrued revenues, accrued expenses, unearned revenues, prepaid expenses, and depreciation.

Accrued Revenues

An adjusting entry to accrue revenues is necessary when revenues have been earned but not yet recorded. Examples of unrecorded revenues may involve interest revenue and completed services or delivered goods that, for any number of reasons, have not been billed to customers. Suppose a customer owes 6% interest on a three-year, $10,000 note receivable but has not yet made any payments. At the end of each accounting period, the company recognizes the interest revenue that has accrued on this long-term receivable.

Unless otherwise specified, interest is calculated with the following formula: principal × annual interest rate × time period in years.

$$\$10,000 \times 6\% \times \frac{30}{360} = \$50$$

Most textbooks use a 360-day year for interest calculations, which is done here. In practice, however, most lenders make more precise calculations by using a 365-day year.

Since the company accrues $50 in interest revenue during the month, an adjusting entry is made to increase (debit) an asset account (interest receivable) by $50 and to increase (credit) a revenue account (interest revenue) by $50.

General Journal   GJ3

Date	Account Title and Description	Ref.	Debit	Credit
20X7				
Apr. 30	Interest Receivable	115	50	
	Interest Revenue	420		50
	Accrue interest			

Interest Receivable   115

Date	Explanation	Ref.	Debit	Credit	Balance
20X7					
Apr. 30	Accrue interest	GJ3	50		50

Interest Revenue   420

Date	Explanation	Ref.	Debit	Credit	Balance
20X7					
Apr. 30	Accrue interest	GJ3		50	50

If a plumber does $90 worth of work for a customer on the last day of April but doesn't send a bill until May 4, the revenue should be recognized in April's accounting records. Therefore, the plumber makes an adjusting entry to increase (debit) accounts receivable for $90 and to increase (credit) service revenue for $90.

General Journal   GJ4

Date	Account Title and Description	Ref.	Debit	Credit
20X7				
Apr. 30	Accounts Receivable	110	90	
	Service Revenue	400		90
	Accrue unbilled service			

Accounts Receivable   110

Date	Explanation	Ref.	Debit	Credit	Balance
20X7					3,610
Apr. 30	Accrue unbilled service	GJ4	90		3,700

Service Revenue   400

Date	Explanation	Ref.	Debit	Credit	Balance
20X7					12,100
Apr. 30	Accrue unbilled service	GJ4		90	12,190

Accounting records that do not include adjusting entries for accrued revenues understate total assets, total revenues, and net income.

Accrued Expenses

An adjusting entry to accrue expenses is necessary when there are unrecorded expenses and liabilities that apply to a given accounting period. These expenses may include wages for work performed in the current accounting period but not paid until the following accounting period and also the accumulation of interest on notes payable and other debts.

Suppose a company owes its employees $2,000 in unpaid wages at the end of an accounting period. The company makes an adjusting entry to accrue the expense by increasing (debiting) wages expense for $2,000 and by increasing (crediting) wages payable for $2,000.

General Journal   GJ9

Date	Account Title and Description	Ref.	Debit	Credit
20X7				
Oct. 31	Wages Expense	500	2,000	
	Wages Payable	270		2,000
	Accrue wages			

Wages Expense   500

Date	Explanation	Ref.	Debit	Credit	Balance
20X7					20,000
Oct. 31	Accrue wages	GJ9	2,000		22,000

Wages Payable   270

Date	Explanation	Ref.	Debit	Credit	Balance
20X7					
Oct. 31	Accrue wages	GJ9		2,000	2,000

If a long-term note payable of $10,000 carries an annual interest rate of 12%, then $1,200 in interest expense accrues each year. At the close of each month, therefore, the company makes an adjusting entry to increase (debit) interest expense for $100 and to increase (credit) interest payable for $100.

General Journal   GJ5

Date	Account Title and Description	Ref.	Debit	Credit
20X7				
May 31	Interest Expense	530	100	
	Interest Payable	220		100
	Accrue interest			

Interest Expense   530

Date	Explanation	Ref.	Debit	Credit	Balance
20X7					
May 31	Accrue interest	GJ5	100		100

Interest Payable   220

Date	Explanation	Ref.	Debit	Credit	Balance
20X7					
May 31	Accrue interest	GJ5		100	100

Accounting records that do not include adjusting entries for accrued expenses understate total liabilities and total expenses and overstate net income.

Unearned Revenues

Unearned revenues are payments for future services to be performed or goods to be delivered. Advance customer payments for newspaper subscriptions or extended warranties are unearned revenues at the time of sale. At the end of each accounting period, adjusting entries must be made to recognize the portion of unearned revenues that have been earned during the period.

Suppose a customer pays $1,800 for an insurance policy to protect her delivery vehicles for six months. Initially, the insurance company records this transaction by increasing an asset account (cash) with a debit and by increasing a liability account (unearned revenue) with a credit. After one month, the insurance company makes an adjusting entry to decrease (debit) unearned revenue and to increase (credit) revenue by an amount equal to one sixth of the initial payment.

General Journal — GJ1

Date	Account Title and Description	Ref.	Debit	Credit
20X7				
Jan. 31	Unearned Insurance Revenue	250	300	
	Vehicle Insurance Revenue	425		300
	Earned insurance premiums			

Unearned Insurance Revenue — 250

Date	Explanation	Ref.	Debit	Credit	Balance
20X7					1,800
Jan. 31	Earned premiums	GJ1	300		1,500

Vehicle Insurance Revenue — 425

Date	Explanation	Ref.	Debit	Credit	Balance
20X7					
Jan. 31	Earned premiums	GJ1		300	300

Accounting records that do not include adjusting entries to show the earning of previously unearned revenues overstate total liabilities and understate total revenues and net income.

Prepaid Expenses

Prepaid expenses are assets that become expenses as they expire or get used up. For example, office supplies are considered an asset until they are used in the course of doing business, at which time they become an expense. At the end of each accounting period, adjusting entries are necessary to recognize the portion of prepaid expenses that have become actual expenses through use or the passage of time.

Consider the previous example from the point of view of the customer who pays $1,800 for six months of insurance coverage. Initially, she records the transaction by increasing one asset account (prepaid insurance) with a debit and by decreasing another asset account (cash) with a credit. After one month, she makes an adjusting entry to increase (debit) insurance expense for $300 and to decrease (credit) prepaid insurance for $300.

General Journal   GJ1

Date	Account Title and Description	Ref.	Debit	Credit
20X7				
Jan. 31	Insurance Expense	550	300	
	Prepaid Insurance	145		300
	Expired insurance			

Insurance Expense   550

Date	Explanation	Ref.	Debit	Credit	Balance
20X7					
Jan. 31	Expired insurance	GJ1	300		300

Prepaid Insurance   145

Date	Explanation	Ref.	Debit	Credit	Balance
20X7					1,800
Jan. 31	Expired insurance	GJ1		300	1,500

Prepaid expenses in one company's accounting records are often—but not always—unearned revenues in another company's accounting records. Office supplies provide an example of a prepaid expense that does not appear on another company's books as unearned revenue.

Accounting records that do not include adjusting entries to show the expiration or consumption of prepaid expenses overstate assets and net income and understate expenses.

Depreciation

Depreciation is the process of allocating the depreciable cost of a long-lived asset, except for land which is never depreciated, to expense over the asset's estimated service life. **Depreciable cost** includes all costs necessary to acquire an asset and make it ready for use minus the asset's expected **salvage value,** which is the asset's worth at the end of its **service life,** usually the amount of time the asset is expected to be used in the business. For example, if a truck costs $30,000, has an expected salvage value of $6,000, and has an estimated service life of sixty months, then $24,000 is allocated to expense at a rate of $400 each month ($24,000 ÷ 60 = $400). This method of calculating depreciation expense, called **straight-line depreciation,** is the simplest and most widely used method for financial reporting purposes. However, several other methods of calculating depreciation expense are discussed on pages 178–190.

Some accountants treat depreciation as a special type of prepaid expense because the adjusting entries have the same effect on the accounts. Accounting records that do not include adjusting entries for depreciation expense overstate assets and net income and understate expenses. Nevertheless, most accountants consider depreciation to be a distinct type of adjustment because of the special account structure used to report depreciation expense on the balance sheet.

Since the original cost of a long-lived asset should always be readily identifiable, a different type of balance-sheet account, called **a contra-asset account,** is used to record depreciation expense. Increases and normal balances appear on the credit side of a contra-asset account. The **net book value** of long-lived assets is found by subtracting the contra-asset account's credit balance from the corresponding asset account's debit balance. Do not confuse book value with market value. Book value is the portion of the asset's cost that has not been written off to expense. **Market value** is the price someone would pay for the asset. These two values are usually different.

Suppose an accountant calculates that a $125,000 piece of equipment depreciates by $1,000 each month. After one month, he makes an adjusting entry to increase (debit) an expense account (depreciation expense–equipment) by $1,000 and to increase (credit) a contra-asset account (accumulated depreciation–equipment) by $1,000.

General Journal   GJ10

Date	Account Title and Description	Ref.	Debit	Credit
20X7				
Dec. 31	Depreciation Expense–Equipment	560	1,000	
	Accumulated Depreciation–Equipment	160		1,000
	Monthly depreciation			

Depreciation Expense–Equipment   560

Date	Explanation	Ref.	Debit	Credit	Balance
20X7					
Dec. 31	Monthly depreciation	GJ10	1,000		1,000

Accumulated Depreciation–Equipment   160

Date	Explanation	Ref.	Debit	Credit	Balance
20X7					
Dec. 31	Monthly depreciation	GJ10		1,000	1,000

On a balance sheet, the accumulated depreciation account's balance is subtracted from the equipment account's balance to show the equipment's net book value.

ACME Manufacturing
Partial Balance Sheet
December 31, 20X7

Property, Plant, and Equipment		
Equipment	125,000	
Less: Accumulated Depreciation	(1,000)	124,000

The Adjustment Process Illustrated

Accountants prepare a trial balance both before and after making adjusting entries. Reexamine the Greener Landscape Group's unadjusted trial balance for April 30, 20X2.

The Greener Landscape Group
Trial Balance
April 30, 20X2

Account		Debit	Credit
100	Cash	$ 6,355	
110	Accounts Receivable	150	
140	Supplies	50	
145	Prepaid Insurance	1,200	
150	Equipment	3,000	
155	Vehicles	15,000	
200	Accounts Payable		$ 50
250	Unearned Revenue		270
280	Notes Payable		10,000
300	J. Green, Capital		15,000
350	J. Green, Drawing	50	
400	Lawn Cutting Revenue		750
500	Wages Expense	200	
510	Gas Expense	30	
520	Advertising Expense	35	
		$26,070	$26,070

Consider eight adjusting entries recorded in Mr. Green's general journal and posted to his general ledger accounts. Then, see the **adjusted trial balance,** which shows the balance of all accounts after the adjusting entries are journalized and posted to the general ledger accounts.

Adjustment A: During the afternoon of April 30, Mr. Green cuts one lawn, and he agrees to mail the customer a bill for $50, which he does on May 2. In accordance with the revenue recognition principle (page 12), Mr. Green makes an adjusting entry in April to increase (debit) accounts receivable for $50 and to increase (credit) lawn cutting revenue for $50.

General Journal GJ2

Date	Account Title and Description	Ref.	Debit	Credit
30	Cash	100	250	
	Accounts Receivable	110		250
	Received customer payments			
30	Accounts Receivable	110	50	
	Lawn Cutting Revenue	400		50
	Accrue unbilled revenue			

Accounts Receivable 110

Date	Explanation	Ref.	Debit	Credit	Balance
20X2					
Apr. 22	Cut eight lawns	GJ2	400		400
30	Customer payments	GJ2		250	150
30	Accrue unbilled revenue	GJ2	50		200

Lawn Cutting Revenue 400

Date	Explanation	Ref.	Debit	Credit	Balance
20X2					
Apr. 14	Cut seven lawns	GJ1		350	350
22	Cut eight lawns	GJ2		400	750
30	Accrue unbilled revenue	GJ2		50	800

Adjustment B: Mr. Green's $10,000 note payable, which he signed on April 2, carries a 10.2% interest rate. Interest calculations usually exclude the day that loans occur and include the day that loans are paid off. Therefore, Mr. Green uses the formula below to calculate how much interest expense accrued during the final twenty-eight days of April.

$$\$10,000 \times 10.2\% \times \frac{28}{360} = \$79$$

Since the matching principle requires that expenses be reported in the accounting period to which they apply, Mr. Green makes an adjusting entry to increase (debit) interest expense for $79 and to increase (credit) interest payable for $79.

General Journal   GJ2

Date	Account Title and Description	Ref.	Debit	Credit
30	Accounts Receivable	110	50	
	Lawn Cutting Revenue	400		50
	Accrue unbilled revenue			
30	Interest Expense	530	79	
	Interest Payable	220		79
	Accrue interest			

Interest Expense   530

Date	Explanation	Ref.	Debit	Credit	Balance
20X2					
Apr. 30	Accrue interest	GJ2	79		79

Interest Payable   220

Date	Explanation	Ref.	Debit	Credit	Balance
20X2					
Apr. 30	Accrue interest	GJ2		79	79

Adjustment C: Mr. Green's part-time employee earns $80 during the last four days of April but will not be paid until May 10. This requires an adjusting entry that increases (debits) wages expense for $80 and that increases (credits) wages payable for $80.

General Journal   GJ2

Date	Account Title and Description	Ref.	Debit	Credit
30	Interest Expense	530	79	
	Interest Payable	220		79
	Accrue interest			
30	Wages Expense	500	80	
	Wages Payable	210		80
	Accrue wages 4-27 to 4-30			

Wages Expense   500

Date	Explanation	Ref.	Debit	Credit	Balance
20X2					
Apr. 26	Wages through 4-26	GJ2	200		200
30	Accrue wages 4-27 to 4-30	GJ2	80		280

Wages Payable   210

Date	Explanation	Ref.	Debit	Credit	Balance
20X2					
Apr. 30	Accrue wages 4-27 to 4-30	GJ2		80	80

Adjustment D: On April 20 Mr. Green received a $270 prepayment for six future visits. Assuming Mr. Green completed one of these visits in April, he must make a $45 adjusting entry to decrease (debit) unearned revenue and to increase (credit) lawn cutting revenue.

General Journal GJ3

Date	Account Title and Description	Ref.	Debit	Credit
20X2				
Apr. 30	Unearned Revenue	250	45	
	Lawn Cutting Revenue	400		45
	Earned revenue			

Unearned Revenue 250

Date	Explanation	Ref.	Debit	Credit	Balance
20X2					
Apr. 20	Prepayment	GJ1		270	270
30	Earned revenue	GJ3	45		225

Lawn Cutting Revenue 400

Date	Explanation	Ref.	Debit	Credit	Balance
20X2					
Apr. 14	Cut seven lawns	GJ1		350	350
22	Cut eight lawns	GJ2		400	750
30	Accrue unbilled revenue	GJ2		50	800
30	Earned revenue	GJ3		45	845

Adjustment E: Mr. Green discovers that he used $25 worth of office supplies during April. He therefore makes a $25 adjusting entry to increase (debit) supplies expense and to decrease (credit) supplies.

General Journal   GJ3

Date	Account Title and Description	Ref.	Debit	Credit
20X2				
Apr. 30	Unearned Revenue	250	45	
	Lawn Cutting Revenue	400		45
	Earned revenue			
30	Supplies Expense	540	25	
	Supplies	140		25
	Supplies used			

Supplies Expense   540

Date	Explanation	Ref.	Debit	Credit	Balance
20X2					
Apr. 30	Supplies used	GJ3	25		25

Supplies   140

Date	Explanation	Ref.	Debit	Credit	Balance
20X2					
Apr. 5	Bought office supplies	GJ1	50		50
30	Supplies used	GJ3		25	25

Adjustment F: Mr. Green must record the expiration of one twelfth of his company's insurance policy. Since the annual premium is $1,200, he makes a $100 adjusting entry to increase (debit) insurance expense and to decrease (credit) prepaid insurance.

General Journal   GJ3

Date	Account Title and Description	Ref.	Debit	Credit
30	Supplies Expense	540	25	
	Supplies	140		25
	Supplies used			
30	Insurance Expense	545	100	
	Prepaid Insurance	145		100
	Expired insurance			

Insurance Expense   545

Date	Explanation	Ref.	Debit	Credit	Balance
20X2					
Apr. 30	Expired insurance	GJ3	100		100

Prepaid Insurance   145

Date	Explanation	Ref.	Debit	Credit	Balance
20X2					
Apr. 5	Insurance premium	GJ1	1,200		1,200
30	Expired insurance	GJ3		100	1,100

Adjustment G: If depreciation expense on Mr. Green's $15,000 truck is $200 each month, he makes a $200 adjusting entry to increase (debit) an expense account (depreciation expense–vehicles) and to increase (credit) a contra-asset account (accumulated depreciation–vehicles).

General Journal   GJ3

Date	Account Title and Description	Ref.	Debit	Credit
30	Insurance Expense	550	100	
	Prepaid Insurance	145		100
	Expired insurance			
30	Depreciation Expense–Vehicles	556	200	
	Accumulated Depreciation–Vehicles	156		200
	Monthly vehicle depreciation			

Depreciation Expense–Vehicles   556

Date	Explanation	Ref.	Debit	Credit	Balance
20X2					
Apr. 30	Monthly depreciation	GJ3	200		200

Accumulated Depreciation–Vehicles   156

Date	Explanation	Ref.	Debit	Credit	Balance
20X2					
Apr. 30	Monthly depreciation	GJ3		200	200

The truck's net book value is now $14,800, which is calculated by subtracting the $200 credit balance in the accumulated depreciation–vehicles account from the $15,000 debit balance in the vehicles account. Many accountants calculate the depreciation of long-lived assets to the nearest month. Had Mr. Green purchased the truck on April 16 or later, he might not make this adjusting entry until the end of May.

Adjustment H: If depreciation expense on Mr. Green's equipment is $35 each month, he makes a $35 adjusting entry to increase (debit) depreciation expense–equipment and to increase (credit) accumulated depreciation–equipment.

General Journal — GJ3

Date	Account Title and Description	Ref.	Debit	Credit
30	Depreciation Expense–Vehicles	556	200	
	Accumulated Depreciation–Vehicles	156		200
	Monthly vehicle depreciation			
30	Depreciation Expense–Equipment	551	35	
	Accumulated Depreciation–Equipment	151		35
	Monthly equipment depreciation			

Depreciation Expense–Equipment — 551

Date	Explanation	Ref.	Debit	Credit	Balance
20X2					
Apr. 30	Monthly depreciation	GJ3	35		35

Accumulated Depreciation–Equipment — 151

Date	Explanation	Ref.	Debit	Credit	Balance
20X2					
Apr. 30	Monthly depreciation	GJ3		35	35

After journalizing and posting all of the adjusting entries, Mr. Green prepares an adjusted trial balance. The Greener Landscape Group's adjusted trial balance for April 30, 20X2 appears below.

The Greener Landscape Group
Adjusted Trial Balance
April 30, 20X2

	Account	Debit	Credit
100	Cash	$ 6,355	
110	Accounts Receivable	200	
140	Supplies	25	
145	Prepaid Insurance	1,100	
150	Equipment	3,000	
151	Accumulated Depreciation–Equipment		$ 35
155	Vehicles	15,000	
156	Accumulated Depreciation–Vehicles		200
200	Accounts Payable		50
210	Wages Payable		80
220	Interest Payable		79
250	Unearned Revenue		225
280	Notes Payable		10,000
300	J. Green, Capital		15,000
350	J. Green, Drawing	50	
400	Lawn Cutting Revenue		845
500	Wages Expense	280	
510	Gas Expense	30	
520	Advertising Expense	35	
530	Interest Expense	79	
540	Supplies Expense	25	
545	Insurance Expense	100	
551	Depreciation Expense–Equipment	35	
556	Depreciation Expense–Vehicles	200	
		$26,514	$26,514

Financial Statements

Financial statements are prepared immediately after the adjusted trial balance. Although the first chapter of this book introduces the four basic financial statements, knowing how to record transactions, make adjusting entries, and create trial balances gives you a greater understanding of the information financial statements contain.

Income statement. The income statement, which is sometimes called the statement of earnings or statement of operations, lists all revenue and expense account balances and shows the company's net income or net loss for a particular period of time. This statement may be prepared using a single-step or multiple-step format. The single-step format puts revenue and expense accounts into separate groups. Then, total expenses are subtracted from total revenues to determine the net income or loss.

The Greener Landscape Group
Income Statement
For the Month Ended April 30, 20X2

Revenues		
Lawn Cutting Revenue		$845
Expenses		
Wages Expense	$280	
Depreciation Expense–Vehicles	200	
Insurance Expense	100	
Interest Expense	79	
Depreciation Expense–Equipment	35	
Advertising Expense	35	
Gas Expense	30	
Supplies Expense	25	
Total Expenses		784
Net Income		$ 61

The multiple-step format uses the same accounts and balances but separates the cost of services provided from operating expenses and also includes a category for other types of income and expense.

The Greener Landscape Group
Income Statement
For the Month Ended April 30, 20X2

Revenues		
Lawn Cutting Revenue		$845
Cost of Services Provided		
Wages Expense	$280	
Depreciation Expense–Vehicles	200	
Insurance Expense	100	
Depreciation Expense–Equipment	35	
Gas Expense	30	
Total Cost of Services Provided		645
Gross Profit		200
Operating Expenses		
Advertising Expense	35	
Supplies Expense	25	
Total Operating Expenses		60
Operating Income		140
Other Income/(Expense), Net		
Interest Expense		(79)
Net Income		$ 61

Companies may use slightly different categories for expenses, but the overall structure for this type of income statement is essentially the same. For example, merchandising companies include a category for the cost of goods sold, and many companies break operating expenses into two subcategories: selling expenses and general and administrative expenses.

Statement of owner's equity. The statement of owner's equity shows activity in the owner's equity accounts for a particular period of time. The capital account's opening balance is followed by a list of increases and decreases, and the account's closing balance is calculated from this information. Increases include investments made by the owner and net income. Decreases include owner withdrawals and net loss. Since the income statement already shows all revenue and expense account balances, only the company's net income or loss appears on this statement.

The Greener Landscape Group
Statement of Owner's Equity
For the Month Ended April 30, 20X2

J. Green, Capital, April 1		$ 0
Additions		
Investments	$15,000	
Net Income	61	15,061
Withdrawals		(50)
J. Green, Capital, April 30		$15,011

Balance sheet. The balance sheet lists the asset, liability, and owner's equity balances at a specific time. It proves that the accounting equation (Assets = Liabilities + Owner's Equity) is in balance. The ending balance on the statement of owner's equity is used to report owner's equity on the balance sheet.

The Greener Landscape Group
Balance Sheet
April 30, 20X2

Assets		
Cash		$ 6,355
Accounts Receivable		200
Supplies		25
Prepaid Insurance		1,100
Vehicles	$15,000	
Less: Accumulated Depreciation	(200)	
Equipment	3,000	
Less: Accumulated Depreciation	(35)	17,765
Total Assets		$25,445

Liabilities and Owner's Equity		
Liabilities		
Accounts Payable		$ 50
Wages Payable		80
Interest Payable		79
Unearned Revenue		225
Notes Payable		10,000
Total Liabilities		10,434
Owner's Equity		
J. Green, Capital		15,011
Total Liabilities and Owner's Equity		$25,445

To aid readers, most companies prepare a classified balance sheet, which categorizes assets and liabilities. The standard asset categories on a classified balance sheet are current assets; property, plant, and equipment; long-term investments; and intangible assets. Liabilities are generally divided into current liabilities and long-term liabilities. The first chapter includes a detailed description of these categories.

The Greener Landscape Group
Balance Sheet
April 30, 20X2

ASSETS			
Current Assets			
Cash			$ 6,355
Accounts Receivable			200
Supplies			25
Prepaid Insurance			1,100
Total Current Assets			7,680
Property, Plant, and Equipment			
Vehicles	$15,000		
Less: Accumulated Depreciation	(200)	$14,800	
Vehicles	3,000		
Less: Accumulated Depreciation	(35)	2,965	17,765
Total Assets			$25,445
LIABILITIES AND OWNER'S EQUITY			
Current Liabilities			
Accounts Payable			$ 50
Wages Payable			80
Interest Payable			79
Unearned Revenue			225
Total Current Liabilities			434
Long-Term Liabilities			
Notes Payable			10,000
Total Liabilities			10,434
Owner's Equity			
J. Green, Capital			15,011
Total Liabilities and Owner's Equity			$25,445

Statement of cash flows. The statement of cash flows places all cash exchanges into one of three categories—operating, investing, or financing—to calculate the net change in cash during the accounting period. **Operating cash flows** arise from day-to-day business operations such as inventory purchases, sales revenue, and payroll expenses. Note that interest and dividends received from long-term assets (investing activities) and interest payments for long-term loans (financing activities) appear on the income statement, so they would appear as operating cash flows on the statement of cash flows. Income taxes are also included with operating cash flows. **Investing cash flows** relate to cash exchanges involving long-term assets, such as the purchase or sale of land, buildings, equipment, or long-term investments in another company's stock or debt. **Financing cash flows** involve changes in long-term liabilities and owner's equity. Examples include the receipt or early retirement of long-term loans, the sale or repurchase of stock, and the payment of dividends to shareholders.

The Greener Landscape Group
Statement of Cash Flows
For the Month Ended April 30, 20X2

Cash Flows from Operating Activities	
Cash from Customers	$ 870
Cash to Employees	(200)
Cash to Suppliers	(1,265)
Cash Flow Used by Operating Activities	(595)
Cash Flows from Investing Activities	
Purchase of Vehicle	(5,000)
Purchase of Equipment	(3,000)
Cash Flow Used by Investing Activities	(8,000)
Cash Flows from Financing Activities	
Investment by Owner	15,000
Withdrawal by Owner	(50)
Cash Flow Provided by Financing Activities	14,950
Net Increase in Cash	6,355
Beginning Cash, April 1	0
Ending Cash, April 30	$ 6,355

Noncash Financing and Investing Activity
The company purchased a used truck for $15,000, paying $5,000 in cash and signing a note for the remaining balance. The note payable portion of the transaction is not included on this statement.

As its name implies, this statement focuses on cash flows rather than income. For example, the $870 Mr. Green receives from customers includes unearned revenues and excludes accounts receivable. At the bottom of the statement, the net increase or decrease in cash is used to reconcile the accounting period's beginning and ending cash balances. Significant noncash transactions likely to impact cash flow in other accounting periods must also be disclosed, but this does not occur in the body of the statement. The footnote in the illustration shows one way to accomplish such disclosures.

According to current accounting standards, operating cash flows may be disclosed using either the direct or the indirect method. The **direct method,** which appears in the illustration on the previous page, simply lists operating cash flows by type of cash receipt and payment. The direct method is straightforward and easy to interpret, but only a small percentage of companies actually use this method. *Cliffs Quick Review Accounting Principles II* explains the indirect method in detail, but a short description of the indirect method is worth mentioning here because most companies use it. The **indirect method** reports operating cash flows by listing the company's net income or loss and then adjusting this figure because net income is not calculated on the cash basis.

The Work Sheet

Many accountants use a work sheet to prepare the unadjusted trial balance, to assign the adjusting entries to the correct accounts, to create the adjusted trial balance, and then to prepare preliminary financial statements. A work sheet is an optional step in the accounting cycle. It is an informal document that is not considered a financial statement, although it gives management some information about results for a period. Work sheets usually have five sets of debit and credit columns, which are completed from left to right one set at a time. Turn the page to see the Greener Landscape Group's work sheet for the month of April.

Use the first set of columns to prepare a trial balance. List all open accounts on the left side of the work sheet and enter each account's debit or credit balance in the appropriate columns immediately to the right. The trial balance in the sample work sheet includes the same information as the trial balance shown on page 38.

The second set of columns shows how the adjusting entries affect the accounts. While completing these columns, list additional accounts as needed along the left side of the work sheet. Use a letter to index the debit and credit portion of each adjusting entry so that, later, it is easier to journalize and post the adjustments. An explanation of each adjustment may be written at the bottom of the work sheet. If an account has more than one adjustment, each is shown separately, using as many lines as necessary. After entering all the adjustments on the work sheet, make sure the column totals are equal.

The third set of columns contains the adjusted trial balance. The adjusted account balances in these columns equal the sum of the trial balance and adjustments columns. Consider the first three accounts on the Greener Landscape Group's work sheet. Since no adjustments affect the cash account, that account's debit balance carries across to the debit column of the adjusted trial balance. Accounts receivable begins with a $150 debit balance and has a $50 debit in the adjustments column. These amounts combine to give the account a $200 debit balance in the adjusted trial balance. In the supplies account, a $50 debit balance combines with a $25 credit in the adjustments column to yield a $25 debit balance. Although each individual account works this way, the totals at the bottom of the trial balance and adjustments columns cannot be combined to determine the column totals at the bottom of the adjusted trial balance—adding $26,070 to $614 clearly does not yield $26,514. After entering each balance in the work sheet's adjusted trial balance, total each column to make sure the debits and credits are equal.

Each account's adjusted trial balance transfers directly to either the fourth or fifth set of columns. Move all revenue and expense account balances to the income statement columns, and move all other account balances (assets, liabilities, owner's capital, and owner's drawing) to the balance sheet columns. Then total each of the final four columns. Unless net income is zero, the columns have unequal debit and credit totals. If total credits are greater than total debits in the income statement columns, the company has net income, and the difference between these columns is added to the work sheet's income statement debit column and balance sheet credit column on a line labeled *Net Income*. The difference is added to the balance sheet credit column because net income increases owner's equity, and increases to owner's equity are recorded with credits. If total debits are greater than total credits in the income statement columns, a net loss occurs, and the difference between these column totals is added to the work sheet's income statement credit column and balance sheet debit column on a line labeled *Net Loss*. Once the company's net income or net loss is added to the correct income statement and balance sheet columns, each set of debit and credit columns balance, and the work sheet is complete.

Prepare the income statement, statement of owner's equity, and balance sheet from the completed work sheet. The accounts and balances in the work sheet's income statement columns transfer directly to the income statement, which is prepared first. Next, from the work sheet's balance sheet columns, use the owner's capital and drawing account balances and the company's net income or loss to complete the statement of owner's equity. Complete the balance sheet last. When

The Greener Landscape Group
Work Sheet
For the Month Ended April 30, 20X2

Account	Trial Balance Dr.	Trial Balance Cr.	Adjustments Dr.	Adjustments Cr.	Adjusted Trial Balance Dr.	Adjusted Trial Balance Cr.	Income Statement Dr.	Income Statement Cr.	Balance Sheet Dr.	Balance Sheet Cr.
Cash	6,355				6,355				6,355	
Accounts Receivable	150		50 (a)		200				200	
Supplies	50			25 (e)	25				25	
Prepaid Insurance	1,200			100 (f)	1,100				1,100	
Equipment	3,000				3,000				3,000	
Vehicles	15,000				15,000				15,000	
Accounts Payable		50				50				50
Unearned Revenue		270	45 (d)			225				225
Notes Payable		10,000				10,000				10,000
J. Green, Capital		15,000				15,000				15,000
J. Green, Drawing	50				50				50	
Lawn Cutting Revenue		750		50 (a) / 45 (d)		845		845		
Wages Expense	200		80 (c)		280		280			
Gas Expense	30				30		30			
Advertising Expense	35				35		35			
Totals	26,070	26,070								
Interest Expense			79 (b)		79		79			
Interest Payable				79 (b)		79				79
Wages Payable				80 (c)		80				80
Supplies Expense			25 (e)		25		25			
Insurance Expense			100 (f)		100		100			
Depreciation Expense–Vehicles			200 (g)		200		200			
Accumulated Depreciation–Vehicles				200 (g)		200				200
Depreciation Expense–Equipment			35 (h)		35		35			
Accumulated Depreciation–Equipment				35 (h)		35				35
Totals			614	614	26,514	26,514	784	845	25,730	25,669
Net Income							61			61
Totals							845	845	25,730	25,730

preparing the balance sheet, be careful *not* to use the capital account balance on the work sheet because it shows the capital account's beginning balance for the accounting period. Instead, use the ending balance on the statement of owner's equity, which has already adjusted the capital account's balance to reflect the company's net income or loss and any withdrawals made by the owner. After the financial statements are prepared, the adjusting entries are journalized and posted.

Closing Entries

To update the balance in the owner's capital account, accountants close revenue, expense, and drawing accounts at the end of each fiscal year or, occasionally, at the end of each accounting period. For this reason, these types of accounts are called **temporary** or **nominal accounts.** Assets, liabilities, and the owner's capital account, in contrast, are called **permanent** or **real accounts** because their ending balance in one accounting period is always the starting balance in the subsequent accounting period. When an accountant closes an account, the account balance returns to zero. Starting with zero balances in the temporary accounts each year makes it easier to track revenues, expenses, and withdrawals and to compare them from one year to the next. There are four **closing entries,** which transfer all temporary account balances to the owner's capital account.

1. Close the income statement accounts with credit balances (normally revenue accounts) to a special temporary account named *income summary.*

2. Close the income statement accounts with debit balances (normally expense accounts) to the income summary account. After all revenue and expense accounts are closed, the income summary account's balance equals the company's net income or loss for the period.

3. Close income summary to the owner's capital account or, in corporations, to the retained earnings account. The purpose of the income summary account is simply to keep the permanent owner's capital or retained earnings account uncluttered.

4. Close the owner's drawing account to the owner's capital account. In corporations, this entry closes any dividend accounts to the retained earnings account. For purposes of illustration, closing entries for the Greener Landscape Group appear on the next several pages.

Closing entry 1: The lawn cutting revenue account is Mr. Green's only income statement account with a credit balance. Debit this account for an amount equal to the account's balance, and credit income summary for the same amount.

General Journal — GJ3

Date	Account Title and Description	Ref.	Debit	Credit
30	Depreciation Expense–Equipment	551	35	
	Accumulated Depreciation–Equipment	151		35
	Monthly equipment depreciation			
	Closing Entries			
Apr. 30	Lawn Cutting Revenue	400	845	
	Income Summary	600		845
	Close credit-balance accounts			

Lawn Cutting Revenue — 400

Date	Explanation	Ref.	Debit	Credit	Balance
20X2					
Apr. 14	Cut seven lawns	GJ1		350	350
22	Cut eight lawns	GJ2		400	750
30	Accrue unbilled revenue	GJ2		50	800
30	Earned revenue	GJ3		45	845
30	Closing entry	GJ3	845		0

Income Summary — 600

Date	Explanation	Ref.	Debit	Credit	Balance
20X2					
Apr. 30	Credit-balance accounts	GJ3		845	845

Closing entry 2: Mr. Green has eight income statement accounts with debit balances; they are all expense accounts. Close these accounts by debiting income summary for an amount equal to the combined

General Journal — GJ4

Date	Account Title and Description	Ref.	Debit	Credit
20X2				
Apr. 30	Income Summary	600	784	
	Wages Expense	500		280
	Gas Expense	510		30
	Advertising Expense	520		35
	Interest Expense	530		79
	Supplies Expense	540		25
	Insurance Expense	545		100
	Depreciation Expense–Equipment	551		35
	Depreciation Expense–Vehicles	556		200
	Close debit-balance accounts			

Income Summary — 600

Date	Explanation	Ref.	Debit	Credit	Balance
20X2					
Apr. 30	Credit-balance accounts	GJ3		845	845
30	Debit-balance accounts	GJ4	784		61

Wages Expense — 500

Date	Explanation	Ref.	Debit	Credit	Balance
20X2					
Apr. 26	Wages through 4-26	GJ2	200		200
30	Accrue wages 4-27 to 4-30	GJ2	80		280
30	Closing entry	GJ4		280	0

Gas Expense — 510

Date	Explanation	Ref.	Debit	Credit	Balance
20X2					
Apr. 5	Gas for lawnmowers	GJ1	30		30
30	Closing entry	GJ4		30	0

debit balances of all eight expense accounts and by crediting each expense account for an amount equal to its own debit balance.

Advertising Expense 520

Date	Explanation	Ref.	Debit	Credit	Balance
20X2					
Apr. 28	Printed advertisements	GJ2	35		35
30	Closing entry	GJ4		35	0

Interest Expense 530

Date	Explanation	Ref.	Debit	Credit	Balance
20X2					
Apr. 30	Accrue interest	GJ2	79		79
30	Closing entry	GJ4		79	0

Supplies Expense 540

Date	Explanation	Ref.	Debit	Credit	Balance
20X2					
Apr. 30	Supplies used	GJ3	25		25
30	Closing entry	GJ4		25	0

Insurance Expense 545

Date	Explanation	Ref.	Debit	Credit	Balance
20X2					
Apr. 30	Expired insurance	GJ3	100		100
30	Closing entry	GJ4		100	0

Depreciation Expense–Equipment 551

Date	Explanation	Ref.	Debit	Credit	Balance
20X2					
Apr. 30	Monthly depreciation	GJ3	35		35
30	Closing entry	GJ4		35	0

Depreciation Expense–Vehicles 556

Date	Explanation	Ref.	Debit	Credit	Balance
20X2					
Apr. 30	Monthly depreciation	GJ3	200		200
30	Closing entry	GJ4		200	0

Closing entry 3: The income summary account's $61 credit balance equals the company's net income for the month of April. To close income summary, debit the account for $61 and credit the owner's capital account for the same amount.

General Journal — GJ4

Date	Account Title and Description	Ref.	Debit	Credit
20X2				
Apr. 30	Income Summary	600	784	
	Wages Expense	500		280
	Gas Expense	510		30
	Advertising Expense	520		35
	Interest Expense	530		79
	Supplies Expense	540		25
	Insurance Expense	545		100
	Depreciation Expense–Equipment	551		35
	Depreciation Expense–Vehicles	556		200
	Close debit-balance accounts			
30	Income Summary	600	61	
	J. Green, Capital	300		61
	Close income summary			

Income Summary — 600

Date	Explanation	Ref.	Debit	Credit	Balance
20X2					
Apr. 30	Credit-balance accounts	GJ3		845	845
30	Debit-balance accounts	GJ4	784		61
30	Transfer to capital	GJ4	61		0

J. Green, Capital — 300

Date	Explanation	Ref.	Debit	Credit	Balance
20X2					
Apr. 1	Owner investment	GJ1		15,000	15,000
30	Net income	GJ4		61	15,061

In partnerships, a compound entry transfers each partner's share of net income or loss to their own capital account. In corporations, income summary is closed to the retained earnings account.

Closing entry 4: Mr. Green's drawing account has a $50 debit balance. To close the account, credit it for $50 and debit the owner's capital account for the same amount.

General Journal — GJ4

Date	Account Title and Description	Ref.	Debit	Credit
30	Income Summary	600	61	
	J. Green, Capital	300		61
	Close income summary			
30	J. Green, Capital	300	50	
	J. Green, Drawing	350		50
	Close drawing account			

J. Green, Capital — 300

Date	Explanation	Ref.	Debit	Credit	Balance
20X2					
Apr. 1	Owner investment	GJ1		15,000	15,000
30	Net income	GJ4		61	15,061
30	Close drawing account	GJ4	50		15,011

J. Green, Drawing — 350

Date	Explanation	Ref.	Debit	Credit	Balance
20X2					
Apr. 29	Owner withdrawal	GJ2	50		50
30	Closing entry	GJ4		50	0

In a partnership, separate entries are made to close each partner's drawing account to his or her own capital account. If a corporation has more than one class of stock and uses dividend accounts to record dividend payments to investors, it usually uses a separate dividend account for each class. If this is the case, the corporation's accounting department makes a compound entry to close each dividend account to the retained earnings account.

The Post-Closing Trial Balance

After the closing entries are journalized and posted, only permanent, balance sheet accounts remain open. A post-closing trial balance is prepared to check the clerical accuracy of the closing entries and to prove that the accounting equation is in balance before the next accounting period begins.

The Greener Landscape Group
Post-Closing Trial Balance
April 30, 20X2

	Account	Debit	Credit
100	Cash	$ 6,355	
110	Accounts Receivable	200	
140	Supplies	25	
145	Prepaid Insurance	1,100	
150	Equipment	3,000	
151	Accumulated Depreciation–Equipment		$ 35
155	Vehicles	15,000	
156	Accumulated Depreciation–Vehicles		200
200	Accounts Payable		50
210	Wages Payable		80
220	Interest Payable		79
250	Unearned Revenue		225
280	Notes Payable		10,000
300	J. Green, Capital		15,011
		$25,680	$25,680

Page 39 explains how to locate errors when the two columns of a trial balance are unequal. Since there are several types of errors that trial balances fail to uncover, however, each closing entry must be journalized and posted carefully.

A Summary of the Accounting Cycle

The accounting cycle begins with the analysis of transactions recorded on source documents such as invoices and checks; it ends with the completion of a post-closing trial balance. This cycle consists of the following steps:

1. Analyze and journalize transactions.

2. Post the journal entries to the general ledger accounts.

3. Prepare a trial balance.

4. Journalize and post the adjusting entries.

5. Prepare an adjusted trial balance.

6. Prepare financial statements.

7. Journalize and post the closing entries.

8. Prepare a post-closing trial balance.

Steps one and two occur as often as needed during an accounting period. Steps three, four, five, and six occur at the end of each accounting period. Steps seven and eight usually occur only at the end of each fiscal year, but these steps may be completed at the end of each accounting period if the company chooses to do so.

If a work sheet is used, steps three, four, and five are initially recorded on the work sheet, which makes it possible to complete step six more quickly, but all adjusting entries on the work sheet must be journalized and posted before closing entries are made.

Reversing Entries

At the beginning of each accounting period, some accountants use **reversing entries** to cancel out the adjusting entries that were made to accrue revenues and expenses at the end of the previous accounting period. Reversing entries make it easier to record subsequent transactions by eliminating the need for certain compound entries.

Suppose Mr. Green makes an adjusting entry at the end of April to account for $80 in unpaid wages. This adjustment involves an $80 debit to the wages expense account and an $80 credit to the wages payable account.

General Journal   GJ2

Date	Account Title and Description	Ref.	Debit	Credit
30	Interest Expense	530	79	
	Interest Payable	220		79
	Accrue interest			
30	Wages Expense	500	80	
	Wages Payable	210		80
	Accrue wages 4-27 to 4-30			

Wages Expense   500

Date	Explanation	Ref.	Debit	Credit	Balance
20X2					
Apr. 26	Wages through 4-26	GJ2	200		200
30	Accrue wages 4-27 to 4-30	GJ2	80		280

Wages Payable   210

Date	Explanation	Ref.	Debit	Credit	Balance
20X2					
Apr. 30	Accrue wages 4-27 to 4-30	GJ2		80	80

If Mr. Green does not reverse the adjusting entry, he must remember that part of May's first payroll payment (for work completed in April) has already been recorded in the wages payable and wages expense accounts. Assuming Mr. Green pays $200 in wages on May 10, he makes a compound entry that decreases (debits) wages payable to $0, increases (debits) wages expense by an amount equal to the wage expenses for May 1 through May 10, and decreases (credits) cash for an amount equal to the total payment.

General Journal   GJ5

Date	Account Title and Description	Ref.	Debit	Credit
20X2				
May 10	Wages Payable	210	80	
	Wages Expense	500	120	
	Cash	100		200
	Wages 4-27 to 5-10			

Wages Payable   210

Date	Explanation	Ref.	Debit	Credit	Balance
20X2					
Apr. 30	Accrue wages 4-27 to 4-30	GJ2		80	80
May 10	Pay accrued wages	GJ5	80		0

Wages Expense   500

Date	Explanation	Ref.	Debit	Credit	Balance
20X2					
Apr. 26	Wages through 4-26	GJ2	200		200
30	Accrue wages 4-27 to 4-30	GJ2	80		280
May 10	Wages 5-1 to 5-10	GJ5	120		400

Cash   100

Date	Explanation	Ref.	Debit	Credit	Balance
9	Paid for servicing mall	GJ4	500		8,000
10	Wages 4-27 to 5-10	GJ5		200	7,800

To avoid the need for a compound entry like the one shown on the previous page, Mr. Green may choose to reverse the April 30 adjustment for accrued wages when the May accounting period begins. The reversing entry decreases (debits) wages payable for $80 and decreases (credits) wages expense for $80.

General Journal   GJ4

Date	Account Title and Description	Ref.	Debit	Credit
20X2				
May 1	Wages Payable	210	80	
	Wages Expense	500		80
	Reverse wage accrual			

Wages Payable   210

Date	Explanation	Ref.	Debit	Credit	Balance
20X2					
Apr. 30	Accrue wages 4-27 to 4-30	GJ2		80	80
May 1	Reverse accrual	GJ4	80		0

Wages Expense   500

Date	Explanation	Ref.	Debit	Credit	Balance
20X2					
Apr. 26	Wages through 4-26	GJ2	200		200
30	Accrue wages 4-27 to 4-30	GJ2	80		280
May 1	Reverse accrual	GJ4		80	200

If the reversing entry is made, the May 10 payroll payment can be recorded with a simple entry that increases (debits) wages expense for $200 and decreases (credits) cash for $200.

General Journal   GJ5

Date	Account Title and Description	Ref.	Debit	Credit
20X2				
May 10	Wages Expense	500	200	
	Cash	100		200
	Wages 4-27 to 5-10			

Wages Expense   500

Date	Explanation	Ref.	Debit	Credit	Balance
20X2					
Apr. 26	Wages through 4-26	GJ2	200		200
30	Accrue wages 4-27 to 4-30	GJ2	80		280
May 1	Reverse accrual	GJ4		80	200
10	Wages 4-27 to 5-10	GJ5	200		400

Cash   100

Date	Explanation	Ref.	Debit	Credit	Balance
9	Paid for servicing mall	GJ4	500		8,000
10	Wages 4-27 to 5-10	GJ5		200	7,800

Between May 1 when the reversing entry is made and May 10 when the payroll entry is recorded, the company's total liabilities and total expenses are understated. This temporary inaccuracy in the books is acceptable only because financial statements are not prepared during this period.

When the temporary accounts are closed at the end of an accounting period, subsequent reversing entries create abnormal balances in the affected expense and revenue accounts. For example, if the wages expense account is closed on April 30, a reversing entry on May 1 creates a credit balance in the account. The credit balance is offset by the May 10 debit entry, and the account balance then shows current period expenses.

Wages Expense   500

Date	Explanation	Ref.	Debit	Credit	Balance
20X2					
Apr. 26	Wages through 4-26	GJ2	200		200
30	Accrue wages 4-27 to 4-30	GJ2	80		280
30	Closing entry	GJ4		280	0
May 1	Reverse accrual	GJ4		80	(80)
10	Wages 4-27 to 5-10	GJ5	200		120

Correcting Entries

Accountants must make **correcting entries** when they find errors. There are two ways to make correcting entries: reverse the incorrect entry and then use a second journal entry to record the transaction correctly, or make a single journal entry that, when combined with the original but incorrect entry, fixes the error.

After making a credit purchase for supplies worth $50 on April 5, suppose Mr. Green accidently credits accounts receivable instead of accounts payable.

General Journal   GJ1

Date	Account Title and Description	Ref.	Debit	Credit
Apr. 5	Supplies	140	50	
	Accounts Receivable	110		50
	Bought office supplies			

Mr. Green discovers the error on May 2, after receiving a bill for the supplies. He may use two entries to fix the error: one that reverses the incorrect entry by debiting accounts receivable for $50 and crediting supplies for $50, and another that records the transaction correctly by debiting supplies for $50 and crediting accounts payable for $50.

General Journal   GJ4

Date	Account Title and Description	Ref.	Debit	Credit
May 2	Accounts Receivable	110	50	
	Supplies	140		50
	Reverses April 5 error			
2	Supplies	110	50	
	Accounts Payable	200		50
	Correcting entry for April 5			

Or Mr. Green can fix the error with a single entry that debits accounts receivable for $50 and credits accounts payable for $50.

General Journal   GJ4

Date	Account Title and Description	Ref.	Debit	Credit
May 2	Accounts Receivable	110	50	
	Accounts Payable	200		50
	Corrects April 5 error			

Although the accounting cycle and the basic accounting principles are the same for companies that sell merchandise and companies that provide services, merchandising companies use several accounts that service companies do not use. The balance sheet includes an additional current asset called *merchandise inventory,* or simply *inventory,* which records the cost of merchandise held for resale. On balance sheets, the inventory account usually appears just below accounts receivable because inventory is less liquid than accounts receivable.

Music World
Partial Balance Sheet
June 30, 20X3

ASSETS	
Current Assets	
Cash	$10,000
Accounts Receivable	2,000
Inventory	37,000
Supplies	1,000
Prepaid Insurance	2,000
Total Current Assets	$52,000

Merchandising companies also have several specific income statement accounts designed to provide detailed information about revenues and expenses associated with salable merchandise.

Recording Sales

Sales invoices are source documents that provide a record for each sale. For control purposes, sales invoices should be sequentially prenumbered to help the accounting department determine the disposition of every invoice. **Sales revenues** equal the selling price of all products that are sold. In accordance with the revenue recognition principle, sales revenue is recognized when a customer receives title to the merchandise, regardless of when the money changes hands. If a customer purchases merchandise at a sales counter and takes possession of the goods immediately, the sales invoice or cash register receipt is the only source document needed to record the sale. However, if merchandise is shipped to the customer, a delivery record or shipping document is matched with the invoice to prove that the merchandise has been shipped to the customer.

Suppose a company named Music Suppliers, Inc., sells merchandise worth $1,000 on account to a retail store named Music World. Music Suppliers, Inc., records the sale with the journal entry below.

General Journal   GJ27

Date	Account Title and Description	Ref.	Debit	Credit
20X3				
Jun. 10	Accounts Receivable		1,000	
	Sales			1,000
	Invoice #15932—Music World			

For reference purposes, the journal entry's description often includes the invoice number.

Sales Returns and Allowances

Although sales returns and sales allowances are technically two distinct types of transactions, they are generally recorded in the same account. **Sales returns** occur when customers return defective, damaged, or otherwise undesirable products to the seller. **Sales allowances** occur when customers agree to keep such merchandise in return for a reduction in the selling price.

If Music World returns merchandise worth $100, Music Suppliers, Inc., prepares a **credit memorandum** to account for the return. This credit memorandum becomes the source document for a journal entry that increases (debits) the sales returns and allowances account and decreases (credits) accounts receivable.

General Journal   GJ28

Date	Account Title and Description	Ref.	Debit	Credit
20X3				
Jun. 15	Sales Returns & Allowances		100	
	Accounts Receivable			100
	CM #1243—Music World			

A $100 allowance requires the same entry.

In the sales revenue section of an income statement, the sales returns and allowances account is subtracted from sales because these accounts have the opposite effect on net income. Therefore, sales returns and allowances is considered a **contra-revenue account,** which normally has a debit balance. Recording sales returns and allowances in a separate contra-revenue account allows management to monitor returns and allowances as a percentage of overall sales. High return levels may indicate the presence of serious but correctable problems. For example, improved packaging might minimize damage during shipment, new suppliers might reduce the amount of defective merchandise, or better methods for recording and packaging orders might eliminate or reduce incorrect merchandise shipments. The first step in identifying such problems is to carefully monitor sales returns and allowances in a separate, contra-revenue account.

Sales Discounts

A **sales discount** is an incentive the seller offers in exchange for prompt payment on credit sales. Sales discounts are recorded in another contra-revenue account, enabling management to monitor the effectiveness of the company's discount policy. Invoices generally include **credit terms,** which specify when the customer must pay and define the sales discount if one is available. For example, the credit terms on the invoice below are 2/10, n/30, which is read "two-ten, net thirty."

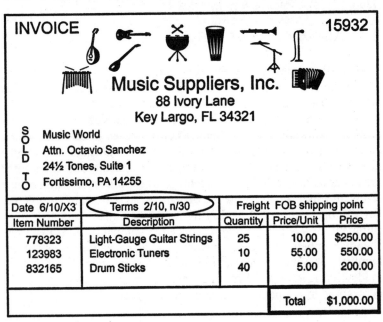

INVOICE			15932	

Music Suppliers, Inc.
88 Ivory Lane
Key Largo, FL 34321

SOLD TO

Music World
Attn. Octavio Sanchez
24½ Tones, Suite 1
Fortissimo, PA 14255

Date 6/10/X3	Terms 2/10, n/30		Freight FOB shipping point	
Item Number	Description	Quantity	Price/Unit	Price
778323	Light-Gauge Guitar Strings	25	10.00	$250.00
123983	Electronic Tuners	10	55.00	550.00
832165	Drum Sticks	40	5.00	200.00
			Total	$1,000.00

The terms 2/10, n/30 mean the customer may take a two percent discount on the outstanding balance (original invoice amount less any returns and allowances) if payment occurs within ten days of the invoice date. If the customer chooses not to take the discount, the outstanding balance is due within thirty days. An abbreviation that sometimes appears in the credit terms section of an invoice is *EOM,* which stands for *end of month*. The terms n/15 EOM indicate that the outstanding balance is due fifteen days after the end of the month in which the invoice is dated.

If Music World returns merchandise worth $100 after receiving a $1,000 order, they still owe Music Suppliers, Inc., $900. Assuming the credit terms are 2/10, n/30 and Music World pays the invoice within ten days, the payment equals $882, an amount calculated by subtracting $18 (2% of $900) from the outstanding balance. To record this payment from Music World, Music Suppliers, Inc., makes a compound journal entry that increases (debits) cash for $882, increases (debits) sales discounts for $18, and decreases (credits) accounts receivable for $900.

General Journal				GJ29
Date	Account Title and Description	Ref.	Debit	Credit
20X3				
Jun. 20	Cash		882	
	Sales Discounts		18	
	Accounts Receivable			900
	Payment for invoice #15932			

Net Sales

Net sales is calculated by subtracting sales returns and allowances and sales discounts from sales. Suppose Music Suppliers, Inc., sells merchandise worth $116,500 during June and, in conjunction with these sales, handles $9,300 in returns and allowances and $1,200 in sales discounts. The company's net sales for June equal $106,000.

Music Suppliers, Inc.
Calculation of Net Sales
For the Month Ended June 30, 20X3

Sales		$116,500
Less: Sales Returns and Allowances	$9,300	
Sales Discounts	1,200	10,500
Net Sales		$106,000

Inventory Systems

There are two systems to account for inventory: the perpetual system and the periodic system. With the **perpetual system,** the inventory account is updated after every inventory purchase or sale. Before computers became widely available, only companies that sold a relatively small number of high-priced items used this system. A complete description of the perpetual system appears later, in the chapter on inventories. The examples in this chapter illustrate the periodic system. Under the **periodic system,** a careful evaluation of inventory occurs only at the end of each accounting period. At that time, each product available for sale is counted and multiplied by its per unit cost, and the total of all such calculations equals the value of inventory.

Recording Purchases

Under the periodic system, a temporary expense account named *merchandise purchases,* or simply *purchases,* is used to record the purchase of goods intended for resale. The source documents used to journalize merchandise purchases include the seller's invoice, the company's purchase order, and a receiving report that verifies the accuracy of the inventory quantities. When Music World receives a shipment of merchandise worth $1,000 on account from Music Suppliers, Inc., Music World increases (debits) the purchases account for $1,000 and increases (credits) accounts payable for $1,000.

General Journal				GJ16
Date	Account Title and Description	Ref.	Debit	Credit
20X3				
Jun. 10	Purchases		1,000	
	Accounts Payable			1,000
	Invoice #15932—Music Suppliers			

For reference purposes, the journal entry's description usually includes the invoice number.

When a seller pays to ship merchandise to a purchaser, the seller records the cost as a delivery expense, which is considered an operating expense and, more specifically, a selling expense. When a purchaser pays the shipping fees, the purchaser considers the fees to be part of the cost of the merchandise. Instead of recording such fees directly in the purchases account, however, they are recorded in a separate expense account named *freight-in* or *transportation-in,* which provides management with a way to monitor these shipping costs.

If Music World pays a shipping company $30 for delivering the merchandise from Music Suppliers, Inc., Music World increases (debits) freight-in for $30 and decreases (credits) cash for $30.

	General Journal			GJ17
Date	Account Title and Description	Ref.	Debit	Credit
20X3				
Jun. 12	Freight-in		30	
	Cash			30
	Shipping fees—invoice #15932			

Freight terms, which indicate whether the purchaser or seller pays the shipping fees, are often specified with the abbreviations FOB shipping point or FOB destination. *FOB* means *free on board.* **FOB shipping point** means the purchaser pays the shipping fees and gains title to the merchandise at the shipping point (the seller's place of business). **FOB destination** means the seller pays the shipping fees and maintains title until the merchandise reaches its destination (the purchaser's place of business).

Purchases Returns and Allowances

When a purchaser receives defective, damaged, or otherwise undesirable merchandise, the purchaser prepares a **debit memorandum** that identifies the items in question and the cost of those items. The purchaser uses the debit memorandum to inform the seller about the return and to prepare a journal entry that decreases (debits) accounts payable and increases (credits) an account named *purchases returns and* *allowances,* which is a contra-expense account. Contra-expense accounts normally have credit balances. On the income statement, the purchases returns and allowances account is subtracted from purchases.

If Music World discovers $100 worth of defective merchandise in the shipment from Music Suppliers, Inc., Music World prepares a debit memorandum, returns the merchandise, and makes a journal entry that decreases (debits) accounts payable for $100 and that increases (credits) purchases returns and allowances for $100.

General Journal   GJ19

Date	Account Title and Description	Ref.	Debit	Credit
20X3				
Jun. 15	Accounts Payable		100	
	Purchases Returns & Allowances			100
	DM #1072, Invoice #15932			

For reference purposes, the journal entry's description may include the debit memorandum number and the seller's invoice number.

Purchases Discounts

Companies that take advantage of sales discounts usually record them in an account named *purchases discounts,* which is another contra-expense account that is subtracted from purchases on the income statement. If Music Suppliers, Inc., offers the terms 2/10, n/30 and Music World pays the invoice's outstanding balance of $900 within ten days, Music World takes an $18 discount. To record this payment to Music Suppliers, Inc., Music World makes a compound journal entry that decreases (debits) accounts payable for $900, decreases (credits) cash for $882, and increases (credits) purchases discounts for $18.

General Journal   GJ20

Date	Account Title and Description	Ref.	Debit	Credit
20X3				
Jun. 20	Accounts Payable		900	
	Cash			882
	Purchases Discounts			18
	Paid invoice #15932			

Net Purchases and the Cost of Goods Purchased

Net purchases is found by subtracting the credit balances in the purchases returns and allowances and purchases discounts accounts from the debit balance in the purchases account. The **cost of goods purchased** equals net purchases plus the freight-in account's debit balance.

```
  Purchases
− Purchases Returns and Allowances
− Purchases Discounts
  Net Purchases
+ Freight-in
= Cost of Goods Purchased
```

The Cost of Goods Available for Sale and the Cost of Goods Sold

The **cost of goods available for sale** equals the beginning value of inventory plus the cost of goods purchased. The **cost of goods sold** equals the cost of goods available for sale less the ending value of inventory.

```
  Beginning Inventory
+ Cost of Goods Purchased
  Cost of Goods Available for Sale
− Ending Inventory
= Cost of Goods Sold
```

Gross Profit

Gross profit, which is also called **gross margin,** represents the company's profit from selling merchandise before deducting operating expenses such as salaries, rent, and delivery expenses. Gross profit equals net sales minus the cost of goods sold.

Net Sales
– Cost of Goods Sold
= Gross Profit

Financial Statements for a Merchandising Company

The statement of owner's equity and the statement of cash flows are the same for merchandising and service companies. Except for the inventory account, the balance sheet is also the same. But a merchandising company's income statement includes categories that service enterprises do not use. A single-step income statement for a merchandising company lists net sales under revenues and the cost of goods sold under expenses.

Music World
Income Statement
For the Year Ended June 30, 20X3

Revenues		
Net Sales		$1,172,000
Interest Income		7,500
Gain on Sale of Equipment		1,500
Total Revenues		1,181,000
Expenses		
Cost of Goods Sold	$596,600	
Selling Expenses	177,000	
General and Administrative Expenses	152,900	
Interest Expense	18,000	
Total Expenses		944,500
Net Income		$ 236,500

Although the single-step format is easier to read than the multiple-step format, most companies produce a multiple-step income statement, which clearly identifies each step in the calculation of net income or net loss.

Music World
Income Statement
For the Year Ended June 30, 20X3

Sales Revenues			
Sales			$1,240,000
Less: Sales Returns and Allowances		$ 65,000	
Sales Discounts		3,000	68,000
Net Sales			1,172,000
Cost of Goods Sold			
Inventory, July 1, 20X2		37,000	
Purchases	$610,000		
Less: Purchases Returns and Allowances	$9,000		
Purchases Discounts	8,000	17,000	
Net Purchases		593,000	
Add: Freight-in		5,600	
Cost of Goods Purchased		598,600	
Cost of Goods Available for Sale		635,600	
Less: Inventory, June 30, 20X3		39,000	
Cost of Goods Sold			596,600
Gross Profit			575,400
Operating Expenses			
Selling Expenses			
Sales Salaries Expense	120,000		
Sales Commission Expense	21,000		
Delivery Expense	15,000		
Store Rent Expense	12,000		
Depreciation Expense–Store Equipment	9,000		
Total Selling Expenses		177,000	
General and Administrative Expenses			
Office Salaries Expense	140,000		
Insurance Expense	6,000		
Depreciation Expense–Office Equipment	5,000		
Office Rent Expense	1,200		
Office Supplies Expense	700		
Total General and Administrative Expenses		152,900	
Total Operating Expenses			329,900
Operating Income			245,500
Other Income/(Expense), Net			
Interest Income		7,500	
Gain on Sale of Equipment		1,500	
Interest Expense		(18,000)	
Other Income/(Expense), Net			(9,000)
Net Income			$ 236,500

Adjusting the Inventory Account

Under the periodic system of accounting for inventory, the inventory account's balance remains unchanged throughout the accounting period and must be updated after a physical count determines the value of inventory at the end of the accounting period. The inventory account's balance may be updated with adjusting entries or as part of the closing entry process. When adjusting entries are used, two separate entries are made. The first adjusting entry clears the inventory account's beginning balance by debiting income summary and crediting inventory for an amount equal to the beginning inventory balance.

General Journal   GJ21

Date	Account Title and Description	Ref.	Debit	Credit
20X3				
Jun. 30	Income Summary	600	37,000	
	Inventory	125		37,000
	Adjust beginning inventory			

Income Summary   600

Date	Explanation	Ref.	Debit	Credit	Balance
20X3					
Jun. 30	Beginning inventory	GJ21	37,000		(37,000)

Inventory   125

Date	Explanation	Ref.	Debit	Credit	Balance
20X2					
Jul. 1	Beginning inventory	GJ1	37,000		37,000
20X3					
Jun. 30	Beginning inventory	GJ21		37,000	0

The second adjusting entry debits inventory and credits income summary for the value of inventory at the end of the accounting period.

General Journal GJ21

Date	Account Title and Description	Ref.	Debit	Credit
20X3				
Jun. 30	Income Summary	600	37,000	
	Inventory	125		37,000
	Adjust beginning inventory			
30	Inventory	125	39,000	
	Income Summary	600		39,000
	Adjust ending inventory			

Inventory 125

Date	Explanation	Ref.	Debit	Credit	Balance
20X2					
Jul. 1	Beginning inventory	GJ1	37,000		37,000
20X3					
Jun. 30	Beginning inventory	GJ21		37,000	0
30	Ending inventory	GJ21	39,000		39,000

Income Summary 600

Date	Explanation	Ref.	Debit	Credit	Balance
20X3					
Jun. 30	Beginning inventory	GJ21	37,000		(37,000)
30	Ending inventory	GJ21		39,000	2,000

Combined, these two adjusting entries update the inventory account's balance and, until closing entries are made, leave income summary with a balance that reflects the increase or decrease in inventory.

Inventory Adjustments on the Work Sheet

On a work sheet, the beginning inventory balance in the trial balance columns combines with the two inventory adjustments to produce the ending inventory balance in the adjusted trial balance columns. This balance carries across to the work sheet's balance sheet columns.

Account	Trial Balance Dr.	Trial Balance Cr.	Adjustments Dr.	Adjustments Cr.	Adjusted Trial Balance Dr.	Adjusted Trial Balance Cr.	Income Statement Dr.	Income Statement Cr.	Balance Sheet Dr.	Balance Sheet Cr.
Inventory	37,000		39,000	37,000	39,000				39,000	

Income summary, which appears on the work sheet whenever adjusting entries are used to update inventory, is always placed at the bottom of the work sheet's list of accounts. The two adjustments to income summary receive special treatment on the work sheet. Instead of combining the adjustments and placing the result in one of the adjusted trial balance columns, both adjustments are transferred to the adjusted trial balance columns and then to the income statement columns. Income summary's debit entry on the work sheet is used to report the beginning inventory balance on the income statement, and income summary's credit entry is used to report the ending inventory balance on the income statement. Each of these amounts is needed to calculate cost of goods sold.

Account	Trial Balance Dr.	Trial Balance Cr.	Adjustments Dr.	Adjustments Cr.	Adjusted Trial Balance Dr.	Adjusted Trial Balance Cr.	Income Statement Dr.	Income Statement Cr.	Balance Sheet Dr.	Balance Sheet Cr.
Income Summary			37,000	39,000	37,000	39,000	37,000	39,000		

Closing Entries for a Merchandising Company

Although merchandising and service companies use the same four closing entries, merchandising companies usually have more temporary accounts to close. The additional accounts include sales, sales returns and allowances, sales discounts, purchases, purchases returns and allowances, purchases discounts, and freight-in. Consider Music World's four closing entries.

1. Close all income statement accounts with credit balances to the income summary account. The entry shown below assumes the inventory account was updated with adjusting entries and, therefore, does not include it.

	General Journal			GJ22
Date	Account Title and Description	Ref.	Debit	Credit
20X3				
Jun. 30	Sales	400	1,240,000	
	Purchases Returns & Allowances	501	9,000	
	Purchases Discounts	502	8,000	
	Interest Income	420	7,500	
	Gain on Sale of Equipment	430	1,500	
	Income Summary	600		1,266,000
	Close credit-balance accounts			

Accountants who choose to update the inventory account during the closing process instead of with adjusting entries include the *ending* inventory balance with this first closing entry.

	General Journal			GJ22
Date	Account Title and Description	Ref.	Debit	Credit
20X3				
Jun. 30	Inventory	125	39,000	
	Sales	400	1,240,000	
	Purchases Returns & Allowances	501	9,000	
	Purchases Discounts	502	8,000	
	Interest Income	420	7,500	
	Gain on Sale of Equipment	430	1,500	
	Income Summary	600		1,305,000
	Close credit-balance accounts			

Notice how this entry has the same effect on the accounts as the closing entry at the top of this page combined with the second of the two adjusting entries discussed on pages 96 and 97.

2. Close all income statement accounts with debit balances to the income summary account. The entry shown below assumes the inventory account was updated with adjusting entries and, therefore, does not include it.

General Journal GJ22

Date	Account Title and Description	Ref.	Debit	Credit
20X3				
Jun. 30	Income Summary	600	1,031,500	
	Sales Returns and Allowances	401		65,000
	Sales Discounts	402		3,000
	Purchases	500		610,000
	Freight-in	510		5,600
	Depreciation Expense–Store Equipment	550		9,000
	Sales Salaries Expense	520		120,000
	Sales Commission Expense	525		21,000
	Store Rent Expense	530		12,000
	Delivery Expense	540		15,000
	Depreciation Expense–Office Equipment	555		5,000
	Office Salaries Expense	521		140,000
	Insurance Expense	560		6,000
	Office Rent Expense	531		1,200
	Office Supplies Expense	545		700
	Interest Expense	570		18,000
	Close debit-balance accounts			

If the inventory account is updated during the closing entry process, this closing entry includes a credit equal to the beginning inventory balance ($37,000), which increases the debit to income summary by a corresponding amount (to $1,068,500).

At this point, income summary has the same balance whether adjusting or closing entries are used to update inventory. If adjusting entries are used, four separate entries contribute to the income summary account's balance.

Income Summary 600

Date	Explanation	Ref.	Debit	Credit	Balance
20X3					
Jun. 30	Beginning inventory	GJ21	37,000		(37,000)
30	Ending inventory	GJ21		39,000	2,000
30	Credit-balance accounts	GJ22		1,266,000	1,268,000
30	Debit-balance accounts	GJ22	1,031,500		236,500

If closing entries are used to update inventory, the first two closing entries establish the income summary account's balance.

Income Summary   600

Date	Explanation	Ref.	Debit	Credit	Balance
20X3					
Jun. 30	Credit-balance accounts	GJ22		1,305,000	1,305,000
30	Debit-balance accounts	GJ22	1,068,500		236,500

The income summary account now has a balance equal to the company's net income or net loss.

3. Close income summary to the owner's capital account.

General Journal   GJ22

Date	Account Title and Description	Ref.	Debit	Credit
20X3				
Jun. 30	Income Summary	600	236,500	
	Octavio Sanchez, Capital	300		236,500
	Close income summary			

4. Close the owner's drawing account to the owner's capital account. Assume the owner's drawing account has a $40,000 balance.

General Journal   GJ22

Date	Account Title and Description	Ref.	Debit	Credit
20X3				
Jun. 30	Octavio Sanchez, Capital	600	40,000	
	Octavio Sanchez, Drawing	300		40,000
	Close drawing account			

The Work Sheet When Closing Entries Update Inventory

If closing entries are used to update inventory, no adjusting entries affect the inventory account, so the beginning inventory balance appears in the work sheet's trial balance and adjusted trial balance columns. This beginning inventory balance is first extended to the income statement debit column. Then, the value of inventory at the end of the accounting period is placed in the work sheet's income statement credit column and balance sheet debit column.

Account	Trial Balance		Adjustments		Adjusted Trial Balance		Income Statement		Balance Sheet	
	Dr.	Cr.	Dr.	Cr.	Dr.	Cr.	Dr.	Cr.	Dr.	Cr.
Inventory	37,000				37,000		37,000	39,000	39,000	

The entries in the work sheet's income statement columns are used in the calculation of cost of goods sold on the income statement, and the entry in the work sheet's balance sheet debit column provides the correct balance for merchandise inventory on the balance sheet.

Subsidiary Ledgers

A **subsidiary ledger** is a group of similar accounts whose combined balances equal the balance in a specific general ledger account. The general ledger account that summarizes a subsidiary ledger's account balances is called a **control account** or **master account.** For example, an accounts receivable subsidiary ledger (customers' subsidiary ledger) includes a separate account for each customer who makes credit purchases. The combined balance of every account in this subsidiary ledger equals the balance of accounts receivable in the general ledger. Posting a debit or credit to a subsidiary ledger account and also to a general ledger control account does not violate the rule that total

Accounts Receivable Subsidiary Ledger

C. Daley   AR1

Date	Ref.	Debit	Credit	Balance
20X1				
Mar. 18		200		200

B. Johnson   AR2

Date	Ref.	Debit	Credit	Balance
20X1				
Mar. 22		700		700

L. Jones   AR3

Date	Ref.	Debit	Credit	Balance
20X1				
Mar. 15		500		500

P. O'Reilly   AR4

Date	Ref.	Debit	Credit	Balance
20X1				
Mar. 5		1,500		1,500
Mar. 29		1,000		2,500

T. Smith   AR5

Date	Ref.	Debit	Credit	Balance
20X1				
Mar. 1		1,000		1,000

Control Account

Accounts Receivable   110

Date	Ref.	Debit	Credit	Balance
20X1				
Mar. 31		4,900		4,900

```
    200
    700
    500
  2,500
+ 1,000
  4,900
```

Here and throughout most of this chapter, each account's explanation column is removed to save space.

debit and credit entries must balance because subsidiary ledger accounts are not part of the general ledger; they are supplemental accounts that provide the detail to support the balance in a control account.

The accounts receivable subsidiary ledger is essential to most businesses. Companies may have hundreds or even thousands of customers who purchase items on credit, who make one or more payments for those items, and who sometimes return items or purchase additional items before they finish paying for prior purchases. Recording all credit purchases, returns, and subsequent payments in a single account would make an individual customer's balance virtually impossible to calculate because the customer's transactions would be interspersed among thousands of other transactions. But the accounts receivable subsidiary ledger provides quick access to each customer's balance and account activity.

Companies create subsidiary ledgers whenever they need to monitor the individual components of a controlling general ledger account. In addition to the accounts receivable subsidiary ledger, companies often use an accounts payable subsidiary ledger (creditors' subsidiary ledger), which has separate accounts for each creditor, an inventory subsidiary ledger, which has separate accounts for each product, and a property, plant, and equipment subsidiary ledger, which has separate accounts for each long-lived asset.

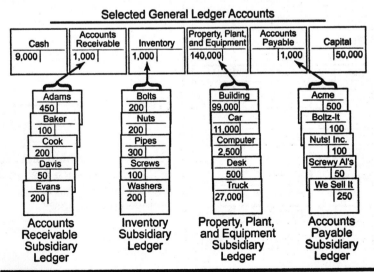

Selected General Ledger Accounts

Cash	Accounts Receivable	Inventory	Property, Plant, and Equipment	Accounts Payable	Capital
9,000	1,000	1,000	140,000	1,000	50,000

Adams	Bolts	Building	Acme
450	200	99,000	500
Baker	**Nuts**	**Car**	**Boltz-It**
100	200	11,000	100
Cook	**Pipes**	**Computer**	**Nuts! Inc.**
200	300	2,500	100
Davis	**Screws**	**Desk**	**Screwy Al's**
50	100	500	50
Evans	**Washers**	**Truck**	**We Sell It**
200	200	27,000	250

Accounts Receivable Subsidiary Ledger	Inventory Subsidiary Ledger	Property, Plant, and Equipment Subsidiary Ledger	Accounts Payable Subsidiary Ledger

Special Journals

Entering transactions in the general journal and posting them to the correct general ledger accounts is time consuming. In the general journal, a simple transaction requires three lines—two to list the accounts and one to describe the transaction. The transaction must then be posted to each general ledger account. If the transaction affects a control account, the posting must be done twice—once to the subsidiary ledger account and once to the controlling general ledger account. To speed up this process, companies use special journals to record repetitive transactions that affect the same set of accounts and have a consistent description. Such transactions can be documented on one line in a special journal. Then, instead of separately posting individual entries, each column's total is posted at the end of the accounting period.

Although companies create special journals for other types of repetitive transactions, almost all merchandising companies use special journals for sales, purchases, cash receipts, and cash disbursements.

Sales Journal   S1

Date	Invoice	Customer	Ref.	Dr. Accounts Receivable / Cr. Sales

• Used for all sales of merchandise on account.
• Each entry debits accounts receivable and credits sales.

Purchases Journal   P1

Date	Supplier	Ref.	Dr. Purchases / Cr. Accounts Payable

• Used for all purchases of merchandise on account.
• Each entry debits purchases and credits accounts payable.

Cash Receipts Journal   CR1

Date	Account	Ref.	Cash Dr.	Sales Discounts Dr.	Accounts Receivable Cr.	Sales Cr.	Other Cr.

• Used for all cash receipts.
• Each entry includes a debit to cash and has equal debits and credits.

Cash Disbursements Journal   CD1

Date	Check	Account	Ref.	Accounts Payable Dr.	Other Dr.	Purchases Discounts Cr.	Cash Cr.

• Used for all cash payments.
• Each entry includes a credit to cash and has equal debits and credits.

Sales journal. The sales journal lists all credit sales made to customers. Sales returns and cash sales are not recorded in this journal. Entries in the sales journal typically include the date, invoice number, customer name, and amount. Invoices are the source documents that provide this information. In its most basic form, a sales journal has only one column for recording transaction amounts. Each entry increases (debits) accounts receivable and increases (credits) sales.

Notice the dates and posting references applied to each entry in the illustration to the right. Each day, individual sales journal entries are posted to the accounts receivable subsidiary ledger accounts so that customer balances remain current. Customer account numbers (or check marks if customer accounts are simply kept in alphabetical order) are placed in the sales journal's reference column to indicate that the entries have been posted. At the end of the accounting period, the column total is posted to the accounts receivable and sales accounts in the general ledger. Account numbers are placed in parentheses below the column to indicate that the total has been posted.

Many companies use a multi-column (columnar) sales journal that provides separate columns for specific sales accounts and for sales tax payable. Each line in a multi-column journal must contain equal debits and credits. For example, the entries in the sales journal to the right appear below in a multi-column sales journal that tracks hardware sales, plumbing sales, wire sales, and sales tax payable. Individual entries are still posted daily to the accounts receivable subsidiary ledger accounts, and each column total is posted at the end of the accounting period to the appropriate general ledger account.

Sales Journal

S1

Date	Invoice	Customer Account Debited	Ref.	Accounts Receivable Dr.	Hardware Sales Cr.	Plumbing Sales Cr.	Wire Sales Cr.	Sales Tax Payable Cr.
20X1								
Mar. 1	1561	Smith	AR5	1,000	200	700	40	60
Mar. 5	1562	O'Reilly	AR4	1,500	1,000	410		90
Mar. 15	1563	Jones	AR3	500			470	30
Mar. 18	1564	Daley	AR1	200			188	12
Mar. 22	1565	Johnson	AR2	700	358	300		42
Mar. 29	1566	O'Reilly	AR4	1,000	940			60
Totals				4,900	2,498	1,410	698	294
				(110)	(410)	(420)	(430)	(290)

Sales Journal   S1

Date	Invoice	Customer Account Debited	Ref.	Dr. Accounts Recievable Cr. Sales
20X1				
Mar. 1	1561	T. Smith	AR5	1,000
Mar. 5	1562	P. O'Reilly	AR4	1,500
Mar. 15	1563	L. Jones	AR3	500
Mar. 18	1564	C. Daley	AR1	200
Mar. 22	1565	B. Johnson	AR2	700
Mar. 29	1566	P. O'Reilly	AR4	1,000
Totals				4,900
				(110) (400)

Individual entries are posted daily
to the accounts receivable
subsidiary ledger accounts.

The column total is posted
at the end of the period to
the general ledger accounts.

C. Daley   AR1

Date	Ref.	Debit	Credit	Balance
20X1				
Mar. 18	S1	200		200

B. Johnson   AR2

Date	Ref.	Debit	Credit	Balance
20X1				
Mar. 22	S1	700		700

L. Jones   AR3

Date	Ref.	Debit	Credit	Balance
20X1				
Mar. 15	S1	500		500

P. O'Reilly   AR4

Date	Ref.	Debit	Credit	Balance
20X1				
Mar. 5	S1	1,500		1,500
Mar. 29	S1	1,000		2,500

T. Smith   AR5

Date	Ref.	Debit	Credit	Balance
20X1				
Mar. 1	S1	1,000		1,000

Accounts Receivable   110

Date	Ref.	Debit	Credit	Balance
20X1				
Mar. 31	S1	4,900		4,900

Sales   400

Date	Ref.	Debit	Credit	Balance
20X1				
Mar. 31	S1		4,900	4,900

Purchases journal. The purchases journal lists all credit purchases of merchandise. Entries in this journal usually include the date of the entry, the name of the supplier, and the amount of the transaction. Some companies include columns to identify the invoice date and credit terms, thereby making the purchases journal a tool that helps the companies take advantage of discounts just before they expire. The purchases journal to the right has only one column for recording transaction amounts. Each entry increases (debits) purchases and increases (credits) accounts payable.

Each day, individual entries are posted to the accounts payable subsidiary ledger accounts. Creditor account numbers (or check marks if the creditor accounts are not numbered) are placed in the purchases journal's reference column to indicate that the entries have been posted. At the end of the accounting period, the column total is posted to purchases and accounts payable in the general ledger. Account numbers are placed in parentheses below the column to indicate that the total has been posted.

Companies that frequently make credit purchases of items other than merchandise use a multi-column purchases journal. For example, the purchases journal below includes columns for supplies and equipment. Of course, every purchase in the journal below must credit accounts payable; equipment purchased with a note payable or supplies purchased with cash would not be recorded in this journal. Individual entries are still posted daily to the accounts payable subsidiary ledger accounts, and each column total is posted at the end of the accounting period to the appropriate general ledger account.

		Purchases Journal				P1
Date	Supplier Account Creditied	Ref.	Purchases Dr.	Supplies Dr.	Equipment Dr.	Accounts Payable Cr.
20X1						
Mar. 2	Dandy One	AP1	800			800
Mar. 7	Supply House	AP6		200		200
Mar. 12	Smith Brothers	AP3	900			900
Mar. 18	Peters & Jones	AP2	600			600
Mar. 23	Equipment Hut	AP5			2,500	2,500
Mar. 28	Woody Blues	AP4	1,400			1,400
Totals			3,700	200	2,500	6,400
			(500)	(140)	(150)	(200)

Purchases Journal — P1

Date	Supplier Account Credited	Invoice Date	Terms	Ref.	Dr. Purchases Cr. Accounts Payable
20X1					
Mar. 2	Dandy One	Mar. 1	n/30	AP1	800
Mar. 12	Smith Brothers	Mar. 10	2/10 n/30	AP3	900
Mar. 18	Peters & Jones	Mar. 18	1/15 n/30	AP2	600
Mar. 28	Woody Blues	Mar. 28	n/10 EOM	AP4	1,400
Totals					3,700
					(500) (200)

Individual entries are posted daily to the accounts payable subsidiary ledger accounts.

The column total is posted at the end of the period to the general ledger accounts.

Dandy One — AP1

Date	Ref.	Debit	Credit	Balance
20X1				
Mar. 2	P1		800	800

Purchases — 500

Date	Ref.	Debit	Credit	Balance
20X1				
Mar. 31	P1	3,700		3,700

Peters & Jones — AP2

Date	Ref.	Debit	Credit	Balance
20X1				
Mar. 18	P1		600	600

Accounts Payable — 200

Date	Ref.	Debit	Credit	Balance
20X1				
Mar. 31	P1		3,700	3,700

Smith Brothers — AP3

Date	Ref.	Debit	Credit	Balance
20X1				
Mar. 12	P1		900	900

Woody Blues — AP4

Date	Ref.	Debit	Credit	Balance
20X1				
Mar. 28	P1		1,400	1,400

Cash receipts journal. Transactions that increase cash are recorded in a multi-column cash receipts journal. If sales discounts are offered to customers, the journal includes a separate debit column for sales discounts. Credit columns for accounts receivable and for sales are normally present, but companies that frequently receive cash from other, specific sources use additional columns to record those types of cash receipts. In addition, the cash receipts journal includes a column named *Other,* which is used to record various types of cash receipts that occur infrequently and therefore do not warrant a separate column. For example, cash receipts from capital investments, bank loans, and interest revenues are generally recorded in the *Other* column. However, a company that provides consumer loans and receives interest payments from many customers would probably include a separate column for interest revenue. Whenever a credit entry affects accounts receivable or appears in the *Other* column, the specific account is identified in the column named *Account.*

Accounts receivable payments are posted daily to the individual subsidiary ledger accounts, and customer account numbers (or check marks if the customer accounts are not numbered) are placed in the cash receipts journal's reference column. At the end of the accounting period, each column total is posted to the general ledger account listed at the top of the column, and the account number is placed in parentheses below the total. Entries in the *Other* column are posted individually to the general ledger accounts affected, and the account numbers are placed in the cash receipts journal's reference column. A capital *X* is placed below the *Other* column to indicate that the column total cannot be posted to a general ledger account.

Cash Receipts Journal   CR1

Date	Account	Ref.	Cash Dr.	Sales Discounts Dr.	Accounts Receivable Cr.	Sales Cr.	Other Cr.
20X1							
Mar. 2	Gander, Capital	300	5,000				5,000
Mar. 7			2,500			2,500	
Mar. 11	T. Smith	AR5	794	16	800		
Mar. 14			2,800			2,800	
Mar. 21			2,100			2,100	
Mar. 25	L. Jones	AR3	490	10	500		
Mar. 28			2,400			2,400	
Mar. 31	P. O'Reilly	AR4	1,500		1,500		
Mar. 31	Interest Income	420	100				100
Totals			17,674	26	2,800	9,800	5,100
			(100)	(402)	(110)	(400)	X

➤ Entries that affect control accounts are posted daily to the subsidiary ledger accounts.

➤ Column totals (besides *Other*) are posted at the end of the period to the general ledger accounts.

L. Jones   AR3

Date	Ref.	Debit	Credit	Balance
20X1				
Mar. 15	S1	500		500
Mar. 25	CR1		500	0

Cash   100

Date	Ref.	Debit	Credit	Balance
20X1				
Mar. 31	CR1	17,674		17,674

P. O'Reilly   AR4

Date	Ref.	Debit	Credit	Balance
20X1				
Mar. 5	S1	1,500		1,500
Mar. 29	S1	1,000		2,500
Mar. 31	CR1		1,500	1,000

Accounts Receivable   110

Date	Ref.	Debit	Credit	Balance
20X1				
Mar. 31	S1	4,900		4,900
Mar. 31	CR1		2,800	2,100

T. Smith   AR5

Date	Ref.	Debit	Credit	Balance
20X1				
Mar. 1	S1	1,000		1,000
Mar. 5	G.J1		200	800
Mar. 11	CR1		800	0

Sales   400

Date	Ref.	Debit	Credit	Balance
20X1				
Mar. 31	S1		4,900	4,900
Mar. 31	CR1		9,800	14,700

Sales Discounts   402

Date	Ref.	Debit	Credit	Balance
20X1				
Mar. 31	CR1	26		26

Entries in the *Other* column are posted individually to the general ledger accounts. ◄

Gander, Capital   300

Date	Ref.	Debit	Credit	Balance
20X1				
Mar. 2	CR1		5,000	1,200

Interest Income   420

Date	Ref.	Debit	Credit	Balance
20X1				
Mar. 31	CR1		100	100

Cash disbursements journal. Transactions that decrease cash are recorded in the cash disbursements journal. The cash disbursements journal to the right has one debit column for accounts payable and another debit column for all other types of cash payment transactions. It has credit columns for purchases discounts and for cash. Since each entry debits a control account (accounts payable) or an account listed in the column named *Other,* the specific account being debited must be identified on every line.

The nature of each company's transactions determines which columns this journal includes. For example, companies sometimes choose to include separate debit columns for regularly used accounts such as salaries expense, sales commissions expense, or other specific accounts affected by cash disbursements.

Entries that affect accounts payable are posted daily to the individual subsidiary ledger accounts, and creditor account numbers (or check marks if the creditor accounts are not numbered) are placed in the cash disbursements journal's reference column. At the end of the accounting period, each column total is posted to the general ledger account listed at the top of the column, and the account number is placed in parentheses below the total. Entries in the *Other* column are posted individually to the general ledger accounts affected, and the account numbers are placed in the cash disbursements journal's reference column. A capital *X* is placed below the *Other* column to indicate that the column total cannot be posted to a general ledger account.

Cash Disbursements Journal — CD1

Date	Check	Account	Ref.	Accounts Payable Dr.	Other Dr.	Purchases Discounts Cr.	Cash Cr.
20X1							
Mar. 1	1973	Rent Expense	540		1,200		1,200
Mar. 10	1974	Utilities Expense	550		400		400
Mar. 15	1975	Supplies	170		250		250
Mar. 20	1976	Smith Brothers	AP3	900		18	882
Mar. 31	1977	Dandy One	AP1	800			1,000
Totals				1,700	1,850	18	3,732
				(200)	X	(502)	(100)

Entries that affect control accounts are posted daily to the subsidiary ledger accounts.

Column totals (besides *Other*) are posted at the end of the period to the general ledger accounts.

Dandy One — AP1

Date	Ref.	Debit	Credit	Balance
20X1				
Mar. 2	P1		800	800
Mar. 31	CD1	800		0

Cash — 100

Date	Ref.	Debit	Credit	Balance
20X1				
Mar. 31	CR1	17,674		17,674
Mar. 31	CD1		3,732	13,942

Smith Brothers — AP3

Date	Ref.	Debit	Credit	Balance
20X1				
Mar. 12	P1		900	900
Mar. 20	CD1	900		0

Accounts Payable — 200

Date	Ref.	Debit	Credit	Balance
20X1				
Mar. 31	P1		3,700	3,700
Mar. 31	CD1	1,700		2,000

Purchases Discounts — 502

Date	Ref.	Debit	Credit	Balance
20X1				
Mar. 31	CD1		18	18

Entries listed in the *Other* column are posted individually to the general ledger accounts.

Supplies — 170

Date	Ref.	Debit	Credit	Balance
20X1				
Mar. 15	CD1	250		250

Rent Expense — 540

Date	Ref.	Debit	Credit	Balance
20X1				
Mar. 1	CD1	1,200		1,200

Utilities Expense — 550

Date	Ref.	Debit	Credit	Balance
20X1				
Mar. 10	CD1	400		400

General journal entries. The general journal is used for adjusting entries, closing entries, correcting entries, and all transactions that do not belong in one of the special journals. For example, if a company uses only the special journals discussed in this chapter, purchase returns and allowances and sales returns and allowances would have to be recorded in the general journal.

If a general journal entry involves an account in a subsidiary ledger, the transaction must be posted to both the general ledger control account and the subsidiary ledger account. Both account numbers are placed in the general journal's reference column to indicate that the entry has been posted correctly.

General Journal   GJ1

Date	Account Title and Description	Ref.	Debit	Credit
20X1				
Mar. 5	Sales Returns & Allowances	401	200	
	Accounts Receivable–T. Smith	110/AR5		200
	Credit Memo #100–T. Smith			

Sales Returns & Allowances   401

Date	Explanation	Ref.	Debit	Credit	Balance
20X1					
Mar. 5	CM #100–T. Smith	GJ1	200		200

General journal entries that affect control accounts must be posted to both the general ledger and the subsidiary ledger accounts.

Accounts Receivable   110

Date	Explanation	Ref.	Debit	Credit	Balance
20X1					4,500
Mar. 5	CM #100–T. Smith	GJ1		200	4,300

T. Smith   AR5

Date	Explanation	Ref.	Debit	Credit	Balance
20X1					
Mar. 1	Credit purchase	S1	1,000		1,000
Mar. 5	CM #100–T. Smith	GJ1		200	800

Cash is a company's most liquid asset, which means it can easily be used to acquire other assets, buy services, or satisfy obligations. For financial reporting purposes, cash includes currency and coin on hand, money orders and checks made payable to the company, and available balances in checking and savings accounts. Most companies report cash and cash equivalents together. **Cash equivalents** are highly liquid, short-term investments that usually mature within three months of their purchase date. Examples of cash equivalents include U.S. treasury bills, money market funds, and commercial paper, which is short-term corporate debt.

Cash Controls

Cash is a liquid, portable, and desirable asset. Therefore, a company must have adequate controls to prevent theft or other misuses of cash. The same control activities introduced in the first chapter of this book have specific applications when cash is involved. These control activities include segregation of duties, proper authorization, adequate documents and records, physical controls, and independent checks on performance.

- **Segregation of duties.** Cash is generally received at cash registers or through the mail. The employee who receives cash should be different from the employee who records cash receipts, and a third employee should be responsible for making cash deposits at the bank. Having different employees perform these tasks helps minimize the potential for theft.

- **Proper authorization.** Only certain people should be authorized to handle cash or make cash transactions on behalf of the company. In addition, all cash expenses should be authorized by responsible managers.

- **Adequate documents and records.** Company managers and others who are responsible for safeguarding a company's cash assets must have confidence in the accuracy and legitimacy of source documents that involve cash. Important documents such as checks, are prenumbered in sequential order to help managers ascertain the disposition of each document. This helps prevent transactions from being recorded twice or from not being recorded at all. In addition, documents should be forwarded to the accounting department soon after their creation so that recordkeeping can be handled professionally and efficiently. Allowing documents that describe cash transactions to go unrecorded for an unnecessarily long period of time increases the likelihood that fraudulent or inaccurate records will pass undetected through the accounting department.

- **Physical controls.** Cash on hand must be physically secure. This is accomplished in a variety of ways. Cash registers should contain only enough cash to handle customer transactions. When a cashier finishes a shift—or perhaps more frequently—excess cash should be moved from cash registers to a safe or another location that provides additional security. In addition, daily bank deposits are made so that excess cash does not remain on the premises. Blank checks, which can be used for forgery, are stored in locked, fireproof files.

- **Independent checks on performance.** Employees who handle cash or who record cash transactions must be prepared for independent checks on their performance. These checks should be done periodically and may be done without forewarning. Having a supervisor verify the accuracy of a cashier's drawer on a daily basis is an example of this type of control.

- **Other cash controls.** Most companies bond individuals that handle cash. A company **bonds** an employee by paying a bonding company for insurance against theft by the employee. If the employee then steals, the bonding company reimburses the company. Companies may also rotate employees from one task to another. Embezzlement or serious mistakes may be uncovered when a new employee takes over a task. Although specific cash controls vary from one company to the next, all companies must implement effective cash controls.

The Petty Cash Fund

Companies normally use checks to pay their obligations because checks provide a record of each payment. Companies also maintain a **petty cash fund** to pay for small, miscellaneous expenditures such as stamps, small delivery charges, or emergency supplies. The size of a petty cash fund varies depending on the needs of the business. A petty cash fund should be small enough so that it does not unnecessarily tie up company assets or become a target for theft, but it should be large enough to lessen the inconvenience associated with frequently replenishing the fund. For this reason, companies typically establish a petty cash fund that needs to be replenished every two to four weeks.

Companies assign responsibility for the petty cash fund to a person called the petty cash custodian or petty cashier. To establish a petty cash fund, someone must write a check to the petty cash custodian, who cashes the check and keeps the money in a locked file or cash box. The journal entry to record the creation of a petty cash fund appears below.

	General Journal				GJ1
Date	Account Title and Description	Ref.	Debit		Credit
20X8					
Apr. 1	Petty Cash		150		
	Cash				150
	Establish petty cash fund				

Most companies would record this entry—or any other entry that credits cash—in the cash disbursements special journal, but the illustrations in this chapter use the general journal to eliminate journal columns that are not relevant to this discussion and to conform with this subject's presentation in most textbooks.

Whenever someone in the company requests petty cash, the petty cash custodian prepares a voucher that identifies the date, amount, recipient, and reason for the cash disbursement. For control purposes, vouchers are sequentially prenumbered and signed by both the person requesting the cash and the custodian. After the cash is spent, receipts or other relevant documents should be returned to the petty cash custodian, who attaches them to the voucher. All vouchers are kept with the petty cash fund until the fund is replenished, so the total amount of the vouchers and the remaining cash in the fund should always equal the amount assigned to the fund.

When the fund requires more cash or at the end of an accounting period, the petty cash custodian requests a check for the difference between the cash on hand and the total assigned to the fund. At this time, the person who provides cash to the custodian should examine the vouchers to verify their legitimacy. The transaction that replenishes the petty cash fund is recorded with a compound entry that debits all relevant asset or expense accounts and credits cash. Consider the journal entry below, which is made after the custodian requests $130 to replenish the petty cash fund and submits vouchers that fall into one of three categories.

	General Journal			GJ12
Date	Account Title and Description	Ref.	Debit	Credit
20X8				
Apr. 30	Office Supplies		55	
	Postage Expense		40	
	Transportation Expense		35	
	Cash			130
	Replenish petty cash fund			

Notice that the petty cash account is debited or credited only when the fund is established or when the size of the fund is increased or decreased, not when the fund is replenished.

If the voucher amounts do not equal the cash needed to replenish the fund, the difference is recorded in an account named *cash over and short*. This account is debited when there is a cash shortage and credited when there is a cash overage. Cash over and short appears on the income statement as a miscellaneous expense if the account has a debit balance or as a miscellaneous revenue if the account has a credit balance. In the journal entry below, the vouchers total $130 but the fund needs $135, so the entry includes a $5 debit to the cash over and short account.

General Journal — GJ12

Date	Account Title and Description	Ref.	Debit	Credit
20X8				
Apr. 30	Office Supplies		55	
	Postage Expense		40	
	Transportation Expense		35	
	Cash Over and Short		5	
	Cash			135
	Replenish petty cash fund			

If the vouchers total $130 but the fund needs only $125, the journal entry includes a $5 credit to the cash over and short account.

General Journal — GJ12

Date	Account Title and Description	Ref.	Debit	Credit
20X8				
Apr. 30	Office Supplies		55	
	Postage Expense		40	
	Transportation Expense		35	
	Cash			125
	Cash Over and Short			5
	Replenish petty cash fund			

Bank Reconciliation

Banks usually send customers a monthly statement that shows the account's beginning balance (the previous statement's ending balance), all transactions that affect the account's balance during the month, and the account's ending balance.

First National Bank
1234 First Avenue
Primo Vista, CA 90783-1409

Statement of Account
109-654-5454-45

April 30, 20X8

Vector Management Group
3214 Tangent Ln.
Circle Park, CA 90778-3421

Balance Last Statement	7,358
Total Credits	14,083
Total Debits	13,239
Balance This Statement	8,202

Date	Check	Debits		Credits		Balance
4/1/20X8						7,358
4/2/20X8				3,200		10,558
4/2/20X8	1541	152				10,406
4/4/20X8	1547	330				10,076
4/5/20X8	1551	18				10,058
4/6/20X8		20	SC			10,038
4/6/20X8	1553	152				9,886
4/7/20X8	1554	87				9,799
4/9/20X8				2,800		12,599
4/10/20X8	1555	1,524				11,075
4/11/20X8	1556	765				10,310
4/12/20X8		253	DM			10,057
4/12/20X8	1557	32				10,025
4/13/20X8	1558	304				9,721
4/14/20X8	1559	3,227				6,494
4/16/20X8				3,100		9,594
4/17/20X8	1560	81				9,513
4/19/20X8		50	SC			9,463
4/19/20X8	1561	152				9,311
4/20/20X8	1562	66				9,245
4/20/20X8	1563	1,325				7,920
4/21/20X8	1566	358				7,562
4/23/20X8				3,400		10,962
4/24/20X8	1567	429				10,533
4/24/20X8		345	NSF			10,188
4/25/20X8				1,565	CM	11,753
4/27/20X8	1568	3,188				8,565
4/30/20X8	1569	381				8,184
4/30/20X8				18	INT	8,202

Symbol key:
CM = Credit Memo (see attachment)
DD = Direct Deposit
DM = Debit Memo (see attachment)
INT = Interest
NSF = Not Sufficient Funds
SC = Service Charge

The ending balance on a bank statement almost never agrees with the balance in a company's corresponding general ledger account. After receiving the bank statement, therefore, the company prepares a **bank reconciliation**, which identifies each difference between the company's records and the bank's records. The normal differences identified in a bank reconciliation will be discussed separately. These differences are referred to as reconciling items. A bank reconciliation begins by showing the bank statement's ending balance and the company's balance (book balance) in the cash account on the same date.

Vector Management Group
Bank Reconciliation
April 30, 20X8

Bank statement balance	$ 8,202	Book balance	$ 6,370

Deposits in transit. Most companies make frequent cash deposits. Therefore, company records may show one or more deposits, usually made on the last day included on the bank statement, that do not appear on the bank statement. These deposits are called deposits in transit and cause the bank statement balance to understate the company's actual cash balance. Since deposits in transit have already been recorded in the company's books as cash receipts, they must be added to the bank statement balance. The Vector Management Group made a $3,000 deposit on the afternoon of April 30 that does not appear on the statement, so this deposit in transit is added to the bank statement balance.

Vector Management Group
Bank Reconciliation
April 30, 20X8

Bank statement balance	$ 8,202	Book balance	$ 6,370
Add: Deposits in transit	3,000		
	11,202		

Outstanding checks. A check that a company mails to a creditor may take several days to pass through the mail, be processed and deposited by the creditor, and then clear the banking system. Therefore, company records may include a number of checks that do not appear on the bank statement. These checks are called outstanding checks and cause the bank statement balance to overstate the company's actual cash balance. Since outstanding checks have already been recorded in the company's books as cash disbursements, they must be subtracted from the bank statement balance.

Vector Management Group
Bank Reconciliation
April 30, 20X8

Bank statement balance	$ 8,202	Book balance	$ 6,370
Add: Deposits in transit	3,000		
	11,202		

Less: Outstanding checks

1552	$1,057	
1564	245	
1565	108	
1570	359	
1571	802	
1572	1,409	(3,980)

Adjusted bank balance $ 7,222

Automatic withdrawals and deposits. Companies may authorize a bank to automatically transfer funds into or out of their account. Automatic withdrawals from the account are used to pay for loans (notes or mortgages payable), monthly utility bills, or other liabilities. Automatic deposits occur when the company's checking account receives automatic fund transfers from customers or other sources or when the bank collects notes receivable payments on behalf of the company.

Banks use **debit memoranda** to notify companies about automatic withdrawals, and they use **credit memoranda** to notify companies about automatic deposits. The names applied to these memoranda may seem confusing at first glance because the company credits (decreases) its cash account upon receiving debit memoranda from the bank, and the company debits (increases) its cash account upon receiving credit memoranda from the bank. To the bank, however, a company's checking account balance is a liability rather than an asset. Therefore, from the bank's perspective, the terms *debit* and *credit* are correctly applied to the memoranda. If this still seems confusing, you may want to review the chart on page 19 and think about how the company classifies their account as an asset while the bank classifies the company's account as a liability.

A credit memorandum attached to the Vector Management Group's bank statement describes the bank's collection of a $1,500 note receivable along with $90 in interest. The bank deducted $25 for this service, so the automatic deposit was for $1,565. The bank statement also includes a debit memorandum describing a $253 automatic withdrawal for a utility payment. Unlike deposits in transit or outstanding checks, which are already recorded in the company's books, automatic withdrawals and deposits are often brought to the company's attention for the first time when the bank statement is received. On the bank reconciliation, add unrecorded automatic deposits to the company's book balance, and subtract unrecorded automatic withdrawals.

Vector Management Group
Bank Reconciliation
April 30, 20X8

Bank statement balance	$ 8,202	Book balance		$ 6,370
Add: Deposits in transit	3,000	Add: Note collection		
	11,202	plus interest		
		less bank fee	$1,565	
Less: Outstanding checks		Less: Utility payment	$253	
1552	$1,057			
1564	245			
1565	108			
1570	359			
1571	802			
1572	1,409	(3,980)		
Adjusted bank balance		$ 7,222		

Because reconciling items that affect the book balance on a bank reconciliation have not been recorded in the company's books, they must be journalized and posted to the general ledger accounts. The $1,565 credit memorandum requires a compound journal entry involving four accounts. Cash is debited for $1,565, bank fees expense is debited for $25, notes receivable is credited for $1,500, and interest revenue is credited for $90.

General Journal GJ14

Date	Account Title and Description	Ref.	Debit	Credit
20X8				
Apr. 30	Cash		1,565	
	Bank Fees Expense		25	
	Notes Receivable			1,500
	Interest Revenue			90
	Bank collection of note			

If the Vector Management Group had previously made adjusting entries to accrue all of the interest revenue (by debiting interest receivable and crediting interest revenue), then interest receivable rather than interest revenue would need to be credited for $90 in the journal entry shown above.

The automatic withdrawal requires a simple journal entry that debits utilities expense and credits cash for $253.

General Journal GJ14

Date	Account Title and Description	Ref.	Debit	Credit
20X8				
Apr. 30	Utilities Expense		253	
	Cash			253
	Utility payment made by bank			

Interest earned. Banks often pay interest on checking account balances. Interest income reported on the bank statement has usually not been accrued by the company and, therefore, must be added to the company's book balance on the bank reconciliation. The final transaction listed on the Vector Management Group's bank statement on page 120 is for $18 in interest that has not been accrued, so this amount is added to the right side of the bank reconciliation shown below.

Vector Management Group
Bank Reconciliation
April 30, 20X8

Bank statement balance	$ 8,202	Book balance			$ 6,370
Add: Deposits in transit	3,000	Add: Note collection			
	11,202	plus interest			
		less bank fee	$1,565		
		Interest earned	18	1,583	
					7,953
Less: Outstanding checks		Less: Utility payment	$253		
1552	$1,057				
1564	245				
1565	108				
1570	359				
1571	802				
1572	1,409	(3,980)			
Adjusted bank balance	$ 7,222				

The interest revenue must be journalized and posted to the general ledger cash account. In the journal entry below, cash is debited for $18 and interest revenue is credited for $18.

General Journal   GJ14

Date	Account Title and Description	Ref.	Debit	Credit
20X8				
Apr. 30	Cash		18	
	Interest Revenue			18
	Checking account interest			

Bank service charges. Banks often require customers to pay monthly account fees, check printing fees, safe-deposit box rental fees, and other fees. Unrecorded service charges must be subtracted from the company's book balance on the bank reconciliation. The Vector Management Group's bank statement on page 120 includes a $20 service charge for check printing and a $50 service charge for the rental of a safe-deposit box.

Vector Management Group
Bank Reconciliation
April 30, 20X8

Bank statement balance	$ 8,202	Book balance			$ 6,370
Add: Deposits in transit	3,000	Add: Note collection			
	11,202	plus interest			
		less bank fee	$1,565		
		Interest earned	18	1,583	
					7,953
Less: Outstanding checks		Less: Utility payment	$253		
1552	$1,057	Check printing	20		
1564	245	Safe-deposit box			
1565	108	rental	50		
1570	359				
1571	802				
1572	1,409	(3,980)			
Adjusted bank balance	$ 7,222				

Although separate journal entries for each expense can be made, it is simpler to combine them, so bank fees expense is debited for $70 and cash is credited for $70.

General Journal   GJ14

Date	Account Title and Description	Ref.	Debit	Credit
20X8				
Apr. 30	Bank Fees Expense		70	
	Cash			70
	Check printing/deposit box			

NSF (not sufficient funds) checks. A check previously recorded as part of a deposit may bounce because there are not sufficient funds in the issuer's checking account. When this happens, the bank returns the check to the depositor and deducts the check amount from the depositor's account. Therefore, NSF checks must be subtracted from the company's book balance on the bank reconciliation. The Vector Management Group's bank statement includes an NSF check for $345 from Hosta, Inc.

Vector Management Group
Bank Reconciliation
April 30, 20X8

Bank statement balance	$ 8,202	Book balance		$ 6,370
Add: Deposits in transit	3,000	Add: Note collection		
	11,202	plus interest		
		less bank fee	$1,565	
		Interest earned	18	1,583
				7,953
Less: Outstanding checks		Less: Utility payment	$253	
1552 $1,057		Check printing	20	
1564 245		Safe deposit box		
1565 108		rental	50	
1570 359		NSF Hosta, Inc.	345	
1571 802				
1572 1,409	(3,980)			
Adjusted bank balance	$ 7,222			

Since the NSF check has previously been recorded as a cash receipt, a journal entry is necessary to update the company's books. Therefore, a $345 debit is made to increase the accounts receivable balance of Hosta, Inc., and a $345 credit is made to decrease cash.

General Journal   GJ14

Date	Account Title and Description	Ref.	Debit	Credit
20X8				
Apr. 30	Accounts Receivable–Hosta, Inc.		345	
	Cash			345
	NSF from Hosta, Inc.			

Errors. Companies and banks sometimes make errors. Therefore, each transaction on the bank statement should be double-checked. If the bank incorrectly recorded a transaction, the bank must be contacted, and the bank balance must be adjusted on the bank reconciliation. If the company incorrectly recorded a transaction, the book balance must be adjusted on the bank reconciliation and a correcting entry must be journalized and posted to the general ledger. While reviewing the bank statement, Vector Management Group discovers that check #1569 for $381, which was made payable to an advertising agency named Ad It Up, had been incorrectly entered in the cash disbursements journal for $318. This error is a reconciling item because the company's general ledger cash account is overstated by $63.

Vector Management Group
Bank Reconciliation
April 30, 20X8

Bank statement balance	$ 8,202	Book balance			$ 6,370
Add: Deposits in transit	3,000	Add: Note collection			
	11,202	plus interest			
		less bank fee	$1,565		
		Interest earned		18	1,583
					7,953
Less: Outstanding checks		Less: Utility payment	$253		
1552	$1,057	Check printing	20		
1564	245	Safe deposit box			
1565	108	rental	50		
1570	359	NSF Hosta, Inc.	345		
1571	802	Error check #1569	63	(731)	
1572	1,409 (3,980)				
Adjusted bank balance	$ 7,222	Adjusted book balance			$ 7,222

When all differences between the ending bank statement balance and book balance have been identified and entered on the bank reconciliation, the adjusted bank balance and adjusted book balance are identical.

Since the Vector Management Group paid Ad It Up $63 more than the books show, a $63 debit is made to decrease the accounts payable balance owed to Ad It Up, and a $63 credit is made to decrease cash.

General Journal   GJ14

Date	Account Title and Description	Ref.	Debit	Credit
20X8				
Apr. 30	Accounts Payable–Ad It Up		63	
	Cash			63
	Correction check #1569			

Credit Card Sales

Retail companies, which sell merchandise in small quantities directly to consumers, often receive a significant portion of their revenue through credit card sales. Some credit card receipts, specifically those involving credit cards issued by banks, are deposited along with cash and checks made payable to the company. The company receives cash for these credit card sales immediately. Because banks that issue credit cards to customers handle billing, collections, and related expenses, they usually charge companies between 2% and 5% of the sales price. This fee is deducted when the receipts are deposited in the company's bank account, so these credit card receipts are slightly more complicated to record than other types of cash deposits. If a company deposits credit card receipts totaling $1,000 and the fee is 3%, the company makes a compound entry that debits cash for $970, debits credit card expense for $30 (3% of $1,000), and credits sales for $1,000.

General Journal   GJ64

Date	Account Title and Description	Ref.	Debit	Credit
20X5				
Dec. 17	Cash		970	
	Credit Card Expense		30	
	Sales			1,000
	Deposit credit card receipts			

Some credit card receipts must be treated as receivables rather than cash. For example, many gas stations and department stores provide customers with credit cards that can be used to buy goods or services only at the issuer's place of business. When a customer makes a purchase, the company must debit the customer's account and credit the sales account. There are also some major credit cards that are not issued by banks, and receipts from these cards must be sent to the credit card company for reimbursement rather than deposited at a bank. After submitting credit card receipts totaling $1,000 directly to a credit card company, the company that makes the sale records the entry by debiting accounts receivable and crediting sales.

General Journal — GJ64

Date	Account Title and Description	Ref.	Debit	Credit
20X5				
Dec. 17	Accounts Receivable–Card Issuer		1,000	
	Sales			1,000
	Credit card sales			

The credit card company deducts their fee before paying the company that made the sale. Upon receiving payment, the company that made the sale debits cash, debits credit card expense, and credits accounts receivable.

General Journal — GJ64

Date	Account Title and Description	Ref.	Debit	Credit
20X5				
Dec. 29	Cash		970	
	Credit Card Expense		30	
	Accounts Receivable–Card Issuer			1,000
	Payment from card issuer			

Recording credit card expenses after receiving payment, as in the example above, is convenient because a compound journal entry is all that is needed. However, if the sale occurs during one accounting period and the payment is not received until the next accounting period, an adjusting entry must be made, if the amount of credit card expense is significant, to prevent the matching principle from being violated. The matching principle requires that expenses be recognized during the same accounting period as the revenues they help to generate. If the payment in the previous example had not yet been received at the close of an accounting period, the company would make an adjusting entry that debits credit card expense for $30 and credits accounts receivable for $30.

General Journal — GJ64

Date	Account Title and Description	Ref.	Debit	Credit
20X5				
Dec. 31	Credit Card Expense		30	
	Accounts Receivable–Card Issuer			30
	Accrue credit expense			

Then, after the payment arrives, cash is debited for $970 and accounts receivable is credited for $970.

General Journal — GJ65

Date	Account Title and Description	Ref.	Debit	Credit
20X6				
Jan. 5	Cash		970	
	Accounts Receivable–Card Issuer			970
	Payment from card issuer			

Accounts receivable are amounts that customers owe the company for normal credit purchases. Since accounts receivable are generally collected within two months of the sale, they are considered a current asset and usually appear on balance sheets below short-term investments and above inventory.

Notes receivable are amounts owed to the company by customers or others who have signed formal promissory notes in acknowledgment of their debts. Promissory notes strengthen a company's legal claim against those who fail to pay as promised. The maturity date of a note determines whether it is placed with current assets or long-term assets on the balance sheet. Notes that are due in one year or less are considered current assets, and notes that are due in more than one year are considered long-term assets.

Accounts receivable and notes receivable that result from company sales are called **trade receivables,** but there are other types of receivables as well. For example, interest revenue from notes or other interest-bearing assets is accrued at the end of each accounting period and placed in an account named *interest receivable.* Wage advances, formal loans to employees, or loans to other companies create other types of receivables. If significant, these nontrade receivables are usually listed in separate categories on the balance sheet because each type of nontrade receivable has distinct risk factors and liquidity characteristics.

Receivables of all types are normally reported on the balance sheet at their **net realizable value,** which is the amount the company expects to receive in cash.

Evaluating Accounts Receivable

Business owners know that some customers who receive credit will never pay their account balances. These uncollectible accounts are also called bad debts. Companies use two methods to account for bad debts: the direct write-off method and the allowance method.

Direct write-off method. For tax purposes, companies must use the direct write-off method, under which bad debts are recognized only after the company is certain the debt will not be paid. Before determining that an account balance is uncollectible, a company generally makes several attempts to collect the debt from the customer. Recognizing the bad debt requires a journal entry that increases a bad debts expense account and decreases accounts receivable. If a customer named J. Smith fails to pay a $225 balance, for example, the company records the write-off by debiting bad debts expense and crediting accounts receivable from J. Smith.

	General Journal			GJ48
Date	Account Title and Description	Ref.	Debit	Credit
20X6				
May 31	Bad Debts Expense		225	
	Accounts Receivable–J. Smith			225
	Write off J. Smith's account			

The Internal Revenue Service permits companies to take a tax deduction for bad debts only after specific uncollectible accounts have been identified. Unless a company's uncollectible accounts represent an insignificant percentage of their sales, however, they may not use the direct write-off method for financial reporting purposes. Since several months may pass between the time that a sale occurs and the time that a company realizes that a customer's account is uncollectible, the matching principle, which requires that revenues and related expenses be matched in the same accounting period, would often be violated if the direct write-off method were used. Therefore, most companies use the direct write-off method on their tax returns but use the allowance method on financial statements.

Allowance method. Under the allowance method, an adjustment is made at the end of each accounting period to estimate bad debts based on the business activity from that accounting period. Established companies rely on past experience to estimate unrealized bad debts, but new companies must rely on published industry averages until they have sufficient experience to make their own estimates.

The adjusting entry to estimate the expected value of bad debts does not reduce accounts receivable directly. Accounts receivable is a control account that must have the same balance as the combined balance of every individual account in the accounts receivable subsidiary ledger. Since the specific customer accounts that will become uncollectible are not yet known when the adjusting entry is made, a contra-asset account named *allowance for bad debts,* which is sometimes called *allowance for doubtful accounts,* is subtracted from accounts receivable to show the net realizable value of accounts receivable on the balance sheet.

If at the end of its first accounting period a company estimates that $5,000 in accounts receivable will become uncollectible, the necessary adjusting entry debits bad debts expense for $5,000 and credits allowance for bad debts for $5,000.

General Journal   GJ32

Date	Account Title and Description	Ref.	Debit	Credit
20X5				
Dec. 31	Bad Debts Expense		5,000	
	Allowance for Bad Debts			5,000
	Estimate of bad debts			

After the entry shown above is made, the accounts receivable subsidiary ledger still shows the full amount each customer owes, the balance of the control account (accounts receivable) agrees with the total balance in the subsidiary ledger, the credit balance in the contra asset account (allowance for bad debts) can be subtracted from the debit balance in accounts receivable to show the net realizable value of accounts receivable, and a reasonable estimate of bad debts expense is recognized in the appropriate accounting period.

When a specific customer's account is identified as uncollectible, it is written off against the balance in the allowance for bad debts account. For example, J. Smith's uncollectible balance of $225 is removed from the books by debiting allowance for bad debts and crediting accounts receivable. Remember, general journal entries that affect a control account must be posted to both the control account and the specific account in the subsidiary ledger.

General Journal GJ48

Date	Account Title and Description	Ref.	Debit	Credit
20X6				
May 31	Allowance for Bad Debts	115	225	
	Accounts Receivable–J. Smith	110/AR91		225
	Write off J. Smith's account			

General Ledger Accounts

Allowance for Bad Debts 115

Date	Ref.	Debit	Credit	Balance
20X6				5,000
May 31	GJ48	225		4,775

Accounts Receivable 110

Date	Ref.	Debit	Credit	Balance
20X6				100,000
May 31	GJ48		225	99,775

Accounts Receivable Subsidiary Ledger

J. Smith AR91

Date	Ref.	Debit	Credit	Balance
20X6				225
May 31	GJ48		225	0

Under the allowance method, a write-off does not change the net realizable value of accounts receivable. It simply reduces accounts receivable and allowance for bad debts by equivalent amounts.

	Before writing off J. Smith's account	After writing off J. Smith's account
Accounts Receivable	$100,000	$99,775
Less: Allowance for Bad Debts	(5,000)	(4,775)
Net Realizable Value	$ 95,000	$95,000

Customers whose accounts have already been written off as uncollectible will sometimes pay their debts. When this happens, two entries are needed to correct the company's accounting records and show that the customer paid the outstanding balance. The first entry reinstates the customer's accounts receivable balance by debiting accounts receivable and crediting allowance for bad debts. As in the previous example, the debit to accounts receivable must be posted to the general ledger control account and to the appropriate subsidiary ledger account.

General Journal   GJ56

Date	Account Title and Description	Ref.	Debit	Credit
20X6				
Aug. 11	Accounts Receivable–J. Smith	110/AR91	225	
	Allowance for Bad Debts	115		225
	Reverse J. Smith write-off			

General Ledger Accounts

Accounts Receivable   110

Date	Ref.	Debit	Credit	Balance
20X6				100,000
May 31	GJ48		225	99,775
Aug. 11	GJ56	225		100,000

Allowance for Bad Debts 115

Date	Ref.	Debit	Credit	Balance
20X6				5,000
May 31	GJ48	225		4,775
Aug. 11	GJ56		225	5,000

Accounts Receivable Subsidiary Ledger

J. Smith   AR91

Date	Ref.	Debit	Credit	Balance
20X6				225
May 31	GJ48		225	0
Aug. 11	GJ56	225		225

The second entry records the customer's payment by debiting cash and crediting accounts receivable. Most companies record cash receipts in a cash receipts journal. Since a special journal's column totals are posted to the general ledger at the end of each accounting period, the posting to J. Smith's account is the only one shown with the cash receipts journal entry in the illustration below. Page 110 describes the cash receipts journal in detail.

Cash Receipts Journal   CR81

Date	Account	Ref.	Cash (Dr.)	Sales Discounts (Dr.)	Accounts Receivable (Cr.)	Sales (Cr.)	Other (Cr.)
20X6							
Aug. 11	AR–J. Smith	AR91	225		225		

J. Smith   AR91

Date	Explanation	Ref.	Debit	Credit	Balance
20X6					225
May 31	Write off account	GJ48		225	0
Aug. 11	Reverse write-off	GJ56	225		225
11	Payment	CR81		225	0

In the future when management looks at J. Smith's payment history, the account's activity will show the eventual collection of the amount owed.

Textbooks usually explain the repayment of previously written-off debts using the general journal. If you use the general journal for the entry shown in the cash receipts journal on the previous page, you post the entry directly to cash and accounts receivable in the general ledger and also to J. Smith's account in the accounts receivable subsidiary ledger.

General Journal GJ56

Date	Account Title and Description	Ref.	Debit	Credit
20X6				
Aug. 11	Accounts Receivable–J. Smith	110/AR91	225	
	Allowance for Bad Debts	115		225
	Reverse J. Smith write-off			
11	Cash	100	225	
	Accounts Receivable–J. Smith	110/AR91		225
	Received payment from J. Smith			

General Ledger Accounts

Cash 100

Date	Ref.	Debit	Credit	Balance
20X6				6,075
Aug. 11	GJ56	225		6,300

Accounts Receivable 110

Date	Ref.	Debit	Credit	Balance
20X6				100,000
May 31	GJ48		225	99,775
Aug. 11	GJ56	225		100,000
11	GJ56		225	99,775

Accounts Receivable Subsidiary Ledger

J. Smith AR91

Date	Ref.	Debit	Credit	Balance
20X6				225
May 31	GJ48		225	0
Aug. 11	GJ56	225		225
11	GJ56		225	0

Estimating Bad Debts Under the Allowance Method

Percentage of total accounts receivable method. One way companies derive an estimate for the value of bad debts under the allowance method is to calculate bad debts as a percentage of the accounts receivable balance. If a company has $100,000 in accounts receivable at the end of an accounting period and company records indicate that, on average, 5% of total accounts receivable become uncollectible, the allowance for bad debts account must be adjusted to have a credit balance of $5,000 (5% of $100,000).

Unless actual write-offs during the just-completed accounting period perfectly matched the balance assigned to the allowance for bad debts account at the close of the previous accounting period, the account will have an existing balance. If write-offs were less than expected, the account will have a credit balance, and if write-offs were greater than expected, the account will have a debit balance. Assuming that the allowance for bad debts account has a $200 debit balance when the adjusting entry is made, a $5,200 adjusting entry is necessary to give the account a credit balance of $5,000.

General Journal — GJ64

Date	Account Title and Description	Ref.	Debit	Credit
20X6				
Dec. 31	Bad Debts Expense	570	5,200	
	Allowance for Bad Debts	115		5,200
	Estimate of bad debts			

Bad Debts Expense — 570

Date	Explanation	Ref.	Debit	Credit	Balance
20X6					
Dec. 31	Estimate of bad debts	GJ64	5,200		5,200

Allowance for Bad Debts — 115

Date	Explanation	Ref.	Debit	Credit	Balance
20X6					(200)
Dec. 31	Estimate of bad debts	GJ64		5,200	5,000

If the allowance for bad debts account had a $300 credit balance instead of a $200 debit balance, a $4,700 adjusting entry would be needed to give the account a credit balance of $5,000.

Aging method. In general, the longer an account balance is overdue, the less likely the debt is to be paid. Therefore, many companies maintain an **accounts receivable aging schedule,** which categorizes each customer's credit purchases by the length of time they have been outstanding. Each category's overall balance is multiplied by an estimated percentage of uncollectibility for that category, and the total of all such calculations serves as the estimate of bad debts. The accounts receivable aging schedule shown below includes five categories for classifying the age of unpaid credit purchases.

Accounts Receivable Aging Schedule
December 31, 20X6

Customer	Balance	Current	Days Past Due			
			1 to 30	31 to 60	61 to 90	Over 90
C. Aaron	$ 2,000	$ 2,000				
B. Ambroz	1,900	1,100	$ 800			
J. Baker	1,300			$1,100	$ 200	
W. Bruce	1,500	800	700			
H. Bunica	2,000	2,000				
K. Carter	600					$ 600
E. Cline	2,700	2,700				
All Others	88,000	71,400	12,500	1,900	800	1,400
Totals	$100,000	$80,000	$14,000	$3,000	$1,000	$2,000
Percentage		1%	10%	30%	50%	70%
Estimated Bad Debts	$ 5,000	$ 800	$ 1,400	$ 900	$ 500	$1,400

In this example, estimated bad debts are $5,000. If the account has an existing credit balance of $400, the adjusting entry includes a $4,600 debit to bad debts expense and a $4,600 credit to allowance for bad debts.

General Journal				GJ64
Date	Account Title and Description	Ref.	Debit	Credit
20X6				
Dec. 31	Bad Debts Expense		4,600	
	Allowance for Bad Debts			4,600
	Estimate of bad debts			

Percentage of credit sales method. Some companies estimate bad debts as a percentage of credit sales. If a company has $500,000 in credit sales during an accounting period and company records indicate that, on average, 1% of credit sales become uncollectible, the adjusting entry at the end of the accounting period debits bad debts expense for $5,000 and credits allowance for bad debts for $5,000.

General Journal					GJ64
Date	Account Title and Description	Ref.	Debit	Credit
20X6				
Dec. 31	Bad Debts Expense		5,000	
	Allowance for Bad Debts			5,000
	Estimate of bad debts			

Companies that use the percentage of credit sales method base the adjusting entry solely on total credit sales and ignore any existing balance in the allowance for bad debts account. If estimates fail to match actual bad debts, the percentage rate used to estimate bad debts is adjusted on future estimates.

Factoring Receivables

Companies sometimes need cash before customers pay their account balances. In such situations, the company may choose to sell accounts receivable to another company that specializes in collections. This process is called factoring, and the company that purchases accounts receivable is often called a factor. The factor usually charges between one and fifteen percent of the account balances. The reason for such a wide range in fees is that the receivables may be factored with or without recourse. **Recourse** means the company factoring the receivables agrees to reimburse the factor for uncollectible accounts. Low percentage rates are usually offered only when recourse is provided.

Suppose a company factors $500,000 in accounts receivable at a rate of 3%. The company records this sale of accounts receivable by debiting cash for $485,000, debiting factoring expense (or service charge expense) for $15,000, and crediting accounts receivable for $500,000.

	General Journal			GJ44
Date	Account Title and Description	Ref.	Debit	Credit
20X1				
May 14	Cash		485,000	
	Factoring Expense		15,000	
	Accounts Receivable			500,000
	Factor accounts worth $500,000			

In practice, the credit to accounts receivable would need to identify the specific subsidiary ledger accounts that were factored, although to simplify the example this is not done here.

Notes Receivable

Companies classify the promissory notes they hold as notes receivable. A simple promissory note appears below.

$1,000   Surf City, California   June 18, 20X1
(Principal Amount)   (Location and Date)

4 months after date   Jim Radd   promises to pay
                          (Name of Maker)

to the order of   Surf Breaker West
                          (Name of Payee)

for value received with annual interest at   9 %
                          (Interest Rate)

                                    Jim Radd
                          (Signature of Maker)

The face value of a note is called the **principal,** which equals the initial amount of credit provided. The **maker** of a note is the party who receives the credit and promises to pay the note's holder. The maker classifies the note as a note payable. The **payee** is the party that holds the note and receives payment from the maker when the note is due. The payee classifies the note as a note receivable.

Calculating interest. Notes generally specify an interest rate, which is used to determine how much interest the maker of the note must pay in addition to the principal. Interest on short-term notes is calculated according to the following formula:

$$\text{Principal} \times \frac{\text{Annual}}{\text{Interest Rate}} \times \frac{\text{Time Period}}{\text{in Years}} = \text{Interest}$$

For example, interest on a four-month, 9%, $1,000 note equals $30.

$$\$1,000 \times .09 \times \frac{4}{12} = \$30$$

When a note's due date is expressed in days, the specified number of days is divided by 360 or 365 in the interest calculation. You may see either of these figures because accountants used a 360-day year to simplify their calculations before computers and calculators became widely available, and many textbooks still follow this convention. In current practice, however, financial institutions and other companies generally use a 365-day year to calculate interest. Therefore, you should be prepared to calculate interest either way.

The interest on a 90-day, 12%, $10,000 note equals $300 if a 360-day year is used to calculate interest, and the interest equals $295.89 if a 365-day year is used.

$$\$10,000 \times .12 \times \frac{90}{360} = \$300$$

$$\$10,000 \times .12 \times \frac{90}{365} = \$295.89$$

Even when a note's due date is not expressed in days, adjusting entries that recognize accrued interest are often calculated in terms of days. Suppose a company holds a four-month, 10%, $10,000 note dated October 19, 20X2. If the company uses an annual accounting period that ends on December 31, an adjusting entry that recognizes 73 days of accrued interest revenue must be made on December 31, 20X2. To determine the number of days in this situation, subtract the date of issue from the number of days in October and then add the result to the number of days in November and December $(31-19=12; 12+30+31=73)$. Notice that when you count days, you omit the note's issue date but include the note's due date or, in this situation, the date that the adjusting entry is made. Assuming the interest calculation uses a 365-day year, the accrued interest revenue equals $200.

$$\$10,000 \times .10 \times \frac{73}{365} = \$200$$

The adjusting entry debits interest receivable and credits interest revenue.

	General Journal			GJ85
Date	Account Title and Description	Ref.	Debit	Credit
20X2				
Dec. 31	Interest Receivable		200	
	Interest Revenue			200
	Accrue interest on note			

Interest on long-term notes is calculated using the same formula that is used with short-term notes, but unpaid interest is usually added to the principal to determine interest in subsequent years. For example, a two-year, 10%, $10,000 note accrues $1,000 in interest during the first year. The principal and first year's interest equal $11,000 when compounded, so $1,100 in interest accrues during the second year.

$$\$10,000 \times .10 \times 1 = \$1,000 \quad \text{(First Year's Interest)}$$
$$\$11,000 \times .10 \times 1 = \$1,100 \quad \text{(Second Year's Interest)}$$

Recording Notes Receivable Transactions

Customers frequently sign promissory notes to settle overdue accounts receivable balances. For example, if a customer named D. Brown signs a six-month, 10%, $2,500 promissory note after falling 90 days past due on her account, the business records the event by debiting notes receivable for $2,500 and crediting accounts receivable from D. Brown for $2,500. Notice that the entry does not include interest revenue, which is not recorded until it is earned.

General Journal				GJ33
Date	Account Title and Description	Ref.	Debit	Credit
20X8				
Apr. 26	Notes Receivable		2,500	
	Accounts Receivable–D. Brown			2,500
	Note for D. Brown's balance			

If a customer signs a promissory note in exchange for merchandise, the entry is recorded by debiting notes receivable and crediting sales.

General Journal				GJ33
Date	Account Title and Description	Ref.	Debit	Credit
20X8				
Apr. 26	Notes Receivable		2,500	
	Sales			2,500
	Goods purchased with note			

A company that frequently exchanges goods or services for notes would probably include a debit column for notes receivable in the sales journal so that such transactions would not need to be recorded in the general journal. A separate subsidiary ledger for notes receivable may also be created. If the amount of notes receivable is significant, a company should establish a separate allowance for bad debts account for notes receivable.

When a note's maker pays according to the terms specified on the note, the note is said to be honored. Assuming that no adjusting entries have been made to accrue interest revenue, the honored note is recorded by debiting cash for the amount the customer pays, crediting notes receivable for the principal value of the note, and crediting interest revenue for the interest earned. The total interest on a six-month, 10%, $2,500 note is $125, so if D. Brown honors her note, the entry includes a $2,625 debit to cash, a $2,500 credit to notes receivable, and a $125 credit to interest revenue.

General Journal					GJ42
Date	Account Title and Description	Ref.	Debit	Credit
20X8				
Oct. 26	Cash		2,625	
	Notes Receivable			2,500
	Interest Revenue			125
	Collect note–D. Brown			

If some of the interest has already been accrued (through adjusting entries that debited interest receivable and credited interest revenue), then the previously accrued interest is credited to interest receivable and the remainder of the interest is credited to interest revenue.

When the maker of a promissory note fails to pay, the note is said to be dishonored. The dishonored note may be recorded in one of two ways, depending upon whether or not the payee expects to collect the debt. If payment is expected, the company transfers the principal and interest to accounts receivable, removes the face value of the note from notes receivable, and recognizes the interest revenue. Assuming D. Brown dishonors the note but payment is expected, the company records the event by debiting accounts receivable from D. Brown for

$2,625, crediting notes receivable for $2,500, and crediting interest revenue for $125.

	General Journal			GJ42
Date	Account Title and Description	Ref.	Debit	Credit
20X8				
Oct. 26	Accounts Receivable–D. Brown		2,625	
	Notes Receivable			2,500
	Interest Revenue			125
	Dishonor note–D. Brown			

If D. Brown dishonors the note and the company believes the note is a bad debt, allowance for bad debts is debited for $2,500 and notes receivable is credited for $2,500. No interest revenue is recognized because none will ever be received.

	General Journal			GJ42
Date	Account Title and Description	Ref.	Debit	Credit
20X8				
Oct. 26	Allowance for Bad Debts		2,500	
	Notes Receivable			2,500
	Uncollectible note–D. Brown			

If interest on a bad debt had previously been accrued, then a correcting entry is needed to remove the accrued interest from interest revenue and interest receivable (by debiting interest revenue and crediting interest receivable). Although interest revenue would have been overstated in the accounting periods when the interest was accrued and would be understated in the period when the correcting entry occurs, efforts to amend prior statements or recognize the error in footnotes on forthcoming statements are not necessary except in rare situations where the bad debt changes reported revenue so much that the judgment of those who use financial statements is materially affected by the disclosure.

Discounting Notes Receivable

Just as accounts receivable can be factored, notes can be converted into cash by selling them to a financial institution at a discount. Notes are usually sold (discounted) with recourse, which means the company discounting the note agrees to pay the financial institution if the maker dishonors the note. When notes receivable are sold with recourse, the company has a contingent liability that must be disclosed in the notes accompanying the financial statements. A **contingent liability** is an obligation to pay an amount in the future, if and when an uncertain event occurs.

The **discount rate** is the annual percentage rate that the financial institution charges for buying a note and collecting the debt. The **discount period** is the length of time between a note's sale and its due date. The **discount,** which is the fee that the financial institution charges, is found by multiplying the note's maturity value by the discount rate and the discount period.

$$\text{Maturity Value of Note} \times \text{Discount Rate} \times \text{Discount Period} = \text{Discount}$$

Suppose a company accepts a 90-day, 9%, $5,000 note, which has a maturity value (principal + interest) of $5,110.96. In this example, precise calculations are made by using a 365-day year and by rounding results to the nearest penny.

Principal	$5,000.00
Interest ($5,000 × .09 × $\frac{90}{365}$)	110.96
Maturity Value	$5,110.96

If the company immediately discounts with recourse the note to a bank that offers a 15% discount rate, the bank's discount is $189.04

$$\$5,110.96 \times .15 \times \frac{90}{365} = \$189.04$$

The bank subtracts the discount from the note's maturity value and pays the company $4,921.92 for the note.

Maturity Value	$5,110.96
Discount	(189.04)
Discounted Value of Note	$4,921.92

The company determines the interest expense associated with this transaction by subtracting the discounted value of the note from the note's face value plus any interest revenue the company has earned from the note. Since the company discounts the note before earning any interest revenue, interest expense is $78.08 ($5000.00 − $4,921.92). The company records this transaction by debiting cash for $4,921.92, debiting interest expense for $78.08, and crediting notes receivable for $5,000.00.

	General Journal				GJ23
Date	Account Title and Description	Ref.	Debit	Credit	
20X1					
Jan. 15	Cash		4921.92		
	Interest Expense		78.08		
	Notes Receivable			5,000.00	
	Discounted note to bank				

Suppose the company holds the note for 60 days before discounting it. After 60 days, the company has earned interest revenue of $73.97.

$$\$5,000.00 \times .09 \times \frac{60}{365} = \$73.97$$

Since the note's due date is 30 days away, the bank's discount is $63.01. The bank subtracts the discount from the note's maturity value and pays the company $5,047.95 for the note.

$$\text{Discount} = \$5,110.96 \times .15 \times \frac{30}{365} = \$63.01$$

Maturity Value	$5,110.96
Discount	(63.01)
Discounted Value of Note	$5,047.95

The company subtracts the discounted value of the note from the note's face value plus the interest revenue the company has earned from the note to determine the interest expense, if any, associated with discounting the note. In this example, the interest expense equals $26.02.

Note's Face Value + Interest Revenue Earned	$5,073.97
Discounted Value of Note	(5,047.95)
Interest Expense	$ 26.02

The company records this transaction by debiting cash for $5,047.95, debiting interest expense for $26.02, crediting notes receivable for $5,000.00, and crediting interest revenue for $73.97.

	General Journal			GJ23
Date	Account Title and Description	Ref.	Debit	Credit
20X1				
Mar. 16	Cash		5047.95	
	Interest Expense		26.02	
	Notes Receivable			5,000.00
	Interest Revenue			73.97
	Discounted note to bank			

Merchandising and manufacturing companies keep an **inventory** of goods held for sale. Management is responsible for determining and maintaining the proper level of goods in inventory. If inventory contains too few items, sales may be missed. If inventory contains too many items, the business pays unnecessary amounts to warehouse, secure, and insure the items, and the company's cash flow becomes one sided—cash flows out to purchase inventory but cash does not flow in from sales.

Merchandising companies classify all goods available for sale in one inventory category. Manufacturing companies generally use three inventory categories: finished products, work in process, and raw materials. This chapter focuses on inventory for merchandising companies, but many of the principles and practices that are discussed apply to manufacturing companies as well. *Cliffs Quick Review Accounting Principles II* explains inventory accounting for manufacturing companies.

Determining Quantities of Merchandise in Inventory

Companies take **physical inventories** to count how many (or measure how much) of each item the company owns. Inventory is easier to count when sales and deliveries are not occurring, so many companies take inventory when the business is closed.

Taking a physical inventory involves the same types of internal control principles discussed in the first chapter of this book and in the chapter entitled "Cash." Some examples of these internal control principles appear below.

- **Segregation of duties.** Specific items should be counted by employees who do not have custody of the items.

- **Proper authorization.** Managers are responsible for assigning each employee to a specific set of inventory tasks. In addition, employees who help take inventory are responsible for verifying the contents of boxes, barrels, and other containers.

- **Adequate documents and records.** Prenumbered count sheets are provided to all employees involved in taking inventory. These count sheets provide evidence to support reported inventory levels and, when signed, show exactly who is responsible for the information they include.

- **Physical controls.** Access to inventory should be limited until the physical inventory is completed. If the company plans to ship inventory items during a physical inventory, these items should be placed in a separate area. Similarly, if the company receives inventory items during a physical inventory, these items should be kept in a designated area and counted separately.

- **Independent checks on performance.** After the employees finish counting, a supervisor should verify that all items have been counted and that none have been counted twice. Some companies use a second counter to check the first counter's results.

Consigned merchandise. Consigned merchandise is merchandise sold on behalf of another company or individual, who retains title to it. Although the seller (consignee) of the merchandise displays the items, only the owner (consignor) includes the items in inventory. Therefore, companies that sell goods on consignment must be careful to exclude from inventory those items provided by consignors.

Goods in transit. Goods in transit must be included in either the seller's or the buyer's inventory. When merchandise is shipped **FOB (free on board) shipping point,** the purchaser pays the shipping fees and gains title to the merchandise once it is shipped. Therefore, the merchandise must be included in the purchaser's inventory even if the purchaser has not yet received it. When merchandise is shipped **FOB (free on board) destination,** the seller pays the shipping fees and maintains title until the merchandise reaches the purchaser's place of business. Such merchandise must be included in the seller's inventory until the purchaser receives it. In addition to counting merchandise on hand, therefore, someone must examine the freight terms and shipping and receiving documents on purchases and sales just before and just after the count takes place to establish a more complete and accurate inventory count.

The Cost of Inventory

The cost of inventory includes the cost of purchased merchandise, less discounts that are taken, plus any duties and transportation costs paid by the purchaser. If the merchandise must be assembled or otherwise prepared for sale, then the cost of getting the product ready for sale is considered part of the cost of inventory. Technically, inventory costs include warehousing and insurance expenses associated with storing unsold merchandise. However, the cost of tracking this information often outweighs the benefits of allocating these costs to each unit of inventory, so many companies simply apply these costs directly to the cost of goods sold as the expenses are incurred.

The Valuation of Merchandise

To ensure the proper matching of expenses and revenues, decreases in the value of inventory due to usage, damage, deterioration, obsolescence, and other factors must be recognized in the accounting period during which the decrease occurs rather than the period during which the merchandise sells. Inventory should never be valued at more than its **net realizable value,** which equals its expected sales price minus any associated selling expenses. For example, if a storm damages a car that cost an automobile dealer $25,000, and if the car can now be sold for no more than $23,000, then the value of the car must be reported at $23,000. This decrease in the value of inventory is recognized by debiting the loss on inventory write-down account, which is an expense account, and by crediting inventory.

General Journal GJ11

Date	Account Title and Description	Ref.	Debit	Credit
20X5				
Jun. 30	Loss on Inventory Write-Down	525	2,000	
	Inventory	125		2,000
	Write down car's value			

Loss on Inventory Write-Down 525

Date	Explanation	Ref.	Debit	Credit	Balance
20X5					
Jun. 30	Write down car's value	GJ11	2,000		2,000

Inventory 125

Date	Explanation	Ref.	Debit	Credit	Balance
20X5					896,000
Jun. 30	Write down car's value	GJ11		2,000	894,000

Some companies attribute inventory write-downs directly to the cost of goods sold, and some companies use other expense accounts for this purpose, so write-downs are not usually identified separately on financial statements.

Market value generally equals the replacement cost of inventory. Items sometimes decrease in value because they become less expensive to purchase. In other words, the market value drops. The **lower-of-cost-or-market (LCM) rule** is used to determine the value of merchandise inventory.

Suppose a retail computer store purchases one hundred computers for $3,000 each. After the store sells fifty of them, the manufacturer decreases the computer's price, enabling the store—as well as the store's competitors—to purchase the same type of computer for $2,500. Applying the lower-of-cost-or-market rule means the value of the fifty remaining computers equals $125,000 (50 × $2,500) rather than $150,000 (50 × $3,000). This $25,000 write-down is recorded by debiting the loss on inventory write-down account and by crediting inventory.

General Journal GJ64

Date	Account Title and Description	Ref.	Debit	Credit
20X5				
Aug. 30	Loss on Inventory Write-Down	525	25,000	
	Inventory	125		25,000
	Write down computers			

Loss on Inventory Write-Down 525

Date	Explanation	Ref.	Debit	Credit	Balance
20X5					
Aug. 30	Write down computers	GJ64	25,000		25,000

Inventory 125

Date	Explanation	Ref.	Debit	Credit	Balance
20X5					481,000
Aug. 30	Write down computers	GJ64		25,000	456,000

Again, many companies choose to record write-downs using a different expense account than the one shown above.

The LCM rule may be applied to individual inventory items, to groups of similar items, or if the inventory consists of related items, to the entire inventory. As the chart below indicates, applying the LCM rule to individual items produces the most conservative valuation of inventory. As the number of items grouped together increases, the reported value of inventory tends to increase because increases in the market value of some items may partially offset decreases in the market value of other items in the same group.

			LCM Rule applied to		
	Cost	Market	Items	Groups	Entire Inventory
Computers					
Model EX7	$150,000	$125,000	$125,000		
Model NX8	30,000	32,000	30,000		
Model VX9	50,000	55,000	50,000		
Total	230,000	212,000		$212,000	
Printers					
Model PL30	30,000	34,000	30,000		
Model PL60	15,000	18,000	15,000		
Model PL90	25,000	24,000	24,000		
Total	70,000	76,000		70,000	
Total inventory	$300,000	$288,000	$274,000	$282,000	$288,000

After the value of inventory has been written down, an increase in net realizable value or market value is not recorded. Instead, such increases are recognized as revenue when sales actually occur. Because companies must estimate net realizable value and because applying the LCM rule to individual items or groups of items yields different inventory values, financial statements should disclose the company's basis for determining the value of inventory.

Comparing Perpetual and Periodic Inventory Systems

Companies may use either the perpetual system or the periodic system to account for inventory. Under the **periodic system,** merchandise purchases are recorded in the purchases account, and the inventory account balance is updated only at the end of each accounting period. The chapter entitled "Accounting for a Merchandising Company," which begins on page 85, describes the periodic system in detail. Perpetual inventory systems have traditionally been associated with companies that sell small numbers of high-priced items, but the development of modern scanning and computer technology has enabled almost any type of merchandiser to consider using this system.

Under the **perpetual system,** purchases, purchase returns and allowances, purchase discounts, sales, and sales returns are immediately recognized in the inventory account, so the inventory account balance should always remain accurate, assuming there is no theft, spoilage, or other losses. Consider several entries under both systems. The reference columns are removed from the illustration to save space.

Periodic Method

General Journal GJ11

Date	Accounts/Description	Dr.	Cr.
20X5			
Apr. 1	Purchases	800	
	AP–ACME		800
	Buy eight tires/$100 each		
4	AP–ACME	100	
	Purchases Returns & Allowances		100
	Return one tire to ACME		
10	AP–ACME	700	
	Cash		686
	Purchases Discounts		14
	Pay for seven tires		
22	AR–M. Guittar	300	
	Sales		300
	Sell two tires/$150 each		
24	Sales Returns & Allow.	150	
	AR–M. Guittar		150
	Return of one tire		
30	Cash	150	
	AR–M. Guittar		150
	Payment from M. Guittar		

Perpetual Method

General Journal GJ11

Date	Accounts/Description	Dr.	Cr.
20X5			
Apr. 1	Inventory–Tires	800	
	AP–ACME		800
	Buy eight tires/$100 each		
4	AP–ACME	100	
	Inventory–Tires		100
	Return one tire to ACME		
10	AP–ACME	700	
	Cash		686
	Inventory–Tires		14
	Pay for seven tires		
22	AR–M. Guittar	300	
	Sales		300
	Sell two tires/$150 each		
22	Cost of Goods Sold	200	
	Inventory–Tires		200
	Cost of tires/$100 each		
24	Sales Returns & Allow.	150	
	AR–M. Guittar		150
	Return of one tire		
24	Inventory–Tires	100	
	Cost of Goods Sold		100
	Add return to inventory		
30	Cash	150	
	AR–M. Guittar		150
	Payment from M. Guittar		

Note: AP stands for accounts payable, and AR stands for accounts receivable.

As the two sets of circled entries on the previous page indicate, two things happen when there is a sale or a sales return. First, the sales transaction's effect on revenue must be recognized by making an entry to increase accounts receivable and the sales account. Second, the flow of merchandise between inventory (an asset) and cost of goods sold (an expense) is recorded in accordance with the matching principle. A sales return has the opposite effect on the same accounts. Under the periodic system, the inventory and cost of goods sold accounts are updated only periodically, but under the perpetual system, entries that recognize a transaction's effect on these accounts occur when the revenue from the sale is recognized.

For convenience, a sale or sales return can be recorded under the perpetual system with a compound entry that lists all four accounts.

General Journal — GJ11

Date	Account Title and Description	Ref.	Debit	Credit
20X5				
Apr. 22	Accounts Receivable–M. Guittar	AR94	300	
	Cost of Goods Sold	560	200	
	Sales	400		300
	Inventory–Tires	I-635		200
	Sell two tires for $300 (cost of tires = $200)			

See pages 105–107 to review some background information about special journals and the sales journal. Textbooks almost always use a general journal to explain inventory accounting because the general journal provides a simple, consistent format to present new information. However, most companies would record the sale in a sales journal.

Inventory Subsidiary Ledger Accounts

Companies that use the perpetual system maintain an inventory control account and an inventory subsidiary ledger with separate accounts for each type of item the business sells. Whenever a transaction affects inventory, the specific item's subsidiary ledger account is also updated. Inventory subsidiary ledger accounts usually contain separate sets of columns for purchases, sales, and the account balance. Each set has three columns, which are used to record the number of units, the cost of each unit, and the total cost. The inventory–tires account from the previous example appears below.

Inventory–Tires   I-635

Max. 15 Min. 7		Purchases				Sales			Overall Balance		
Date	Description	Ref.	Units	Cost	Total	Units	Cost	Total	Units	Cost	Total
Apr. 1	Beginning inventory								7	$100	$ 700
1	Purchase	GJ1	8	$100	$800				15	100	1,500
4	Purchase return	GJ1	(1)	(100)	(100)				14	100	1,400
10	Purchase discount	GJ1		(2)	(14)				14	99	1,386
22	Sale	GJ1				2	99	198	12	99	1,188
24	Sales return	GJ1				1	(99)	(99)	13	99	1,287

The numbers in the maximum and minimum fields near the upper left corner of the account are optional control fields designed to prevent the company from having too many or too few of the items in stock. In this example, the company purchases new tires whenever the overall number of units in stock drops to seven or less, and the number purchased should never cause the company's stock to exceed fifteen units.

If you study the journal entries on page 159 and the subsidiary ledger account above, you will notice that the cost of the tires sold on April 22 changes from $100 in the journal entries to $99 in the inventory account. These examples illustrate two different cost flow methods, so they are intended to be used for illustration purposes only. A company must use one cost flow method consistently. The next section of this chapter explains in detail the methods that companies use to determine the cost of goods sold.

Cost Flow Methods

The cost of items remaining in inventory and the cost of goods sold are easy to determine if purchase prices and other inventory costs never change, but price fluctuations may force a company to make certain assumptions about which items have sold and which items remain in inventory. There are four generally accepted methods for assigning costs to ending inventory and cost of goods sold: specific cost; average cost; first-in, first-out (FIFO); and last-in, first-out (LIFO). On the next several pages, each method is applied to the information below, which summarizes the activity in one inventory subsidiary ledger account at a company named Zapp Electronics.

January 1	Beginning inventory—100 units @ $14/unit
March 20	Sale of 50 units
April 10	Purchase of 150 units @ $16/unit
July 15	Sale of 100 units
September 30	Sale of 50 units
October 10	Purchase of 200 units @ $17/unit
December 15	Sale of 150 units
December 31	Ending inventory—100 units

The cost of goods available for sale equals the beginning value of inventory plus the cost of goods purchased. Two purchases occurred during the year, so the cost of goods available for sale is $7,200.

	Units		Per Unit Cost		Total Cost
Beginning Inventory	100	×	$14	=	$1,400
+ Purchase—April 10	150	×	$16	=	2,400
+ Purchase—October 10	200	×	$17	=	3,400
= Cost of Goods Available for Sale	450				$7,200

Specific cost. Companies can use the specific cost method only when the purchase date and cost of each unit in inventory is identifiable. For the most part, companies that use this method sell a small number of expensive items, such as automobiles or appliances.

If specially coded price tags or some other technique enables Zapp Electronics to determine that 15 units in ending inventory were purchased on April 10 and the remaining 85 units were purchased on October 10, then the ending value of inventory and the cost of goods sold can be determined precisely.

	Units	Per Unit Cost	Total Cost
Purchased April 10	15 ×	$16 =	$ 240
Purchased October 10	85 ×	$17 =	1,445
Ending Inventory	100		$1,685

Cost of Goods Available for Sale	$7,200
− Ending Inventory	(1,685)
= Cost of Goods Sold	$5,515

Since the specific cost of each unit is known, the resulting values for ending inventory and cost of goods sold are not affected by whether the company uses a periodic or perpetual system to account for inventory. The only difference between the systems is that the value of inventory and the cost of goods sold is determined every time a sale occurs under the perpetual system, and these amounts are calculated at the end of the accounting period under the periodic system. Check the value found for cost of goods sold by multiplying the 350 units that sold by their per unit cost.

	Units	Per Unit Cost	Total Cost
Beginning Inventory	100 ×	$14 =	$1,400
Purchased April 10	135 ×	$16 =	2,160
Purchased October 10	115 ×	$17 =	1,955
Cost of Goods Sold	350		$5,515

Companies that sell a large number of inexpensive items generally do not track the specific cost of each unit in inventory. Instead, they use one of the other three methods to allocate inventoriable costs. These other methods (average cost, FIFO, and LIFO) are built upon certain assumptions about how merchandise flows through the company, so they are often referred to as **assumed cost flow methods** or **cost flow assumptions**. Accounting principles do not require companies to choose a cost flow method that approximates the actual movement of inventory items.

Average cost. Companies that use the periodic system and want to apply the same cost to all units in an inventory account use the **weighted average cost method.** The weighted average cost per unit equals the cost of goods available for sale divided by the number of units available for sale.

For Zapp Electronics, the cost of goods available for sale is $7,200 and the number of units available for sale is 450, so the weighted average cost per unit is $16.

$$\frac{\$7,200}{450} = \$16$$

The weighted average cost per unit multiplied by the number of units remaining in inventory determines the ending value of inventory. Subtracting this amount from the cost of goods available for sale equals the cost of goods sold.

Cost of Goods Available for Sale	$7,200
− Ending Inventory (100 × $16)	(1,600)
= Cost of Goods Sold	$5,600

Check the value found for cost of goods sold by multiplying the 350 units that sold by the weighted average cost per unit.

Cost of Goods Sold (350 × $16) = $5,600

Companies that use the perpetual system and want to apply the average cost to all units in an inventory account use the **moving average method.** Every time a purchase occurs under this method, a new weighted average cost per unit is calculated and applied to the items.

As the chart below indicates, the moving average cost per unit changes from $14.00 to $15.50 after the purchase on April 10 and becomes $16.70 after the purchase on October 10.

Date	Purchases	Sales	Balance
Jan. 1			100 @ $14.00 = $1,400
Mar. 20		50 @ $14.00 = $ 700	50 @ $14.00 = $ 700
Apr. 10	150 @ $16.00 = $2,400		200 @ $15.50 = $3,100
July 15		100 @ $15.50 = $1,550	100 @ $15.50 = $1,550
Sep. 30		50 @ $15.50 = $ 775	50 @ $15.50 = $ 775
Oct. 10	200 @ $17.00 = $3,400		250 @ $16.70 = $4,175
Dec. 15		150 @ $16.70 = $2,505	100 @ $16.70 = $1,670

Use the final moving average cost per unit to calculate the ending value of inventory and the cost of goods sold.

Cost of Goods Available for Sale	$7,200
− Ending Inventory (100 × $16.70)	(1,670)
= Cost of Goods Sold	$5,530

First-in, first-out. The first-in, first-out (FIFO) method assumes the first units purchased are the first to be sold. In other words, the last units purchased are always the ones remaining in inventory. Using this method, Zapp Electronics assumes that all 100 units in ending inventory were purchased on October 10.

Cost of Goods Available for Sale	$7,200
− Ending Inventory (100 × $17)	(1,700)
= Cost of Goods Sold	$5,500

Check the value found for cost of goods sold by multiplying the 350 units that sold by their per unit cost.

	Units	Per Unit Cost	Total Cost
Beginning Inventory	100 ×	$14 =	$1,400
Purchased April 10	150 ×	$16 =	2,400
Purchased October 10	100 ×	$17 =	1,700
Cost of Goods Sold	350		$5,500

The first-in, first-out method yields the same result whether the company uses a periodic or perpetual system. Under the perpetual system, the first-in, first-out method is applied at the time of sale. The earliest purchases on hand at the time of sale are assumed to be sold.

Date	Purchases	Sales	Balance
Jan. 1			100 @ $14.00 = $1,400
Mar. 20		50 @ $14.00 = $ 700	50 @ $14.00 = $ 700
Apr. 10	150 @ $16.00 = $2,400		50 @ $14.00 } $3,100 150 @ $16.00
July 15		50 @ $14.00 } $1,500 50 @ $16.00	100 @ $16.00 = $1,600
Sep. 30		50 @ $16.00 = $ 800	50 @ $16.00 = $ 800
Oct. 10	200 @ $17.00 = $3,400		50 @ $16.00 } $4,200 200 @ $17.00
Dec. 15		50 @ $16.00 } $2,500 100 @ $17.00	100 @ $17.00 = $1,700

Last-in, first-out. The last-in, first-out (LIFO) method assumes the last units purchased are the first to be sold. Therefore, the first units purchased always remain in inventory. This method usually produces different results depending on whether the company uses a periodic or perpetual system.

If Zapp Electronics uses the last-in, first-out method with a periodic system, the 100 units remaining at the end of the period are assumed to be the same 100 units in beginning inventory.

Cost of Goods Available for Sale	$7,200
− Ending Inventory (100 × $14)	(1,400)
= Cost of Goods Sold	$5,800

Check the value found for cost of goods sold by multiplying the 350 units that sold by their per unit cost.

	Units	Per Unit Cost	Total Cost
Purchased October 10	200 ×	$17 =	$3,400
Purchased April 10	150 ×	$16 =	2,400
Cost of Goods Sold	350		$5,800

If Zapp Electronics uses the last-in, first-out method with a perpetual system, the cost of the last units purchased is allocated to cost of goods sold whenever a sale occurs. Therefore, the assumption would be that the 50 units sold on March 20 came from beginning inventory, the units sold on July 15 and September 30 were all purchased on April 10, and the units sold on December 15 were all purchased on October 10. Therefore ending inventory consists of 50 units from beginning inventory and 50 units from the October 10 purchase.

Date	Purchases	Sales	Balance
Jan. 1			100 @ $14.00 = $1,400
Mar. 20		50 @ $14.00 = $ 700	50 @ $14.00 = $ 700
Apr. 10	150 @ $16.00 = $2,400		50 @ $14.00 150 @ $16.00 } $3,100
July 15		100 @ $16.00 = $1,600	50 @ $14.00 50 @ $16.00 } $1,500
Sep. 30		50 @ $16.00 = $ 800	50 @ $14.00 = $ 700
Oct. 10	200 @ $17.00 = $3,400		50 @ $14.00 200 @ $17.00 } $4,100
Dec. 15		150 @ $17.00 = $2,550	50 @ $14.00 50 @ $17.00 } $1,550

	Units	Per Unit Cost	Total Cost
Beginning Inventory	50 ×	$14 =	$ 700
Purchased October 10	50 ×	$17 =	850
Ending Inventory	100		$1,550

Cost of Goods Available for Sale	$7,200
– Ending Inventory	(1,550)
= Cost of Goods Sold	$5,650

Check the value found for cost of goods sold by multiplying the 350 units that sold by their per unit cost.

	Units	Per Unit Cost	Total Cost
Beginning Inventory	50 ×	$14 =	$ 700
Purchased April 10	150 ×	$16 =	2,400
Purchased October 10	150 ×	$17 =	2,550
Cost of Goods Sold	350		$5,650

Comparing the assumed cost flow methods. Although the cost of goods available for sale is the same under each cost flow method, each method allocates costs to ending inventory and cost of goods sold differently. Compare the values found for ending inventory and cost of goods sold under the various assumed cost flow methods in the previous examples.

	Weighted Average (Periodic)	Moving Average (Perpetual)	FIFO (Periodic or Perpetual)	LIFO (Periodic)	LIFO (Perpetual)
Ending Inventory	$1,600	$1,670	$1,700	$1,400	$1,550
Cost of Goods Sold	5,600	5,530	5,500	5,800	5,650
Cost of Goods Available for Sale	$7,200	$7,200	$7,200	$7,200	$7,200

If the cost of goods sold varies, net income varies. Less net income means a smaller tax bill. In times of rising prices, LIFO (especially LIFO in a periodic system) produces the lowest ending inventory value, the highest cost of goods sold, and the lowest net income. Therefore, many companies in the United States use LIFO even if the method does not accurately reflect the actual flow of merchandise through the company. The Internal Revenue Service accepts LIFO as long as the same method is used for financial reporting purposes.

The Effect of Inventory Errors on Financial Statements

Income statement effects. An incorrect inventory balance causes an error in the calculation of cost of goods sold and, therefore, an error in the calculation of gross profit and net income. Left unchanged, the error has the opposite effect on cost of goods sold, gross profit, and net income in the following accounting period because the first accounting period's ending inventory is the second period's beginning inventory. The total cost of goods sold, gross profit, and net income for the two periods will be correct, but the allocation of these amounts between periods will be incorrect. Since financial statement users depend upon accurate statements, care must be taken to ensure that the inventory balance at the end of each accounting period is correct. The chart below identifies the effect that an incorrect inventory balance has on the income statement.

	Impact of Error on		
Error in Inventory	Cost of Goods Sold	Gross Profit	Net Income
Ending Inventory			
Understated	Overstated	Understated	Understated
Overstated	Understated	Overstated	Overstated
Beginning Inventory			
Understated	Understated	Overstated	Overstated
Overstated	Overstated	Understated	Understated

Balance sheet effects. An incorrect inventory balance causes the reported value of assets and owner's equity on the balance sheet to be wrong. This error does not affect the balance sheet in the following accounting period, assuming the company accurately determines the inventory balance for that period.

	Impact of Error on				
Error in Inventory	Assets	=	Liabilities	+	Owner's Equity
Understated	Understated		No Effect		Understated
Overstated	Overstated		No Effect		Overstated

Estimating Inventories

Companies sometimes need to determine the value of inventory when a physical count is impossible or impractical. For example, a company may need to know how much inventory was destroyed in a fire. Companies using the perpetual system simply report the inventory account balance in such situations, but companies using the periodic system must estimate the value of inventory. Two ways of estimating inventory levels are the gross profit method and the retail inventory method.

Gross profit method. The gross profit method estimates the value of inventory by applying the company's historical gross profit percentage to current-period information about net sales and the cost of goods available for sale. **Gross profit equals net sales minus the cost of goods sold. The gross profit margin** equals gross profit divided by net sales. If a company had net sales of $4,000,000 during the previous year and the cost of goods sold during that year was $2,600,000, then gross profit was $1,400,000 and the gross profit margin was 35%.

Net Sales	$4,000,000
Less: Cost of Goods Sold	(2,600,000)
Gross Profit	$1,400,000

$$\text{Gross Profit Margin} = \frac{\$1,400,000}{\$4,000,000} = 35\%$$

If gross profit margin is 35%, then cost of goods sold is 65% of net sales.

Suppose that one month into the current fiscal year, the company decides to use the gross profit margin from the previous year to estimate inventory. Net sales for the month were $500,000, beginning inventory was $50,000, and purchases during the month totaled $300,000. First, the company multiplies net sales for the month by the historical gross profit margin to estimate gross profit.

Net Sales × Gross Profit Margin = Gross Profit

$500,000 × 35% = $175,000

Next, estimated gross profit is subtracted from net sales to estimate the cost of goods sold.

Net Sales	$500,000
Gross Profit	(175,000)
Cost of Goods Sold	$325,000

Alternatively, cost of goods sold may be determined by multiplying net sales by 65% (100% – gross profit margin of 35%).

Finally, the estimated cost of goods sold is subtracted from the cost of goods available for sale to estimate the value of inventory.

Beginning Inventory	$ 50,000
Purchases	300,000
Cost of Goods Available for Sale	350,000
Less: Cost of Goods Sold	(325,000)
Ending Inventory	$ 25,000

The gross profit method produces a reasonably accurate result as long as the historical gross profit margin still applies to the current period. However, increasing competition, new market conditions, and other factors may cause the historical gross profit margin to change over time.

Retail inventory method. Retail businesses track both the cost and retail sales price of inventory. This information provides another way to estimate ending inventory. Suppose a retail store wants to estimate the cost of ending inventory using the information shown below.

	Cost	Retail
Beginning Inventory	$ 49,000	$ 80,000
Purchases	209,000	350,000
Goods Available for Sale	$258,000	430,000
Net Sales		$400,000

The first step is to calculate the retail value of ending inventory by subtracting net sales from the retail value of goods available for sale.

	Cost	Retail
Beginning Inventory	$ 49,000	$ 80,000
Purchases	209,000	350,000
Goods Available for Sale	$258,000	430,000
Net Sales		400,000
Ending Inventory (Retail)		$ 30,000

Next, the cost-to-retail ratio is calculated by dividing the cost of goods available for sale by the retail value of goods available for sale.

	Cost	Retail
Beginning Inventory	$ 49,000	$ 80,000
Purchases	209,000	350,000
Goods Available for Sale	$258,000	430,000
Net Sales		400,000
Ending Inventory (Retail)		$ 30,000
Cost to Retail Ratio ($258,000 + $430,000 = 60%)		

Then, the estimated cost of ending inventory is found by multiplying the retail value of ending inventory by the cost-to-retail ratio.

	Cost	Retail
Beginning Inventory	$ 49,000	$ 80,000
Purchases	209,000	350,000
Goods Available for Sale	$258,000	430,000
Net Sales		400,000
Ending Inventory (Retail)		$ 30,000
Cost to Retail Ratio ($258,000 + $430,000 = 60%)		
Ending Inventory (Cost) ($30,000 × 60%)	$ 18,000	

One limitation of the retail inventory method is that a store's cost-to-retail ratio may vary significantly from one type of item to another, but the calculation simply uses an average ratio. If the items that actually sold have a cost-to-retail ratio that differs significantly from the ratio used in the calculation, the estimate will be inaccurate.

Operating assets are long-lived assets that are used in normal business operations. They are not held for resale to customers. Investments in operating assets are essential to the success of most businesses. There are three major categories of operating assets: property, plant, and equipment, which is a category that some textbooks refer to as plant assets or fixed assets; natural resources; and intangible assets. **Property, plant, and equipment** includes land; land improvements, such as driveways, parking lots, fences, and similar items that require periodic repair and replacement; buildings; equipment; vehicles; and furniture. **Natural resources,** such as timber, fossil fuels, and mineral deposits, are created by natural processes that may take thousands or even millions of years to complete. Companies use up natural resources by cutting or extracting them, so natural resources are sometimes called **wasting assets. Intangible assets,** which lack physical substance, may nevertheless provide substantial value to a company. Patents, copyrights, and trademarks are examples of intangible assets.

According to the matching principle, the costs of operating assets other than land must be matched with the revenues they help to generate over their useful lives. Allocating these costs to expense is called depreciation for plant assets, depletion for natural resources, and amortization for intangible assets. The cost of land is never depreciated because land is considered to have an unlimited useful life.

Natural resources are usually listed within the property, plant, and equipment category on the balance sheet. Intangible assets are placed in a separate category.

Digby Pitts Strip Mining
Partial Balance Sheet
December 31, 20X4

ASSETS			
Current Assets			
Cash			$ 16,000
Accounts Receivable			84,000
Inventory			189,000
Supplies			3,000
Prepaid Insurance			8,000
Total Current Assets			300,000
Property, Plant, and Equipment			
Land		$ 300,000	
Buildings and Equipment	$ 500,000		
Less: Accumulated Depreciation	(200,000)	300,000	
Coal Deposits	5,000,000		
Less: Accumulated Depletion	(2,000,000)	3,000,000	3,600,000
Intangible Assets			
Leaseholds		100,000	
Goodwill		400,000	
Less: Accumulated Amortization		(100,000)	400,000
Total Assets			$4,300,000

The Cost of Property, Plant, and Equipment

The cost of property, plant, and equipment includes the purchase price of the asset and all expenditures necessary to prepare the asset for its intended use.

Land. Land purchases often involve real estate commissions, legal fees, bank fees, title search fees, and similar expenses. To be prepared for use, land may need to be cleared of trees, drained and filled, graded to remove small hills and depressions, and landscaped. In addition, old buildings may need to be demolished before the company can use the land. Such demolition expenses are considered part of the land's cost. For example, if a company purchases land for $100,000, pays an additional $3,000 in closing costs, and pays $22,000 to have an old warehouse on the land demolished, then the company records the cost of the land at $125,000.

Land improvements. The cost of land improvements includes all expenditures associated with making the improvements ready for use. For example, when one business contracts with another business to put a parking lot on a piece of land, the cost of the parking lot is simply the agreed-upon price. A company that builds its own parking lot would determine the lot's cost by combining the cost of materials and wages paid to employees for building the lot.

Buildings. The cost of buildings includes the purchase price and all closing costs associated with the acquisition of the buildings, including payments by the purchaser for back taxes owed. Remodeling an acquired building and making repairs necessary for it to be used are also considered part of the cost. If a building is constructed for the company over an extended period, interest payments to finance the structure are included in the cost of the asset only while construction takes place. After construction is complete and the building is ready for productive use, interest payments are classified as interest expense.

Equipment, vehicles, and furniture. The cost of equipment, vehicles, and furniture includes the purchase price, sales taxes, transportation fees, insurance paid to cover the item during shipment, assembly, installation, and all other costs associated with making the item ready for use. These costs do not include such things as motor vehicle licensing and insurance, however, even if they are paid when a vehicle purchase occurs. Expenses of this type are normal, recurring operational expenses that do not add lasting value to the vehicle.

Depreciation

Depreciation is the process of allocating the cost of long-lived plant assets other than land to expense over the asset's estimated useful life. For financial reporting purposes, companies may choose from several different depreciation methods. Before studying some of the methods that companies use to depreciate assets, make sure you understand the definitions below.

> **Useful life** is an estimate of the productive life of an asset. Although usually expressed in years, an asset's useful life may also be based on units of activity, such as items produced, hours used, or miles driven.

> **Salvage value** equals the value, if any, that a company expects to receive by selling or exchanging an asset at the end of its useful life.

> **Depreciable cost** equals an asset's total cost minus the asset's expected salvage value. The total amount of depreciation expense assigned to an asset never exceeds the asset's depreciable cost.

> **Net book value** is an asset's total cost minus the accumulated depreciation assigned to the asset. Net book value rarely equals market value, which is the price someone would pay for the asset. In fact, the market value of an asset, such as a building, may increase while the asset is being depreciated. Net book value simply represents the portion of an asset's cost that has not been allocated to expense.

Straight-line depreciation. There are many depreciation methods available to companies. Straight-line depreciation, introduced on page 48, is the method that companies most frequently use for financial reporting purposes. If **straight-line depreciation** is used, an asset's annual depreciation expense is calculated by dividing the asset's depreciable cost by the number of years in the asset's useful life.

Calculating Straight-Line Depreciation

$$\frac{\text{Depreciable Cost}}{\text{Useful Life in Years}} = \text{Annual Depreciation Expense}$$

Another way to describe this calculation is to say that the asset's depreciable cost is multiplied by the **straight-line rate,** which equals one divided by the number of years in the asset's useful life.

Calculating Straight-Line Depreciation

$$\frac{1}{\text{Useful Life in Years}} = \text{Straight-Line Rate}$$

$$\text{Straight-Line Rate} \times \text{Depreciable Cost} = \text{Annual Depreciation Expense}$$

Suppose a company purchases a $90,000 truck and expects the truck to have a salvage value of $10,000 after five years. The depreciable cost of the truck is $80,000 ($90,000 – $10,000), and the asset's annual depreciation expense using straight-line depreciation is $16,000 ($80,000 ÷ 5).

Cost	$90,000
Less: Salvage Value	(10,000)
Depreciable Cost	$80,000

Calculating Straight-Line Depreciation

$$\frac{\$80,000}{5} = \$16,000 \qquad \text{or:} \qquad \frac{1}{5} = 20\%$$

$$20\% \times \$80,000 = \$16,000$$

The table below summarizes the application of straight-line depreciation during the truck's five-year useful life.

Straight-Line Depreciation

	Straight-Line Rate		Depreciable Cost		Annual Depreciation Expense	Accumulated Depreciation	Net Book Value
Cost							$90,000
Year 1	20%	×	$80,000	=	$16,000	$16,000	74,000
Year 2	20%	×	80,000	=	16,000	32,000	58,000
Year 3	20%	×	80,000	=	16,000	48,000	42,000
Year 4	20%	×	80,000	=	16,000	64,000	26,000
Year 5	20%	×	80,000	=	16,000	80,000	10,000

At the end of year five, the $80,000 shown as accumulated depreciation equals the asset's depreciable cost, and the $10,000 net book value represents its estimated salvage value.

To record depreciation expense on the truck each year, the company debits depreciation expense–vehicles for $16,000 and credits accumulated depreciation–vehicles for $16,000.

General Journal   GJ99

Date	Account Title and Description	Ref.	Debit	Credit
20X0				
Dec. 31	Depreciation Expense–Vehicles	556	16,000	
	Accumulated Depreciation–Vehicles	156		16,000
	Annual depreciation on truck			

Depreciation Expense–Vehicles   556

Date	Explanation	Ref.	Debit	Credit	Balance
20X0					
Dec. 31	Annual depreciation on truck	GJ99	16,000		16,000

Accumulated Depreciation–Vehicles   156

Date	Explanation	Ref.	Debit	Credit	Balance
20X0					
Dec. 31	Annual depreciation on truck	GJ99		16,000	16,000

If another depreciation method had been used, the accounts that appear in the entry would be the same, but the amounts would be different.

Companies use separate accumulated depreciation accounts for buildings, equipment, and other types of depreciable assets. Companies with a large number of depreciable assets may even create subsidiary ledger accounts to track the individual assets and the accumulated depreciation on each asset.

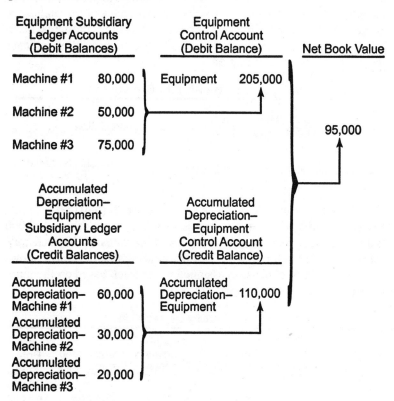

Units-of-activity depreciation. The useful life of some assets, particularly vehicles and equipment, is frequently determined by usage. For example, a toy manufacturer may expect a certain machine to produce one million dolls, or an airline may expect an airplane to provide ten thousand hours of flight time. **Units-of-activity depreciation,** which is sometimes called **units-of-production depreciation,** allocates the depreciable cost of an asset based on its usage. A per-unit cost of usage is found by dividing the asset's depreciable cost by the number of units the asset is expected to produce or by total usage as measured in hours or miles. The per-unit cost times the actual number of units in one year equals the amount of depreciation expense recorded for the asset that year.

Calculating Units-of-Activity Depreciation

$$\frac{\text{Depreciable Cost}}{\text{Units in Useful Life}} = \text{Per-Unit Depreciation}$$

$$\text{Per-Unit Depreciation} \times \text{Units During Year} = \text{Annual Depreciation Expense}$$

If a truck with a depreciable cost of $80,000 ($90,000 cost less $10,000 estimated salvage value) is expected to be driven 400,000 miles during its service life, the truck depreciates $0.20 each mile ($80,000 ÷ 400,000 miles = $0.20 per mile). The table below shows how depreciation expense is assigned to the truck based on the number of miles driven each year.

Units-of-Activity Depreciation

	Units (Miles)		Per-Unit Depreciation		Annual Depreciation Expense	Accumulated Depreciation	Net Book Value
Cost							$90,000
Year 1	110,000	×	$0.20	=	$22,000	$22,000	68,000
Year 2	70,000	×	0.20	=	14,000	36,000	54,000
Year 3	90,000	×	0.20	=	18,000	54,000	36,000
Year 4	80,000	×	0.20	=	16,000	70,000	20,000
Year 5	50,000	×	0.20	=	10,000	80,000	10,000

Sum-of-the-years'-digits depreciation. Equipment and vehicles often provide greater benefits when they are new than when they approach the end of their useful lives and more frequently require repairs. Using **sum-of-the-years'-digits depreciation** is one way for companies to assign a disproportionate share of depreciation expense to the first years of an asset's useful life. Under this method, depreciation expense is calculated using the equation shown below.

Calculating Sum-of-the-Years'-Digits Depreciation

$$\frac{\text{Years Remaining in the Asset's Useful Life at the Beginning of the Year}}{\text{Sum of the Years' Digits (explained below)}} \times \text{Depreciable Cost} = \frac{\text{Annual Depreciation}}{\text{Expense}}$$

The equation's denominator (the sum of the years' digits) can be found by adding each integer from one through the number of years in the asset's useful life $(1 + 2 + 3 \ldots)$ or by substituting the number of years in the asset's useful life for x in the equation below.

$$\frac{x(x + 1)}{2} = \text{Sum of the Years' Digits}$$

The sum of the years' digits for an asset with a five-year useful life is 15.

$$1 + 2 + 3 + 4 + 5 = 15 \quad \text{or} \quad \frac{5(5 + 1)}{2} = 15$$

Therefore, depreciation expense on the asset equals five-fifteenths of the depreciable cost during the first year, four-fifteenths during the second year, three-fifteenths during the third year, two-fifteenths during the fourth year, and one-fifteenth during the last year.

The table below shows how the sum-of-the-years'-digits method allocates depreciation expense to the truck, which has a depreciable cost of $80,000 ($90,000 cost less $10,000 expected salvage value) and a useful life of five years.

Sum-of-the-Years'-Digits Depreciation

	SYD Fraction		Depreciable Cost		Annual Depreciation Expense	Accumulated Depreciation	Net Book Value
Cost							$90,000
Year 1	$5/15$	×	$80,000	=	$26,667	$26,667	63,333
Year 2	$4/15$	×	80,000	=	21,333	48,000	42,000
Year 3	$3/15$	×	80,000	=	16,000	64,000	26,000
Year 4	$2/15$	×	80,000	=	10,667	74,667	15,333
Year 5	$1/15$	×	80,000	=	5,333	80,000	10,000

Declining-balance depreciation. Declining-balance depreciation provides another way for companies to shift a disproportionate amount of depreciation expense to the first years of an asset's useful life. **Declining-balance depreciation** is found by multiplying an asset's net book value (not its depreciable cost) by some multiple of the straight-line rate for the asset. The straight-line rate is one divided by the number of years in the asset's useful life. Companies typically use twice (200%) the straight-line rate, which is called the double-declining-balance rate, but rates of 125%, 150%, or 175% of the straight-line rate are also used. Once the declining-balance depreciation rate is determined, it stays the same for the asset's useful life.

Calculating Declining-Balance Depreciation

$$\frac{1}{\text{Useful Life in Years}} \times \frac{\text{Multiple}}{\text{(200\%, 175\%, 150\%, or 125\%)}} = \begin{array}{c}\text{Declining-Balance}\\\text{Depreciation Rate}\\\text{(DBD Rate)}\end{array}$$

$$\begin{array}{c}\text{Declining-Balance}\\\text{Depreciation Rate}\\\text{(DBD Rate)}\end{array} \times \begin{array}{c}\text{Beginning-of-Year}\\\text{Net Book Value}\end{array} = \begin{array}{c}\text{Annual Depreciation}\\\text{Expense}\end{array}$$

To illustrate double-declining-balance depreciation, consider the truck that has a cost of $90,000, an expected salvage value of $10,000, and a five-year useful life. The truck's net book value at acquisition is also $90,000 because no depreciation expense has been recorded yet. The straight-line rate for an asset with a five-year useful life is 20% (1 ÷ 5 = 20%), so the double-declining-balance rate, which uses the 200% multiple, is 40% (20% × 200% = 40%). The table below shows how the double-declining-balance method allocates depreciation expense to the truck.

Double-Declining-Balance Depreciation

	DBD Rate		Beginning-of-Year Book Value		Annual Depreciation Expense	Accumulated Depreciation	End-of-Year Book Value
Year 1	40%	×	$90,000	=	$36,000	$36,000	$54,000
Year 2	40%	×	54,000	=	21,600	57,600	32,400
Year 3	40%	×	32,400	=	12,960	70,560	19,440
Year 4	40%	×	19,440	=	7,776	78,336	11,664
Year 5	40%	×	11,664		1,664*	80,000	10,000

* Limited to $1,664 so book value does not go below salvage value.

At the end of an asset's useful life, the asset's net book value should equal its salvage value. Although 40% of $11,664 is $4,666, the truck depreciates only $1,664 during year five because net book value must never drop below salvage value. If the truck's salvage value were $5,000, depreciation expense during year five would have been $6,664. If the truck's salvage value were $20,000, then depreciation expense would have been limited to $12,400 during year three, and no depreciation expense would be recorded during year four or year five.

Comparing depreciation methods. All depreciation methods are designed to systematically allocate the depreciable cost of an asset to expense during the asset's useful life. Although total depreciation expense is the same no matter what depreciation method is used, the methods differ from each other in the specific assignment of depreciation expense to each year or accounting period. Consider how the depreciation methods discussed on the last several pages have assigned the truck's depreciable cost of $80,000 to depreciation expense over five years.

Annual Depreciation Expense

	Straight-Line Depreciation	Units-of-Activity Depreciation	Sum-of-the-Years'-Digits Depreciation	Double-Declining-Balance Depreciation
Year 1	$16,000	$22,000	$26,667	$36,000
Year 2	16,000	14,000	21,333	21,600
Year 3	16,000	18,000	16,000	12,960
Year 4	16,000	16,000	10,667	7,776
Year 5	16,000	10,000	5,333	1,664
	$80,000	$80,000	$80,000	$80,000

The sum-of-the-years'-digits and double-declining-balance methods are called accelerated depreciation methods because they allocate more depreciation expense to the first few years of an asset's life than to its later years.

Partial-year depreciation calculations. Partial-year depreciation expense calculations are necessary when depreciable assets are purchased, retired, or sold in the middle of an annual accounting period or when the company produces quarterly or monthly financial statements. The units-of-activity method is unaffected by partial-year depreciation calculations because the per-unit depreciation expense is simply multiplied by the number of units actually used during the period in question. For all other depreciation methods, however, annual depreciation expense is multiplied by a fraction that has the number of months the asset depreciates as its numerator and twelve as its denominator. Since depreciation expense calculations are estimates to begin with, rounding the time period to the nearest month is acceptable for financial reporting purposes.

Suppose the truck is purchased on July 26 and the company's annual accounting period ends on December 31. The company must record five months of depreciation expense on December 31 (August–December).

Under the straight-line method, the first full year's annual depreciation expense of $16,000 is multiplied by five-twelfths to calculate depreciation expense for the truck's first five months of use. $16,000 of depreciation expense is assigned to the truck in each of the next four years, and seven months of depreciation expense is assigned to the truck in the following year.

Straight-Line Depreciation

	Straight-Line Rate	Depreciable Cost	Annual Depreciation Expense	Accumulated Depreciation	Net Book Value
Cost					$90,000
Year 1 (5 mo.)	$5/12 \times 20\%$ ×	$80,000 =	$ 6,667	$ 6,667	83,333
Year 2	20% ×	80,000 =	16,000	22,667	67,333
Year 3	20% ×	80,000 =	16,000	38,667	51,333
Year 4	20% ×	80,000 =	16,000	54,667	35,333
Year 5	20% ×	80,000 =	16,000	70,667	19,333
Year 6 (7 mo.)	$7/12 \times 20\%$ ×	80,000 =	9,333	80,000	10,000

Under the declining-balance method, the first full year's annual depreciation expense of $36,000 is multiplied by five-twelfths to calculate depreciation expense for the truck's first five months of use. In subsequent years, the truck's net book value is higher than it would have been if a full year's depreciation expense had been assigned during the first year, but the declining-balance method's calculation of depreciation expense is otherwise unchanged.

Double-Declining-Balance Depreciation

	DBD Rate	Beginning-of-Year Book Value	Annual Depreciation Expense	Accumulated Depreciation	End-of-Year Book Value
Year 1 (5 mo.)	$5/12 \times 40\%$ ×	$90,000 =	$15,000	$15,000	$75,000
Year 2	40% ×	75,000 =	30,000	45,000	45,000
Year 3	40% ×	45,000 =	18,000	63,000	27,000
Year 4	40% ×	27,000 =	10,800	73,800	16,200
Year 5	40% ×	16,200	6,200*	80,000	10,000
Year 6 (7 mo.)			0	80,000	10,000

* Limited to $6,200 so book value does not go below salvage value.

Under the sum-of-the-years'-digits method, the first full year's annual depreciation expense of $26,667 is multiplied by five-twelfths to calculate depreciation expense for the truck's first five months of use. During the second year, depreciation expense is calculated in two steps. The remaining seven-twelfths of the first full year's annual depreciation expense of $26,667 is added to five-twelfths of the second full year's annual depreciation expense of $21,333. This two-step calculation continues until the truck's final year of use, at which time depreciation expense is calculated by multiplying the last full year's annual depreciation expense of $5,333 by seven-twelfths.

Sum-of-the-Years'-Digits Depreciation

	Portion of Year × SYD Fraction × Depreciable Cost	Annual Depreciation Expense	Accumulated Depreciation	Net Book Value
Cost				$90,000
Year 1 (5 mo.)	$5/12 \times 5/15 \times \$80,000$	$ 11,111	$ 11,111	78,889
Year 2	$7/12 \times 5/15 \times 80,000$ $+ 5/12 \times 4/15 \times 80,000$	24,445	35,556	54,444
Year 3	$7/12 \times 4/15 \times 80,000$ $+ 5/12 \times 3/15 \times 80,000$	19,111	54,667	35,333
Year 4	$7/12 \times 3/15 \times 80,000$ $+ 5/12 \times 2/15 \times 80,000$	13,778	68,445	21,555
Year 5	$7/12 \times 2/15 \times 80,000$ $+ 5/12 \times 1/15 \times 80,000$	8,444	76,889	13,111
Year 6 (7 mo.)	$7/12 \times 1/15 \times 80,000$	3,111	80,000	10,000

Revising depreciation estimates. Depreciation expense calculations depend upon estimates of an asset's useful life and expected salvage value. As time passes, a number of factors may cause these estimates to change. For example, after recording three years of depreciation expense on the truck, suppose the company decides the truck should be useful until it is seven rather than five years old and that its salvage value will be $14,000 instead of $10,000. Prior financial statements are not changed when useful life or salvage value estimates change, but subsequent depreciation expense calculations must be based upon the new estimates of the truck's useful life and depreciable cost.

Under the straight-line method, depreciation expense for years four through seven is calculated according to the equation below.

Revising Straight-Line Depreciation

$$\frac{\text{Net Book Value} - \text{New Salvage Value}}{\text{New Useful Life in Years}} = \frac{\text{New Annual Depreciation}}{\text{Expense}}$$

Assume that the company purchased the truck at the beginning of an annual accounting period. The table on page 180 shows how depreciation expense was calculated during the truck's first three years of use. The truck's net book value of $42,000 at the end of year three is reduced by the new, $14,000 estimate of salvage value to produce a revised depreciable cost of $28,000. The revised depreciable cost is divided by the four years now estimated to remain in the truck's useful life, yielding annual depreciation expense of $7,000.

$$\frac{\$42,000 - \$14,000}{4} = \$7,000$$

Similar revisions are made for each of the other depreciation methods. The asset's net book value when the revision is made along with new estimates of salvage value and useful life—measured in years or units—are used to calculate depreciation expense in subsequent years.

Depreciation for income tax purposes. In the United States, companies frequently use one depreciation method for financial reporting purposes and a different method for income tax purposes. Tax laws are complex and tend to change, at least slightly, from year to year. Therefore, this book does not attempt to explain specific income tax depreciation methods, but it is important to understand why most companies choose different income tax and financial reporting depreciation methods.

For financial reporting purposes, companies often select a depreciation method that apportions an asset's depreciable cost to expense in accordance with the matching principle. For income tax purposes, companies usually select a depreciation method that reduces or postpones taxable income and, therefore, tax payments. In the United States, straight-line depreciation is the method companies most frequently use for financial reporting purposes, and a special type of accelerated depreciation designed for income tax returns is the method they most frequently use for income tax purposes.

Repairs and Improvements

Expenses relating to depreciable assets fall into two broad categories: ordinary expenditures and capital expenditures. **Ordinary expenditures** include normal repairs, maintenance, and upkeep. The costs associated with these items are considered normal operating expenses, and they are recorded by debiting expense accounts and crediting cash or another appropriate account. **Capital expenditures** increase an asset's usefulness or service life, and they are recognized by increasing the asset's net book value.

There are two ways to increase an asset's net book value: the asset account can be debited, thus increasing the recognized cost of the asset, or the asset's corresponding accumulated depreciation account can be debited, thus decreasing the amount of depreciation previously allocated to the asset. If the capital expenditure serves primarily to increase the asset's usefulness or value, the asset account should be debited. On the other hand, if the capital expenditure serves primarily to increase the asset's useful life or salvage value, the accumulated depreciation account should be debited. Such judgments are not always clear cut, and discussions about the best way to record capital expenditures are usually covered in more advanced accounting courses. Nevertheless, you should be prepared to see capital expenditures recorded in either the asset account or the asset's accumulated depreciation account, and you should recognize that the effect on the asset's net book value is the same either way. Consider how a $10,000 capital expenditure changes the truck's net book value.

	Before Capital Expenditure	After $10,000 Capital Expenditure	
		Asset Account Debited	Accumulated Depreciation Debited
Cost	$90,000	100,000	90,000
Accumulated Depreciation	(64,000)	(64,000)	(54,000)
Net Book Value	$26,000	36,000	36,000

When capital expenditures are made, the revised net book value must be used to calculate depreciation expense in subsequent accounting periods.

The Disposition of Depreciable Assets

Depreciable assets are disposed of by retiring, selling, or exchanging them. When a depreciable asset is disposed of, an entry is made to recognize any unrecorded depreciation expense up to the date of the disposition, and then the asset's cost and accumulated depreciation are removed from the respective general ledger accounts. Any recognized losses or gains associated with the disposition are recorded in a separate account and appear in the portion of the income statement named *other income/(expense), net.*

Music World
Partial Income Statement
For the Year Ended June 30, 20X3

Operating Income		
Other Income/(Expense), Net		245,500
Interest Income	$ 7,500	
Gain on Sale of Equipment	1,500	
Interest Expense	(18,000)	
Other Income/(Expense), Net		(9,000)
Net Income		$ 236,500

Retirement of depreciable assets. Retirement occurs when a depreciable asset is taken out of service and no salvage value is received for the asset. In addition to removing the asset's cost and accumulated depreciation from the books, the asset's net book value, if it has any, is written off as a loss.

Suppose the $90,000 truck reaches the end of its useful life with a net book value of $10,000, but the truck is in such poor condition that a salvage yard simply agrees to haul it away for free. The entry to record the truck's retirement debits accumulated depreciation–vehicles for $80,000, debits loss on retirement of vehicles for $10,000, and credits vehicles for $90,000. The loss is considered an expense and decreases net income.

General Journal — GJ451

Date	Account Title and Description	Ref.	Debit	Credit
20X4				
May 31	Accumulated Depreciation–Vehicles	156	80,000	
	Loss on Retirement of Vehicles	590	10,000	
	Vehicles	155		90,000
	Retirement of truck			

A gain never occurs when an asset is retired. If the entire cost of an asset has been depreciated before it is retired, however, there is no loss. For example, if the company using the truck had expected no salvage value and, therefore, had allocated $90,000 in depreciation expense to the truck before its retirement, the disposition would be recorded simply by debiting accumulated depreciation–vehicles for $90,000 and crediting vehicles for $90,000.

General Journal — GJ451

Date	Account Title and Description	Ref.	Debit	Credit
20X4				
May 31	Accumulated Depreciation–Vehicles	156	90,000	
	Vehicles	155		90,000
	Retirement of truck			

Sale of depreciable assets. If an asset is sold for cash, the amount of cash received is compared to the asset's net book value to determine whether a gain or loss has occurred. Suppose the truck sells for $7,000 when its net book value is $10,000, resulting in a loss of $3,000. The sale is recorded by debiting accumulated depreciation–vehicles for $80,000, debiting cash for $7,000, debiting loss on sale of vehicles for $3,000, and crediting vehicles for $90,000.

General Journal · GJ451

Date	Account Title and Description	Ref.	Debit	Credit
20X4				
May 31	Accumulated Depreciation–Vehicles	156	80,000	
	Cash	100	7,000	
	Loss on Sale of Vehicles	591	3,000	
	Vehicles	155		90,000
	Sale of truck			

If the truck sells for $15,000 when its net book value is $10,000, a gain of $5,000 occurs. The sale is recorded by debiting accumulated depreciation–vehicles for $80,000, debiting cash for $15,000, crediting vehicles for $90,000, and crediting gain on sale of vehicles for $5,000.

General Journal · GJ451

Date	Account Title and Description	Ref.	Debit	Credit
20X4				
May 31	Accumulated Depreciation–Vehicles	156	80,000	
	Cash	100	15,000	
	Vehicles	155		90,000
	Gain on Sale of Vehicles	491		5,000
	Sale of truck			

Exchange of depreciable assets. Certain types of assets, particularly vehicles and large pieces of equipment, are frequently exchanged for other tangible assets. For example, an old vehicle and a negotiated amount of cash may be exchanged for a new vehicle.

There are two types of exchanges: similar exchanges and dissimilar exchanges. A **similar exchange** involves the exchange of one asset for another asset that performs the same type of function. Trading in an old delivery truck to purchase a new delivery truck is an example of a similar exchange. A **dissimilar exchange,** which is less common than a similar exchange, involves the exchange of one asset for another asset that performs a different function. Trading in an old truck for a forklift is an example of a dissimilar exchange.

Suppose a $90,000 delivery truck with a net book value of $10,000 is exchanged for a new delivery truck. The company receives a $6,000 trade-in allowance on the old truck and pays an additional $95,000 for the new truck, so a loss on exchange of $4,000 must be recognized.

Cost of Truck Traded In	$90,000
Less: Accumulated Depreciation	(80,000)
Net Book Value	10,000
Trade-in Value	(6,000)
Loss on Exchange	$ 4,000

The cost of the new truck is $101,000 ($95,000 cash + $6,000 trade-in allowance). Therefore, the exchange is recorded by debiting vehicles for $101,000 (to record the new truck's cost), debiting accumulated depreciation–vehicles for $80,000 (to remove the old truck's accumulated depreciation from the books), debiting loss on exchange of vehicles for $4,000, crediting vehicles for $90,000 (to remove the old truck from the books), and crediting cash for $95,000.

	General Journal			GJ451
Date	Account Title and Description	Ref.	Debit	Credit
20X4				
May 31	Vehicles	155	101,000	
	Accumulated Depreciation–Vehicles	156	80,000	
	Loss on Exchange of Vehicles	592	4,000	
	Vehicles	155		90,000
	Cash	100		95,000
	Exchange old truck for new truck			

If the company exchanges its used truck for a forklift, receives a $6,000 trade-in allowance, and pays $20,000 for the forklift, the loss on exchange is still $4,000. Assuming the company uses a separate account to record the cost of forklifts, the journal entry to record this dissimilar exchange debits forklifts for $26,000, debits accumulated depreciation–vehicles for $80,000, debits loss on exchange of vehicles for $4,000, credits vehicles for $90,000, and credits cash for $20,000.

General Journal   GJ451

Date	Account Title and Description	Ref.	Debit	Credit
20X4				
May 31	Forklifts	175	26,000	
	Accumulated Depreciation–Vehicles	156	80,000	
	Loss on Exchange of Vehicles	592	4,000	
	Vehicles	155		90,000
	Cash	100		20,000
	Exchange old truck for new forklift			

If the company receives a $12,000 trade-in allowance, a gain of $2,000 occurs.

Cost of Truck Traded In	$90,000
Less: Accumulated Depreciation	(80,000)
Net Book Value	10,000
Trade-in Value	(12,000)
Gain on Exchange	($ 2,000)

Gains on similar exchanges are handled differently from gains on dissimilar exchanges. On a similar exchange, gains are deferred and reduce the cost of the new asset. For example, after receiving a $12,000 trade-in allowance on a delivery truck with a net book value of $10,000 and paying $89,000 in cash for a new delivery truck, the company records the cost of the new truck at $99,000 instead of $101,000. The $99,000 cost of the new truck equals the $12,000 trade-in allowance plus the $89,000 cash payment minus the $2,000 gain. Since the $12,000 trade-in allowance minus the $2,000 gain equals the old truck's net book value of $10,000, however, it is easier to think of the $99,000 cost as being equal to the old truck's net book value of $10,000 plus the $89,000 paid in cash. To record this exchange, the company debits vehicles for $99,000 (to record the new truck's recognized cost), debits accumulated depreciation–vehicles for $80,000 (to remove the old truck's accumulated depreciation from the books), credits vehicles for $90,000 (to remove the old truck from the books), and credits cash for $89,000.

General Journal — GJ451

Date	Account Title and Description	Ref.	Debit	Credit
20X4				
May 31	Vehicles	155	99,000	
	Accumulated Depreciation–Vehicles	156	80,000	
	Vehicles	155		90,000
	Cash	100		89,000
	Exchange old truck for new truck			

Gains on dissimilar exchanges are recognized when the transaction occurs. After receiving a $12,000 trade-in allowance on a truck with a $10,000 net book value and paying $14,000 in cash for a forklift, the company debits forklifts for $26,000, debits accumulated depreciation–vehicles for $80,000, credits vehicles for $90,000, credits cash for $14,000, and credits gain on exchange of vehicles for $2,000.

General Journal — GJ451

Date	Account Title and Description	Ref.	Debit	Credit
20X4				
May 31	Forklifts	175	26,000	
	Accumulated Depreciation–Vehicles	156	80,000	
	Vehicles	155		90,000
	Cash	100		14,000
	Gain on Exchange of Vehicles	492		2,000
	Exchange old truck for new forklift			

Natural Resources

Timber, fossil fuels, mineral deposits, and other natural resources are different from depreciable assets because they are physically extracted during company operations and they are replaceable only through natural processes.

Cost of natural resources. The cost of natural resources includes all costs necessary to acquire the resource and prepare it for extraction. If the property must be restored after the natural resources are removed, the restoration costs are also considered to be part of the cost.

Companies that search for new natural resources determine cost using one of two approaches: the successful-efforts approach or the full-cost approach. Under the **successful-efforts approach,** exploration costs are considered part of the cost of natural resources only when a productive natural resource is found. Unsuccessful exploration costs are treated as expenses in the period during which they occur. Under the **full-cost approach,** all exploration costs are included in the cost of natural resources. The approach that a company selects should be disclosed in the notes that accompany the financial statements.

Depletion. Depletion is the process of allocating the depletable cost of natural resources to expense as individual units of the resource are extracted. **Depletable cost** equals the total cost of natural resources less any salvage value remaining after the company finishes extracting them. Depletion expense is generally calculated using the units-of-activity method. Under this method, a per-unit cost of depletion is found by dividing the depletable cost by the estimated number of units the resource contains. The per-unit cost times the actual number of units extracted and sold in one year equals the amount of depletion expense recorded for the asset during that year.

Calculating Units-of-Activity Depletion

$$\frac{\text{Depletable Cost}}{\text{Units of Resource}} = \text{Per-Unit Depletion}$$

$$\text{Per-Unit Depletion} \times \text{Units During Year} = \text{Annual Depletion Expense}$$

Suppose a company pays $50,000,000 for an existing gold mine estimated to contain 1,000,000 ounces of gold. The mine has no salvage value, so the depletable cost of $50,000,000 is divided by 1,000,000 ounces to calculate a per-unit depletion cost of $50 per ounce. If the company extracts and then sells 100,000 ounces of gold during the year, depletion expense equals $5,000,000.

Calculating Units-of-Activity Depletion

$$\frac{\$50,000,000}{1,000,000 \text{ ounces}} = \$50 \text{ per ounce}$$

$$\$50 \text{ per ounce} \times 100,000 \text{ ounces} = \$5,000,000$$

One way to record depletion expense of $5,000,000 is to debit depletion expense for $5,000,000 and credit accumulated depletion–mine for $5,000,000.

General Journal   **GJ98**

Date	Account Title and Description	Ref.	Debit	Credit
20X9				
Dec. 31	Depletion Expense	566	5,000,000	
	Accumulated Depletion–Mine	166		5,000,000
	Depletion of 100,000 ounces			

Instead of using a contra-asset account to record accumulated depletion, companies may also decrease the balance of natural resources directly. Therefore, depletion expense of $5,000,000 might be recorded by debiting depletion expense for $5,000,000 and crediting the gold mine for $5,000,000.

General Journal   **GJ98**

Date	Account Title and Description	Ref.	Debit	Credit
20X9				
Dec. 31	Depletion Expense	566	5,000,000	
	Mine	165		5,000,000
	Depletion of 100,000 ounces			

Intangible Assets

Intangible assets include patents, copyrights, trademarks, trade names, franchise licenses, government licenses, goodwill, and other items that lack physical substance but provide long-term benefits to the company. Companies account for intangible assets much as they account for depreciable assets and natural resources. The cost of intangible assets is systematically allocated to expense during the asset's useful life or legal life, whichever is shorter, and this life is never allowed to exceed forty years. The process of allocating the cost of intangible assets to expense is called amortization, and companies almost always use the straight-line method to amortize intangible assets.

Patents. Patents provide exclusive rights to produce or sell new inventions. When a patent is purchased from another company, the cost of the patent is the purchase price. If a company invents a new product and receives a patent for it, the cost includes only registration, documentation, and legal fees associated with acquiring the patent and defending it against unlawful use by other companies. **Research and development costs,** which are spent to improve existing products or create new ones, are never included in the cost of a patent; such costs are recorded as operating expenses when they are incurred because of the uncertainty surrounding the benefits they will provide.

The legal life of a patent is seventeen years, which often exceeds the patent's useful life. Suppose a company buys an existing, five-year-old patent for $100,000. The patent's remaining legal life is twelve years. If the company believes the patent's remaining useful life is only ten years, they use the straight-line method to calculate that $10,000 ($100,000 ÷ 10 = $10,000) must be recorded as amortization expense each year.

One way to record amortization expense of $10,000 is to debit amortization expense for $10,000 and credit accumulated amortization–patent for $10,000.

General Journal　　　　　　GJ848

Date	Account Title and Description	Ref.	Debit	Credit
20X6				
Dec. 31	Amortization Expense	576	10,000	
	Accumulated Amortization–Patent	176		10,000
	Annual amortization of patent			

Instead of using a contra-asset account to record accumulated amortization, most companies decrease the balance of the intangible asset directly. In such cases, amortization expense of $10,000 is recorded by debiting amortization expense for $10,000 and crediting the patent for $10,000.

General Journal　　　　　　GJ848

Date	Account Title and Description	Ref.	Debit	Credit
20X6				
Dec. 31	Amortization Expense	576	10,000	
	Patent	175		10,000
	Annual amortization of patent			

A similar entry would be made to record amortization expense for each type of intangible asset. The entry would include a debit to amortization expense and a credit to the accumulated amortization or intangible asset account.

Copyrights. Companies amortize a variety of intangible assets, depending on the nature of the business. **Copyrights** provide their owner with the exclusive right to reproduce and sell artistic works, such as books, songs, or movies. The cost of copyrights includes a nominal registration fee and any expenditures associated with defending the copyright. If a copyright is purchased, the purchase price determines the amortizable cost. Although the legal life of a copyright is extensive, copyrights are often fully amortized within a relatively short period of time. The amortizable life of a copyright, like other intangible assets, may never exceed forty years.

Trademarks and trade names. **Trademarks** and **trade names** include corporate logos, advertising jingles, and product names that have been registered with the government and serve to identify specific companies and products. All expenditures associated with securing and defending trademarks and trade names are amortizable.

Franchise licenses. The purchaser of a **franchise license** receives the right to sell certain products or services and to use certain trademarks or trade names. These rights are valuable because they provide the purchaser with immediate customer recognition. Many fast-food restaurants, hotels, gas stations, and automobile dealerships are owned by individuals who have paid a company for a franchise license. The cost of a franchise license is amortized over its useful life, often its contractual life, which is not to exceed forty years.

Government licenses. The purchaser of a **government license** receives the right to engage in regulated business activities. For example, government licenses are required to broadcast on specific frequencies and to transport certain materials. The cost of government licenses is amortizable in the same way as franchise licenses.

Goodwill. **Goodwill** equals the amount paid to acquire a company in excess of its net assets at fair market value. The excess payment may result from the value of the company's reputation, location, customer list, management team, or other intangible factors. Goodwill may be recorded only after the purchase of a company occurs because such a transaction provides an objective measure of goodwill as recognized by the purchaser. The value of goodwill is calculated by first subtracting the purchased company's liabilities from the fair market value (not the net book value) of its assets and then subtracting this result from the purchase price of the company.

Fair Market Value of Assets
− Liabilities
= Net Assets at Fair Market Value

Purchase Price of Company
− Net Assets at Fair Market Value
= Goodwill

Suppose Yard Apes, Inc., purchases the Greener Landscape Group for $50,000. When the purchase takes place, the Greener Landscape Group has assets with a fair market value of $45,000 and liabilities of $15,000, so the company would seem to be worth only $30,000.

The Greener Landscape Group
Fair Market Value of Assets and Liabilities
July 31, 20X5

Assets		Liabilities	
Cash	$ 6,000	Accounts Payable	$ 3,000
Accounts Receivable	4,000	Wages Payable	1,000
Supplies	1,000	Unearned Revenue	2,000
Prepaid Insurance	2,000	Notes Payable	9,000
Equipment	12,000	Total Liabilities	$15,000
Vehicles	20,000		
Total Assets	$45,000		

Since Yard Apes, Inc., is willing to pay $50,000, they must recognize that the Greener Landscape Group's value includes $20,000 in goodwill. Yard Apes, Inc., makes the entry shown below to record the purchase of the Greener Landscape Group.

General Journal   GJ97

Date	Account Title and Description	Ref.	Debit	Credit
20X5				
July 31	Cash	100	6,000	
	Accounts Receivable	110	4,000	
	Supplies	140	1,000	
	Prepaid Insurance	145	2,000	
	Equipment	150	12,000	
	Vehicles	155	20,000	
	Goodwill	190	20,000	
	Accounts Payable	200		3,000
	Wages Payable	210		1,000
	Unearned Revenue	250		2,000
	Notes Payable	280		9,000
	Cash	100		50,000
	Purchase Greener Landscape			
	Group for $50,000 in cash			

Yard Apes, Inc., believes the useful life of the goodwill is five years. Using the straight-line method, Yard Apes, Inc., calculates that $4,000 in goodwill must be amortized each year ($20,000 ÷ 5 = $4,000). To record a full year's amortization expense, they debit amortization expense for $4,000 and credit goodwill for $4,000.

General Journal   GJ164

Date	Account Title and Description	Ref.	Debit	Credit
20X6				
July 31	Amortization Expense	576	4,000	
	Goodwill	190		4,000
	Annual amortization of goodwill			